D1391328

Social Dictatorships

Praise for the book

"Why do authoritarian regimes provide strikingly different levels of social welfare provision to their citizens and why does such variation persist over time? Focusing on the Middle East's populous authoritarian regimes, this book offers a seminal take on this puzzle and offers an argument that is both theoretically rigorous and empirically rich. In seeking to understand the politics of social service provision, Eibl puts together a highly original and sophisticated argument that considers the role of such diverse factors as intra-elite conflict, resource endowments, external threat and communal cleavages. It beautifully situates the study of Middle Eastern authoritarianism in a global comparative perspective in ways that has not been attempted before. In doing so, the book's relevance goes far beyond its stipulated focus on social welfare and the Middle East, and sheds new light on the everyday politics of authoritarian rule. This study offers the very best of political science and Middle Eastern studies and will serve as the gold standard against which future work on the subject will be judged."

Adeel Malik, *Globe Fellow in the Economies of Muslim Societies and Associate Professor*, University of Oxford

"In *Social Dictatorships*, Ferdinand Eibl makes a valuable contribution to studies of welfare regimes in developing countries and autocracies. Focusing on labor abundant countries in the Middle East – a region that has been neglected thus far in the literature on welfare politics – he explains variation in social spending and policies across the region. Eibl's logically rigorous explanation articulates the conditions under which authoritarian rulers develop broad support coalitions, which in turn incentivizes them to expand public services. A sophisticated combination of original quantitative and qualitative data and analyses provides ample evidence to support his nuanced arguments. As Eibl so convincingly shows, social dictators are not more benign and generous than their less generous counterparts, but their populations benefit from greater investment in social sectors."

Melani Cammett, *Clarence Dillon Professor of International Affairs*, Harvard University

"*Social Dictatorships* is remarkable for both its theoretical synthesis and its empirical sweep. Ambitiously drawing together insights from across the rational-choice and historical-institutionalist traditions, Ferdinand Eibl carefully develops and compellingly delivers the bold argument that welfare states in labor-abundant Middle Eastern dictatorships have only substantially expanded when conflicts among elites could neither be reconciled nor repressed. A monumental contribution to our knowledge of Middle Eastern political economy and the historical development of authoritarian welfare states."

Dan Slater, *Ronald and Eileen Weiser Professor of Emerging Democracies*, University of Michigan

"When scholars mix qualitative and quantitative methods, one of them usually gets short-changed. Ferdinand Eibl's book is a rare exception to this rule: his field research is of as high quality as his quantitative analysis. He has undertaken remarkable detective work through interviews with decision-makers and access to (now closed off) national archives, getting as close to elite decision-making as is humanly possible in authoritarian systems. At the same time, he has collected unique primary data to identify the long-term distributional consequences of these decisions across the MENA region. His findings are of great relevance for scholars of both authoritarianism and social policy."

Steffen Hertog, *Associate Professor in Comparative Politics*, London School of Economics

Social Dictatorships

The Political Economy of the Welfare State in the Middle East and North Africa

FERDINAND EIBL

OXFORD
UNIVERSITY PRESS

OXFORD
UNIVERSITY PRESS

Great Clarendon Street, Oxford, OX2 6DP,
United Kingdom

Oxford University Press is a department of the University of Oxford.
It furthers the University's objective of excellence in research, scholarship,
and education by publishing worldwide. Oxford is a registered trade mark of
Oxford University Press in the UK and in certain other countries

Published in the United States of America by Oxford University Press
198 Madison Avenue, New York, NY 10016, United States of America

British Library Cataloguing in Publication Data
Data available

Library of Congress Control Number: 2019949439

ISBN 978-0-19-883427-4

DOI: 10.1093/oso/9780198834274.001.0001

Printed and bound in Great Britain by
Clays Ltd, Elcograf S.p.A.

To my mother

Acknowledgements

I have incurred numerous debts in writing this book. Nancy Bermeo, my PhD supervisor, was an important source of guidance during my doctoral studies at Oxford and her experienced advice as a comparative scholar has immensely enriched my work. My thinking about the Middle East and North Africa has been profoundly shaped by two other Oxford academics, Michael Willis and Adeel Malik, who both taught me during my MPhil degree at Oxford and were important mentors throughout my PhD. To be able to count them amongst my friends today fills me with great joy. I would also like to thank my esteemed friend and colleague Steffen Hertog at LSE for his meticulous reading of the text and key inputs in the writing up of the manuscript. My PhD examiners, Ben Ansell and Melani Cammett, both read an earlier version of the manuscript and provided detailed comments that were an invaluable source of guidance while revising the text. Finally, I would like to express my gratitude to Erzsébet Bukodi at the Department of Social Policy in Oxford who encouraged me to pursue an academic career in a moment of great doubt.

This book has not less benefited from numerous discussions with my academic friends and peers, whose comments on my work have been insightful, incisive, and supremely generous: special thanks to Dina Bishara, Holger Albrecht, Halfdan Lynge-Mangueira, Viola Lucas, and Thomas Richter for their precious time. I am also immensely grateful to Henning Tamm who has been a great intellectual companion and dearest friend during all these years, and helped me keep sane during the various stages of my project.

When I joined King's College London as an Assistant Professor, I found great colleagues and friends in Jeroen Gunning, Michael Farquhar, and Neil Ketchley, who offered valuable advice on the initial book proposal and provided much-needed moral support when the finishing line seemed to be fading, again, on the horizon.

In conducting the research for this book, I greatly benefited from a visiting fellowship at the German Institute of Global and Area Studies (GIGA) in Hamburg. A special thanks to Thomas Richter for associating me to his research project and generously sharing his data. In Egypt and Tunisia, my gratitude goes to my numerous interviewees who shared their precious time, thoughts, and memories with me and profoundly shaped my thinking about their countries. In particular, I would like to thank Mohamed Ennaceur for his invaluable insights into post-independence social policy in Tunisia. I was also greatly supported by the staff at the Fondation Temimi and the National Archives in Tunis, as well as the Egyptian

National Archives in Cairo, who provided me a warm welcome and helped me locate relevant documents.

The research upon which this dissertation is based received generous financial support from a number of institutions: the Star Award and travel grants from St Antony's College, Oxford; a writing-up studentship and travel grants from the Department of Politics and International Relations at Oxford; a doctoral studentship from the German National Academic Foundation, whose generous financial support has enabled me to pursue my passion for academic research; and the Kuwait Foundation for the Advancement of Sciences (KFAS) which funded my postdoctoral fellowship at the LSE Middle East Centre.

Finally, my deepest thanks to—as it happens—three women without whom this book would not have been possible: my late grandmother, Irmgard Eibl, for her unconditional and generous support; RP who—with her joy, love, and kindness—showed me a way out of the seemingly endless life as a perpetual student and has become my beloved companion for the journeys ahead; she was an unfailing source of confidence whenever I was lost; and finally my mother, Ulla Lorenz, whose profound trust and unwavering belief in my abilities enabled me to take on this journey. While she often told me that going on fieldwork to remote places seemed very brave to her, it was her bravery—much earlier—that now enables me to write these lines. For this—and so many other things—I shall always be grateful. This book is dedicated to her.

Contents

List of Illustrations

List of Tables

1

Welfare States in the Middle East and North Africa: Puzzles and Answers

In January 2013, the Moroccan king Mohamed VI was visiting the Ibn Rochd hospital in Casablanca when a woman screamed at him and begged him to buy blood for her mother, waiting for an emergency operation in the nearby Baouafi hospital. In the same hospital, deficient equipment had led to the death of an infant earlier the same month. Lacking a respirator, the doctors had only been able to rub the child's chest.[1] In stark contrast, neighbouring Tunisia has repeatedly been sent British patients because of a shortage of beds in the United Kingdom.[2] Such diverging health outcomes are not a legacy of past performance: upon independence, child mortality was *lower* in Morocco than in Tunisia; by 2005, it was twice as high.[3] Eastwards, in Manshiet Nasser, one of Cairo's biggest shanty towns, one school caters for 2,000 pupils, with more than seventy pupils per classroom.[4] Reflecting decades of under-investment, Egypt's literacy rate in the mid-2000s stood at 66 per cent, almost 20 per cent lower than in Iran, the second most populous country in the region.[5] On the eve of the Iranian Revolution, this difference had amounted to only 5 per cent. As examples abound, it becomes clear that in a region usually considered as a whole,[6] states have invested very differently in the social welfare of their citizens.

Despite these contrasts, comparative politics has little to offer to explain the divergence of welfare efforts across the Middle East and North Africa (MENA). This has to do with a triple neglect. First of all, welfare states have historically emerged in advanced industrialized nations as the culmination of a century-long struggle for social protection. Distributing resources amounting to considerable shares of GDP, welfare states have become a fundamental part of modern capitalism in industrialized societies. As a result, the comparative politics literature has seen a proliferation of studies explaining the, in global comparison rather subtle, differences between Western welfare states, whilst neglecting developing

---

[1] New York Times 2013.   [2] See, for instance, The Telegraph 2002.
[3] 220 deaths per 1,000 births in Morocco compared to 280 in Tunisia; in 2005, the rate was 40 in Morocco as opposed to 20 in Tunisia; see UNDP 2015.
[4] IRIN 2014.   [5] World Bank 2010c.
[6] For a critique of this holistic view, see Rauch and Kostyshak 2009.

Social Dictatorships: The Political Economy of the Welfare State in the Middle East and North Africa. Ferdinand Eibl, Oxford University Press (2020). © Ferdinand Eibl. DOI: 10.1093/oso/9780198834274.001.0001

countries.[7] Second, as the literature has recently pivoted to social policies in developing countries, the MENA region has received only scant attention. As a consequence, welfare provision in the Middle East 'has so far been under-represented in the mainstream social policy and development studies literatures'.[8] Third, while the welfare state literature has predominantly focused on democracies and adduced autocracies mostly to contrast differences *across regime types*,[9] scholarship on authoritarianism has paid little attention to policy differences *within regime types*.[10]

These differences are of a considerable magnitude, however. Figure 1.1 depicts the divergence of welfare efforts across authoritarian regimes. To facilitate comparison, the graph focuses on labour-abundant, in contrast to labour-scarce and resource-rich, regimes which represent the modal type of economy among autocracies.[11] Contrasting the average welfare effort with the average annual change of welfare effort, the figure highlights three important observations.[12] First, spending patterns have been very stable and annually vary only little—about 2.9 per cent.[13] In fact, cross-regime differences dwarf any changes in spending over time. Second, most but not all authoritarian regimes spend relatively little on social welfare. Whilst circa 75 per cent of all regimes commit a third or less of their budget to welfare, a number of regimes have made social welfare a clear spending priority, approximating or exceeding 50 per cent of their budget. Third, and most importantly, labour-abundant MENA regimes can be found among low- and high-spenders and, thus, represent a microcosm of a more general divergence in welfare provision across the authoritarian regime spectrum. Given the persistence of social spending patterns, it is of critical importance to understand what *initially* caused this divergence.

---

[7] The literature on the welfare state is too vast to be cited at length. Suffice it to refer to the handbook by Castles et al. 2010 which gives a succinct overview of the field.

[8] Gal and Jawad 2013, p. 242.

[9] Avelino, D. S. Brown, and Hunter 2005; Baqir 2002; Blaydes and Kayser 2011; Habibi 1994; Barroso 2009; Stasavage 2005; Dodlova and Giolbas 2015; and Ansell 2008 all find a positive effect of democracy on social welfare. The literature emphasizes the possibility of leader removal and citizen empowerment as the main mechanisms linking democracy to better welfare provision. See Lieberman 2018. For contradicting findings, see D. S. Brown and Hunter 1999; Kaufman and Segura-Ubiergo 2001; Lott 1999; McGuire 2013; Deacon 2009; and Mulligan, Gil, and Sala-i-Martin 2004.

[10] This is noted by Mares and Carnes 2009, p. 101; Bank 2009, p. 33; Charron and Lapuente 2011, p. 398; Escribà-Folch 2013, p. 3; Wright 2008b, p. 334; and Richter 2012a, p. 2.

[11] Labour-abundant regimes can be resource-rich, such as Algeria or Iran. Yet, given a sizeable population, the political economy of distribution in these regimes is assumed to be characterized by scarcity and thus conflict, not abundance.

[12] Only regimes with a minimum duration of five years have been considered. As spending data are not always complete for non-MENA countries, the averages of regimes outside the MENA region should be taken as a rough indication only.

[13] The pattern is very similar when using social spending as a share of GDP as an indicator.

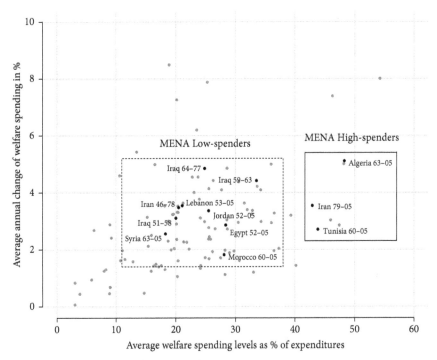

Figure 1.1 Welfare efforts in labour-abundant authoritarian regimes

Note: Regime data for non-MENA countries are based on Svolik 2012; spending data are taken from V. Lucas and Richter 2016; and IMF 2011. The MENA pattern is robust to different time period specifications.

This study thus asks two interrelated research questions:

1. Why have social spending levels and social policy trajectories writ large diverged so drastically across labour-abundant MENA regimes?
2. And how can we explain the marked persistence of spending levels after divergence?

In answering these questions, this study combines existing strands of literature in a novel theoretical framework explaining the emergence of authoritarian welfare states and tests existing arguments pertaining to the path dependence of social spending trajectories developed for democratic welfare states in an autocratic setting. Doing so, the book contends that the varying trajectories of these regimes are far from idiosyncratic, but follow a systematic, potentially generalizable pattern with relevance to labour-abundant authoritarian regimes in general. Understanding this pattern is of importance to the fields of comparative politics and Middle Eastern studies alike.

Given recent upheaval in the MENA region, it seems important to clarify the time period under study before proceeding. Systematic, comparable spending data are available for most countries analysed herein from the early 1950s until 2005; for some countries until 2010. The empirical claims put forward thus refer to the Middle East before the advent of the Arab Spring, while the theoretical argument, within its scope conditions of postcolonial capitalism, strives for relevance beyond any specific time frame. Given the shortcomings of spending data in researching welfare states—inefficient allocation, wastage through corruption, etc.[14]—I will supplement my analysis with data on welfare outcomes and social insurance coverage, the details of which are outlined in Chapter 2. These limitations notwithstanding, relative spending measures, which the theory's core predictions are about, remain a reasonable proxy for authoritarian regimes' political priorities and are significantly correlated with welfare outcomes.[15] What is more, given that high shares of spending mean something different at later stages of development, observing spending shares over long stretches of time allows us to gauge the extent to which regimes have been able to deepen their welfare effort after early human development gains have been achieved. Finally, in a region where, by and large, the state has been the main provider of social welfare,[16] this study analyses *public* provision of social welfare delivered by the institutions of the state. This is not to downplay the importance of non-state welfare provision in developing countries,[17] in particular as a tool for parties to provide patronage and for social movements to embed themselves in civil society.[18]

The remainder of this introductory chapter is structured as follows. Section 1.1 adumbrates my argument, highlighting its theory generating and theory testing elements. Section 1.2 lays out in greater detail how the argument contributes to the existing literatures on the welfare state, authoritarianism, and socioeconomic development in the Middle East. Section 1.3 examines alternative explanations, emphasizing their inability to explain the variation at hand. Section 1.4 outlines the particular research design of this study and describes the organization of the manuscript.

1.1 The Argument

Scholars never start from a white canvass and this book is certainly no exception. In combining different strands in the literature, my theoretical framework

---

[14] Esping-Andersen 1990, p. 107 famously called social spending 'epiphenomenal'.
[15] Rudra and Haggard 2005; and Haile and Niño-Zarazúa 2017.
[16] Even in cases where non-state welfare provision has been extensive, such as through the Muslim Brotherhood in Egypt, only 2 to 6 per cent of the population were reached. See Brooke 2015 and 2017. The only real exception is Lebanon where the state is only a marginal provider. See Cammett 2014a and 2014b for an in-depth analysis of this case.
[17] Cammett and L. M. MacLean 2014b; and Geof Wood and Gough 2006.
[18] See, for example, De Elvira and Zintl 2014; and Clark 2004a.

has taken great inspiration from existing works on the political economy of authoritarianism and distribution. With its focus on the formative, long-term effects of political conflict during regime formation, the book stands in a tradition of macro-historical, comparative analysis for which the emergence of political institutions, such as welfare states, is the product of power struggles during specific historical contexts.[19] Like others,[20] I combine the historical framework with a rational action perspective to explain the behaviour of key actors during critical junctures. In doing so, the framework is kept purposefully simple and stylized, focusing on the way in which key actors navigate through conflict under a set of structural constraints.

Beyond these meta-theoretical underpinnings, my framework rests upon four distinct bodies of literature: (i) elite-centric works in explaining the emergence of authoritarian coalitions, in particular works by Waldner, Slater, and Yom;[21] (ii) the literature on communal cleavages and how they shape distributive outcomes;[22] (iii) the rentier state framework and its conditionalist refinement;[23] and (iv) the literature on the political economy of war and external threats.[24] While readers familiar with these literatures will recognize the intellectual debts I have incurred to their work, in the following discussion I also highlight areas of disagreement and divergence. The novelty of my argument lies in combining these strands into an explanatory framework capable of explaining the varying welfare efforts in a broader group of countries. My assertion is that none of these literatures individually is able to do so.

1.1.1 Theoretical foundations

Elites represent the key actors in my theoretical framework. While I do not propose a specific definition of elites, they are understood to exhibit two key characteristics that set them apart from ordinary citizens. They are (a) *endowed with power*, derived from a disproportionately high amount of political and economic resources; and (b) *interested in power* in that they will seek to maintain or improve their access to power. Pursuing their interests, elites stand in competition with each other, and it is the dynamic pattern of cooperation and conflict between competitive elites that represents one of the key pillars of my argument. The argument is thus inspired by and contributes to theories that have highlighted interaction

[19] See Mahoney and Rueschemeyer 2003a; Mahoney and Thelen 2015; and Hall and Taylor 1996.
[20] See, for example, Hall 2010.
[21] Waldner 1999; Slater 2010; and Yom 2016. See also Albertus 2015a.
[22] See, for instance, Corstange 2016; and Habyarimana et al. 2007.
[23] For the original rentier state argument, see Beblawi 1987; and Luciani 1987. On conditionality in the resource curse literature, see Herb 2017. For empirical examples, see Hertog 2010; Chaudhry 1997; and Yom 2011, amongst others.
[24] See, for instance, Doner, Ritchie, and Slater 2005; and Thies 2004. For the seminal argument on war and state formation, see Tilly 1985.

between elites as the primary driver of political change and stability, particularly in the absence of meaningful democratic elections.[25] Moreover, given the particular opportunity structure of episodes of regime formation, elite interaction is assumed to be momentous in these contexts.[26]

The specific pattern of elite interaction is assumed to follow a rational logic shaped by the imperatives of political survival. Similar to other rational action approaches to authoritarian politics,[27] I hold that the key concern of elites, notably autocratic rulers, is the conquest of and the survival in political power.[28] This has two important implications. First, countering a tendency to attribute the policies of authoritarian regimes to the personal predilections of its ruler,[29] I maintain that any kind of social policies in stable autocracies must be compatible with the imperative of regime and ruler survival. Second, and following from that, I attribute only a marginal role to what might be called 'regime ideologies'. Following Pepinsky,[30] I view these ideologies as a reflection of the preferences of a regime's supporters and a mechanism to cement its underlying coalition.

Regarding the structure of my argument (see Figure 1.2), I distinguish between two fundamental conditions that must be present to enable the emergence of an authoritarian welfare state. Regime-building elites need to have an *incentive* to provide extensive welfare to a broad cross-section of the population. In addition, elites must have the *ability* to provide welfare, provided a sufficiently strong incentive. Both are necessary and jointly sufficient conditions for a regime to provide extensive social welfare. While most scholarship on authoritarian regimes has uniquely focused on domestic politics as the arena in which incentives and abilities are generated,[31] the proposed theoretical framework emphasizes the

Figure 1.2 The logic of the argument

[25] Elite-based approaches are numerous in the literature. Tilly 1978, Tarrow 2011, and O'Donnell, P. C. Schmitter and Whitehead 1986, for example, consider elite division an important causal factor enabling political change through mass mobilization. For North, Wallis, and Weingast 2009, elite competition drives the transformation of social orders. Slater 2010 and Slater and N. R. Smith 2016 emphasize threat-induced elite cohesion to explain the emergence of counter-revolutionary regimes.

[26] For a similar argument, see Hertog 2010, p. 3.

[27] See, for instance, Albertus 2015a; Bueno de Mesquita, A. Smith et al. 2003; Magaloni 2008; Svolik 2012; and Wright 2008a.

[28] Tullock 1987.

[29] This tendency has been criticized by T. Cook 2002, pp. 188–9; and, in the MENA context, by Richards and Waterbury 2008, p. 289.

[30] Pepinsky 2009, p. 18.

[31] A notable exception is Levitsky and Way's 2010 explanation of regime survival past the third wave of democratization.

important interrelation between domestic and external environment. As regimes are embedded in a system of states that poses specific challenges, their policies cannot be understood in relation to their societies alone.[32] This is particularly true in the MENA region where both spheres, domestic and external, have been highly permeable.[33] Inasmuch as the survival of regimes and rulers also depends on external forces and the behaviour of surrounding regimes,[34] this inter-penetration can be considered a general characteristic of authoritarian politics. Only by taking both spheres into account—so the argument goes—are we able to explain the divergent pattern of welfare provision in autocracies.

1.1.2 Coalitions and the politics of distribution in autocracies

Since Aristotle we know that it is often more revealing to ask *not by whom* a regime is ruled, *but for whom*. As authoritarian regimes are exclusively, not electorally responsive like democracies,[35] identifying those constituencies to which an authoritarian regime is responsive provides key insights to explain their social policies.[36] In line with recent scholarship on authoritarian regimes,[37] I argue that constituencies of authoritarian regimes are assembled in the form of *authoritarian support coalitions* and that the composition and shape of these coalitions determine a regime's incentive to distribute social welfare.[38] Following Pepinsky, I define authoritarian support coalitions as groups of supporters who (i) voluntarily bestow upon political leaders economic, coercive, and/or ideological resources; (ii) benefit from existing public policies; (iii) and thence guarantee and favour the reproduction of the political and allocational regime.[39] Political regimes, in turn, can be understood as 'a set of formal and/or informal rules for choosing leaders and policies'.[40] To the extent that no single person, even in autocracies, can

---

[32] Rueschemeyer, Huber, and J. D. Stephens 1992, p. 63. See also Barnett 1992, p. 7.

[33] Halliday 2005, p. 68.   [34] See Yom 2016; and Allinson 2016.

[35] Albrecht and Frankenberger 2010. Changes in welfare spending induced by regime setbacks in authoritarian elections, as found by Miller 2015a, are minor compared to the large differences in welfare efforts across autocracies.

[36] Mares and Carnes 2009, p. 101.

[37] The critical importance of coalitions has been highlighted by, amongst others, Waterbury 1993; Bueno de Mesquita, A. Smith et al. 2003; and Pepinsky 2008a. However, coalitional politics has a longer tradition in comparative politics, harking back to a literature on cross-class coalitions in the history of Europe and Latin America. See, for example, B. Moore 1967; Luebbert 1991; and Berins Collier and D. Collier 1991.

[38] Coalitions conceptually overlap with the notion of political settlements, which has been described as a balance of power between societal groups, with elites being central actors. Like coalitions, political settlements entail processes of path dependency. See Di John and Putzel 2009; Parks and Cole 2010; and Kelsall 2016.

[39] Pepinsky 2008a, p. 450. It is important to note that the concept of support coalition is related to, but not commensurate with the notion of a ruling coalition, which generally designates a narrower circle of decision-makers in an authoritarian regime. See, for instance, Svolik 2009.

[40] Geddes, Wright, and Frantz 2018, detailed coding scheme p. 1.

determine these rules on their own, the emergence of any authoritarian regime necessitates the formation of an authoritarian support coalition. Regime formation and coalition building are interdependent processes.

I further distinguish between two types of coalition in this study: *narrow coalitions* are composed almost exclusively of a country's political and economic elites and predominantly respond to their specific policy preferences; *broad coalitions* are composed of a broad cross-section of social classes, including lower and middle classes. The fundamental distinction between both types is therefore the extent to which elites are willing to include popular sectors into the coalition and allow them to benefit from public policies.[41] Narrow and broad coalitions, in turn, need to be distinguished from two related concepts in the literature proposed by Slater, namely protection and provision pacts.[42] The underlying logic in his typology is the motivation of elite support for an authoritarian regime and, by consequence, the direction of the flow of resources: protection pacts are formed in response to existential threats to elites, who in turn willingly bestow vast resources upon the regime to ensure their protection; in provision pacts, elites support authoritarian regimes because of rent flows from the regime toward elites. While focused primarily on regime–elite relations and authoritarian durability as an outcome, Slater's framework is not incompatible with the typology of coalitions proposed above. Narrow coalitions can occur as either protection or provision pacts, yielding stronger or weaker political regimes. Broad coalitions, however, seem to be incommensurate with the notion of protection pacts insofar as such pacts are formed as bulwarks against mass-based class conflict.[43]

Given the difference in size and social origins of broad as opposed to narrow coalitions, there are two distinct logics of how coalition type affects welfare provision. First, authoritarian coalitions spawn social orders in which the distribution of benefits is congruent with the distribution of power in society.[44] Inasmuch as popular classes in broad coalitions endow these coalitions with power, broad coalitions should be more representative of the policy interests of lower income groups. Lower endowment with socioeconomic resources means that lower and middle classes cannot privately purchase services, such as education, or insure themselves against life-course risks, such as illness. This entails a preference for the public distribution of these services.[45] Moreover, even if elites had the same preference for public welfare distribution, the smaller size of narrow coalitions would be reflected in a much lower welfare effort in these regimes, even if welfare were provided extensively to elites. The second mechanism linking broad coalitions to higher welfare provision pertains to the size of the coalition rather than its social origins. In principle, authoritarian regimes can distribute benefits to their

---

[41] Class-centric approaches have a long tradition in political science. See, for instance, B. Moore 1967; Luebbert 1991; and Rueschemeyer, Huber, and J. D. Stephens 1992.
[42] Slater 2010.   [43] Slater 2010, p. 14.   [44] Khan 2010.   [45] Korpi 2006, p. 168.

support coalition in manifold ways, ranging from individualized, highly targeted benefits, such as a job in the bureaucracy or an import licence for businessmen, to open-access public goods. So why should a broad coalition necessarily entail high levels of social spending on services with a predominantly public-goods character? The reason social spending covaries with coalition size is that, as support coalitions grow, 'leaders reduce their provision of private goods in favor of the now relatively cheaper public goods'.[46] Taken together, broad coalitions should spend relatively larger shares of public expenditures on social welfare and provide social policies with low barriers to access. Narrow coalitions should spend relatively less on welfare, even when welfare is publicly provided to elites, and show a predilection for more targeted private goods and/or social policies with high barriers to access.

Importantly, this logic of authoritarian exchange or 'bargains'[47] should not be viewed in overly benign terms. As Albertus et al. point out, distribution and coercion are often co-products, rather than substitutes.[48] By crafting strategies of economic distribution that enmesh and control the vast majority of the citizenry, while at the same time undercutting rival elites as alternative welfare providers, distribution in authoritarian regimes always has elements of coercion and control as constitutive dimensions. That said, the scope and relative importance of welfare provision still varies considerably from regime to regime and begs an explanation. Another questionable assumption in the political economy literature has been the alleged inability of spending as a credible commitment device in authoritarian regimes. This assertion has most prominently been put forward by Acemoglu and Robinson: '[Elites] can promise to make transfers in the future, but these promises may be noncredible. Tomorrow, they get to decide these transfers and, if it is not in their interest to be making them tomorrow, they will not make them.'[49] Building on this claim, the literature on authoritarianism has come to consider only institutions as credible commitment devices as these are costly to establish and difficult to tear down;[50] spending, by contrast, is deemed discretionary and thus non-credible. This, however, elides the highly institutionalized nature of welfare provision. As Knutsen and Rasmussen remark with regard to old-age pensions, these programmes are 'not easy to reverse without substantial costs for the rulers'.[51] I would extend this claim to the bulk of social policy programmes that drive social spending: mass schooling involves substantial sunk costs in building the institutions delivering education, in addition to the teaching personnel who normally end up on the public payroll; universalizing health care requires a vast and costly infrastructure; and social security programmes are difficult to reverse because of the accruing nature of benefits and contributions. Thus, if we take seriously the claim that welfare states are difficult to retrench, let

---

[46] Bueno de Mesquita, A. Smith et al. 2003, p. 91.   [47] R. M. Desai, Yousef, and Anders 2007.
[48] Albertus, Fenner, and Slater 2018.   [49] Acemoglu and J. A. Robinson 2006, p. 133.
[50] See, for example, Gandhi 2008; and Wright 2008a.   [51] Knutsen and Rasmussen 2018, p. 661.

alone reverse,[52] we must consider social policies a credible way of committing to authoritarian support coalitions.

Related to the foregoing, it is also important to clarify that welfare efforts provided by authoritarian regimes are not simply commensurate with political patronage. In authoritarian settings, patronage has been a major driver of distributive politics, shaping industrial policies, facilitating cross-ethnic electoral coalitions, and ensuring continued support for dominant ruling parties.[53] It is usually understood as an exchange of political support (e.g. a vote) in return for direct payments or continuing access to goods.[54] Therefore, for patronage to be fully effective as a political tool, it requires contingency and the credible threat that goods provision can be withdrawn if political support fails to materialize. In addition, patronage has been shown to be most effective when delivered through a political mass organization that is directly linked to the regime, most often a ruling party.[55] Given that, it becomes clear that social policies are not the ideal instrument to provide patronage. First, as I argued above, many social policies are costly to withdraw; at the very least, retrenchment would take a long time making social policies a highly inflexible instrument for patronage. Second, social policies are often delivered by institutions of the state, rather than parties, which means they are not directly linked to political machines. Third, many social policies can have a quasi public-goods character, which makes them a blunt instrument for targeting specific groups. This is not to say that there can be no patronage for specific social policy programmes, such as social housing, which are more amenable to clientelistic exchange.[56] It is also the case that, if welfare provision is not broad-based and spending levels are low, targeting limited-access social policies to key constituencies becomes easier. This means that patronage-driven social policies should be more likely in regimes with rudimentary welfare provision.[57] Finally, even in authoritarian welfare states social policies can be characterized by regional favouritism, which could be considered a form of group patronage. As I will show later, this is particularly pronounced if ethnic groups close to the regime are regionally segregated.[58]

A coalitional approach to authoritarian politics is arguably more fruitful than alternative frameworks that have emphasized the difference between authoritarian regime types or their different institutional setup. Regarding regime typologies, it has been pointed out that policy preferences are difficult to derive from a taxonomy of who rules the country (military, parties, monarchies).[59] This is also due to the

---

[52] See, most prominently, Pierson 1994.

[53] See Hong and S. Park 2016; Arriola 2009; Baldwin 2013; Greene 2009; Magaloni 2006; and Blaydes 2010, amongst others.

[54] Kitschelt and S. Wilkinson 2007.   [55] Handlin 2016.

[56] Marschall, Aydogan, and Bulut 2016.   [57] See, for example, Cammett 2014a.

[58] On regional favouritism, see Hodler and Raschky 2014. See also De Luca et al. 2018; and Ejdemyr, Kramon, and A. L. Robinson 2018.

[59] Geddes 1999a, p. 11; and Falleti 2011. See also Haggard and Kaufman 2008, p. 357.

fact that a number of regimes exhibit a hybrid mix of these three and are thus not easy to classify.[60] As for institutional variation, the literature has almost exclusively focused on legislatures, with mixed findings regarding social policies.[61] To the extent that political institutions are underpinned by social coalitions,[62] an analysis of coalitions should yield greater insights into the distributional preferences of an authoritarian regime. And as I show later in this chapter, authoritarian institutions do not meaningfully covary with levels of welfare provision in MENA. In sum, maximizing the gains of their members, support coalitions critically regulate material exchange in society and, by providing various incentives to authoritarian rulers, drive the politics of distribution in autocracies. In other words, coalitions are the proximate cause of varying policies of welfare provision.

1.1.3 Forming incentives: explaining the emergence of different support coalitions

My theoretical argument starts from the assumption that, in authoritarian settings, coalitions need to be self-enforcing as agreements between different actors cannot be enforced externally.[63] In other words, they must be incentive compatible such that no member wants to defect from it. Two main factors affect the dynamics of coalition formation in particular, as described below.

Rivalling elites
Regarding the shape of coalitions, elites have a preference for narrow instead of broad coalitions.[64] These coalitions are small in size, which means that the resources and surplus generated from political power are distributed over a smaller number of people. This, in turn, entails a higher payoff for each individual member of the elite. Such coalitions run for elites and by elites have historically existed in different fashions, be it family dictatorships like the Somoza regime in Nicaragua, labour-repressive military regimes such as the Pinochet regime in Chile, or rentier kleptocracies such as the Obiang regime in Equatorial Guinea.[65] In the Middle East, the Pahlavi regime in Iran probably came closest to this narrow coalition ideal type.[66] There are two interrelated conditions for such narrow coalitions to be self-enforcing. First, elites must be able to forge a compromise amongst themselves

---

[60] Geddes 1999b, pp. 123–4.
[61] See, for instance, Gandhi and Przeworski 2006; Gandhi 2008; Wright 2008a; Escribà-Folch 2008; and N. K. Kim and Kroeger 2018.
[62] Hall 2010, p. 206; and Hall 2013, p. 26.
[63] Acemoglu, Egorov, and Sonin 2006; and Pepinsky 2008b.
[64] Geddes 2004; and Peters and P. Moore 2009, p. 259.
[65] See Booth 1998; Huneeus and Sagaris 2007; and Geoffrey Wood 2004 on the three countries respectively.
[66] Katouzian 1998.

about how to share political power and economic resources, and about a set of rules for choosing the political leadership of the regime. If such a compromise is achievable at the moment of regime formation—in other words, if elites are cohesive—they will seek to form a narrow support coalition with limited or no side-payments in the form of social welfare.[67] Thus, unlike Hinnebusch,[68] I do not assume that all regime-building elites have an incentive to broaden coalitions. The second condition for the emergence of a narrow coalition is that elites successfully convert their higher endowment with power resources into building a reliable coercive apparatus in order to defend this power-sharing arrangement against potential threats emanating from ordinary citizens. The overall claim here is that elite cohesion make the emergence of narrow coalitions more likely.

While this requires minimal collective action on the part of elites, it stays well below the level of elite collective action that Slater sees at work in the creation of high-capacity authoritarian Leviathans, where elites endow the regime with extraordinary resources in the face of endemic threats.[69] The understanding of elite cohesion here is more minimalist and denotes the idea of a basic power-sharing arrangement in which elites can, and in MENA often do, mostly focus on building up repressive capacity.[70] Such low-intensity elite cohesion can originate from multiple sources: for example, elites can coalesce around a traditional social status order; a shared ethnic origin; possibly a shared ideology; or cohesion stems from a unified command structure, like in military regimes where the coercive apparatus itself becomes the core of the support coalition. Empirically, a more minimalist understanding of elite cohesion takes inspiration from the fact that seemingly weak, yet enduring elite-based regimes have existed—be it the aforementioned Shah regime or personalist dictatorships in Latin America and Africa. They occupy the space between broad coalitions and counter-revolutionary Leviathans as in Slater.

Under what conditions, then, are elites willing to broaden their coalition to include popular classes? A vast literature in comparative politics has emphasized the formative impact of virulent intra-elite conflict on coalitional dynamics. As Theda Skocpol, for example, remarks, 'competition among elites for coercive and authoritative control spurs certain leadership groups to mobilize previously politically excluded popular forces'.[71] Shefter argues that '[p]oliticians will have an

---

[67] Whether or not elites are capable of coming to an internal agreement hinges on conditions antecedent to coalition formation, which are not explicitly theorized, though I highlight the sources of elite cohesion in the case narratives. Most seem exogenous and idiosyncratic, at least in the short run. There was no evidence for settler colonialism as a consistent cause of intra-elite conflict as per Waldner, Peterson, and Shoup (2017). For potential sources of elite cohesion, see Slater 2010. For the concept of antecedent conditions, see Slater and E. Simmons 2010.

[68] Hinnebusch 2010, p. 204.

[69] For Slater 2010, these threats need to be endemic, urban-based, and communal to trigger elite collective action of such intensity.

[70] See Bellin 2004 and 2012.   [71] Skocpol 1988, p. 149.

incentive to embark upon a strategy of mass mobilization [...] if a serious cleavage opens up within the political class that divides it along functional or sectoral lines, and that leaders cannot readily compromise or smooth over'.[72] In a similar vein, Albertus maintains that elite splits between landed elites and ruling political elites lead to redistributive land reforms.[73] It needs to be noted, though, that his argument concerns two specific types of elite and a specific type of redistribution— land reform. The mechanisms is also slightly different: land reform is not a result of coalitional broadening, but rather of the elites' eagerness to wipe out rivalling elites and *forestall* popular mobilization rather than encourage it.

In the literature on the Global South, Waldner has been the most prominent proponent of the argument that intra-elite conflicts broaden coalitions.[74] The bare-bone logic of the argument goes as follows. Intra-elite conflict that cannot be resolved entails the risk of permanent exclusion from the support coalition for certain elite groups. Facing 'an absolute loss of [the] capacity to extract surplus',[75] elites have an incentive to broaden their coalition to outcompete their elite rival by including segments of the lower and middle classes.[76] Whilst their incorporation means a permanently reduced payoff for the victorious elites, this situation is still preferable to the risk of ultimate elimination from the support coalition, assuming risk-averse elites. Existing game-theoretic models have argued that such elite–lower class alliances are not self-enforcing as, once the elite rival is eliminated, the remaining elite would turn against their lower-class partners and oust them from the coalition, yielding a higher payoff.[77] This crucially hinges on the assumption that sidelined elite groups cannot return.[78] However, if elite groups are rather understood as social groups, such as capital owners or religious elites, their future return seems indeed quite plausible, and under these conditions such coalitions are self-enforcing.

While my argument follows the broad logic outlined by Waldner, there is need for further clarification and refinements. For starters, it is important to distinguish conceptually between elite factionalism and intra-elite conflict. Competitive discord is an omnipresent feature of all political action and, as Slater rightly points out, particularly 'elite politics is rife with factionalism and parochialism'.[79] The notion

---

[72] Shefter 1994, p. 10. See also Schattschneider 1960.

[73] Albertus 2015a and 2015b.

[74] Waldner 1999; and Waldner, Peterson, and Shoup 2017. See also Brownlee 2007.

[75] Waldner 1999, p. 29.

[76] Again, sources of intra-elite conflict can be various and are not explicitly modelled in the argument here. Waldner, Peterson, and Shoup 2017 emphasize colonialism and the pattern of decolonization as an important variable. As I show in the case narratives later, this explains a fair share of, yet not all, incidents of elite conflicts in the MENA region. On the whole, the sources of intra-elite conflict appear mostly exogenous to the outcome of welfare provision.

[77] Acemoglu, Egorov, and Sonin 2006; and Pepinsky 2008b.

[78] The most prominent example is the repeated purges carried out by Stalin, which permanently narrowed his ruling coalition.

[79] Slater 2010, p. 10.

of intra-elite cohesion therefore does not imply that competition between elites will ever cease completely; rather, it seems that some forms of elite competition are reconcilable with the imperatives of forging a minimal power-sharing arrangement as outlined above, while other forms of conflict render such arrangements unachievable. Hence the question is what type of intra-elite conflict it takes to make elites broaden the coalition. There are two considerations here. First, can conflicting elites be reconciled, for instance, through a change in policy, a shift in the distribution of resources within the coalition, or rotation within the inner circle of power? If this is not the case, intra-elite conflict is *irreconcilable*, which is the first necessary condition to trigger coalitional dynamics. Second, can one elite group end the conflict by coercing their rival elites, generally by some form of violent repression? If not, intra-elite conflict is *irrepressible*. I argue that only such forms of irreconcilable and irrepressible elite conflict trigger the mechanism of coalitional broadening outlined above.

It is worth dwelling on the second point of repression a bit more as this will be important for the empirical analysis. As Khan points out, political actors have varying ability to prevail in conflict.[80] This means that intra-elite conflict only triggers the outlined mechanism if the elites' coercive capacity breaks rather evenly along the fault lines of elite dispute. This is most likely to be the case if elite conflict divides the coercive apparatus itself, or an organized, reliable repressive apparatus is not present. This can be the case in postcolonial regimes where either the colonial power left no organized military or police force, or the coercive apparatus has broken down. Conversely, if conflict breaks out *between* civilian and military elites, the military would be expected not to broaden their coalition but to use their coercive capacity to sideline civilian elites. Importantly, repressive capacity does not necessarily have to originate domestically from power resources intrinsic to elite actors. As Yom convincingly argues,[81] access to external patrons can shape authoritarian coalitions by enabling elite factions to fend off vital threats, usually through a mix of financial and military assistance. This is an important insight which I incorporate in my framework. Unlike Yom, however, I argue and later empirically demonstrate that the availability of external patrons does not generally and directly affect the shape of coalitions; it does so conditionally by turning irrepressible into repressible intra-elite conflicts, thus obviating the incentives to open up coalitions.

This is related to another point of disagreement with Yom, Smith, and others who have argued that mobilization from below leads to accommodation in the form of broader support coalitions.[82] In the words of Smith, 'in the face of a well-organized opposition, state leader are likely to build early alliances with powerful social groups and to make significant concessions to those groups in return

---

[80] Khan 2010, p. 6.   [81] Yom 2016.
[82] See ibid. 2016; B. Smith 2007; and Doner, Ritchie, and Slater 2005, amongst others.

for their support'.[83] Despite the mechanism's intuitive appeal, it has theoretical and empirical problems. At the theoretical level, I see a number of issues: (i) If popular mobilization is episodic, to borrow Slater's notion,[84] elites will likely seek to get away with a temporary buy-off—that is, one-off measures that are unlikely to shift the tectonic plates of the coalition; such measures do not entail the type of institution building characteristic of authoritarian welfare states. (ii) If popular mobilization is endemic and opposition is well organized, threats to the elites' status from popular classes are real but it is questionable why elites would co-opt popular segments into their coalition given the real threat of being completely sidelined. Opening up the coalition under these circumstances may be too risky a strategy, prompting repression instead of accommodation. (iii) More generally, as Yom rightly points out, 'regimes are threatened when their coercive units such as armies, security agencies, and police forces are unwilling or unable to disperse challengers and impose political closure'.[85] But is it not too late to widen the coalition under these circumstances of, essentially, a revolutionary moment when the regime has lost control? Why would the revolutionaries accept co-optation when they can oust the regime? Finally, as Wood has argued, preferences for political inclusion as a result of changing cost–benefit calculations emerge only slowly among elites.[86] This means that, at the very least, it necessitates a very specific type of enduring popular mobilization to crack open narrow coalitions. Theoretically, it therefore seems unlikely that social conflict will often reach the 'bittersweet spot'[87] where elites deem social mobilization too strong to be bought off and weak enough to broaden the coalition.[88]

Empirically, voluntarist theories of democratization have long argued that 'no transition can be forced purely by opponents against a regime which maintains the cohesion, capacity, and disposition to apply repression'.[89] This chimes with the empirical fact that, on the one hand, ousters of authoritarian regimes through revolutions are rare[90] and, on the other hand, authoritarian regimes have frequently managed to wipe out even highly organized, mass-based opposition groups. The eradication of the organized Left under the Indonesian Suharto regime is a case in point. In sum, it seems that the effect of popular mobilization on authoritarian support coalitions is ambiguous, to say the least, and as Yashar remarks, insufficient on their own to beget cross-class coalitions.[91]

---

[83] B. Smith 2007, p. 51.   [84] Slater 2010, p. 13.   [85] Yom 2016, p. 29.
[86] E. J. Wood 2000.
[87] The term is borrowed from Slater and Wong 2013.
[88] The elite rationale for accommodation may be different in resource-rich, labour-scarce regimes where the relative cost of accommodation through welfare is much lower compared to repression. See Eibl and Hertog 2018.
[89] Guillermo and P. Schmitter 1986, p. 21.   [90] Goemans, K. S. Gleditsch, and Chiozza 2009.
[91] Yashar 1997, pp. 15–17.

Communal salience

Underpinning the elite-based argument above is a social conflict theory of inter-class struggle. Yet class is not the only social category that matters. A long-standing tradition in comparative politics has emphasized communal cleavages as an important shaper of authoritarian coalitions.[92] Counteracting the broadening effect of intra-elite conflict, communal cleavages, whenever sufficiently salient, incentivize elites to build coalitions around communally confined sub-groups of the population.[93] Two main mechanisms explain this communal narrowing of coalitions.

From social psychology and the cognitive sciences, we know that group boundaries can lead to bias in favour of in-group members, who in turn may seek to maximize the reward for their own group relative to the out-group.[94] In punishment experiments, Bernhard et al. found that individuals expect more lenient punishment from their own in-group members.[95] This does not seem to be motivated by hostility toward out-groups. Rather, it is the preferential treatment of in-group members that matters.[96] Given that 'the expectation of reciprocity is greatest with mutually acknowledged ingroup members',[97] elite and non-elite members of the same community expect mutual support.[98] In the context of Africa, Posner argues that these self-fulling expectations of communal favouritism are widely established.[99] Two-edged in nature, these expectations render intra-communal coalitions more cohesive whilst they also represent an important source of instability if these expectations were to be disappointed.

Another strand in the literature has pointed to the varying ability to monitor and sanction coalition members in order to explain communal narrowing of coalitions. The reasoning here is that all coalitions necessarily entail degrees of delegation between coalition members or groups within the coalition, which in turn trigger principal–agent dynamics. As both sides want to ensure no one is shirking, the ability to monitor and, if necessary, sanction coalition members is vital. Information is a vital prerequisite for successful monitoring but, transmitted through networks, it does not flow equally across communal boundaries: 'To the degree that people's social networks are densest at low-level units, and those units are embedded within a broader ethnic community, information flows are much stronger and cheaper within ethnic groups than across them.'[100] In other words, because of language, geographic accessibility or otherwise, certain communities are less legible

---

[92] See, for instance, the seminal work by Bates 1983.

[93] Building on Whitefield 2002, p. 181, I define communal cleavages as strongly structured and persistent lines of division among different ethno-linguistic or religious groups.

[94] Tajfel et al. 1971.   [95] Bernhard, Fischbacher, and Fehr 2006.   [96] Brewer 1999.

[97] Ejdemyr, Kramon, and A. L. Robinson 2018, p. 5; see also Charnysh, C. Lucas, and Singh 2015.

[98] Wimmer 2002, p. 93.

[99] Posner 2005, p. 2. See Greif 1994; and Bowles and Gintis 2004 for a game-theoretic approach to these cultural norms of strong reciprocity.

[100] Corstange 2016, p. 13. See also Fearon and Laitin 1996.

for political elites than others.[101] Given that monitoring and sanctioning is easier within communities,[102] the costs of building cross-ethnic coalitions can thus be prohibitively high. Similarly, because cross-communal coalitions in the presence of inter-communal fray are impaired by heightened distrust between communities,[103] collective action and high-cost political activities are discouraged.[104] By forming intra-communal coalitions, elites thus reduce uncertainty,[105] increase the collective action capacity of their coalition, and heighten their chances of outcompeting their rivals. Having said this, it it important to acknowledge that relative group sizes matter for this mechanism to kick in. As Lieberman rightly points out: 'A society is highly fragmented when relatively strong boundaries separate many discrete social groups. If a single group constitutes the vast majority of the population—say 90 per cent or more—then irrespective of the strength of boundaries that separate ethnic minorities, that polity is not described as fragmented.'[106]

Why, then, does communal narrowing translate into lower levels of welfare provision?[107] Some authors have emphasized differences in preferences and tastes between communities,[108] but it is not clear why communities should have varying preferences for essential goods, such as health care or insurance against life-course risk. Instead, it seems that the effect is mediated by the size of the coalition and the type of spending. As for the coalition size mechanism, intra-communal coalitions tend to be smaller than coalitions unfettered by communal cleavages, entailing preferential welfare provision to in-group members at the expense of out-groups and likely lower levels of welfare spending overall. Regarding the spending type mechanism, elites will be more willing to use welfare provision—which often has a public-goods character—to cater to their in-group if communities are sufficiently geographically segregated because in this case welfare provision is unlikely to spill over into out-groups.[109] Communities are never perfectly segregated, however, and thus spill-overs remain potentially problematic in communally mixed territories and urban areas. Thus, coalition-building elites will always have an incentive to substitute some welfare provision with more clientelistic private goods, such as public sector jobs, to cater to their in-group coalition members.[110] Welfare spending will consequently be crowded out by other types of spending. In reality,

---

[101] Blaydes 2018, p. 14.   [102] Habyarimana et al. 2007.   [103] Cohen 1974.
[104] Petersen 2001, p. 15.   [105] Hale 2004.   [106] Lieberman 2009, p. 33.
[107] Suppressed provision of public goods in the presence of ethnic fractionalization is a recurrent empirical pattern. See seminally Easterly and Levine 1997; and Jensen and Skaaning 2015. But see also Gibson and Hoffman 2013; and Gao 2016 for contrary evidence. De Luca et al. 2018 find that communal favouritism is a general global phenomenon, whereas Hodler and Raschky 2014 observe it mostly in regimes with weak political accountability.
[108] See, for instance, Lieberman and McClendon 2013.
[109] Ejdemyr, Kramon, and A. L. Robinson 2018.
[110] Corstange 2016, chapter 7. See also Bueno de Mesquita, A. Smith et al. 2003.

both effects will probably occur as elites may want to ensure the support of their co-ethnics through a mix of selective private and public goods provision.

I mentioned above that communal cleavages must be salient in order to narrow coalitions, but this leaves open the question of where the cleavages come from in the first place and how they become salient. As for the *existence* of communal cleavages, it is important to point out that diversity does not automatically translate into polarization.[111] Also, communal identities exhibit a high level of fluidity and are constantly re-negotiated in everyday practice.[112] This is one of the reasons why the literature has struggled to explain why some ascriptive features become markers of distinction, and not others.[113] Given diversity, the creation of a shared narrative of descent and belonging depends to a large extent on the strategic action of elites.[114] Administrative procedures, such as the way in which states conduct censuses, can also institutionalize communal identities and practices.[115] Finally, colonialism can have an important impact in undermining state centralization while relying on local communities for indirect rule, thus engraining communal cleavages.[116] On the whole, there seems to be an emerging consensus that communal diversity itself is endogenous to legacies of weak statehood in the long run.[117]

Colonialism has also been highlighted as one of the key factors in heightening the *salience* of existing group boundaries. By applying divide and rule tactics and promoting minority groups within the state administration, colonial powers have frequently sown the seeds for communal strife in the postcolonial period. In the Middle East, this was particularly acutely felt in Syria and Lebanon where colonial encroachment coupled with Ottoman modernization sharpened and politicized communal boundaries.[118] Blaydes identifies another mechanism in the form of a negative feedback loop between low legibility of certain communities by the regime and a resulting tendency for collective, untargeted repression, which in turn reinforces communal identities.[119] Yet the most powerful mobilizer of communal identities are elites themselves as they find it opportune to activate communal sentiments for political objectives. This logic of strategically instrumentalizing communal cleavages has been highlighted by numerous authors, inside and outside of MENA, as the key driver of ethnic politics.[120] Given that, elites are more likely to 'activate' communal identities in the presence of severe intra-elite conflict.[121] In other words, rivalling elites tend to increase the salience of communal cleavages, making broad cross-class coalitions less likely.[122]

---

[111] Singh 2011.   [112] Nucho 2018.   [113] Brubaker 2004.
[114] See, for example, Singh 2011; and Varshney 2009.
[115] Lieberman and Singh 2012 and 2017.   [116] Ali et al. 2018.
[117] Wimmer 2016; and Singh and vom Hau 2016.
[118] Makdisi 2000.   [119] Blaydes 2018.
[120] For representatives of this instrumentalist approach in MENA, see Hashemi and Postel 2017; and Hazran 2017. For a general overview, see Varshney 2009.
[121] Fearon and Laitin 2000.
[122] Given the context of authoritarian political regimes, I do not consider here Posner's 2005 argument that democratic institutions can varyingly politicize communal cleavages.

Critics will likely point out that my approach to coalition formation is highly simplified and stylized. There is indeed no point denying that the empirical reality will be infinitely more complex than this model. For starters, for coalition formation to unfold in this manner, elites need to perceive their strategic environment in a way that is congruent with the logic outlined above. This leaves room for strategic misperceptions which can consequently embark regimes upon alternative paths. While perceptions can be empirically difficult to capture, especially in macro-comparative research, the case narratives in Chapter 3 seek to shed some light on the inner motivations of elite actors. Another valid objection is nuance: in the empirical reality, forms of narrow and broad coalitions are gradual, rather than dichotomous; communal favouritism and neglect can be partial, rather than total. Again, this does not undermine the logic of the model, but requires careful empirical analysis to ascertain if the model has heuristic value for concrete historical cases. Finally, the rather crude division into elites and non-elites defies the variety of actors within these two groups. At the end of this chapter, I give some indication as to how welfare efforts could vary depending on the specific type of actors forming the coalition. That said, for the purpose of establishing a theoretical framework with wider relevance for authoritarian regimes, focusing on these two groups gets us a very long way in explaining the nature of authoritarian social policies.

In sum, the two core predictions from the foregoing are (see Figure 1.3): (i) intra-elite conflict in the absence of salient communal cleavages increases the

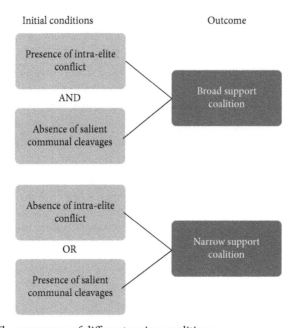

Figure 1.3 The emergence of different regime coalitions

likelihood of broad support coalitions; (ii) the absence of intra-elite conflict or the presence of salient communal cleavages makes narrow coalitions more likely. Predictions for the other two combinations are harder to make. Elite conflict combined with communal cleavages may lead to lopsided cross-class coalitions, entailing a contradictory mix of universalist social policies and communal favouritism. Cohesive elites in the presence of salient communal cleavages may decide to privilege some of their non-elite co-ethnics materially, probably depending on how precarious the communal balance of power and how trustworthy the level of elite cohesion is. In both cases, however, we should not expect the emergence of authoritarian welfare states.

1.1.4 Ability constrained: coalitions in their geostrategic environment

Thus far, I have argued that elite interaction at the moment of regime formation shapes a regime's incentives to provide social welfare. Conditioned by internal conflict and communal cleavages, the pattern of coalition formation is thus predominantly rooted in the domestic politics of a regime. Yet, given the 'porous boundary between domestic and international alliance making',[123] regimes have to respond to challenges of regime survival emanating from the geostrategic environment. This environment can be either constraining or enabling. This claim has most prominently been made by Doner, Ritchie, and Slater who argue that, given a broad coalition, developmental states emerge as a result of the interplay between scarce resource endowments and severe security threats.[124] Their argument, in turn, takes inspiration from the rentier state paradigm which, at least in its Middle Eastern variant, posits that large resource endowments enable ruling elites to buy their citizens' political acquiescence in return for generous welfare provision.[125]

Developmental states have been ostensibly absent from the MENA region although, as I will empirically demonstrate, a number of countries have been affected by the conundrum of broad coalitions, threats, and resource scarcity that Doner et al. associate with developmental states. This notwithstanding,[126] the notion of systemic vulnerability remains analytically useful in explaining regimes' varying ability to build authoritarian welfare states. Specifically, building on the systemic vulnerability and rentier state literature, I argue that the ability to build an authoritarian welfare state critically hinges on the two variables of external threats and resource endowments.

---

[123] Allinson 2016, p. 316.   [124] See Doner, Ritchie, and Slater 2005; and Ritchie 2010.
[125] For the original rentier state argument, see Beblawi 1987; and Luciani 1987.
[126] In the concluding chapter, I speculate about the reasons why systemic vulnerability failed to bring about developmental states in MENA.

External threats

In line with Doner et al.,[127] the occurrence of severe external threats during regime formation can undermine the establishment of an authoritarian welfare state by shifting a regime's spending priority from welfare to national defence. Specifically, threats need to exhibit three main characteristics in order to undermine a regime's welfare effort in the long run.

First, the external threat must pose an imminent danger for the survival of an authoritarian regime and its rulers. Crucially, severe here does not only denote the possibility of military defeat and loss of territory. Severe external threats are perceived by the rulers as representing a danger to the regime as a whole and, constituting an acute short-term risk, need to be addressed swiftly. The fact that external conflict can dethrone authoritarian regimes is well established in the literature. For example, military defeat in interstate wars has been shown to increase the probability of military coups.[128] And if the final stab does not come from within, leaders can 'lose power at the hands of their foreign enemy's military forces [as] foreign forces typically remove any impediment or potential source of opposition to their rule and hence exile, imprison, or outright eliminate the former leaders'.[129] Conversely, threats that do not endanger the political or physical survival of the regime are not expected lastingly to undermine welfare.

Second, the external threat must be enduring in the sense that it cannot be easily removed through military victory. This is the case if the threat emanates from, most often neighbouring, states that cannot be defeated in a way that guarantees the absence of any future threats—for example, by taking complete control of their industrial production, ensuring complete demilitarization, or continuous occupation. Save for making lasting peace, the infeasibility of any of these options makes fending off such threats an enduring political and fiscal burden.

Third, threats need to be external to the national territory in order to trigger this dynamic. This is because internal threats in the form of centre-seeking rebellions—those seeking to seize power by overthrowing the incumbent regime— are routinely fought in a way that associates civilian and military agencies in a 'joint project' comprising significant welfare measures as part of a 'hearts and minds' campaign.[130] Such counter-revolutionary constellations see a rise of social spending in parallel to security-related expenditures. As Stubbs notes in the case of Malaysia, the Federal and the state governments significantly increased their spending on education and health during the Emergency.[131] Regional rebellions, in turn, that seek separation or autonomy from the political centre are often not perceived as severe threats to the survival of the regime, making governments reluctant to shift significant resources towards the military—especially if such shifts would mean jeopardizing their own political coalitions.[132]

---

[127] Doner, Ritchie, and Slater 2005.   [128] Bueno de Mesquita, Siverson et al. 1992.
[129] Goemans 2008, p. 778.   [130] Slater 2018.   [131] Stubbs 1989, pp. 168–89.
[132] Slater 2018.

Such enduring, regime-threatening, external threats entail a significant shift in the regime's fiscal priorities. As Carter points out, between 1950 and 2001 war mobilization and fighting has been associated with a significant squeeze in non-military expenditures.[133] While during peace time about 75 per cent of the budget is spent on non-military items, this proportion shrinks to about 50 per cent in times of conflict. He further notes that '[t]his reduction in nonmilitary expenditures often includes cuts to social spending. From 1960 to 1999, governments allocated 16.2 per cent less of their annual GDP to health care spending during an interstate war than they did during peacetime'.[134]

Rulers are usually aware that this spending shift entails a domestic political risk as resources are turned away from key constituencies of the support coalition. Yet, given the imminence of the threat, they prefer the possibility of short-term survival irrespective of later negative repercussions. Furthermore, since the threat is severe, it is visible and common knowledge to all members of the support coalition. As a result, coalition members do not perceive the spending shift as a 'power grab'[135] by rulers revoking the social contract. In view of the reduction of their side-payment,[136] coalition members have two choices. They can abandon the coalition and thereby risk the breakdown of the regime, or accept lower side-payments and maintain their support. For two reasons, they will be likely to choose the latter option. First, they cannot be certain to be part of any newly formed regime coalition and will thus prefer a permanent, albeit reduced, side-payment to the risk of exclusion.[137] Second, it is likely that even a newly formed regime will have to deter the external threat, and thus cannot credibly commit to higher side-payments. Note, however, that even if the threat is present before regime formation, intra-elite conflict still entails an incentive to form broad coalitions. From the elites' point of view, support continues to be needed against elite rivals. And from the ordinary citizens' point of view, any level of side-payment is still preferable to no side-payments at all. Broad coalitions facing a severe external threat therefore face a dilemma of contravening incentives in the presence of limited resources. It is the erosion of their fiscal capacity to provide 'butter and guns' that undermines their ability to establish authoritarian welfare states.

Two significant objections may be raised to this argument which need to be addressed: First, in the western European context war making and preparation have been associated with an increase in redistributive public policies as compensation for the hardship lower-income groups endured during the war,[138] and with enhancement of state capacity and in particular the ability to extract resources from society.[139] There is empirical evidence for the latter outside Europe as

---

[133] J. Carter 2017.   [134] ibid., p. 1772.   [135] Svolik 2009.

[136] Those working in the military will obviously see their side-payments increase, which, as argued below, can have important distributive consequences at later stages.

[137] Bueno de Mesquita, A. Smith et al. 2003.   [138] Scheve and Stasavage 2010.

[139] Tilly 1985.

well.[140] Both of these mechanisms should in principle counteract the fiscally detrimental effects of external threats. In practice, however, the countervailing effects are limited for the following reasons. First, the 'conscription of wealth'[141] argument relies on *progressive* taxation of income, in particular from the wealthy in society. Yet even high-capacity developing countries have struggled to extract revenue from economic elites.[142] One of the main reasons is that income tax relies on a sophisticated system of monitoring, enforcement, and compliance.[143] In addition, the ability to tax income is positively correlated with political competition, which means autocratic regimes are particularly disadvantaged in this respect.[144] In sum, developing countries have 'failed to emulate the hallmark of 20th-century Western taxation: a strong and progressive personal income tax',[145] making 'conscription of wealth' effects unlikely.[146]

As for the Tilly mechanism, Lu and Thies have shown that enhanced extractive capacity from war making occurs only under specific scope conditions, which in the case of external threats of the nature described above are rarely met, in particular in the Middle East:[147] in Tilly's argument, wars and war preparation are viewed as sporadic features of politics, whereas threats here are defined as enduring and endemic. In the Middle East especially, interstate wars have been highly destructive and been frequently followed by debt traps. The availability of external patrons—which is also a common feature of Middle East politics—further erodes extractive capacity as elites seek to extract resources from the international system rather than from their own society.[148] This is not to deny that external threats can enhance a state's non-fiscal abilities. For example, war preparation and making can heighten infrastructural power by increasing the legibility and penetration of society by the state through compulsory conscription, censuses, and population mapping.[149] But unless this infrastructural power can in turn be converted into increased fiscal resources—which I argue is unlikely—severe external threats prevent the emergence of authoritarian welfare states.

The second major objection concerns the enduring effect of severe external threats on welfare spending *after the threat has subsided*. While they can last for decades, most severe external threats eventually subside, which should in principle open an opportunity for a 'peace dividend' and a significant shift in the spending priorities of the regime. The reason why broad-coalition regimes after the threat has faded hardly ever pivot to a full-blown authoritarian welfare state is that external threat situations entail processes of path dependence. More

---

[140] Thies 2004; and Thies 2005.   [141] Scheve and Stasavage 2010.
[142] Lust and Rakner 2018.
[143] Besley and Persson 2014, p. 103.   [144] Yogo and Ngo Njib 2018.
[145] Genschel and Seelkopf 2016, p. 316.
[146] This is one of the reasons why in the Global South the welfare state debate does not systematically revolve around the trade-off between high welfare spending and disincentives from high taxes.
[147] Lu and Thies 2012.   [148] Heydemann 2000a, p. 13.   [149] Mann 1993, p. 59.

specifically, long-lasting external threats and the attendant shifts in fiscal resources towards security empower a very specific segment within the support coalition: the military. And just like welfare states over time reinforce initial advantages given to beneficiaries (see below), external threats heighten the power asymmetries between military and non-military actors in the coalition. Simply channelling vast sums from warfare back to welfare after the end of conflict is thus not an option. Related to that, Perthes rightly remarks that militarization induced by external threats can itself morph into a survival strategy for the regime as it not only affords high levels of control over society, but also allows for the continued extraction of external support in the presence of external patrons.[150] Taken together, both mechanisms prevent easy post-conflict shifts towards authoritarian welfare.

Resource endowments

At this point, yet only here, resource endowment begins to matter (see Figure 1.4). As the literature on the 'rentier state' has argued, the availability of significant fiscal surpluses stemming from the export of natural resources, specifically hydrocarbons in the Middle East, has enabled rentier states to flush their citizens with welfare measures.[151] In its Middle Eastern variant, resource-driven generosity has often been considered quasi-natural. For example, Beblawi remarks that the 'rent

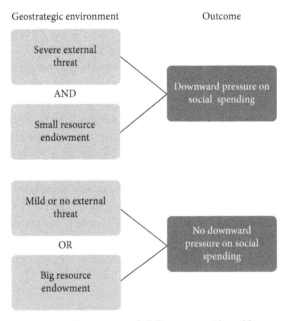

Figure 1.4 Geostrategic environment and ability to provide welfare

---

[150] Perthes 2000.
[151] Beblawi and Luciani 1987. See also Hertog 2010; Soares de Oliviera 2007; and Heilbrunn 2014.

that is held in the hands of the government *has to be* redistributed among the population'.[152] Similarly, Luciani asserts that 'a rentier state will *inevitably* end up performing the role of allocating the income that it receives from the rest of the world'.[153] Yet in light of very ungenerous resource-rich countries—Oman, for example, has the same level of rents per capita as Equatorial Guinea but its secondary enrolment is 234 per cent and its life expectancy 34 per cent higher[154]—this automatism is not warranted. Instead, as Yom rightly notes, rentierism can occur in a 'despotic' variant, with a narrow coalition that keeps itself in power through repressive closure.[155] There is thus no mechanism that links fiscal surpluses from rents directly to either coalition size or social welfare.[156]

Given the political incentives of a broad-coalition regime, however, rent surpluses should enable rulers to simultaneously engage in military expansion *and* maintain a high level of social spending. Whilst scarce resources drag social spending levels to the bottom if threats are severe, abundant resource surpluses provide the regime with sufficient fiscal capacity to honour both defence and welfare commitments. That said, long-lasting, full-scale interstate war can make shielding welfare from warfare difficult even in regimes with large resource endowments. However, given that open warfare is rather exceptional and temporary in nature, these situations can hamper yet not undermine the emergence of authoritarian welfare states.

Could we see a similar dynamic in regimes relying on other forms of external rents, such as foreign aid and grants from foreign patrons? The short answer is no. For starters, grants and foreign aid do not reach the level of resource rents, especially not oil and gas rents. In the period from 2000 until 2012, the highest level of foreign aid in a non-micro island state was 368 USD per capita (Kosovo).[157] In the Middle East, Iraq received most aid per capita (178 USD p.c.), followed by Jordan (141 USD p.c.). By comparison, the labour-abundant oil exporters Iran and Algeria earned an average of 1,782 and 2,217 USD per capita respectively from resource rents. Even the minor exporter Malaysia exported hydrocarbons worth 1,122 USD per capita. Moreover, external aid flows are frequently link to the military and geopolitical position of a state. They therefore often supplement rather than substitute a regime's domestic defence effort and make the continued flow of resources contingent upon the continued presence of external threats.

---

[152] Beblawi 1987, p. 53; emphasis added.   [153] Luciani 1987, p. 69; emphasis added.
[154] World Bank 2017.   [155] Yom 2011.
[156] Eibl and Hertog 2018 maintain that in resource-rich, labour-scarce regimes welfare distribution bears lower marginal costs than repression, which is why such regimes are expected to respond with distribution to bottom-up threats. But even this mechanism is conditional and relies on the prior occurrence of popular threats. To reiterate, I would expect the opposite mechanism in labour-abundant regimes analysed here.
[157] World Bank 2017. Micronesia, the Marshall Islands, and Palau received foreign aid between 1,074 and 1,472 per capita.

To put it more bluntly, the United States would not have bankrolled a welfare state in South Korea during the Cold War.

Towards the end of this section, two further questions need to be answered—one substantive, one epistemological. First, what justifies the narrow focus on abilities understood as fiscal capacity? There is no point denying that the institutional capacity of the state and its bureaucracy significantly influence how resources are translated into outcomes. Social policies are no exception in this respect and Wood and Gough point out that the capabilities of state institutions have an important role in shaping welfare outcomes.[158] That said, I would submit that state capacity at regime onset was largely comparable across the cases examined herein. I provide empirical evidence corroborating this claim later in this chapter. Second, to some readers my theoretical framework may have the smack of determinism. This is not the case. In keeping with Lieberman's position,[159] the mechanisms outlined above are underpinned by a logic of at least partial indeterminacy. In a world governed by structure and agency, processes such as intra-elite conflict raise the likelihood of coalitional broadening, but this is not a guaranteed outcome. The partial indeterminacy of critical junctures is precisely a function of the probabilistic nature of causation, which in critical junctures gives more room to agency than during 'normal' times but does not mean that the interaction of structure and agency is not characterized by recurrent patterns of the type I emphasize here.[160]

1.1.5 Three different pathways of welfare provision

Figure 1.5 and Table 1.1 provide an overview of the argument thus far and succinctly summarize the determinants of welfare provision in autocracies. The realignment of societal actors during the moment of regime formation is structured by the interplay of intra-elite conflict, communal cleavages, external threats, and abundant resources. These 'discontinuities in patterns of political domination,' as Haggard and Kaufman call it,[161] determine the constituencies to which ruling elites respond. Social policy regimes shaped by these coalitional dynamics do not map easily onto the distinction between clientelistic and policy-driven distributive policies.[162] On the one hand, they lack the contingency upon imminent, contextualized political support, such as clientelistic distribution during an election. Most often, the criteria for distribution are also formal and public, akin to programmatic forms of distribution. On the other hand, in specific contexts they can be utilized

---

[158] Geof Wood and Gough 2006. See also Cammett and Sasmaz 2016.
[159] Lieberman 2015, p. 241.
[160] See Pierson 2004, p. 51; and Slater and E. Simmons 2010 for a similar understanding of critical junctures. The arguments in favour of complete indeterminacy are represented by Mahoney 2000; and Capoccia and Kelemen 2007.
[161] Haggard and Kaufman 2008, p. 7.   [162] Stokes et al. 2013; see also Harding 2015.

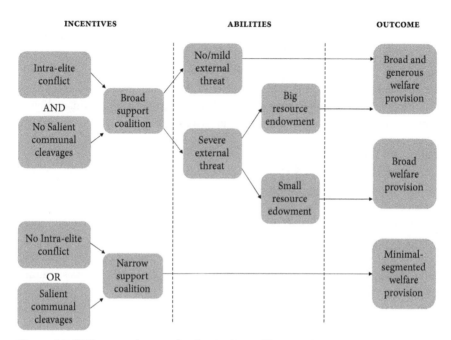

Figure 1.5 Different pathways of authoritarian welfare provision

Table 1.1 Determinants of authoritarian welfare provision

	High ability	Low ability
High incentive	Broad and generous welfare provision	Broad welfare provision
Low incentive	Segmented or minimal welfare provision	Segmented or minimal welfare provision

in a targeted manner and are thus not safe from clientelistic practices. Moreover, understanding the social policy regimes outlined below as programmatic would ignore the coercive aspect embedded in them which seeks to tie strategically relevant groups to the regime and render them dependent upon it.[163] Three pathways of welfare provision emerge out of the dynamics of coalition formation.[164]

Pathway 1: broad and generous welfare provision
Broad coalitions that are unconstrained by their geostrategic environment provide generous levels of welfare spending to a broad cross-section of the population.

---

[163] Albertus, Fenner, and Slater 2018. Gerschewski 2013 defines the process of co-optation in autocracies along similar lines.

[164] See Chapter 2 for a more detailed description of these pathways.

This is expressed by high welfare efforts, measured as the relative amount of state spending allocated to social welfare, and by social policies widely, often universally, accessible to the population. Social policies tend to be highly inclusive, with no or very few barriers to access for groups within society.[165] Social security and assistance programmes are characterized by a high rate of coverage that sets these regimes apart from those based on narrow coalitions. This pathway represents what can be called authoritarian welfare states.

Pathway 2: broad welfare provision

Broad coalitions with scarce resources and facing a severe external threat provide welfare broadly, but not generously. This reflects the fact that the politics of distribution is shaped by incentives stemming from coalition types, whilst the politics of allocation responds to challenges from the external environment. Such regimes seek to make social policies widely accessible and inclusive, with access often based on citizenship only and coverage rates being rather high. They fail, however, to underpin access with a sufficient stream of financial resources, leading to generally underfunded social policies.

Emanating from the specific combination of high incentives and low abilities, these regimes, furthermore, engage in what can be called 'cheap social policies', which are characterized by (i) insufficient financial commitment; (ii) a strong reliance on 'free' social policies distributing rent-generating statutory rights to lower and middle classes; (iii) the use of windfalls to finance social expenditures, such as expropriations or privatizations; (iv) devising social policies that alleviate the regime's shortage of resources.

Pathway 3: minimal-segmented welfare provision

Narrow coalition regimes, regardless of the geostrategic environment, are characterized by minimal-segmented welfare provision. This pathway features generally low welfare efforts expressed in relative shares of social spending significantly below those of authoritarian welfare states. It comes in two main variants. *Minimal* welfare provision is reflected in a low welfare effort and minimal financial commitments to social policies. Social security is provided rudimentarily, covering only a small number of life-course risks.[166] Coverage rates of social security and assistance programme are low. *Segmented* welfare provision differs in that social policies are not underfunded or ungenerous, but they are highly exclusive, accessible mostly to small set of strategic groups in society only. This type of welfare provision is characterized by a high level of segmentation into in-groups and out-groups, but access is not systematically conditional on individual political

---

[165] See Cammett 2014a on the notion of inclusive and exclusive welfare provision.
[166] Lebanon, which is not covered here because of its lack of spending data, falls into this category. See Chen and Cammett 2012.

support in a clientelistic fashion. Depending on the exact size of in-groups catered to, coverage and spending levels can be higher than in the minimalist type. That said, the exclusion of large parts of society from social policies means that even in segmented policy regimes the overall share of social spending will be significantly lower than in authoritarian welfare states. This is partly due to the fact that generosity towards in-group members in a small coalition regime is often expressed by distributing strictly private goods, rather than social policies, to coalition members to ensure exclusivity. Genuine high-spenders with limited access do not exist.

While my framework based on elites and non-elites gives preference to parsimony, there are nonetheless patterns that emerge depending on the type of non-elite group that is included in the coalition. First, regimes characterized by high levels of rural incorporation with important agricultural constituencies in the countryside tend to give particular attention to primary schooling, literacy, and health care needs. The establishment of 'low tech, high results' health houses in post-1979 Iran is a good example.[167] Regimes with more urban constituencies are often characterized by an extensive subsidy regime, ensuring cheap food and energy to urban dwellers.[168] From a class perspective, the incorporation of large middle-class groups tends to shift educational policies towards the secondary and tertiary sector, whereas working-class constituencies are often rewarded with classical decommodifying policies in the area of social security. While these are discernible trends, it is important to point out that (i) actors' policy preference are dynamic, not fixed; (ii) these different non-elite groups do not necessarily have organizational capacity, but if they have they will be more forceful in shaping social policies; (iii) broad-coalition regimes need to cater to a number of different groups, such that no single social policy will ever completely dominate; and (iv) importantly welfare states are generative of new groups in society through the very policies they implement (e.g. education and middle classes).

Regarding the incorporation of working classes specifically, Bellin has argued that giving a privileged position to organized labour segments the working class, which in turn can lead to segmented and dualistic policy regimes that sharply delineate insiders and outsiders.[169] I would argue, though, that the ability of organized labour to undermine the emergence of broad and generous welfare provision is limited for the following reasons. First, as a result of incomplete commodification organized labour has been notoriously weak in the Global South, in particular in authoritarian regimes.[170] Its ability to shape social policies has therefore often been curtailed. Second, the 'labour aristocracy' argument is not as relevant during periods of extension, but rather during welfare

---

[167] K. Harris 2017, chapter 4.   [168] This trend has been well established since Bates 1983.
[169] Bellin 2000; Ragui Assaad 2014; and Hertog 2016.
[170] Rudra 2002; Rudra 2007; and Cammett and Sasmaz 2016.

stagnation and retrenchment when established benefits need to be defended in a zero-sum situation. Third, as mentioned above authoritarian regimes can shape and generate new societal groups in the process of establishing welfare states, which can counteract monopolizing tendencies within labour. In fact, once social policy has been established as the key mechanism of legitimation, authoritarian regimes often seek to reach out to new segments in the economy beyond the group of initial core supporters by, for instance, opening social security to parts of the informal sector. I provide examples of this process in Chapter 2.

1.1.6 Mechanisms of path dependence

The above explanation combines existing arguments in a novel framework and, thus, generates theory. The explanation of the persistence of welfare trajectories exclusively resorts to the body of existing literature on path dependence and applies it to an authoritarian context.[171] While the institutionalization of coalitions in social policies reflects underlying balances of power and, as a result, does not fundamentally differ from patterns of institutionalization in democracies,[172] the persistence of coalitions is reinforced in a non-democratic context. This is because, in contrast to democracies, autocracies lack an institutional mechanism—that is, electoral competition for power—to organize the reformation of coalitions. By consequence, the substitution of support groups by others becomes more difficult and more risky, considering the negative consequences of such an endeavour which surpass the troubles inflected by electoral defeat.[173] This is not to say that change and reform have been absent. Broadly speaking, however, regimes have remained on their specific pathways of spending and distribution.

Regarding the specific mechanisms of path dependence relevant to this study, two can be highlighted in particular.

Initial advantages reinforced over time

It has been argued that initial advantages conferred on societal actors can be significantly reinforced over time, which turns the beneficiaries of policies into important gatekeepers guaranteeing their continuation.[174] The reason for this is twofold. First, groups targeted by specific social policies can, over time, substantially grow in size, which reinforces their political weight. Consider the example

---

[171] The study of path dependence has been prolific. See Ikenberry 1994; Thelen 2003; Pierson 2004; and Beyer 2010 for a selective overview.

[172] This has been the key tenet of historical institutionalism, which conceptualizes institutions as distributional instruments. See Hall 2010; and Mahoney and Thelen 2010. This stands in contrast to approaches that view institutions primarily as commitment devices. See, in an authoritarian context, Gandhi 2008; Magaloni 2008; and Wright 2008a.

[173] Martin 2005, p. 29.   [174] Skocpol 1992.

of free university education. Instituted, say, in the 1950s, the policy benefits a manageable section of the middle class, barely surpassing a few thousand families. Forty years later, free higher education has become a privilege of millions of families, who consider it their right and are ready to stand up for its continuation. Second, policies implemented by specific coalitions tend to maintain, if not increase, power asymmetries between members and non-members of the support coalition.[175] In this context, it is important to realize that the decisive victory achieved by societal groups during the moment of regime formation shift resources in a lasting manner, which they can deploy in future rounds of contestation.[176] Based on this dynamic feedback between policies and power rooted in coalitions, we should expect a perpetuation of welfare trajectories.

Initial divergence reinforcing the power of groups in society is also the reason why resource-scarce broad coalitions facing a severe external threat cannot easily transform into authoritarian welfare states. Following a sustained empowerment of the regime's military, the military develops considerable veto power itself, able to influence budgetary decisions and ready to defend privileges, even once external threats have waned.[177]

Unintended beneficiaries

The second mechanism concerns the expansion of the number of beneficiaries to groups that were not initially targeted by policies, but that, over time, have become powerful stakeholders in the current status quo.[178] With regard to social policies, this group of unintended beneficiaries can be found especially in the area of food and energy subsidies. As the two case studies on Egypt and Tunisia will show, subsidies that initially targeted urban middle classes—they were never really intended to target the poor—have gradually come to benefit a politically powerful network of local producers and traders that reap enormous benefits from the subsidy system as it is currently in place.

Yet, unintended beneficiaries also exist for countries following pathway 2, the broad but not generous welfare providers. Due to the sustained financial commitment to the army in these regimes, a similar network of beneficiaries can come into place that strives for the perpetuation of a high financial stream to the armed forces. These beneficiaries include, on the one hand, the military-industrial complex, which in the MENA region has grown to a considerable size and vested its interests in the status quo.[179] On the other hand, the army itself can transform into an economic actor by venturing into sectors of civilian production and thus

---

[175] Ikenberry 1994, p. 8; and Pierson 2004, p. 30.   [176] Pierson 2015, p. 134.
[177] See Perlmutter 1977; P. Collier and Hoeffler 2002; Gupta et al. 2004; Rasler and Thompson 1985; and Lektzian and Prins 2008 for examples outside the MENA region. In the context of the Middle East, see Kamrava 2000; S. Cook 2007; and Droz-Vincent 2011.
[178] Thelen 2003.   [179] Richards and Waterbury 2008, p. 354; and Halliday 2005.

aggrandize the pool of people who directly or indirectly benefit from military expenditures.

1.2 Contribution to the Literature

1.2.1 Middle Eastern studies

Social policies have received increasing attention by scholars of the Middle East,[180] but the literature has been dominated by individual case studies, in contrast to other world regions where a cross-regional research agenda on the welfare state is well established.[181] In the Middle East, there is a marked absence of explicitly macro-comparative work which seeks to explain the variety of social policy trajectories across the region in a coherent analytical framework.[182] This study represents an attempt to remedy this shortcoming by, first, laying out empirically the extent of regional divergence with regards to social policy trajectories and, second, establishing a framework capable of explaining the causes of this long-term divergence. Looking at Middle Eastern social policies through a comparative lens has a number of analytical advantages.

First, it counters the existing tendency in the literature to generalize from heavily researched cases to the region as a whole. This has been particularly the case with Egypt which, due to size, geopolitics, and accessibility, has received disproportionate attention. As a result, the country has frequently been portrayed as the epitome of extensive populist welfare distribution in the region.[183] In reality, Egypt's historical welfare effort has been mediocre and its social policy ambitions were stunted early on. Conversely, authoritarian welfare states, such as Tunisia or Algeria, that have been trailblazers in the field of social policies, have not had the same impact on social policy research. The cross-regional typology of welfare efforts developed in this study not only enables us to gauge the relative importance of social policies in different regimes, but also guides us in the expectation as to which kind of social policies (e.g. open access vs. segmented) we should expect to see.

Second, comparing allows us to better understand the conditions in which key variables begin to matter. In this respect, the best example in the Middle East is probably oil, the effect of which has both been over- and under-estimated in individual country studies. 'Rentier state' theory in its original form saw an intrinsic

---

[180] See, for example, Cammett 2014a; Brooke 2019; K. Harris 2017; and Loewe 2010.
[181] For example, Segura-Ubiergo 2007; C.-U. Park and Jung 2009; Kwon 1997; L. J. Cook 2007; and Cerami 2013.
[182] Karshena and Moghadam's 2006 insightful volume represents a collection of individual country studies.
[183] See, for instance, Richards and Waterbury 2008, p. 31.

link between oil rents and welfare distribution, which was largely a function of its theorizing based on a number of Gulf states.[184] At the other end of the spectrum, in Harris' path-breaking study of the Iranian welfare state oil is literally a non-variable and thus deemed to be causally insignificant for the social policy shift after 1979.[185] He thereby underestimates the role oil has played in enabling the post-revolutionary regime to eschew the 'butter or guns' trade-off. More generally, nothing, *per se*, prevents a resource-scarce regime from spending half of its budget on welfare; and nothing, *per se*, predisposes a resource-rich regime to do so. Continuing the conditionalist revision of the resource curse literature,[186] this study situates resource endowments in an analytical framework that explains under what conditions oil rents and external threats matter for social policies. It is the implicit counterfactuals at the heart of this comparison which provide, in my view, hitherto untapped analytical leverage to study social policies in MENA.

Another empirical contribution of this book lies in the collection of original data on welfare spending in the countries analysed herein. By compiling a novel dataset on social spending reaching back to the moments of regime formation—often in the early to mid-1950s—this book critically expands our empirical knowledge of welfare distribution in labour-abundant MENA regimes. The data were collected from archival material of the International Monetary Fund and from a selected number of statistical yearbooks.[187] Whilst data collection itself is sometimes undervalued as descriptive, the availability of new, mostly historical data has been crucial for this study. First, only by tracing spending data back to the origins of these regimes was I able to identify regime formation as the moment of spending divergence. With pre-existing data only,[188] it would have been impossible to eliminate other potential moments of social policy divergence, such as the oil boom in the early 1970s.

Second, overlooking social spending patterns for the entire post-independence period, this study sounds a cautioning note on the argument that the advent of neoliberalism in the region has led to general welfare retrenchment across the region.[189] Granted, neoliberal transformation has had profound effects on livelihoods across the region. Fiscal constraints imposed by austerity have slowed down progress in the area of human development.[190] The reversal of land reforms

---

[184] Beblawi and Luciani 1987.   [185] K. Harris 2017.

[186] E.g. Herb 2014; Dunning 2008; Peters and P. Moore 2009; Yom 2011; Luong and Weinthal 2010; and Caselli and Tesei 2016.

[187] The dataset and the method of data collection are presented in greater detail in a data note in Appendix A. Data collection was carried out in association with a research project on authoritarian stability at the GIGA Institute in Hamburg. The project has yielded a large dataset on Global State Revenues and Expenditures, parts of which are used in this book. See V. Lucas and Richter 2016.

[188] Staring in the early 1970s, IMF data have important temporal limitations and are incomplete for a number of MENA countries, such as Algeria. See IMF 2011.

[189] For examples of this claim, see Baylouny 2010; Clark 2004a; Murphy 1999; King 2010; Hinnebusch 2006; Hinnebusch 2010; and Bozarslan 2011.

[190] Diwan and Akin 2015, p. 18.

acutely heightened inequality in rural sectors.[191] And structural adjustment had a negative effect on poverty in Egypt, Jordan, and Morocco.[192] That said, this study emphasizes and helps explain variation in the application of neoliberalism in the Middle East. First, this study shows that historically welfare efforts were not uniform, which is important if we want to gauge the relative severity of cutbacks. Ascribing a 'previously wide-ranging commitment to social welfare' to segmented-minimalist welfare providers, such as Jordan, is symptomatic of a widespread broad-brush approach in the literature, which views both welfare expansion and cutbacks across the region as universal.[193] This study seeks to nuance that. Second, while the partial exemption of health and education from cutbacks has been acknowledged,[194] this study provides quantitative empirical evidence that welfare retrenchment was systematically conditioned by the type of support coalition formed at the moment of regime formation. Given that, it becomes much less surprising that welfare was cutback in Jordan or outsourced to charities in Syria during neoliberal transformation, but relatively untouched in Tunisia.[195] In other words, social spending in the Middle East was adjusted as a function of the way in which welfare states had been created.

1.2.2 Comparative social policies

This study also contributes to the comparative research on the welfare state and continues recent attempts to broaden the geographical scope of this literature.[196] Regrettably, the literature on welfare states in the Global South has taken very little notice of the Middle East. For example, Haggard and Kaufman's seminal cross-regional study omits the Middle East entirely.[197] Similarly, *The Oxford Handbook of the Welfare State* contains no entry on the Middle East, although 'emerging welfare states' in Latin America, Eastern Europe, and Asia are included.[198] This relative neglect is particularly surprising given the scope and fiscal weight of public welfare provision in the region, roughly on a par with Latin America and only just behind post-Communist Central Asia. With the Middle East often viewed as a region pervaded by exceptionalism stemming from abundant resources, violent conflict, and the lack of democracy, this books attempts to build an analytical map for non-MENA specialists interested in the region's social policies. By the same token, the book also highlights that blanket cross-regional comparisons of social policies can be problematic.[199]

---

[191] Bush 2011; Bush and Ayeb 2012; and Hanieh 2013.   [192] El-Said and Harrigan 2014.
[193] Martínez 2017, p. 476.   [194] Cammett and Diwan 2016.
[195] Baylouny 2010; De Elvira and Zintl 2014; and El-Said and Harrigan 2014.
[196] Examples of this new focus on less developed countries are Rudra 2007; and Rudra 2008.
[197] Haggard and Kaufman 2008.   [198] Castles et al. 2010.
[199] For examples of cross-regional approaches, see Haggard and Kaufman 2008; and Mares and Carnes 2009.

While borrowing heavily from the literature on (advanced) welfare states, this book also seeks to contribute to theory development by emphasizing war making and preparation as major determinants of social policies, which finds expression in the concept of 'cheap social policies' introduced in this book. Despite the ubiquity of war in politics, the comparative politics literature on war has predominantly been focused on the nexus with state formation,[200] and to a lesser extent economic development.[201] Major exceptions are Skocpol's seminal study *Protecting Soldiers and Mothers* and Harris' recent work on Iran's 'martyr's welfare state',[202] yet neither of them explores the effect of war in a broader comparative setting. Through the conceptual lens of 'cheap social policies', this study emphasizes that the impact of war on social policies is contingent upon the incumbent political coalition,[203] while demonstrating how political elites seek to juggle the conflicting incentives of defending the country and catering to large popular constituencies. This concept should prove useful for analysing the interaction between conflict and social policies beyond the Middle East.

1.2.3 Authoritarianism studies

As a legacy to its origins, scholarship on authoritarianism has been predominantly concerned with the question of regime breakdown and survival.[204] This means that 'current theoretical research has neglected much of the interesting everyday politics of authoritarian rule, consigning this to the realm of case studies by country experts.'[205] While the political economy literature on authoritarianism has elucidated many differences in *economic policies* across autocracies in the last decade,[206] the variation of *social policies* across authoritarian regimes has not been systematically studied.[207] By furnishing a novel explanatory framework for the study of authoritarian welfare states, this study sheds systematic light on the conditions under which authoritarian regimes make extensive welfare commitments to large cross-sections of the population and, in doing so, many times outperform developing democracies. At the same time, this study shows that theories developed in democratic welfare states, notably explanations of path dependent social policies, travel fairly well to autocracies where the sustained

---

[200] For example, Tilly 1985; Thies 2004; and Scheve and Stasavage 2010. In the Middle East, see Heydemann 2000b.

[201] Stubbs 1999; and Doner, Ritchie, and Slater 2005.

[202] Skocpol 1992; K. Harris 2013; and K. Harris 2017.

[203] For a similar argument regarding war and debt servicing, see Saylor and Wheeler 2017.

[204] Bank 2009, p. 33.   [205] Pepinsky 2008b, p. 1.

[206] See, for example, Steinberg and Malhotra 2014; Hankla and Kuthy 2013; and Knutsen and Fjelde 2013.

[207] Social policies have most often been analysed across regime types (democracy and autocracy). See, most recently, Knutsen and Rasmussen 2018.

empowerment of societal groups by institutionalized social spending imposes severe political constraints on the regime.

In addition, by showing the crucial importance of support coalitions for the political economy of distribution in authoritarian regimes, this study urges an analytic shift away from the category of regime type to explain divergent spending patterns in autocracies. Granted, the proposed categories of broad and narrow coalitions are still very broad; yet they appear more appropriate to capture varying incentives for authoritarian rulers than focusing on nominal differences in the composition of the ruling elite (e.g. civilian, military). Coalitional approaches also guard against the problematic assumption that authoritarianism means government for and by the elite.[208] Autocracies can built distributive, universalist welfare states for lower and middle classes and this book spells out under what conditions this is possible.

Finally, the book seeks to restore the role of spending, in particular social spending, as a credible commitment device in autocracies. Coined 'transfers'[209] or 'rents',[210] pro-majority spending has generally been conceptualized as a highly discretionary tool for short-term appeasement which can be withdrawn with virtually no political costs. As a result, spending has been ruled out as a mechanism autocrats can use to make credible commitments to their support coalitions. While this stance has always been at odds with the retrenchment literature, which has highlighted the politics of 'taking away' as one of the thorniest issues for politicians,[211] it equally fails to acknowledge the extent to which *spending is institutionalized* in authoritarian regimes. Delivered through innumerable public institutions enshrined in law and populated by actors, social policies in autocracies are most often highly formalized and defy any notion that they can be retracted at the whim of the ruler. Knutsen and Rasmussen made this point recently for pension policies[212]—this study extends the argument to authoritarian welfare distribution more widely.

1.3 Why Conventional Wisdom Does not Work

A number of alternative explanations have been utilized to explain cross-country differences in welfare efforts. Some of these theoretical arguments, such as the ideological orientation of the autocratic ruler, cannot be easily rejected at the macro-level and, therefore, will be examined in greater detail in later case study chapters. Others can be evaluated and refuted more easily here.[213]

---

[208] For example, Acemoglu and J. A. Robinson 2006; Ansell 2010; and Jensen and Skaaning 2015. For a critique, see Albertus 2015a.

[209] Acemoglu and J. A. Robinson 2006.   [210] Gandhi and Przeworski 2006.

[211] E.g. Pierson 1994.   [212] Knutsen and Rasmussen 2018.

[213] While this study is focused on public welfare policies, it is important to acknowledge the huge importance of social and lifestyle determinants of human development outcomes, a literature that is not reviewed systematically here. See, for example, R. Wilkinson and Marmot 2003.

1.3.1 Socioeconomic determinants

The literature has highlighted a number of macro-structural variables to explain varying levels of social expenditures. Following a 'logic of industrialism,'[214] some scholars have viewed increasing social expenditures as a quasi-natural accompaniment of economic wealth and modernization, as income growth is believed to bring about new constituencies in demand for social welfare.[215] Theoretically and empirically, however, development as a predictor of welfare spending is problematic. On the one hand, either the 'logic of industrialism' assumes a pluralistic political framework for its causal mechanisms to work,[216] or the causal effects of development are understood as unmediated by the political process.[217] On the other hand, reflecting mixed findings for democracies,[218] wealth seems to be a rather bad predictor of social spending levels, in the Middle East and autocracies at large.[219] Looking at Figure 1.6(a), it becomes clear that welfare spending has remained markedly constant despite the considerable increase of GDP per capita

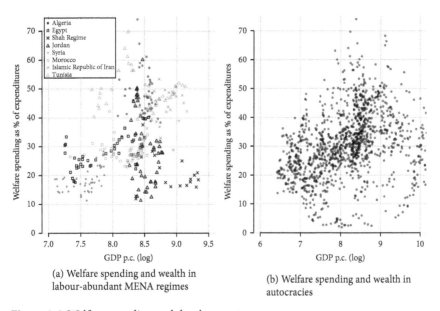

(a) Welfare spending and wealth in labour-abundant MENA regimes

(b) Welfare spending and wealth in autocracies

Figure 1.6 Welfare spending and development

Note: Regime data for non-MENA countries are based on Svolik 2012; spending data are taken from V. Lucas and Richter 2016; and IMF 2011; GDP data are taken from Heston, Summers, and Aten 2006.

---

[214] C. Kerr 1964.   [215] Wilensky 1975; Lindert 2005; and Obinger and Wagschal 2010.
[216] Myles 1984.   [217] Hicks and Misra 1993, p. 674.
[218] See Huber and J. D. Stephens 2001, p. 335; Baqir 2002, p. 23; Mares and Carnes 2009, p. 96; and Gandhi 2008, p. 147. Flora and Alber 1981 argue that economic development is a bad predictor of the timing of social insurance adoption.
[219] M. N. Islam 2015 finds a negative effect of growth on non-defence spending in autocracies.

that has occurred in labour-abundant MENA regimes over time.[220] At the global level, depicted in Figure 1.6(b), high spending levels are only empirically absent in very poor autocracies, suggesting a minimum threshold of development as a necessary condition for a high welfare effort.[221]

Development strategies and openness to world trade have been put forward as another explanation for varying welfare efforts. Wibbels and Ahlquist, for example, have proposed a theory in which factor endowments determine development strategies, which, in turn, produce distinct patterns of social spending.[222] As for trade, two rival hypotheses, a 'compensation hypothesis' and an 'efficiency hypothesis', exist, with each of them claiming some empirical evidence in their favour.[223] Problems, again, emerge at the theoretical and empirical level. Whilst varying factor endowments predict the emergence of specific cleavages, they do not preclude any particular distributional outcome and, by consequence, spending level.[224] Moreover, these theoretical claims seem to be vitiated by the uniformity of development strategies in the MENA region. Richards and Waterbury note 'the relative lack of variation in the degree and scope of state intervention across countries that otherwise differ greatly'.[225] Likewise, trade restrictions have been high in the Middle East and, in contrast to social spending, differed very little across countries (see Figure 1.7).[226]

Non-tax revenues, such as resource rents and aid, have also been conjectured to affect social spending levels positively.[227] Its intuitive appeal notwithstanding, rentier state theory struggles to provide convincing causal mechanisms that link rent income to social spending. Certainly, rents directly increase state revenues which, in turn, can be distributed as social benefits to the population. Yet rents also tend to displace taxation which means that the overall level of income does not necessarily increase.[228] Moreover, the crucial question is why autocrats should actually distribute the rents rather than keeping them for themselves. Beck suggests that by distributing rents, autocrats seek to depoliticize their population;[229] yet this also holds for social spending in non-rentier states. Schlumberger argues that rentier states do not have to reinvest rent income and can therefore use it to bolster their grip on power;[230] but this strangely suggests that most state revenue in non-rentier states is productively reinvested, which is empirically not true. Finally, Anderson

---

[220]   See also Loewe 2010, p. 136; and Salbah and Yartey 2004 on this point.

[221]   All graphs in this section look very similar when using social expenditures as a share of GDP.

[222]   Wibbels and Ahlquist 2011; see also Haggard and Kaufman 2008, pp. 8–10.

[223]   Compare Segura-Ubiergo 2007, p. 167 with contradictory evidence in Mares 2005; Kaufman and Segura-Ubiergo 2001; and Nooruddin and J. W. Simmons 2009. In a vast sample of autocracies, Gandhi 2008, p. 136 finds a negligible impact of trade on social spending.

[224]   Rogowski 1989.

[225]   Richards and Waterbury 2008, p. 179; see also Cammett and Sasmaz 2016, p. 245.

[226]   See Figure 1.7 and Noland and Pack 2007, p. 105.

[227]   Beblawi 1987, p. 53; Morrison 2009; and Frazier 2006, p. 23. In the Middle East, see Beblawi and Luciani 1987.

[228]   Dunning 2008, p. 7.   [229]   M. Beck 2007b, p. 46.   [230]   Schlumberger 2008a, p. 118.

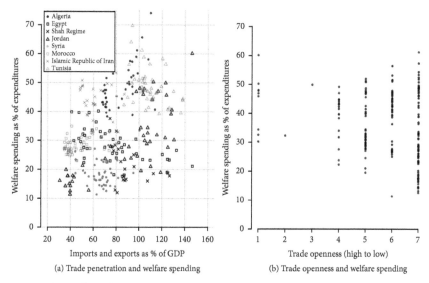

Figure 1.7 Trade and welfare spending in labour-abundant MENA regimes

Note: Regime data for non-MENA countries are based on Svolik 2012; spending data are taken from V. Lucas and Richter 2016; and IMF 2011; GDP data are taken from Heston, Summers, and Aten 2006; and the measure for trade openness is taken from Martin 2005.

remarks that rents make state elites autonomous, which is why they seek legitimacy through distribution rather than taxation and representation.[231] Yet would it not be more plausible to expect tax-paying citizens to demand more social welfare than those exempted from taxation? The state costs them more and they should logically ask for more in return.[232] Conversely, 'despotic rentierism'[233] based on exclusionary policies and repression exists, albeit not in MENA. Overall, it is problematic to attribute deterministic features to economic rents as nothing conditions their use solely for the purpose of social welfare.[234] Regarding my country sample, Figure 1.8 indeed suggests no systematic link between non-tax revenues and social spending.

1.3.2 Political and historical determinants

From the MENA-specific literature, two rival explanations need to be highlighted, which are neo-patrimonialism and legitimation ideologies. Neo-patrimonialism in the Middle East has been associated with paternalistic tendencies and, hence, a tendency to legitimate non-democratic rule by the distribution of welfare

---

[231] Anderson 1986, p. 10.   [232] Ross 2004, pp. 243–5.
[233] Yom 2011, p. 223; see also Peters and P. Moore 2009, p. 280.
[234] Richter 2009, p. 71; Herb 2005, p. 302; and Herb 2009, p. 391.

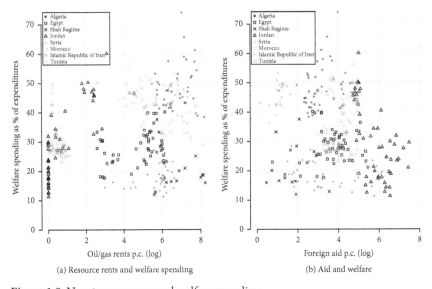

Figure 1.8 Non-tax revenues and welfare spending

Note: Regime data for non-MENA countries are based on Svolik 2012; spending data are taken from V. Lucas and Richter 2016; and IMF 2011; data on resources rents are taken from Ross 2013; and the data for aid are taken from World Bank 2010c.

goods.[235] From a slightly different angle, Loewe has argued that legitimation ideologies strongly influence a ruler's propensity to provide social welfare. He thus claims that the fault line in terms of welfare spending runs along a division between conservative-monarchical (Jordan, Morocco) and (post)socialist-republican (Algeria, Tunisia, Egypt, Syria) regimes.[236] Yet, whilst the focus on the legitimizing effect of welfare distribution is certainly warranted, theories of neo-patrimonial rule have failed to make strong predictive claims about the type and, most importantly, the extent of distribution. I should also add that almost all regimes in the region have been attributed neo-patrimonial characteristics, albeit to different degrees.[237] Finally, outside the Middle East, neo-patrimonialism is seen as a system of elite distribution that leaves precious little for the larger population.[238] Regarding the role of ideology, most area study scholars have been reluctant to view ideology—apart from nationalism and Islamism—as a driving force in Middle Eastern politics.[239] Furthermore, strong ideological commitments have not been a hallmark of neo-patrimonialism.[240] In view of Figure 1.1, the fault

---

[235] Schlumberger 2008a, pp. 111–12. For a summary of the debate on neo-patrimonialism, see Erdmann and Engel 2007.

[236] Loewe 2010, pp. 157–8.   [237] Pawelka 2002.   [238] Seminally Médard 1982.

[239] On the MENA region in general, see Ayubi 1992; Anderson 1987, p. 11; and Perlmutter 1977, p. 164. On Egypt, see Bayat 2006; and Beinin and Lockman 1988, chapter 13. On Algeria, see D. Ottaway and M. Ottaway 1970, p. 286; Quandt 1969, p. 172; and Knauss 1980, p. 71. On Tunisia, see C. H. Moore 1970, p. 315.

[240] Bratton and Van de Walle 1994, p. 548.

line seems to run right through the group of republican party regimes, which also makes regime type implausible as an explanation.

At the level below regime type, there has been a resurgence of research on authoritarian institutions in recent decades, in particular legislatures, parties, and elections.[241] Some authors have found a significant positive effect of these institutions on human development outcomes and welfare spending,[242] In a similar vein, Mares and Carnes propose three types of institutional equilibria in authoritarian regimes depending on how autocrats interact with the 'launching organization' that brought them to power.[243] In their organization proliferation scenario, social policies are expected to have broad coverage, albeit split over a multitude of programmes.[244] Could it be that the observed social policy divergence in the Middle East is driven by different institutional setups?

Four reasons make this rather unlikely. First, the positive effect of institutions on welfare has been contested. For example, Gandhi's findings do not 'indicate a significant impact for institutions on social spending'.[245] Nor are health outcomes in MENA systematically correlated with Polity scores, which in turn are associated with institutions.[246] Second, the effect of institutions is likely to be limited to short-term variations, such as distributive responses to weak electoral results as Miller finds,[247] rather than long-term, sustained, and drastic divergences into welfare state types. Third, regarding Mares and Carnes' argument their framework is mostly descriptive as they do not provide an explanation as to why autocrats choose a specific strategy of interacting with their launching organization over another. Fourth, in view of Table 1.2 institutional variation across the eight regimes studied here does not coincide with welfare divergence.

Table 1.2 Political institutions and welfare spending in labour-abundant MENA regimes

Regime	Legislature at regime formation		Outcome
	Legislature	*Parties*	*Welfare provision*
Algeria	Elected until 1965	Single party	Broad and generous
Egypt	Closed until 1963	Single party	Broad
Shah Regime	Elected	Multi-party	Minimal-segmented
Islamic Republic of Iran	Elected	Multi-party	Broad and generous
Jordan	Elected	Multi-party until 1956	Minimal-segmented
Morocco	Appointed	Multi-party	Minimal-segmented
Syria	Closed	Single party (de facto)	Broad
Tunisia	Elected	Multi-party until 1962	Broad and generous

Note: Data on institutions from Cheibub, Gandhi and J. Vreeland 2010.

---

[241] For example, Wright 2008a; and Magaloni 2008.   [242] Miller 2015b.
[243] Mares and Carnes 2009.   [244] Ibid., pp. 99–100.
[245] Gandhi 2008, p. 136. See also N. K. Kim and Kroeger 2018.   [246] Batniji et al. 2014.
[247] Miller 2015a.

Turning to the welfare state literature, working-class mobilization has been viewed as a driving force behind both programme enactment[248] and expansion of expenditures,[249] as well as an influential veto player capable of inhibiting welfare retrenchment.[250] Distributional conflict between competing interests, determined by relative balances of power, are a key feature of this demand-based approach.[251] Welfare state development is thus conceived as a result of a societal demand from below, with the power resources of organized labour as the key determinant of the outcome.[252] However, this power resource approach cannot be easily transferred to an authoritarian context because it generally assumes an even playing field in which societal actors can organize. In autocracies, the organizational strength of labour might be seriously hampered by regime repression, or at least considerably limited as a result of organizational co-optation into state-led unions, bans on strikes or severe restrictions on wage bargaining. Harris' argument that the universalization of health care was driven by lobbying from professional associations during moments of political opening and heightened political competition faces equal challenges as such conditions have mostly, and certainly historically, been absent in the Middle East.[253]

In the Middle East, the industrial working class has remained relatively small[254] and the existence of a sizeable population of low-skilled workers, often working in the informal sector, has complicated labour organization.[255] Moreover, labour incorporation in the region has been rather repressive[256] and, as a result, labour has remained relatively weak.[257] In Algeria—a high-spending regime—the central labour union has been described as 'the region's most coopted, divided and political inconsequential union organization'.[258] Similarly, Iranian labour unions were heavily repressed under the Shah and, lacking coordinated labour organization after the Islamic Revolution, were quickly brought under control in the early 1980s, despite their mobilization during the revolution.[259] In contrast, labour in Morocco was well organized, mobilized, and relatively independent

---

[248] Hicks, Misra, and Ng 1995.
[249] Esping-Andersen 1990; Hicks 1999; and Ebbinghaus 2010.
[250] Huber and J. D. Stephens 2001; and Rudra 2002.   [251] Hicks and Misra 1993.
[252] Korpi 1983.   [253] J. Harris 2017.   [254] Ayubi 1995, p. 176.
[255] Rudra 2002, p. 413 notes that the abundance of low-skilled workers makes collective action for labour more difficult.
[256] Gobe 2008.
[257] Comparing labour strength across the Middle East is a complicated undertaking either because the standard measure, i.e. the level of unionization, is not available for the early periods of regime formation or because existing data seem to have little reliability. Therefore, one is left with case studies as the only way to compare labour strength across the region. For a comparative analysis of different *labour regimes* in MENA, see Cammett and Posusney 2010.
[258] Alexander 1996, p. 50.   [259] Bayat 1988.

until the mid-1960s,[260] yet remarkably inconsequential for social spending. As Cammett and Sasmaz conclude, '[t]heories linking the origins and variation of social policies to power resources, developmental strategies, or political regime type cannot adequately explain the diversity of welfare regimes across the Middle East. Autocratic leaders in the region introduced social policies with minimal pressure from below: organized labor and other mass-based social groups have been notoriously weak or fragmented.'[261]

Highlighting the historical origins of welfare states, a number of authors have emphasized the colonial origins of social policies in developing countries.[262] Desai shows that the Kerala monarchy expanded welfare distribution to ward off annexation by the British.[263] Grier notices higher levels of postcolonial growth in countries with longer histories of colonization, which could have a positive spillover effect on social policies.[264] Acemoglu et al. emphasize the type of colonialism in explaining postcolonial development by emphasizing the legacies of extractive and inclusive colonial institutions, the latter being generally associated with larger settler colonies.[265] Certainly, colonialism left an imprint on the *institutional design of social policies*, which is particularly visible in the countries of the Maghrib (see Chapter 2). As an explanation for our puzzle, however, colonialism faces problems.

As Veit et al. remark, there is considerable variation in the way in which the same colonial power affected social policies, depending on the specific timing and historical context.[266] This makes it difficult to derive predictive hypotheses based on the identity of the colonizing power. Moreover, it is striking that the country with arguably the most extractive colonial institutions—Algeria—developed the most progressive social policies after independence, which casts doubt on explanations based on type of colonialism. Finally, neither the identity of the colonizer nor the length of colonial rule easily maps on the variation of social spending and the type of postcolonial welfare state (see Table 1.3). Other factors emphasized in the literature, such as religion,[267] are held constant by design.

Finally, as I mentioned above, the abilities of regimes to distribute welfare could be plausibly hampered by weak state capacity. Indeed, Cammett and Sasmaz in their analysis of social policy in developing countries place great emphasis on this factor, arguing that 'the administrative [...] capacities of the state are often not sufficiently articulated to sustain an extensive mix of policies.'[268] State capacity

---

[260] Douglas Elliott Ashford 1961, p. 270; Benseddik 1990, p. 574; Bouzaine 1989, p. 66; Benhlal 1984; and Monjib 1992, p. 158.

[261] Cammett and Sasmaz 2016, p. 245.   [262] Bailey 2004; and Barbone and Sanchez 1999.

[263] M. Desai 2005.   [264] Grier 1999.

[265] Acemoglu, Johnson, J. A. Robinson, and Albouy 2012.

[266] Veit, Schlichte, and Karadag 2017.

[267] Jawad and Yakut-Cakar 2010.   [268] Cammett and Sasmaz 2016, p. 241.

Table 1.3 Colonialism and welfare spending in labour-Abundant MENA regimes

Regime	Colonial power	Years non-autonomous since 1900	Welfare provision
Algeria	France	62	Broad and generous
Egypt	Britain	53	Broad
Shah Regime	Britain*	33	Minimal-segmented
Islamic Republic of Iran	Britain*	33	Broad and generous
Jordan	Britain	24	Minimal-segmented
Morocco	France	43	Minimal-segmented
Syria	France	29	Broad
Tunisia	France	57	Broad and generous

Note: Iran was never colonized but came under strong British influence at the beginning of the twentieth century. Data on non-autonomous years from Coppedge et al. 2017.

itself has been shown to be endogenous to a number of factors, ranging from geographical features, such as the size and the ruggedness of the territory which prevent state penetration,[269] to war and threats along a Tillyan logic discussed above.

Empirically, however, state capacity indicators displayed in Table 1.4 do not show systematic variation across my sample of countries. Territorial size and ruggedness, which have been linked to weak statehood, are highest in Algeria and Iran respectively, both authoritarian welfare states. Tunisia, which also falls into this category, is territorially smaller and not very mountainous, but is by no means a regional outlier in this respect. Bockstette et al.'s State Antiquity Index shows high- and low-spenders equally distributed across the whole spectrum.[270] When it comes to extractive measures, Syria, Morocco, the Pahlavi regime, and partly Jordan all score higher than Tunisia in the late 1950s to early 1960s. If we take census activity as an indicator of a state's infrastructural power,[271] differences are starker—with Algeria and Egypt clearly topping the list, in line with the extractive data—but they do not map straightforwardly onto types of welfare state.[272] Most notably Iran had conducted no census by 1945 and only three by 1979, while oil rents had further eroded the state's extractive capacity. Finally, although the plausibility of Tilly's mechanism in the Middle East has been challenged empirically and theoretically (see above), it would suggest higher state capacity in cases that are nearly all low-spenders. Irrespective of the fact that state capacity is partly endogenous to a regime's political incentives, the data below do not suggest that authoritarian welfare states were unachievable in any country due to lacking state capacity.

[269] Herbst 2000; and Jimenez-Ayora and Ulubaşoğlu 2015.
[270] Bockstette, Chanda, and Putterman 2002.   [271] Soifer 2012.
[272] The quality of the pre-1945 censuses listed below varies and the data need to be interpreted with caution.

Table 1.4 State capacity across labour-abundant MENA regimes

Regime	Territorial size	Terrain ruggedness	State Antiquity Index	Tax/GDP	Direct tax/GDP	Pre-1945 censuses	Interstate conflicts 1945–80
Algeria	238,174	0.51	25	15.2% (1963)	3.6% (1963)	18	1
Egypt	99,545	0.72	33	20.2% (1952)	4.9% (1952)	6	9
Shah Regime	162,855	2.45	50	14.6% (1946)	3.8% (1946)	0	2
Islamic Republic of Iran	162,855	2.45	50	6.7% (1980)	2.0% (1980)	0*	2
Jordan	8,824	1.10	25	8.7% (1960)	1.6% (1960)	2	3
Morocco	44,630	2.41	50	12.5% (1958)	2.8% (1958)	5	1
Syria	18,378	0.76	25	12.6% (1963)	2.5% (1963)	1	4
Tunisia	15,536	0.73	33	8.6% (1960)	2.2% (1960)	4	1

Note: Territorial size is measured in thousands of hectares. Ruggedness is measured in hundreds of metres of elevation difference for grid points 30 arc-seconds (926 metres on a meridian) apart based on Nunn and Puga 2012. The State Antiquity Index measures the cumulatively discounted presence of state infrastructure in a given territory at a point in time (here by 1900). The measure varies from 0 to 50 and is based on Bockstette, Chanda, and Putterman 2002. Taxation data are taken from V. Lucas and Richter 2016; and IMF 2011. Census dates are taken from various sources, amongst others Soifer 2012. Interstate conflict data are from N. P. Gleditsch et al. 2002. *3 censuses pre-1979.

1.4 Research Design and Outline

1.4.1 The case for studying labour-abundant MENA regimes

The rationale for choosing cases from the same geographical area is often a concern for comparability.[273] Units from the same region are expected to be similar and therefore causal processes are assumed to be broadly comparable. Yet my argument for selecting eight MENA regimes differs from such a purely taxonomic approach to area studies.[274] In fact, MENA is socioeconomically one of the most diverse regions,[275] so that claims of similarity are not easily warranted. Besides, case selection based on region can lead to serious inferential bias.[276] What matters are *theoretically relevant similarities*, which can only be specified in relation to the relevant universe of cases and the scope conditions of the proposed theory.[277] What will follow is a five-step procedure of case selection that delineates the boundaries of theory and generalization of this study.[278]

From among all authoritarian regimes for which data are available, I propose, first, to select only regimes with relatively long duration.[279] On the one hand, the budgetary effect of social policies can take some time to be visible and, on the other hand, welfare efforts are affected by business cycles. Longevity also affects a ruler's discount rate and political horizon, making long-term decision making more likely.[280] Therefore, short-term data might be seriously distorted and inferences biased as a result. I therefore propose a fifteen-year threshold to circumvent that problem.[281] Second, given the high persistence of social spending levels over time, I propose to compare only those countries that have not (yet) experienced longer periods of democracy, generally not longer than one election period of four years. Theory suggests that democracy has a positive impact on social spending. It is thus important to ensure the welfare effort of an authoritarian regime is not confounded by the welfare effort of its democratic predecessor regime.

Third, taking into account the relationship between economic development and welfare effort, I suggest 720 USD per capita as a minimum threshold of development for case selection.[282] The threshold was determined empirically and corresponds to the income level of the poorest high-spender that could be found: that is, Tunisia in the 1960s. This case selection based on a minimum level of development follows the 'possibility principle',[283] which advises the selection only

---

[273] Basedau and Köllner 2007, pp. 118–19.

[274] Ahram 2009, p. 4.

[275] Rauch and Kostyshak 2009. Richards and Waterbury 2008, p. 45 note that the MENA region exhibits more variation in per capita income than any other region.

[276] Geddes 2003, pp. 101–2.   [277] Munck 2004, p. 107; and Nome 2011.

[278] See Appendix A, Table A.1 for a schematic overview.

[279] Regime codings for non-MENA regimes are based on Svolik 2012.

[280] Blaydes and Chaney 2013; and Caselli and Cunningham 2009.

[281] Varying this threshold does not substantially vary the composition of the sample.

[282] Dollars are in constant 2000 prices. Data are taken from World Bank 2010c.

[283] Goertz and Mahoney 2004.

of cases where the outcome of interest is at least possible. Fourth, given the small number of resource-rich and labour-scarce rentier autocracies, it seems sensible to select regimes with a broadly similar socioeconomic profile. Thus, labour-scarce, resource-abundant rentier autocracies have not been considered for case selection. This does not mean, however, that my sample includes only resource-scarce regimes. In fact, to avoid selection bias it is important to maintain a number of resource-rich regimes in the sample. But these regimes are both resource-rich and labour-abundant. Fifth, and finally, cases were selected so as to ensure sufficient variation of the causal conditions of interest.

At this point, an explanation for the exclusion of Iraq and Lebanon is in order. Iraq was excluded because of lacking social spending data after 1977. This is unfortunate as the particular combination of a broad coalition, communal cleavages, oil, and interstate war would have made Iraq a pathway case to test the predicted negative effect of communal cleavages on welfare distribution. The data which are available (see Figure 1.1) suggest, however, that Iraq was not a high-spender on social welfare, in line with my theoretical argument. As for Lebanon, twenty-five years of civil war coupled with its sectarian electoral regime means a theory on welfare states in relatively enduring authoritarian regimes is not a particularly good fit.[284]

In summary, the proposed theory aims to be valid for rather enduring, fairly developed, labour-abundant autocracies without any prior experience of democratic rule. In light of these scope conditions, I would argue that the selected sample of eight MENA cases is indeed relatively representative of the relevant population. The region is renowned for its long-standing legacy of autocratic rule,[285] and thus any theory of welfare efforts in enduring autocracies would be evaluated according to how well it can explain the variation of social spending in the world's most authoritarian region. Besides, labour-abundant MENA regimes feature a number of theoretical 'anomalies' (see Table 1.5), which make them an interesting starting point for analysis.[286]

Table 1.5 Labour-abundant MENA regimes as a challenge to theoretical expectations

Theoretical expectation	Middle Eastern 'anomaly'
Rents boost social spending	*Shah Regime* / Tunisia
Party regimes are more pro-welfare	*Syria, Egypt* / Islamic Republic of Iran
Strong labour unions foster high social spending	*Morocco* / Algeria, Islamic Republic of Iran
Left-wing regimes create welfare states	*Egypt, Syria* / Islamic Republic of Iran

Note: Cases in italics exhibit the hypothetical cause but not the outcome; non-italicized cases exhibit the outcome without the cause. Table inspired by Slater 2010, p. 10.

[284] For an excellent analysis of social policies in Lebanon, see Cammett 2014a; and Cammett 2015.
[285] Schlumberger 2007.
[286] Within the MENA region, Owen 2000 argues that North African states are good counterfactuals for Levantine states, especially when it comes to the effects of war.

1.4.2 Claiming causality: a funnel mixed-methods design

This study broadly falls within the research agenda of comparative historical analysis (CHA).[287] It is 'concerned with explanation and the identification of causal configurations that produce major outcomes of interest'.[288] My theory aims at 'contingent generalizations'[289] and therefore mirrors CHA's attempt to reconcile external and internal validity.[290] Its propositions are best formulated in terms of necessary and sufficient conditions, which has been a main feature of CHA.[291] Although methodologically diverse,[292] CHA has shown a strong affinity with (comparative) case studies.[293]

By contrast, this dissertation proposes a 'funnel approach' that tries to maximize inferential leverage by combining qualitative and quantitative methods in a mixed-methods design.[294] In view of the methodological trade-offs each single method entails,[295] I aim to work gradually 'downwards' from the macro-comparative to the case level with different methods jointly testing my theoretical propositions. This has a number of advantages.

First, the funnel design reflects the dual interest of this study in theory generation, which has an important macro-comparative element, and theory testing, which in light of the theories requires detailed attention to cases. Second, the evaluation of the theoretical argument at hand requires a good balance between macro-comparative and case study level, and thus between external and internal validity. On the one hand, delving into causal mechanisms using process tracing in case studies might overlook inconsistencies at the macro, cross-country level that invalidate the theoretical claim.[296] I therefore start by testing whether the theoretical argument broadly holds at the macro level: that is, whether the causal factors hypothesized to explain the outcome are actually present.[297] Methodologically, this is done by a structured, focused comparison of coalition formation in the selected MENA regimes.[298] As the theory makes a number of concrete predictions as to when we should see the emergence of broad regime coalitions and how the

---

[287] Mahoney and Rueschemeyer 2003a; and Mahoney and Thelen 2015.
[288] Mahoney and Rueschemeyer 2003b, p. 11.   [289] George and Bennett 2005, p. 235.
[290] Janoski 1991.   [291] Mahoney, Kimball, and Koivu 2008.
[292] Amenta 2003; Hall 2013 argues that CHA is distinguished by its subject-matter, rather than a specific method.
[293] Rueschemeyer 2003.
[294] See Seawright 2016 for a discussion of the philosophical underpinnings and understandings of causality in multi-method research.
[295] As Gerring 2001 and 2011 rightly points out, every research design represents an arbitration between trade-offs. For arguments in support of a mixed-methods design, see Pickel 2009; and Seawright 2011.
[296] On process tracing, see Mahoney and Goertz 2006; Checkel 2006; Vennesson 2008; Mahoney 2012; Beach 2012; Rohlfing 2013; and Hall 2013.
[297] Mahoney 2012, p. 589.
[298] On structured, focused comparison as a method, see George and Bennett 2005, chapter 3; see Slater and Ziblatt 2013 for a related approach.

external environment affects these, it is important to ensure that the cross-country pattern is consistent before tracing any causal mechanism. Evidence at this stage will be mainly from secondary accounts and a selected number of primary sources.

On the other hand, a causal relationship based on a consistent cross-country pattern might be spurious if there is no evidence of the causal mechanism.[299] For the theory at hand, it is thus crucial to demonstrate that intra-elite conflict incentivized elites to broaden their coalition *using social expenditures as a tool to do so*, and that external threats made it impossible for broad-based regimes to establish authoritarian welfare states. Regarding the mechanisms underpinning path dependence, it needs to be demonstrated how initial advantages were reinforced over time and how unintended beneficiaries became major stakeholders in the status quo. This is best done by bringing the analysis to the case level. This book thus includes two in-depth case studies, Tunisia and Egypt, to trace the outlined causal mechanisms.[300] Both cases represent typical cases of one causal pathway. Tunisia represents a typical authoritarian welfare state, whereas Egypt followed a trajectory of broad, yet not generous welfare provision due to the external environment.[301] The evidence presented in these two case studies is based on documents, including cabinet minutes, from the national archives of both countries and elite interviews with former politicians and bureaucrats.

Finally, I draw on the rich time series data on social spending to test important observable implications from my theoretical framework. For instance, my theory relies on the existence of a trade-off between welfare and defence spending, which can be tested using statistical analysis. Other assumptions include the likelihood of welfare retrenchment and how different regimes deal with free resources. If coalitions are as powerful as I claim, they should have left a traceable impact on the pattern of social spending over time, which these tests aim to bring to light.

1.4.3 Organization of the manuscript

The remainder of the book is organized as follows. Chapter 2 turns the empirical focus to the MENA region by providing an analytical overview of welfare provision in labour-abundant MENA regimes. Covering the period from regime formation until the late 2000s, the chapter gives particular attention to spending levels and the accessibility of social policies and maps the eight regimes onto the three different

---

[299] Hedström and Ylikoski 2010, p. 54.

[300] This corresponds to Beach and Derek's 2013 theory-testing type of process tracing. As causal processes are often difficult to observe directly, I also examine observable implications of the hypothesis's causal mechanism at the case level. See Bennett and Checkel 2015, pp. 7–8.

[301] According to Gerring 2007; and Seawright and Gerring 2008, p. 297, typical cases are well suited to process trace causal hypotheses. Egypt, in addition to being a typical case, is also a pathway case in the sense that it is the only regime representing this pathway. On pathway cases, see Schneider and Rohlfing 2013.

pathways of welfare provision outlined above. It also diversifies the picture by examining policies of education, health, and social protection separately. Whilst the argument is descriptive, the chapter lays important groundwork for further analyses and gives a better sense of the outcome than bare-bone spending figures.

Chapters 3 is macro-comparative in nature and examines whether coalition formation followed the expected pattern, structured by intra-elite conflict and communal cleavages. In addition, the chapter also maps out the variation of the geostrategic environment, highlighting differences in the exposure to external threat and the endowment with resources. It does so in the form of comparative narratives of coalition formation and the geostrategic context and, whilst outlining broad trends, demonstrates how elite competition and communal cleavages widened or narrowed the support coalitions.

Chapter 4 uses statistical methods to test observable implications of my argument visible in the spending patterns over time. Establishing an important crowding-out effect between military and social spending, the chapter empirically corroborates a key mechanism of the outlined theory. It further demonstrates the importance of different coalition types for welfare retrenchment and the distribution of resource windfalls.

In Chapters 5 and 6, I substantiate the causal mechanism at the micro-level by retracing the emergence and development of social policies in two regimes, Tunisia and Egypt. As both regimes were based on broad coalitions unconstrained by communal cleavages, a primary goal of the case studies is to provide empirical evidence for a link between intra-elite conflict and social policies and spending. To to so, I rely on three types of primary sources archival material, including cabinet minutes, from the Tunisian, Egyptian, and IMF archives; autobiographies of key actors of regime formation; and interviews with former policy makers who have all been involved in the budget-making process. Especially in Tunisia, I was fortunate to find a number of the founding figures of the regime still alive and ready to answer my questions.

Given the geostrategic situation of Egypt, my analysis of archival material emphasizes in particular how external threat made high social spending levels financially impossible, albeit politically desirable. It also demonstrates the specific types of 'cheap social policies' the regime utilized to deal with this dilemma. For example, based on my archival research, I can show that the establishment of Egypt's social insurance scheme in 1955 was partly, if not mainly, motivated by the country's defence policies. Finally, in both countries, I specifically focus on the role of the ruler, Bourguiba and Nasser, and their impact on early social policies. Highlighting important about-faces in the case of Nasser and opposition to social policy reforms in the case of Bourguiba, I back up my claim that ideas played a secondary role in shaping social policies.

Regarding the persistence of social spending following divergence, I focus on a number of key periods of reform or, as in Egypt, attempted reform, to demonstrate the mechanisms underpinning path dependence. Specifically, I analyse the system of food and energy subsidization in both countries, demonstrating how a group of producers and traders has become a major stakeholder in the status quo. I also focus on health care reforms in the 2000s, highlighting failed reform in Egypt and successful reform in Tunisia as evidence illustrating a continuation of their specific welfare trajectory. With regard to Egypt in particular, I show how the military has become a key player in the budget-making process and how this has undermined a reversal of the regime's welfare path after the Camp David peace treaty.

In Chapter 7, I draw out the implications of my argument, both at the scholarly and at the policy level. I outline future comparative research to assess the validity of my theory beyond the MENA region. Finally, in the light of recent episodes of regime breakdown in Tunisia and Egypt, I reflect on the ambiguous link between social policies and autocratic survival.

2

Welfare Efforts in Comparative Perspective

The introductory chapter briefly outlined the pattern of welfare provision in labour-rich MENA countries, highlighting an initial divergence between high- and low-spenders and the persistence of this divergence until present days. It proposed a typology of welfare trajectories in the region, distinguishing between broad and generous, broad only, and minimal-segmented welfare provision. Supported by a cursory overview of social spending, this stylized description requires further scrutiny. This chapter therefore aims to substantiate empirically the validity of this distinction. To do so, I comparatively analyse social policy trajectories from the moment of regime formation until the late 2000s using three types of evidence: (i) social spending data over time, at both the aggregate and the more fine-grained level, focusing on education and health spending; (ii) the extent of social protection provided by public social security systems, most notably health care and pension schemes; (iii) changes in outcome indicators over time in the area of education and health, such as enrolment rates and infant mortality rates. Regarding the latter, literacy, enrolment, and mortality indicators have been considered good indicators of inequalities in human development and should reflect different patterns of welfare provision.[1]

Combining these different data has a number of advantages. First, as stated in Chapter 1, the underlying dataset on social spending relies on novel historical data from IMF archival material, so juxtaposing spending, insurance coverage, and outcome data serves as an important cross-check for the new dataset and its validity as a first-hand indicator of welfare effort.[2] The triangulation of data confirms that, despite its drawbacks (e.g. inefficient allocation, corruption), spending remains a reliable indicator of a regime's policy preferences and is well correlated to welfare outcomes.[3] Second, and more importantly, only the combination of multidimensional data brings to light the three different pathways of welfare provision prevalent in the MENA region. Ideally, the quality of welfare provision should equally be taken into account as degrading quality can inhibit access and

---

[1] Ross 2006; Gerring, Thacker, and Alfaro 2012; and Miller 2015b. I focus on changes in outcomes over time rather than than absolute levels as these largely depend on a country's point of departure, which is historically contingent. In addition to public policies, it is important to point out that social factors and lifestyle choices have a significant effect on these outcomes. See R. Wilkinson and Marmot 2003.

[2] For a detailed description of the dataset, see the data note in Appendix A.

[3] Haile and Niño-Zarazúa 2017.

Social Dictatorships: The Political Economy of the Welfare State in the Middle East and North Africa. Ferdinand Eibl, Oxford University Press (2020). © Ferdinand Eibl. DOI: 10.1093/oso/9780198834274.001.0001

hence coverage.[4] Using outcome indicators as a proxy is only a partial remedy as outcomes can 'linger on' while quality has declined. Unfortunately, systematic, let alone time-varying data on quality of provision are hard to come by, even in high-income countries.[5]

To foreshadow, I argue in this chapter that broad and generous welfare providers have not only exhibited consistently high levels of welfare spending,[6] they have also established extensive social insurance systems, which protect their population from life-course risks, such as old age and illness. Including large parts of the workforce, their coverage levels are the highest in the region. Broadness and generosity of welfare provision are also reflected in outcome indicators, which demonstrate the fastest changes in literacy, enrolment, and child mortality in these regimes.

Broad welfare providers lack the resources to financially honour their commitment to social welfare, as they are impeded by perceived risks from the external environment which drive up defence spending. Yet, while spending levels are generally low and social policies are underfunded, these regimes still provide welfare broadly among their population as barriers to social services are low and access is usually granted universally based on citizenship. This fact is most notable in the area of health care which has been accessible to the large majority of the population at zero cost or highly subsidized rates. In turn, nearly universal access is mirrored in positive outcome indicators, most notably in the area of health where broad welfare providers are nearly on a par with their generous counterparts. Similarly, broad welfare providers have established relatively comprehensive social insurance systems.[7]

Finally, minimal-segmented welfare provision neither exhibits high levels of aggregate welfare spending nor is there a noticeable effort to distribute welfare broadly. Its *minimal* variant features underfunded social policies and a rudimentary social security system, covering few life-course risks with coverage limited to key constituencies, such as a civil service and the military. Social policies do not play a prominent role in the regime's political survival strategy. Under segmented, rather than minimal, welfare provision, benefit levels for these key constituencies are not ungenerous and social policies for these insider groups are relatively sophisticated and well funded. Access to social policies is exclusive, however, entailing highly segmented welfare provision with low-coverage social security systems that provide relatively generous benefits to insiders. Due to the small coalition size, aggregate levels of welfare spending remain low. In terms of outcomes, limited access in minimal-segmented providers has caused them to

---

[4] Cammett and L. MacLean 2014, p. 34.   [5] Papanicolas and Cylus 2017.

[6] According to Theborn 1983, welfare states spend about half their budget on social policies.

[7] 'Cheap social policies' as a unique variant of social policies of broad welfare providers are addressed in detail in Section 2.1.

Table 2.1 Typology of welfare provision in MENA

		Generosity	
		High	*Low*
Barriers to Access	*Low*	**Authoritarian welfare states** Expectations: High aggregate welfare spending; well-funded policies High social security coverage	**Broad welfare provision** Expectations: Low aggregate welfare spending; poorly funded policies Medium social security coverage
	High	**Segmented welfare provision** Expectations: Low aggregate welfare spending; well-funded policies Low-medium social security coverage	**Minimal welfare provision** Expectations: Low aggregate welfare spending; poorly funded policies Low social security coverage

narrow coalition
broad coalition

lag behind in the extension of school enrolment and the improvement of health, as evidenced by slower changes in child mortality and life expectancy. Table 2.1 summarizes the typology and the empirical expectations about social policies in each type.

Two caveats need to be mentioned before proceeding. First, while this typology distinguishes types of welfare provision based on a sparse set of criteria, it is analytically much less ambitious than alternative frameworks, such as the one developed by Gough et al.,[8] which are explicitly anchored in a normative framework and seek to encapsulate state and non-state social policies in holistic welfare *regimes*. In contrast, the focus in this book lies decidedly more on welfare *states* and the proposed framework essentially seeks to evaluate the role of the state in providing social policies. That said, Iran, Tunisia, and Algeria similarly fall into the highest category of welfare provision in the Gough et al. framework,[9] which increases confidence in the validity of my typology.

Second, emphasizing differences in welfare provision should not disregard influential global trends that have affected social policies across the region. The most important one of these is the trend towards 'health universalism'.[10] Whilst

---

[8] Gough et al. 2004; and Geof Wood and Gough 2006.   [9] Ibid.; and Gough 2014.
[10] J. Harris 2017.

'health universalism' has been a hallmark of authoritarian welfare states since the beginning, universal health coverage has become a national aspiration in many parts of the developing world.[11] This agenda is forcefully driven by the United Nations and international agencies, such as the World Health Organization (WHO), which provide both technical assistance and funding. In the MENA region, this has been accompanied by health care reforms across regime types and a catching up of health care spending among low-spenders (see below). However, the transformation of historically segmented social insurance schemes is far from complete and liable to political slippage and reversal (see the Moroccan example).

The organization of the chapter closely follows the typology of welfare provision outlined above. Section 2.1 describes welfare provision of the broad and generous type in Tunisia, Algeria, and the Islamic Republic of Iran. Along with an analysis of the data, the section also briefly addresses social policies in the colonial period to underline that postcolonial welfare provision was not conditioned by a propitious colonial legacy. Section 2.2 analyses Egypt and Syria as broad welfare providers. Section 2.3 turns to minimal-segmented welfare provision in Jordan, Morocco, and Pahlavi Iran. A conclusion summarizes the findings.

2.1 Broad and Generous Welfare Provision

Broad and generous welfare providers are what I consider authoritarian welfare states among labour-abundant MENA regimes. Whilst their per capita spending has not reached levels of OECD countries, the share of resources allocated to social welfare rivals those in developed democracies, with spending levels near or above 50 per cent of total government expenditures. Their spending patterns have thus been distinctive from those of low-spenders. Moreover, authoritarian welfare states have succeeded in establishing comprehensive social security systems covering, at least, two-thirds of their workforce. Their intensive and extensive welfare effort, sustained over long periods of time, is reflected in the fastest changes in child mortality, enrolment, and literacy in the region. Three regimes in the region have followed this path: Tunisia, Algeria, and the Islamic Republic of Iran.

2.1.1 Tunisia

Tunisia has stood out for its level of social expenditures and the scope and coverage of its social security system.[12] Since 1960, the country has spent on average 44 per cent of its budget on social welfare, reaching a peak of 56 per cent in

---

[11] Reich et al. 2016.
[12] Karshenas and Moghadam 2006b, p. 22; Chaabane 2002, p. 1; and M. Q. Islam 2000, p. 105.

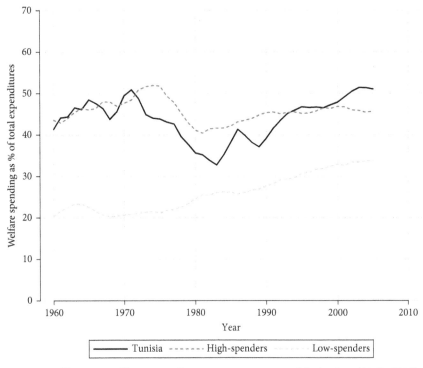

Figure 2.1 Tunisian welfare expenditures as a percentage of the budget (1960–2005)

Note: High-spenders include Tunisia, Algeria, and the Islamic Republic of Iran; low-spenders include Egypt, Jordan, Morocco, Syria, and Pahlavi Iran. Line plots were smoothed using a three-year moving average. The pattern looks similar when using welfare spending as a percentage of GDP. Data from V. Lucas and Richter 2016; and IMF 2011.

1971 (see Figure 2.1).[13] From the late 1970s until the mid-1980s, when Tunisia went through a period of meagre growth and economic readjustment, followed by an IMF agreement in 1986, social spending dropped below 40 per cent, only to pick up again from the early 1990s onwards.[14] Quite remarkably, changing economic policies did not entail major social disruption and the government was anxious to shield welfare spending from austerity cuts.[15] On the contrary, the period witnessed a number of major social policy reforms, including a significant extension of the coverage of social security.[16] In the late 2000s, the Tunisian social security system covered circa 85 per cent of the country's workforce,[17] and

---

[13] See also Ben Romdhane 2006, p. 31.

[14] Murphy 1999, p. 153.

[15] Ben Romdhane 2006, p. 52; Willis 2012, p. 241; El-Said and Harrigan 2014; and Alexander 2010, p. 116.

[16] Catusse and Karam 2009, pp. 19–20; and Erdle 2010, p. 130.

[17] Catusse and Karam 2009, p. 22. Kasmi 2008b indicates a coverage rate of 92 per cent while CRES 2016 estimates 72.5 per cent.

80 per cent were entitled to a pension.[18] Over 60 per cent of the elderly population were in receipt of a pension.[19] Tunisia has thus achieved a remarkable success in gradually extending social insurance to an ever-growing number of socio-professional categories.[20] Reflecting its high welfare effort, Tunisia witnessed the most rapid extension of primary and secondary enrolment among all countries in my sample, the second-fastest reduction of child mortality, and the fastest increase in life expectancy (see Table 2.2).[21]

Nothing had predestined Tunisia to take this trajectory, however. When the French protectorate ended in 1956, after seventy-four years of colonial rule, the former rulers had left a framework of rudimentary social policies, geared to the minuscule elite of white-collar workers, most frequently French nationals, and the nascent industrial proletariat.[22] The most long-lasting impact was made by family allowances (*allocations familiales*), introduced in 1918, which became a major pillar of post-independence social policy. Upon independence, the health infrastructure was largely insufficient, leaving a country of almost 4 million people with only 548 doctors.[23] Nor had education been a priority of the French. Primary school enrolment stood at 35 per cent in 1950[24] and only 15 per cent of the population were literate.[25]

To address these shortcomings, education was made a key priority in post-independence Tunisia. In absolute terms, education spending tripled in the first ten years after independence,[26] amounting to 8.2 per cent of GDP in 1968—at the time the highest share of educational spending in the world.[27] In budgetary terms, education spending doubled to nearly a third of all government expenditure in the early 1970s. The government's effort in the realm of education had a sizeable effect both on enrolment and on literacy rates. Thanks to a major educational reform adopted in 1958 under Mahmoud Messaadi, Minister of Education and head of the Secondary Teachers' Federation in the National Trade Union, UGTT, Tunisia achieved nearly complete primary school enrolment by 1968. With an

[18] Loewe 2010, p. 224; Boudahrain 2003, p. 134; and Ben Braham and Marouani 2016, p. 14.

[19] El Mekkaoui 2019.

[20] Destremeau, 2009, 130; Catusse and Karam 2009, p. 32; and Sraïeb 1971, p. 426.

[21] While within-country inequality in welfare provision is not the central topic of this study, the benefits of social policies have been particularly concentrated in the coastal areas, leading to a notable divergence in welfare outcomes. The extent to which regional inequalities are particularly pronounced in Tunisia compared to other MENA countries is difficult to assess with available data. See AfDB 2014; and Thyen 2019.

[22] A provident society was established for civil servants in 1889. In 1921, the authorities set up a workmen's compensation scheme, followed by a programme for single-income families in 1944. See Chaabane 2002, p. 3; Duwaji 1967, p. 167; and Amin 1966, p. 236.

[23] Guen 1961, p. 112.

[24] World Bank 2008, p. 314. Granai and Fanton 1965, p. 221 advance a much lower figure of 26 per cent.

[25] World Bank 2008, p. 337.

[26] Ben Romdhane 2006, p. 36, 38; Alexander 1996, p. 117; Micaud, L. C. Brown, and C. H. Moore 1964, p. 150; and Poncet 1970, p. 108.

[27] Sraïeb 1971, p. 110.

Table 2.2 Summary of welfare provision in labour-abundant MENA regimes

Regime	Type of welfare provision	Social spending	Extent of social protection		Education performance				Health performance	
			Pension entitlement (% of workforce)	Access to health care, health insurance coverage (% of workforce)	Average annual growth of primary enrolment in %	Average annual growth of secondary enrolment in %	Average annual growth of primary and secondary education in %	Average annual growth of literacy in %	Average annual reduction of child mortality in %	Average annual change of life expectancy in %
Tunisia	Broad and generous	High	80	Universal, 85	3.56	1.40	2.48	1.23	−5.45	1.13
Algeria	Broad and generous	High	75	Universal, 75	1.80	1.56	1.68	1.37	−4.57	0.83
Islamic Republic of Iran	Broad and generous	High	66	Universal, 90	2.20	1.77	1.99	1.31	−5.52	0.88
Egypt	Broad	Low	55	Universal, 55	0.97	1.75	1.36	0.86	−4.97	0.75
Syria	Broad-minimal hybrid	Low	35	Universal, 35	1.44	0.66	1.05	1.11	−4.63	0.65
Morocco	Minimal	Low	22	Restricted,16	1.62	0.83	1.23	0.87	−3.84	0.73
Pahlavi Iran	Minimal	Low	18	Restricted, 18	1.98	1.01	1.50	0.64	−2.41	0.85
Jordan	Minimal	Low	50	Restricted, 50	0.65	1.54	1.10	1.16	−3.95	0.65

Note: Education performance based on the following time periods: Tunisia 1955–2000, Algeria 1965–2000, Egypt 1950–2000, Syria 1965–2000, Morocco 1955–2000, Pahlavi Iran 1950–1980, Jordan 1955–2000. Health performance is based on the time period from 1960 to 2010, except for Iran where the period from 1950 to 1980 is used for the Pahlavi regime, and the period from 1980 until 2010 for the Islamic Republic. Data from World Bank 2008; Abrahamian 2008, p. 142; United Nations 2012; Loewe 2010; and K. Harris 2013.

average annual enrolment growth of 3.6 per cent, Tunisia even stands out among other high-spenders (see Table 2.2). Similarly, literacy levels increased at one of the fastest rates in the region.[28] Complete primary school enrolment having been achieved in the early 1970s, education spending decreased but has remained consistently above levels of low-spenders and 'far above the corresponding percentage for the OECD [...] and lower-middle income countries'.[29]

In contrast to other countries in the region, access to secondary education was kept relatively selective until the early 1990s,[30] when the entrance exam for secondary education was abolished. That said, a bursary scheme was set up to broaden access to, in particular, higher education.[31] While other regimes in the region have embarked on a programme of privatization of education since the late 1990s to alleviate the financial burden on the state budget, private education has remained marginal in Tunisia, representing the lowest share of private education in the sample.[32]

A similar effort was exerted in the field of health policies.[33] Hospital capacity, for instance, increased by 89 per cent between 1956 and 1961.[34] In addition, 1960 saw the establishment of the country's public social security scheme, which incorporated compensation for accidents and work-related illnesses, granted in 1957, alongside a maternity leave scheme, a survivorship annuity, and health insurance.[35] Public pensions were initially limited to state employees and extended to private sector employees in the mid-1960s. As health insurance was initially limited to formal sector workers in the non-agricultural sector, the government provided a parallel tax-based health care system, which was practically free of charge until 1969, when the government introduced a small mandatory contribution, coupled with a compensation scheme for low-income families.[36]

This is reflected in comparatively high health spending until the early 1980s. With increasing social security coverage, the weight of health expenditures in the Tunisian state budget gradually declined as the social security fund was stepping in to cover the costs. The Tunisian public health insurance, CNAM (*Caisse nationale d'assurance maladie*), which merged the public and private sector health insurances in the 2000s and insures both the policy holder and dependent family members,

---

[28] See Table 2.2 and World Bank 2008, p. 176.

[29] Galal and Kanaan 2010, p. 118. See also Erdle 2010, p. 350.

[30] Allman 1979, p. 62; and Micaud, L. C. Brown, and C. H. Moore 1964, p. 150.

[31] Until the mid-1980s, 50 per cent of all students were in receipt of government bursaries, a number which declined to 30 per cent in 2007. See Galal and Kanaan 2010, p. 124.

[32] World Bank 2008, p. 191.   [33] Perkins 1997, p. 58; and Alexander 2010, p. 73.

[34] Ben Romdhane 1984, p. 264.

[35] There are two main social security funds in Tunisia. The *Caisse de retraite et de prévoyance sociale* (CNRPS) covers the public sector. Private sector employees subscribe to the *Caisse nationale de sécurité sociale* (CNSS).

[36] Camau, Zaïem, and Bahri 1990, p. 184. Until today, there is a non-prohibitive out-of-pocket contribution to health care in Tunisia. See Chaabane 2002, p. 6.

covers 68 per cent of the population.[37] A Free Medical Assistance Programme (*Assistance médicale graduite*, AMG), established in 1991 and consolidated in 2009, provides subsidized or free medical health care to 20 to 27 per cent of the population.[38] The AMG is fully funded from the state budget while the CNAM receives tax subsidies.[39] In an attempt to ensure the allegiance of working-class constituents, the regime has continuously sought to grant social security access to large segments of the informal and low-income sectors,[40] including most recently construction workers and domestic employees.[41] Social security coverage for the self-employed is mandatory and coverage in the largely informal non-salaried private sector reached nearly 50 per cent in the late 2000s.[42] On the whole, pension and health insurance coverage is high, covering 80 and 85 per cent of the workforce respectively.

Another pillar of social protection has been the subsidization of energy and consumable durables, such as flour and oil, with the stated goal to preserve the purchasing power of low-income families. In this respect, Tunisia has followed a widespread pattern of subsidization prevalent across the region. The system has been reformed incrementally since the 1990s by introducing self-targeting for food subsidies and reducing the number of subsidized food items. An indexation mechanism of energy prices to the world market was introduced in 2009, but repealed shortly after the uprisings in 2011.[43] To alleviate the impact of structural adjustment, the government also introduced a social safety net (SSN) programme for families in need (*Programme National d'Aide aux Familles Nécessiteuses*, PNAFN) in 1986, which covers 9 per cent of the population.[44] Finally, in the mid-1990s, the National Solidarity Fund (NSF) and National Employment Fund (NEF) were created under the explicit auspices of President Ben Ali.[45] Spending and coverage data for these SSN schemes is hard to come by. Given the small size of their target group, their financial weight is likely to be fairly limited.

2.1.2 Algeria

Similar to Tunisia, Algeria made social spending its key priority after gaining independence in 1962. Since its first post-independence budget, the country has

---

[37] Arfa and Elgazzar 2013, p. 3.
[38] AfDB 2014, p. 4; Arfa and Elgazzar 2013, p. 6; and Ayadi and Zouari 2017, p. 5.
[39] The CNRPS and the CNSS also receive cash injections from the budget to cover deficits.
[40] Chaabane 2002, p. 11.   [41] Boudahrain 2003, p. 134.
[42] Gatti et al. 2014, p. 279; and CRES 2016, p. 69.
[43] The indexation mechanism was later reintroduced in January 2014. See Cuesta, El-Lahga and Lara Ibarra 2015.
[44] Silva, Levin, and Morgandi 2013, p. 256. According to Tzannatos 2000, p. 26, it covered about 72 per cent of the target group in the mid-1990s.
[45] Hibou 2006, pp. 230–6; and Erdle 2010, p. 256.

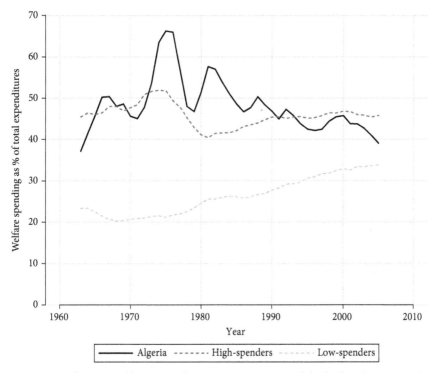

Figure 2.2 Algerian welfare expenditures as a percentage of the budget (1960–2005)

Note: High-spenders include Tunisia, Algeria, and the Islamic Republic of Iran; low-spenders include Egypt, Jordan, Morocco, Syria, and Pahlavi Iran. Line plots were smoothed using a three-year moving average. The pattern looks similar when using welfare spending as a percentage of GDP. Data from V. Lucas and Richter 2016; and IMF 2011.

dedicated on average 48 per cent of all expenditures to social welfare, culminating in a historical peak of 74 per cent at the height of the oil boom in 1975 (see Figure 2.2). When oil prices started to decline in the 1980s, social expenditures also contracted, an effect which was further compounded by violent conflict with Islamist insurgents in the 1990s. Yet despite these upheavals, social spending still amounted to approximately 45 per cent of the state budget in the period from 1985 until 2005, leaving the country's distributive policies largely intact.[46] To alleviate the negative effects of an IMF structural adjustment programme starting in 1994, the Algerian regime responded by considerably enlarging the scope of its social security system. In the mid-2000s, three-quarters of the country's workforce were contributing to a public pension scheme and health insurance.[47] This has

---

[46] Safar Zitoun 2009, p. 54.

[47] Loewe 2010, p. 244. In terms of pensions recipients, 70 per cent of men and 21 per cent of women receive a pension from the social insurance funds. This partly reflects the very low female labour force participation in Algeria (15 per cent). See Merouani, N.-E. Hammouda, and El Moudden 2014, p. 134.

left Algeria with one of the most sophisticated social security systems in the region.[48] In terms of human development outcomes, Algeria has had the third largest annual growth of primary and secondary enrolment behind Tunisia and the Islamic Republic of Iran, the biggest annual growth of literacy, and a rapid reduction in child mortality on a par with other broad welfare providers.[49]

Like in Tunisia, Algeria's postcolonial welfare trajectory represented a remarkable break with the colonial past. While the French government introduced free medical assistance (*assistance médicale gratuite*) in Algeria for the poorest segments of the French settler population in 1902, the much more numerous Algerian native population was left at the mercy of charitable organizations, both Christian and Muslim, to meet their basic sanitary needs.[50] In 1920 the French authorities extended the provisions for industrial injuries to the Algerian territory, followed by the introduction of family benefits (*allocations familiales*) in 1941, again only targeted at the French settler population. This situation started to change in the wake of the Algerian war of independence as France abandoned its policy of social discrimination in 1956 and extended the social security regime to parts of the Algerian population.[51] In an attempt to undercut popular support for the Algerian National Liberation Front (*Front de Libération Nationale*, FLN), the authorities also launched an extensive social assistance programme (*Service de l'action sociale*, SAS) that specifically targeted the native population.[52] Yet this belated attempt could not alleviate the devastating effects of more than a century of neglect. On the eve of the war, Algerians died of diseases that had ravaged Europe in the nineteenth century, and the mass flight of Europeans in 1962 left a country of 11 million inhabitants with merely 600 doctors.[53] In 1954, only 8 per cent of Algerian children went to school,[54] and 80 per cent of all Algerians were illiterate.[55]

After independence was achieved education was made one of the most favoured sectors in the allocation of state resources. Whilst the country was recovering from a disruptive war and public resources were depleted,[56] the government set itself the ambitious goal to reach universal primary enrolment by 1978, for which it tripled the share of education in the budget from 10 per cent in 1963 to nearly 30 per cent by the early 1970s. As a result, Algeria witnessed the second fastest increase in primary enrolment between 1965 and 1985 after Tunisia, and the third fastest growth in combined enrolment figures amongst all labour-abundant

---

[48] The main social security funds are the *Caisse nationales des assurances sociales des travailleurs salariés* (CNAS), the *Caisse des non salariés* (CASNOS), the *Caisse nationale de retraite* (CNR), and the *Caisse nationale d'assurance chômage* (CNAC). Special funds exist for high-level bureaucrats (*Fonds spécial des retraites*, FSR) and the military (*Caisse militaire de sécurité sociale et prévoyance*, CAMSSP).
[49] See Table 2.2.   [50] Kaddar 1989, p. 3.   [51] Safar Zitoun 2009, p. 56.
[52] The financial impact of this programme should not be overstated. Actually, the share of social spending declined between 1954 and 1961, from 25.7 to 16.2 per cent. See Amin 1966, p. 221.
[53] Ouchfoun and Hammouda 1993, p. 2.   [54] Stora 2001, p. 24.
[55] Ouchfoun and Hammouda 1993, pp. 4–5.   [56] Buy 1965, p. 42.

MENA regimes.[57] Despite initial disadvantages, Algeria thus quickly caught up with other countries in terms of literacy levels.[58] Government scholarships, which, by the late 1970s, were being granted to 65 per cent of all pupils and nearly all university students, sought to guarantee equitable access to education, especially for underprivileged segments of society.[59] In addition, the regime's firm financial commitment to education guarded the educational system from potentially deleterious effects of a rapidly growing population, particularly in the 1970s and 1980s.[60] To be sure, the decline in oil prices and the Algerian civil war during the 1990s dampened education spending, yet this decrease occurred from particularly high levels.[61] Private education has also remained marginal at all levels and the Algerian state still shoulders the brunt of educational expenditures.[62]

In the area of health, the regime pursued a policy of marginalizing private health care, which had been predominant under colonial rule, whilst rapidly expanding hospital capacity and the number of trained personnel after independence.[63] To improve access, the government introduced a system of means-tested free medical assistance to the poor shortly after independence, which made health care affordable for the majority of Algeria's low-income population.[64] With improved financial resources after the oil boom, free universal health care was introduced in 1974, and all medical fees and means-tests were abolished.[65] The policy shift was accompanied by a parallel 'de-budgetization'[66] of health expenditures. This meant that the government gradually apportioned the costs of health care to public social insurance, the share of which increased from 29 per cent in 1974 to 65.8 per cent in 1987.[67] On balance, Algeria's somewhat lower health expenditures compared to other high-spenders are reflected in the outcome indicators, which show for child mortality and life expectancy slower average changes than Tunisia and Iran. That said, with these figures, Algeria still ranges in the top tier of broad welfare providers and noticeably above the levels of minimal providers.

Since the 1990s, government health spending has nearly doubled whilst social security coverage has increased further, from 66 per cent in 1984 to nearly 75 per cent in the mid-2000s.[68] In addition to pensions and health care this includes further benefits, such as sick-pay and disability pensions, for the insured and all dependent members of the household. It is also remarkable that the Algerian social security system started to reach out into the agricultural sector early on, granting family benefits to agricultural workers in 1971.[69] At 17 per cent, coverage in the agricultural sector is low, however, similar to coverage of the self-employed

[57] See World Bank 2008, pp. 314–15 and Figure 2.2.   [58] Ibid., p. 337.
[59] Korany 1984, p. 82; and Bennoune 1988, p. 226.   [60] Abdoun 1989, p. 8.
[61] World Bank 2008, p. 105.   [62] Ibid., p. 27.   [63] Bennoune 1988, p. 247, 249.
[64] Grangaud 1984, p. 5.   [65] CERMOC 1992, p. 115.   [66] Kaddar 1989, p. 15.
[67] Fatima-Zohra 1990, p. 15. Combined, social security and government spending represented one of the highest levels of health expenditures among developing countries in the late 1980s. See Zine Barka 1991, p. 2.
[68] Loewe 1998, p. 7; Loewe 2010, p. 244; Grangaud 1984, p. 4.   [69] Ibid., p. 12.

(22 per cent), for whom social security coverage is non-mandatory.[70] Coverage to these groups is provided by the *Agence de développement social* (ADS), which administers Algeria's social safety nets, amongst others the *Allocation forfaitaire de solidarité* (AFS) covering all Algerians without income unable to work and a public works programme (*Indemnité pour activité d'intérêt général*, IAIG). A supplementary pension is also granted to former civil war fighter (*mujahidin*) and daughters of martyrs of the civil war (*shuhada*). Combined, these programmes reached 2.3 per cent of the population in the late 2000s.[71] Finally, like all MENA regimes, Algeria has also pursued an extensive policy of subsidization of durables and energy, which has been easier to finance in view of the country's oil and gas reserves. Despite occasional price increases, no major reform had occurred by the end of the 2000s.

2.1.3 The Islamic Republic of Iran

The downfall of the Shah and the establishment of the Islamic Republic of Iran in 1979 heralded a period of steady increase in social spending, which has set the new regime in sharp contrast to the policy of minimal welfare provision under Mohamed Reza Shah.[72] In its first year, the new Iranian government boosted the share of social spending in the budget by nearly 10 per cent compared to pre-revolutionary levels, reaching a third of the state budget in 1980.[73] A drastic decline in real output and the war with Iraq, which started in September 1980 and lasted until 1988, caused welfare expenditures to decline slightly between 1981 and 1984, but spending levels quickly rebounded and, by the late 1980s, spending levels had doubled compared to pre-revolutionary levels. When the pressure for acute defence spending abated with the end of the Iran–Iraq War, welfare spending rose even further to more than half of the government budget under the first five-year plan in the early 1990s.[74] Since then, spending levels have fluctuated between 40 and 50 per cent of the state budget (see Figure 2.3) making welfare provision a major characteristic of the regime.[75] The fact that this spending expansion coincided with Iran fighting one of the deadliest and most destructive wars in the twentieth century demonstrates remarkably the new regime's political commitment to social welfare. Alongside expenditures, the Iranian regime also improved social safety nets and insurance, such that, by the mid-2000s, over

---

[70] Merouani, N.-E. Hammouda, and El Moudden 2014, pp. 129–31; and Gatti et al. 2014.
[71] See Perret 2012.
[72] Amuzegar 1993, p. 87; and Maloney 2000, p. 163. As welfare provision under the Shah is analysed later in the chapter, I refrain here from describing the legacy of past provision. Like in Tunisia and Algeria, Iran's welfare trajectory post-1979 represents a marked deviation from the past.
[73] K. Harris 2010a, p. 731.   [74] Messkoub 2006b, p. 240.   [75] Doostgharin 2012, p. 55.

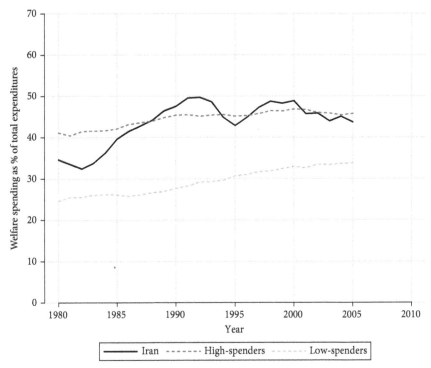

Figure 2.3 Iranian welfare expenditures as a percentage of the budget (1980–2005)

Note: High-spenders include Tunisia, Algeria, and the Islamic Republic of Iran; low-spenders include Egypt, Jordan, Morocco, Syria, and Pahlavi Iran. Line plots were smoothed using a three-year moving average. The pattern looks similar when using welfare spending as a percentage of GDP. Data from V. Lucas and Richter 2016; and IMF 2011.

90 per cent of the Iranian workforce were covered by health insurance.[76] Social security as a whole covers two-thirds of the Iranian workforce.[77]

To combat illiteracy and achieve universal primary enrolment, the new leadership intensified spending efforts in the field of education. Its share of the national budget doubled from 10 per cent in the last decade of the Shah to a fifth by the mid-2000s. Literacy rates and school enrolment improved markedly as a result, making Iran one of the most successful MENA country's in this field.[78] The annual growth of literacy was second highest after Algeria and enrolment grew at the third highest rate after Algeria and Tunisia.[79] Despite strong population

---

[76] K. Harris 2010a, p. 736.   [77] K. Harris 2013, p. 234.

[78] World Bank 2008, p. 176; and Abrahamian 2008, p. 180.

[79] See Table 2.2. Note that these outcome figures underestimate the performance of the Islamic Republic while they overestimate the performance of the Pahlavi regime. The reason for this lies in the different time periods used to calculate the percentage changes. While for all other regimes I look at comparably long time periods, comprising periods of early and late development, in Iran figures for the Pahlavi regime reflect an early development period, which generally features much faster changes

growth in the 1990s, there was no outsourcing to private education for primary and secondary education.[80] However, spending priorities gradually shifted to university education, which has entailed greater class sizes and, in some places, the running of two classes a day.[81]

Likewise, spending on health care also doubled compared to the 1970s, amounting to roughly 7 per cent of the state budget. Major sums were spent on the construction of so-called health houses, which provide free health care to the poor, especially in rural areas. Their number increased from 1,800 in 1985 to 12,000 in 1992.[82] In 1994, the government went one step further and extended the coverage of the public Medical Care Insurance Organization (MCIO) to the entire population, including the self-employed.[83] Although the implementation of this law has met some difficulty,[84] over 90 per cent of all Iranians were covered by a public health insurance or an assistance scheme by the mid-2000s.[85] To fully honour article 29 of the post-revolutionary constitution, which stipulates the right to social security in very broad terms, the regime also extended the coverage and scope of public social insurance bodies.[86] Having established an insurance scheme for unemployment in the early 1990s, the country's largest fund, the Social Security Organization (SSO), opened up to the informal sector and the self-employed in 2002 and thereby provided coverage to socio-professional categories that had hitherto been excluded.[87] Under President Ahmadinejad (2005–2013), the social insurance system was finally opened up to the entire workforce.[88] The regime's effort to broaden access to health care has had a conspicuously positive impact on human development. Child mortality witnessed the most rapid decrease in the sample and improvements in life expectancy were only topped by Tunisia.

The particular context of a revolutionary regime moulded by the ravages of war also led to the emergence of special revolutionary institutions (*nahadha-ye Enghelabi*), which have become a major provider of welfare alongside the classical institutions of social security. These para-statal charities and foundations (*boniyads*), currently more than thirty in number, provide a wide range of social services, such as medical assistance, studentships, and family benefits, and have

---

in mortality, life expectancy, and enrolment. By contrast, the figures for the Islamic Republic represent a period of late development, where gains in outcome indicators are much more difficult to achieve. The fact that the Islamic Republic still compares well with other high-spenders in terms of outcome performance makes their welfare record all the more remarkable.

[80] World Bank 2008, pp. 332–3.   [81] Messkoub 2006b, p. 241.   [82] Rastegar 1996, p. 226.
[83] The MCIO had been set up in 1972 to provide medical insurance for public servants. See Messkoub 2006a, p. 210.
[84] K. Harris 2010a, p. 735.
[85] This has gradually shifted the financial burden of health care away from the state budget to the social security sector, which is visible in the spending plot.
[86] The major social security funds are the Social Security Organization (SSO) and the Medical Service Insurance Organization (MSIO).
[87] K. Harris 2010a, p. 735.   [88] K. Harris 2017, p. 151.

over time amassed an enormous economic weight. Financed by donations and, mainly, public subsidies, their financial structure has been opaque. The World Bank estimates that their combined expenditures amount to half of the annual state budget.[89] Taken together, they might control up to 40 per cent of the country's GDP.[90] Some of these *boniyads*, such as the Foundation of the Martyrs of the Islamic Revolution (*Boniyad-e Shadi-e Enghelab-e Eslami*), built their endowment by appropriating the former estates and industries of the Pahlavi family and their cronies. Other foundations, such as the Imam Khomeini Relief Committee (*Komiteh-e Emdad-e Emam Khomeini*), were born out of the concern to support the victims of war and destruction. The latter organization assisted in 2001 over 6 million people, delivering services such as health care, housing loans, and stipends, and received the lion's share of its funds from the state budget.[91]

Finally, the post-revolutionary regime also heavily engaged in subsidizing food essentials and energy. The government has spent between a quarter and a third of current expenditures on these subsidies, which, in the light of recent international sanctions, have become a considerable burden on the state budget.[92] Therefore, the regime initiated a major reform of the system in late 2010, which aimed to transform in-kind subsidies into cash transfers, which could be better geared toward the target population.[93] Energy and wheat prices increased substantially as part of the reform process.

2.2 Broad Welfare Provision

Broad welfare provision results from the combination of an incentive to provide social welfare, stemming from a broad regime coalition, and the inability to do so as a result of strong external threats. It is thus characterized by wide, often universal access to social services without being underpinned by a strong financial commitment to social welfare. Broad providers also feature social security systems that reach out beyond labour market elites in the public sector or the army. Broad provision is most obvious in the area of health care which is accessible universally. This has lifted broad providers above minimal-segmented providers in terms of human development improvements, most notably child mortality and, to a lesser extent, enrolment. Egypt is the exemplary case in this category. Syria is a hybrid case featuring elements of communal favouritism, but its universal access

---

[89] World Bank 2006a, p. 35.   [90] Longuenesse, Catusse, and Destremeau 2005, p. 27.
[91] K. Harris 2012.
[92] Messkoub 2006b, p. 246; and Abrahamian 2008, p. 180.
[93] Segal 2012; and K. Harris 2010b. Initially the cash grants were envisaged to be conditional upon a means test, but for political reasons they ended up being extended to the entire population. See K. Harris 2017, p. 213.

regime coupled with its human development record distinguishes it from minimal providers.[94]

2.2.1 Egypt

Egypt has long been considered the epitome of populist authoritarianism under Gamal Abdel Nasser (1952–70), whose legacy was supposedly dismantled by neoliberal reforms introduced under his successors, Anwar Al-Sadat (1970–81) and Husni Mubarak (1981–2011).[95] Both parts of the story are not entirely accurate and misrepresent the particular welfare trajectory of Egypt since the 1950s. Certainly, Nasser, who increasingly turned toward socialism from the mid-1950s, introduced numerous social reforms and significantly broadened access to social services.[96] This is reflected in marked improvements in human development, such as life expectancy, child mortality, and enrolment.[97] Yet, this was not underpinned by a major financial commitment to social welfare, an assessment which is supported by the evolution of social spending under his rule (see Figure 2.4).

After an initial boost upon the Free Officers' seizure of power in 1952, the share of social spending in the budget gradually declined, not exceeding an average of a third in the 1950s and a quarter in the 1960s.[98] Social spending remained at this level under Anwar Al-Sadat and stepped up again to about a third in the first decade of Mubarak's presidency. With the onset of a severe economic crisis in the early 1990s, social spending had declined to about a quarter of the budget by the late 1990s, only to bounce back to a third, on average, until the mid-2000s. While it is true that neither Sadat nor Mubarak continued Nasser's verve in the realm of social policies—no major social policy reform has been passed since the mid-1960s—the narrative of a dismantling of Nasser's legacy is not supported by empirical evidence.

Regarding education, Nasser abolished all remaining fees for primary and secondary education in 1956, and this was followed by the suspension of university fees in 1961. The early Nasser years also witnessed a rapid expansion of primary education, with the number of primary schools doubling between 1952 and 1976.[99] Primary education was increasingly neglected, however, at the expense of secondary education, the expansion of which was only faster in the Islamic Republic of Iran.[100] This is reflected in the particularly slow increase in literacy

---

[94] Broad welfare providers can also engage in what I call 'cheap social policies', which are analysed in Chapter 6.

[95] See, amongst others, Posusney 1997; and King 2010.

[96] British colonial authorities had taken no great interest in introducing social policies in Egypt. See Veit, Schlichte, and Karadag 2017.

[97] See Table 2.2.   [98] See also Issawi 1963, p. 277.   [99] Waterbury 1983, p. 219.

[100] See Table 2.2.

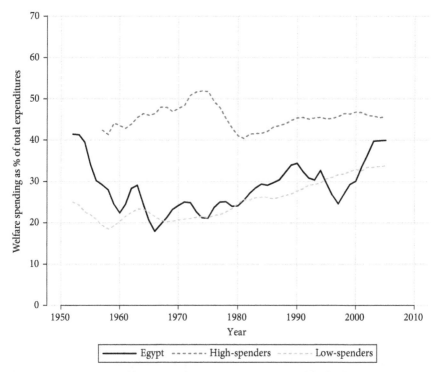

Figure 2.4 Egyptian welfare expenditures as a percentage of the budget (1952–2005)

Note: High-spenders include Tunisia, Algeria, and the Islamic Republic of Iran; low-spenders include Egypt, Jordan, Morocco, Syria, and Pahlavi Iran. Line plots were smoothed using a three-year moving average. The pattern looks similar when using welfare spending as a percentage of GDP. Data from V. Lucas and Richter 2016; and IMF 2011.

in Egypt.[101] Education spending did not significantly increase following the Free Officers' coup.[102] By the late 1980s, the share of educational spending in the budget had declined dramatically,[103] teachers were being poorly remunerated, and 40 per cent of all schools were operating more than one shift to cope with the ever growing number of pupils.[104] Under Mubarak, a programme to build 1,000 new schools yielded a meagre 140.[105] And although educational spending had picked up again towards the end of the 1990s, lifting the country to a position between the low- and high-spender averages, Egypt in the mid-2000s exhibited considerably lower levels of education expenditure than other lower-middle income

---

[101] See Table 2.2.

[102] Issawi 1963, pp. 97–9; and Hinnebusch 1985, p. 268. It is noteworthy that educational spending had noticeably increased prior to 1952. See Mabro 1974, p. 109.

[103] G. Amin 1995, p. 125.   [104] Harik 1997, p. 142.   [105] Arafat 2009, p. 69.

countries.[106] As a result, there has been a growing tendency to privatize education in Egypt to compensate for the lack of quality in the public education system.[107]

Health care followed a similar trajectory. Free basic health care was introduced in 1959 for those not covered by health insurance. At the same time, health insurance has been gradually extended to new socio-professional groups. For instance, in 1973 social security coverage was extended to permanent agricultural workers, self-employed persons and, on a voluntary basis, Egyptians working abroad. In 1993, the government gave access to health insurance to more than 14 million pupils and university students at a highly subsidized rate. Coverage extension has been hampered, however, by the fact that Egyptian social insurance does not insure dependants. An attempted reform of the health insurance system failed during the 2000s, essentially because the government was reluctant to foot the bill (see Chapter 6). In the mid-2000s, 43 per cent of the workforce were covered by social insurance and about 50 per cent contributed to the public pension scheme.[108] Just over 50 per cent of the population received a pension.[109] On the whole, the architecture of the Egyptian health care system means that access is universal, which is expressed by the country's remarkable reduction in child mortality—on a par with high-spenders—and an increase in life expectancy above the levels of minimal-segmented welfare providers, such as Jordan.[110]

Broad access was not accompanied by high expenditures on health, however, which means that the public health infrastructure has been chronically underfunded.[111] Although the share of health spending increased under Nasser and the regime attempted to bring health care to the countryside, only 10 per cent of all planned social service units were eventually built.[112] In the 1970s, 'public hospitals fell into abysmal squalor'[113] and health spending reached an all time low of 2 per cent of the state budget in 1992. At the same time, out-of-pocket expenditures amounted to 60 per cent of all health expenditures, with often impoverishing effects for lower-income groups.[114] Though health spending soared between 2002 and 2004, this was not sustained and by the mid-2000s, every other patient was using private health care; only a fifth relied on the free public services.[115]

Finally, Egypt, like all countries in the region, has subsidized consumer durables and energy in order to preserve the purchasing power of the lower and middle classes. Dating back to the period of food rationing during the First World War, the subsidy system was considerably extended under Nasser, but, due to propitious world market prices, was financially endurable.[116] Yet when food prices started to

---

[106] Soliman 2011, p. 66; and Galal and Kanaan 2010, p. 13.
[107] World Bank 2008, pp. 332–3.
[108] Roushdy and Selwaness 2014, p. 16; and Loewe 2010, p. 244.
[109] El Mekkaoui 2019.   [110] See Table 2.2.   [111] CERMOC 1992, p. 117.
[112] Baker 1978, p. 221.   [113] Hinnebusch 1985, p. 272.
[114] Chiffoleau 1990, p. 88; and Rashad and Sharaf 2015.   [115] Clark 2004b, p. 74.
[116] Soliman 2011, p. 123. Based on my own data, subsidies amounted to an average of 8 per cent of all expenditures between 1952 and 1970. The Egyptian subsidy system is discussed in greater detail in Chapter 6.

climb in the 1970s, subsidies increasingly strained the state budget, representing 15.5 per cent of all expenditures in 1977. In the same year, Anwar al-Sadat's attempt to reduce food subsidies resulted in notorious 'bread riots' and the plan to cut back subsidies was abandoned. After subsidies peaked at 20.5 per cent of total expenditures in 1980/1, they were gradually reduced back to levels of around 8 per cent under the presidency of Husni Mubarak.[117] Thanks, again, to low world market prices and a growing economy, the subsidy bill was manageable by the mid-2000s.[118] In addition to subsidies, Egypt has an array of social safety nets of varying size, the largest of which is a social pension scheme for vulnerable groups among the elderly, using categorical targeting. In 2010, it covered 1.4 per cent of the Egyptian population.[119]

2.2.2 Syria

The Syrian welfare trajectory exhibits many similarities with Egypt. In fact, some of the most important social policy reforms in Syria were implemented when Egypt and Syria unified briefly under the banner of the United Arab Republic (UAR, 1958–63).[120] Syrian social policies are characterized by the same combination of universalism and insufficient spending. As Hinnebusch remarks, social policies remain 'unenforced for failure of the government to assign sufficient resources or to develop policy instruments to enforce them'.[121] That said, Syria's commitment to welfare was hampered not only by its external environment, but also by the lopsided nature of its regime coalition, characterized by communal favouritism (see below).[122] This, in turn, meant that welfare was provided less broadly than in Egypt and, honouring the regime's communal base, particularly furthered the social development of specific regions.[123]

Spending levels have been even lower than in Egypt, which brings Syria closer to the pattern of minimal-segmented welfare provision prevalent in other low-spending countries (see Figure 2.5). While average spending amounted to 22 per cent of the state budget in the period 1953–62, the Ba'th regime, which came to power through a coup d'état on 8 March 1963, cut back spending levels, so that by the end of the 1960s social spending represented a meagre 14 per cent of the state budget.[124] In the aftermath of the 1973 war with Israel, spending levels picked

---

[117] Ibid., pp. 57–9. Subsidies on meat, fish, tea, and rice were removed between 1990 and 1992.

[118] A number of subsidy reforms have been carried out by post-2011 governments, which lies beyond the time frame of this study. See, amongst others, Eibl 2017; and Lorenzon 2016.

[119] Silva, Levin, and Morgandi 2013, p. 269.

[120] Heydemann 1999, pp. 122–6.   [121] Hinnebusch 1986, p. 95.

[122] Balanche 2017. See Chapter 3 for more details on the coalition formation process.

[123] G. E. Robinson 1998, p. 161; and Hinnebusch and Ehteshami 2002, p. 10.

[124] This figure is also reported by Waldner 1999, p. 108. Yet while he views this as an indicator of high welfare effort, this chapter should have made clear that such spending levels are dwarfed by the financial commitment to welfare in high-spending regimes.

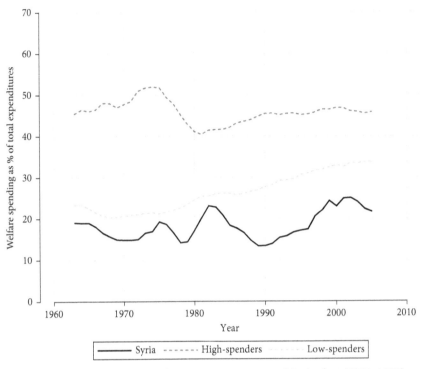

Figure 2.5 Syrian welfare expenditures as a percentage of the budget (1966–1999)

Note: High-spenders include Tunisia, Algeria, and the Islamic Republic of Iran; low-spenders include Egypt, Jordan, Morocco, Syria, and Pahlavi Iran. Line plots were smoothed using a three-year moving average. The pattern looks similar when using welfare spending as a percentage of GDP. Data from V. Lucas and Richter 2016; and IMF 2011.

up slightly and peaked at 26 per cent in 1983, after which declining oil prices and the ensuing economic slowdown led to a period of social spending contraction. Towards the end of Hafiz Al-Asad's rule (1970–2000) and in particular after the takeover by his son, Bashar Al-Asad, in 2000, welfare expenditures experienced a noticeable increase, rising to about a quarter of the state budget by the mid-2000s. Yet this merely meant that Syria was catching up with the average level of low-spenders. A parallel trend in the 2000s was the outsourcing of welfare provision to charities run by regime cronies.[125]

Universalism and low spending has also characterized Syria's educational policies. The Syrian Ba'th regime followed the example of Egypt in abolishing tuition fees and making all levels of education free of charge. In addition, after elementary education was made compulsory in 1970, Syria witnessed a rapid expansion of primary school enrolment.[126] The number of primary students doubled between 1964 and 1977 and, by the early 1980s, the country had

[125] De Elvira and Zintl 2014.   [126] Owen and Şevket 1998, pp. 157–8.

reached nearly universal primary school enrolment.[127] While most regimes have a preference for the politically more volatile urban centres, the Syrian regime's focus on the countryside, where the Ba'th was historically strong, meant that rural areas benefited more from social development than elsewhere, which is visible in the regime's human development record. For instance, the annual growth in primary school enrolment was noticeably higher than amongst other low-spenders, such as Jordan, and higher than in Egypt.[128] Moreover, in terms of literacy, the regime holds a middle position between high- and low-spenders and, again, outperforms Egypt.[129] Syria's outcome performance contrasts with spending levels which had actually been in constant decline since the mid-1960s and levelled off at an average of 8 per cent in the 1980s. By that time, many schools were in decay, classrooms were crowded, and minuscule salaries forced many teachers into moonlighting.[130] Drop-out rates were also very high.[131] Education spending increased slightly until the end of the 1990s but still ranked among the lowest shares in the world.[132] This had led to the development of a considerable private sector for higher education by the mid-2000s.[133]

As regards health care, Syria gradually established a universal health care system by increasing the number of those holding health cards which allowed access to free health care following a means test. The regime finally abandoned means testing and introduced a national health service free of charge and accessible to all Syrian citizens.[134] However, the gradual and lengthy introduction of universal health care meant that, for a long time, between a third and a quarter of the country's population was covered neither by the means-tested system nor by any other social insurance.[135] Spending levels have been extremely low, barely exceeding 1.7 per cent of the state budget in the period from 1972 until 1999. This has negatively affected the quality of the health care infrastructure, with 'public health institutions' being understaffed and poorly equipped'.[136] Yet, again, the combination of broad access and the regime's advertence to the countryside entailed relatively good performance in terms of health outcomes. Child mortality, for instance, decreased faster on average than in Algeria—a high-spender—and other minimal-segmented welfare providers, such as Morocco and Jordan.[137]

In terms of social protection, at 35 per cent Syria's social security coverage lies in between Egypt's medium-range coverage and the very rudimentary systems in minimal-segmented welfare providers, such as Morocco, which underlines the regime's status as a hybrid between both types. The number of actual pension beneficiaries was less than 20 per cent of the elderly population.[138] There has been no major reform since the introduction of social insurance in 1959 during the union

[127] Drysdale 1981a, p. 102.   [128] See Table 2.2.   [129] See Table 2.2.
[130] Batatu 1999, p. 71.   [131] Ma'oz 1988, p. 80.   [132] Galal and Kanaan 2010, p. 104.
[133] Ibid., p. 106.   [134] CERMOC 1992, p. 119.   [135] Drysdale 1981a, p. 100.
[136] Perthes 1997, p. 128.   [137] See Table 2.2.   [138] El Mekkaoui 2019.

with Egypt.[139] An reform attempt to unify the schemes of the public and private sectors in 1979 failed because of the staunch resistance of labour unions.[140] As a result, coverage rates have remained stagnant and the current system privileges a minority of white-collar public sector workers.[141] Social safety nets outside the contributory system are underdeveloped, comprising a public works programme and the Social Welfare Fund, which both suffer from underfunding.[142] Following the regional pattern, Syria has sought to guarantee social protection for low-income groups by extensively subsidizing food and energy.[143]

The particular rural focus of the regime's social policies stems partly from the fact that the Syrian Ba'th party had considerably more followers in the countryside as compared to the predominantly Sunni urban centres.[144] However, it also reflects patterns of favouritism towards the regime's communal base, in particular the Druze and the Alawis. Both groups are regionally clustered in the Dar'a and Latakia provinces respectively. As Balanche notes, Alawis have not only benefited from preferential public goods delivery and private goods like public employment, but have also managed to safeguard their privileges better during cutbacks by levering their political connections.[145] In the mid-2000s, the Latakia province exhibited not only the highest regional levels of public employment—64.5 per cent compared to 26.7 per cent nationally—but also above-average literacy levels and the highest secondary enrolment rate.[146] This trend towards communal favouritism became noticeable shortly after the Ba'th party took over in 1963. Drysdale notes that 'al-Ladhiqiyah and Dar'a provinces have enjoyed disproportionate [school enrolment] growth, possibly because of government favoritism. [...] The tremendous growth of enrollment in the province is especially significant, because since 1971 the government has guaranteed all graduates from secondary school admission to university or to other institutions of higher education. [...] It seems likely that the ties of many of Syria's leaders with the region have worked to its advantage.'[147]

Drysdale further suggests that any over-provision in the Dar'a and Latakia provinces is a reflection of the fact that both provinces were strongly over-represented in the Regional Command (RC) of the Ba'th party, which formed the centre of political decision-making after the 1963 coup.[148] Using his historical data of regional shares in the RC, the assertion of a positive association between RC representation and welfare provision appears warranted in light of Figure 2.6, which

[139] CERMOC 1992, p. 119.
[140] Ibid., p. 120. Labour unions mostly comprise public sector workers.   [141] Perthes 1997, p. 128.
[142] Silva, Levin, and Morgandi 2013, p. 271.
[143] In 2008, the government increased the price of diesel to bring it closer to world market prices. In the wake of the Syrian civil war, both food and energy subsidies have been cut back substantially. See IMF 2014, p. 87.
[144] Hinnebusch 2002.   [145] Balanche 2018, p. 117.   [146] Balanche 2006, p. 64, 120.
[147] Drysdale 1981a, p. 109, 103.   [148] Drysdale 1981b.

shows a positive gradient in particular for changes in primary and secondary enrolment between 1966 and 1976. Importantly, the initial distribution of power among regions appears to have had a lasting effect on welfare provision, as the historical RC shares also correlate with indicators of welfare provision from the 2004 census (see Figures 2.6 and 2.7).[149] The bivariate plots further suggest that this effect goes over and above what can be explained by regional representation in the RC alone. Instead, the figures indicate that the Latakia province in particular has received better welfare provision than its historical political weight in the Ba'th party would have warranted. Combined with the qualitative evidence cited, this underlines the particular communal slant of social policies in Syria.

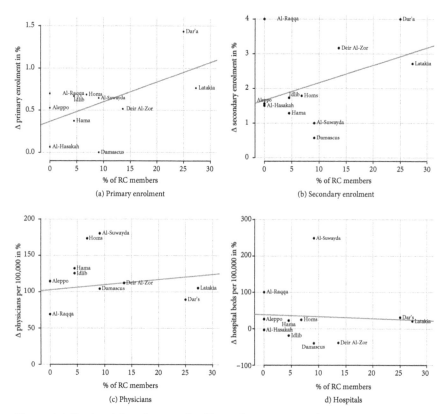

Figure 2.6 Regional distribution of welfare infrastructure and outcomes in Syria (late 1970s)

Note: RC = Regional Command of the Ba'th party. All data are taken from Drysdale 1981a.

---

[149] Unfortunately it was not possible to use the same set indicators for the historical and contemporary period. That said, both sets cover the key areas of health and education.

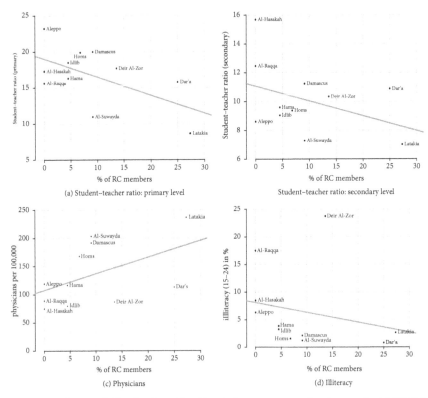

Figure 2.7 Regional distribution of welfare infrastructure and outcomes (mid-2000s)

Note: RC = Regional Command of the Ba'th party. Data on RC composition taken from Drysdale 1981a. Data on health and education outcomes from Central Bureau of Statistics 2004.

2.3 Minimal-Segmented Welfare Provision

Minimal-segmented welfare provision is the third social policy trajectory observed among labour-rich MENA countries. Generally, this type lacks the universal access policies characteristic of broad welfare provision and authoritarian welfare states. The underlying authoritarian support coalition being narrow, this type exhibits noticeably lower social spending levels than authoritarian welfare states. It comes in two variants. *Minimal* welfare provision is characterized by rudimentary social policies and an underdeveloped social security system covering few life-course risks only. As a result, coverage rates of social insurance and assistance are low. In cases of minimal welfare provision, even for core regime constituencies social policies do not play a major role in the regime's legitimation strategy. *Segmented* welfare provision features well-developed but exclusive social policies, catering predominantly to the regime's core constituencies. This has abetted the sharp segmentation of social policies and the social security system into in- and out-groups, which is reflected in lower coverage rates than broad (and generous) welfare providers, but a rather generous provision for in-groups. In terms of human development outcomes, minimal-segmented provision has entailed slower reductions in child mortality, slower improvements in life expectancy and literacy, and a less vigorous expansion of enrolment.

2.3.1 Morocco

Like no other regime in the region, the Kingdom of Morocco stands for a policy of minimal welfare provision. Since the country's independence from France in 1956, social protection has never been a priority. Instead, it has been considered ancillary to growth and economic development, turning social policies into a residual category of state activity.[150] This is clearly reflected in the regime's pattern of social spending. Between 1960 and 2005, the average share of social expenditure in the

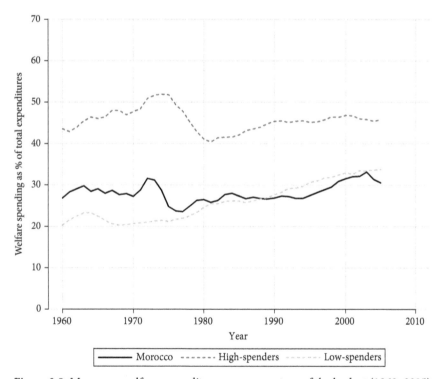

Figure 2.8 Moroccan welfare expenditures as a percentage of the budget (1960–2005)

Note: High-spenders include Tunisia, Algeria, and the Islamic Republic of Iran; low-spenders include Egypt, Jordan, Morocco, Syria, and Pahlavi Iran. Line plots were smoothed using a three-year moving average. The pattern looks similar when using welfare spending as a percentage of GDP. Data from V. Lucas and Richter 2016; and IMF 2011.

---

[150] Catusse and Zaki 2009, p. 188.

state budget has approximated a third of total expenditures (see Figure 2.8). Only in the wake of a phosphate boom, parallel to the oil boom in the early 1970s,[151] did social spending hike up rapidly, reaching an all-time high of 35 per cent in 1973. However, this spree was short-lived as the rapid fall in phosphate prices entailed a steady contraction of spending levels until the late 1970s. The IMF structural adjustment programme in the 1980s did not noticeably affect social spending levels as the country kept its, admittedly rudimentary, social policies intact.[152] Since the early 1990s, spending levels have fluctuated around the long-term average of 28 per cent. In this respect, the transition from King Hassan II to his son Mohammed VI has not entailed any marked change.

This assessment is shared by a World Bank report from 2002, which notes: 'public expenditures in social sectors, although increasing, are still (i) insufficient for lifting people out of poverty and reducing vulnerabilities; (ii) skewed toward the better-off; and (iii) inefficient'.[153] This bias toward the better-off is equally visible in Morocco's weakly developed social insurance system. By the mid-2000s, only one in four Moroccans was covered by a public pension scheme.[154] The number of pension beneficiaries above the age of sixty is even lower (10 per cent).[155] Access to health insurance is equally low, covering only 15 per cent of the entire population,[156] which is reflected in the the slowest decrease of child mortality in the whole sample.[157] Until 2002, health insurance was not even part of the social insurance scheme, not even for public sector workers, who were only offered optional complementary insurance.[158] Self-employed Moroccans are totally excluded from social insurance as there is no possibility of voluntary self-enrolment. This underlines the minimalist nature of Morocco's social policies. Minimalist welfare provision has also affected the educational sector. Reduction in illiteracy was slow and Morocco achieved universal primary enrolment only belatedly, in the early 2000s.[159]

Looking at education more specifically, independence was not accompanied by a major effort to achieve mass education. On the contrary, Hassan II's infamous declaration that he wished Moroccans had remained illiterate gives an

---

[151] Morocco holds 75 per cent of the world's phosphate reserves and is the second largest exporter worldwide.

[152] Mouline 2005, p. 54.   [153] World Bank 2002, i.

[154] Loewe 2010, p. 244. The main schemes for the public sector are the *Caisse marocaine des retraites* (CMR) and the *Régime collectif d'allocation de retraite* (RCAR). The principal private sector scheme is the *Caisse nationale de sécurité sociale* (CNSS).

[155] World Bank 2015b, p. 16. El Mekkaoui 2019 indicates a higher rate of 30 per cent, which still ranges at the bottom of the spectrum observed in labour-abundant MENA countries.

[156] Catusse and Zaki 2009, p. 200. Coverage rates have improved since the the health care reforms in the mid-2000s (see below).

[157] See Table 2.2.   [158] World Bank 2001, p. 34.

[159] See Table 2.2; and World Bank 2008, pp. 314–15.

impression of the insignificance of education for postcolonial regime building.[160] Expenditures thus barely increased after independence and constituted 15 to 20 per cent of the state budget from 1960 until the late 2000s. In addition, educational policies have also been biased in favour of secondary and higher education,[161] which explains the comparatively slow decline of illiteracy in Morocco.[162] Another factor that has contributed to the persistence of illiteracy is a particularly high dropout rate from school. According to Galal and Kanaan, only 46 per cent of all children starting school reach the final year of compulsory education.[163] With the ascension of Mohammed VI to the Moroccan throne in 2000, the so-called 'King of the Poor' placed a greater emphasis on human development, which led to an increase of education's share in the state budget. Increased spending, however, has as yet not been able to make up the accumulated leeway over the past decades. By the mid-2000s, Morocco's education sector remained 'poorly funded and equipped'.[164]

In the field of health care, Morocco established a centralized health care system after independence, in which the state was the unique provider.[165] Yet, in contrast to broad welfare providers, these services were not provided universally and came with prohibitively high costs for the country's poor. To build the necessary infrastructure, health expenditures expanded during the first decade after independence, but thereafter set on a permanent decline until the late 1970s. Since then, the share of health expenditure has barely exceeded 3 per cent of the budget. In contrast to broad welfare providers, health services have not been provided universally and come with prohibitively high costs, particularly for the country's poor, with out-of-pocket costs for health care exceeding 50 per cent.[166] Until the health care reform in 2002, the lowest income brackets had access to subsidized health care, subject to a means test, which in reality many poor Moroccans were unable to afford. Moreover, coverage was weak, reaching only 5 per cent of the population.[167] This meant that, by the mid-2000s, about 80 per cent of all Moroccans had to pay their health expenses entirely out of their own pockets. This had visible repercussions on Morocco's human development record as mortality rates and life expectancy range at the very bottom of my sample of countries.[168]

As part of the international effort to universalize health care and propelled by international agencies, the Moroccan government introduced compulsory health insurance (*Assurance maladie obligatoire*, AMO) alongside a tax-based scheme for low-income groups (*Régime d'assistance médicale*, RAMED) in 2002. AMO came into effect in 2002; RAMED was piloted between 2008 and 2012, and then rolled

---

[160] The literal quote reads as follows: 'It would be better if you were illiterate because illiterates are less dangerous to the state than so-called intellectuals.' The declaration was made when addressing the nation on 29 March 1965 in response to civil unrest in Casablanca and Rabat. See Rollinde 2002, p. 123.   [161] World Bank 2008, p. 33.   [162] See Table 2.2.   [163] Galal and Kanaan 2010, p. 89.   [164] Sater 2010, p. 116.   [165] Belghiti Allaoui 2006.   [166] Belouas 2017.   [167] Loewe 2010, pp. 251–2.   [168] See Table 2.2.

out countrywide. While the reform certainly represents an improvement, it has thus far failed to universalize access to health, setting Morocco apart from broad welfare providers with open access policies. Between 40 and 60 per cent of the population remain outside either RAMED and AMO, as the latter covers only employees in the formal sector.[169] Non-poor informal workers remain excluded from either scheme. RAMED, which is intended to cover 25 per cent of the population, has its own significant shortcomings. Although it targets only the lowest consumption quintile, up to 72 per cent of this group remain excluded from the scheme due to design issues in the proxy means test.[170] And RAMED does not cover chronic diseases or the costs of medication. Health professionals and politicians agree that it remains chronically underfunded.[171]

These weaknesses of the social insurance scheme have been partly attenuated by a number of social assistance programmes. The National Initiative for Human Development (*Initiative nationale pour le développement humain*, INDH), established in 2005 under the auspices of the King, uses geographical targeting to fund public infrastructure, as well as cultural and sports events in poor communities. The initiative 'covered' circa 20 per cent of the population in 2008,[172] but given that it contains few revenue-generating or cash transfer components, its impact on poverty alleviation has been limited.[173] School feeding and supplies programmes covered 7 per cent of the population, the flagship cash transfer programme Tayssir only 0.5.[174] This means that the subsidization of food and energy has remained the most important safety net component in Morocco. Sugar subsidies for food-processing industries were faded out in 1999.[175]

2.3.2 Pahlavi Iran

Iran under the rule of Mohamed Reza Shah Pahlavi (1953–79) is another example of an authoritarian regime with only minimal provision of welfare. While Iran's considerable oil reserves made it by far the most affluent labour-rich MENA country—GDP per capita levels exceeded all other regimes until the late 1970s—copious oil rents did not entail high social spending. On the contrary, save the momentary spending surge in the wake of the White Revolution in the early 1960s,[176] welfare spending was low throughout and rarely exceeded 20 per cent

---

[169] Estimates of coverage vary. Compare Mahmoud 2019 and Ismaili 2019.
[170] World Bank 2015b, p. 29.   [171] Huffpost 2019.
[172] Silva, Levin, and Morgandi 2013, p. 271.   [173] Benkassmi, Abdelkhalek, and Ejjanoui 2017.
[174] Silva, Levin, and Morgandi 2013, p. 271.
[175] In 2013, the government further introduced an indexation system for energy subsidies to rein in their cost.
[176] The White Revolution was a reform and modernization programme of the Shah, initiated in 1963, which aimed to undercut the influence of the country's landed upper class and promote social and economic development. See Milani 1994, pp. 43–47.

of the state budget (see Figure 2.9).[177] Against claims of a quasi-natural link between rent income and welfare provision, spending remained flat with the onset of the oil price boom in the early 1970s and only picked up slightly when prices started to drop again by the end of the decade. Another indicator of the regime's weak commitment to welfare provision is the belated established of a Ministry of Social Affairs, which was set up only five years before the Shah's ouster during the Iranian Revolution.[178] Social insurance was also a latecomer in Iran and remained a privilege of urban white-collar employees, mainly working in the public sector. By the end of the Shah's regime, Iran exhibited the slowest reductions of illiteracy and child mortality in the entire sample.[179] The International Labour Organization (ILO) considered Pahlavi Iran one of the least egalitarian countries in the world.[180] Social policies were clearly not the preferred legitimation strategy of the regime, including for its supporters.

The regime's disregard for the population's welfare is particularly visible in the field of education. Although the idea of mass education had been part of the Iranian public discourse since the beginning of the twentieth century and the country established its first national university in Tehran in 1934,[181] actual expenditures for education lay bare the regime's unwillingness to honour its political rhetoric. Compared to spending levels under the Shah's father and predecessor, Reza Shah Pahlavi (1925–41),[182] the share of education increased only slightly. Between 1953 and 1963, an average of 13 per cent of the budget was spent on education, and after a temporary hike at the beginning of the White Revolution in 1963, spending quickly reverted to previous levels. In addition, the regime invested very little in the country's educational infrastructure, allocating less than 10 per cent of all development expenditures under the Second (1955–62) and Third Plan (1962–7) to education.[183]

A more fine-grained study of spending further reveals that increasing expenditures clearly favoured higher education.[184] Thus, when education became compulsory and nominally free of charge in the mid-1960s, primary enrolment stood at 63 per cent.[185] It is true that following the establishment of so-called literacy corps in 1963, primary enrolment increased rapidly until the Shah's downfall, amounting to 2 per cent on average between 1950 and 1979.[186] Whilst these figures are high compared to other minimal welfare providers, they need to be put in perspective. As Abrahamian reports, about 60 per cent of all school children did not finish school, which qualifies official enrolment figures.[187] This also explains why Pahlavi

[177] See also Messkoub 2006b, pp. 234–35.
[178] Savory 1978, p. 120.
[179] See Table 2.2. As mentioned above, these estimates probably overestimate the Shah regime's performance as they are measured for a period of more rapid, early development only.
[180] Abrahamian 1982, pp. 447–48.
[181] Messkoub 2006b, p. 228.   [182] Ibid., p. 229.   [183] Messkoub 2006b, p. 233.
[184] Eilers 1978, p. 306.   [185] World Bank 2008, pp. 314–15.   [186] See Table 2.2.
[187] Abrahamian 2008, p. 142.

Figure 2.9 Iranian welfare expenditures as a percentage of the budget (1953–1979)

Note: High-spenders include Tunisia, Algeria, and the Islamic Republic of Iran; low-spenders include Egypt, Jordan, Morocco, Syria, and Pahlavi Iran. Line plots were smoothed using a three-year moving average. The pattern looks similar when using welfare spending as a percentage of GDP. Data from V. Lucas and Richter 2016; and IMF 2011.

Iran achieved the slowest increase in literacy of all countries under observation, amounting to an annual average of 0.64 per cent.[188] On the whole, the education system was clearly biased toward higher-income groups in urban areas.[189]

Rural areas were also largely left out when it came to health care. Despite the creation of health corps to improve sanitary conditions in the countryside in 1964, an estimated 90 per cent of all villages still lacked access to medical facilities by the late 1970s.[190] The medical journal *The Lancet* concluded that 'the interest they [the health corps] have in rural areas remains questionable'.[191] Health spending never exceeded 5 per cent of the budget and was primarily allocated to 'pseudo-modernistic' prestige projects in the big cities.[192] As a result of this weak financial effort, Iran stood out for having one of the worst doctor–patient and hospital bed-to-population ratios in the Middle East.[193] In terms of child

---

[188] See Table 2.2.   [189] Katouzian 1981, pp. 288–9.
[190] Halliday 1979, p. 120.   [191] Cited in K. Harris 2017, p. 72   [192] Katouzian 1981, p. 291.
[193] Abrahamian 1982, p. 447.

mortality, figures reveal almost no change between 1950 and 1969 and the total average reduction amounted to only 0.64 per cent a year—not even half the level of high-spenders.[194] Even an official government report from the late 1970s remarked that 'many of Iran's major health and medical problems remain unsolved'.[195]

The only reasonably protected segments of society were the army and the civil service, which had been offered social insurance schemes in 1957 and 1960 respectively, including pensions and health insurance.[196] In contrast, the establishment of social insurance for the private sector lagged behind. Until the mid-1970s, social protection was limited to work-related accidents and illnesses, based on a law from 1953.[197] In 1975, the regime transferred this minimal scheme for the private sector to the newly founded Social Security Organization (SSO) and extended coverage to include pensions, health, and unemployment. Coverage rates for the private sector remained relatively weak, however. A coverage rate of only 4 per cent of the population in the 1950s increased to about 18 per cent of the population prior to the Shah's ouster.[198] The rural sector was legally included but, again, hardly benefited from these reforms as the government failed to carry social security into the countryside.[199] The regime also lacked a noticeable social assistance programme.

2.3.3 Jordan

The Kingdom of Jordan takes a special position among welfare providers as the coalition that underpins it is shaped by a historical communal cleavage between East Bankers and Palestinian West Bankers (see Chapter 3). While I classify the coalition on the whole as narrow, the logic of communal welfare distribution means that Jordan has been rather generous to communal 'insiders', i.e. East Bankers, and much less generous to communal 'outsiders', i.e. Palestinian West Bankers. Alongside private goods, particularly public employment, social policies have been used to garner the support of the East Bank population for the regime, albeit to a lesser extent. The country's welfare provision is thus best described as segmented, rather than minimal.

Having gained full sovereignty with the end of the British protectorate in 1946, Jordan's first ruler, King Abdullah (1946–51), only paid very scant attention to social welfare.[200] His grandson, King Hussein, who came to power in 1953 after

---

[194] See Table 2.2 and United Nations 2012.

[195] Cited in Halliday 1979, p. 120.

[196] Longuenesse, Catusse, and Destremeau 2005, p. 26; and Messkoub 2006b, p. 243. These schemes had historical predecessors in a retirement law and pension fund for civil servants, passed in 1908 and 1922 respectively, and a nascent contributory scheme for public sector employees beginning in 1931. See K. Harris 2017, p. 50, 54.

[197] Messkoub 2006b, p. 231.   [198] K. Harris 2010a, pp. 728–9.   [199] Ibid., p. 730.

[200] Satloff 1994, p. 11.

a short interregnum, followed in his grandfather's footsteps and mainly focused on foreign and defence policy, which led to 'a deplorable neglect of internal affairs and especially the welfare of his people'.[201] The regime's social policies were thus broadly in line with those of Morocco and the Shah regime at the time, and Jordan exhibited all the key characteristics of a low welfare effort. Social expenditures were low, especially in the 1950s and 1960s, and until the late 1980s always represented less than a third of the state budget. A first seven-year development plan to improve education and health facilities was only adopted sixteen years after the country had gained independence. Social security was non-existent until the late 1970s.[202]

Moreover, social policies were biased against Palestinians, who after the 1948 war with Israel and Jordan's annexation of the West Bank in 1950 represented about half of Jordan's population.[203] This ongoing communal favouritism has reinforced the exclusivist and segmented nature of welfare provision in Jordan. As Loewe argues, the targeting of social policies to key support groups has been more pronounced in Jordan than elsewhere.[204] Since the early 1990s, the existence of a two-tier system has been particularly visible. Whilst the conjuncture of a severe economic crisis in the early-mid 1990s—poverty rates quintupled[205]—the return of more than 100,000 Jordanians in the wake of the Gulf War, and the improvement of social services to buffer the effects of IMF structural adjustment induced an expansion of social and, in particular, health expenditure in the 1990s (see Figure 2.10),[206] this spending spree particularly benefited regime insiders. The spending hike, which abated in the early 2000s as Jordan reverted to levels comparable to other minimal-segmented welfare providers, was predominantly driven by more generous social benefits to civil servants—a sector which has historically been dominated by East Bankers.[207] Military personnel and their families benefited particularly from this new largesse as social services for this already privileged group were further enhanced.[208] Thus, instead of extensive universalism, Jordanian welfare provision has been marked by a striking segmentation and a remarkable generosity toward the country's armed forces.

In the field of education, policies were haphazard and spending increased only piecemeal. In the wake of two wars with Israel in 1967 and 1973, education was nearly squeezed out of the budget, with spending levels reaching an all-time low of 6 per cent in 1973. Although spending recuperated and increased until the early 1990s, education spending by the mid-2000s was lagging behind levels seen in high-spenders. In addition, the establishment of the United Nations Relief and Works Agency for Palestine Refugees (UNRWA) in 1949 allowed the regime to outsource the education of the Palestinian population to an international agency, which provided free education to all Palestinian refugees. Over 80 per cent of UNRWA's budget goes towards education and health, which has

---

[201] Shlaim 2007, p. 472.   [202] Aruri 1972, p. 178.   [203] Baylouny 2010, p. 72.
[204] Loewe 1998, p. 151.   [205] IMF 1995, p. 69.   [206] See also IMF 2004b, p. 119.
[207] Baylouny 2008, p. 281.   [208] Ibid., p. 301.

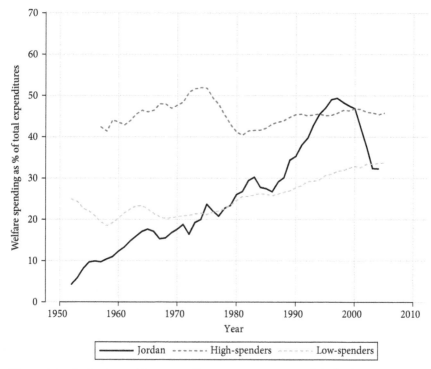

Figure 2.10 Jordanian welfare expenditures as a percentage of the budget (1952–2004)

Note: High-spenders include Tunisia, Algeria, and the Islamic Republic of Iran; low-spenders include Egypt, Jordan, Morocco, Syria, and Pahlavi Iran. Line plots were smoothed using a three-year moving average. The pattern looks similar when using welfare spending as a percentage of GDP. Data from V. Lucas and Richter 2016; and IMF 2011.

taken considerable fiscal pressure off the regime.[209] It is also predominantly thanks to UNRWA that primary enrolment rates jumped by about 30 per cent between 1950 and 1955.[210] Given the country's meagre performance in increasing primary enrolment thereafter—primary enrolment growth after 1955 was the lowest in the entire sample[211]—Jordan's performance would have looked much more like Morocco's without the presence of UNRWA. The influx of the much better educated Palestinian refugees also boosted Jordan's literacy levels,[212] which have been comparatively high given the regime's spending levels. In terms of literacy growth, Jordan clearly ranks below rates of high-spenders.[213]

Educational outsourcing intensified in the late 1980s when the regime decided to alleviate the financial burden of education by encouraging private

[209] IMF 2000, p. 79.   [210] World Bank 2008, pp. 314–15.   [211] See Table 2.2.
[212] Ayal and Chiswick 2013, p. 866.   [213] See Table 2.2.

education and shifting the financial burden onto citizens.[214] Between 1983 and 2003, the private enrolment share in primary education increased from 7.8 to 29.9 per cent. For secondary education, shares increased from zero to 16.6 per cent in the same period.[215] In cooperation with the World Bank, the Jordanian government also initiated a reform of higher education starting in 2000,[216] which has led to a significant hike in tuition fees for students.[217] While higher education is essentially free of charge for members of the military and their families,[218] tuition fees represented, overall, 65.6 per cent of universities, income in the late 2000s.[219]

The health sector has followed a similar trajectory. Apart from a spending surge following the Six-Day War in 1967, health expenditures represented only a minimal share of the state budget until the late 1980s, consuming about 4 per cent on average. In the 1990s, the provision of health care improved as a result of higher expenditures and development loans from the World Bank.[220] Access to health care has remained unequal, however, and clearly privileges public sector employees and the army, both dominated by East Bankers. For instance, 25 per cent of the population can access the Royal Health Services, created in 1963, which provide high-quality health care to members of the army and their dependants.[221] In 1965, the government introduced Civic Health Insurance which provides coverage to another 25 per cent of the population working in the public sector (including dependants).[222] A health card programme provides access to subsidized health care for poor households, covering another 8 per cent of the population in the early 2000s, but coverage has remained hampered by a complicated application process and even reduced fees are often unaffordable.[223] In 2004, the government further extended health insurance to all children under six years of age.[224] On the whole, 40–50 per cent of the population were not covered by health insurance in the mid-2000s and had to self-fund their health care expenses.[225] Restricted access to health care is reflected in Jordan's outcome performance, with improvements in life expectancy and child mortality ranging at the lower end of the spectrum.[226]

The same holds true for pension coverage, which has only been accessible for a minority of the country's workforce. Members of the armed forces have historically benefited from a very generous pension regime, which affords beneficiaries and their survivors final-salary benefits despite low contribution levels with a short minimum pay-in period. The scheme was deemed financially unsustainable and closed for new entrants in 2003.[227] The establishment of a state pension fund for non-military public sector employees occurred late, in 1977. As a result,

[214] Baylouny 2010, p. 56.
[215] World Bank 2008, pp. 332–4.   [216] Knowles 2005, p. 110.   [217] World Bank 2008, p. 191.
[218] Baylouny 2010, p. 54.   [219] Galal and Kanaan 2010, p. 32.   [220] Knowles 2005, p. 110.
[221] CERMOC 1992, p. 123.   [222] Baylouny 2008, p. 297.
[223] Loewe 2010, p. 252; and IMF 1998, p. 126.   [224] IMF 2001, p. 50.
[225] Loewe 2010, p. 251; and IMF 2004b, p. 111, 119. Fifty per cent of all health expenditures were private in 2004.
[226] See Table 2.2.   [227] IMF 2004b, p. 116.

total pension coverage was limited to about a third of the workforce until the mid-1980s.[228] This was reflected in a low number of actual pension beneficiaries amongst the elderly in the mid-2000s (32 per cent).[229] Even after the creation of the Social Security Cooperation (SSC) for private sector employees in 1980, coverage levels increased only very slowly, mainly because the subscription to the SSC has long been limited to large businesses and no concerted effort to reach into the informal sector has been undertaken.[230] Even after the consolidation of public and private pension schemes within the SSC, only 47 per cent of the Jordanian workforce contribute to the public social security scheme.[231] Conversely, nearly 50 per cent of Jordan's workforce did not have access to a pension scheme, private or public. In 2010, the government introduced maternity benefits and an unemployment insurance saving account as part of the SSC, while making SSC enrolment for all private sector companies compulsory.[232] The inclusion of a health insurance component in the SSC was envisaged but not completed at the time.[233]

In terms of non-contributory social protection schemes, food and energy subsidies are the only truly universally accessible policies in Jordan. Food subsidies, save for bread, had been phased out by 1997 but then reintroduced in 2005 to mitigate the effect of an energy subsidies reform.[234] This reform, partly caused by the end of cheap oil deliveries from Iraq, comprised gradual energy price increases culminating in an automatic price indexation to the world market that came into force in 2008.[235] The National Aid Fund (NAF) is Jordan's major cash grant scheme, which provides monetary support and food vouchers to low-income individuals without employment. Working poor households are not included in the programme. The NAF reached 6.5 per cent of the Jordanian population in 2009.[236]

2.4 Conclusion

This chapter has presented a descriptive argument about the divergent welfare trajectories of labour-abundant MENA regimes. Based on my typology of three distinct types of welfare provision—broad and generous, broad, and minimal-segmented—the chapter has mapped out the different welfare trajectories of my

---

[228] Loewe 1998, p. 151.   [229] El Mekkaoui 2019.   [230] CERMOC 1992, p. 124.
[231] Hazaimeh 2012.   [232] Gatti et al. 2014, p. 284.
[233] A health insurance and an unemployment insurance component were added to the SSC after a reform law passed in 2013. See Neimat 2013b; and Neimat 2013a.
[234] IMF 2014, p. 83.
[235] It was abandoned in 2011 in the wake of the Arab Spring and later reintroduced.
[236] Silva, Levin, and Morgandi 2013, p. 270.

eight cases and, in so doing, laid important groundwork for the analysis to come. The key findings are presented in Table 2.2 and can be summarized as follows.

First, based on the foregoing description, the use of social spending data as a first-hand criterion to distinguish welfare efforts in the region seems warranted. High-spenders, such as Tunisia, Algeria, and the Islamic Republic of Iran, have not only allocated more resources to social welfare; their social policies have also reached out to large segments of the population. They all established complex systems of social security that cover not only the white-collar, urban middle classes, but also encompass important segments of the rural and informal sector. Ranging between 66 and 90 per cent of the workforce, the coverage rates of both pension and health insurance schemes are by far the highest in the whole sample. Regarding health care in particular, all high-spenders have ensured universal access to health care by providing far-reaching social security coupled with free or highly subsidized health care for those without coverage. This has had noticeable repercussions on the countries' health outcomes. In terms of life expectancy and child mortality, the three high-spenders have witnessed the fastest improvements across all observed cases. They have also achieved the fastest changes in enrolment and literacy rates. The latter two points further demonstrate a strong link between consistently high spending levels and desired social outcomes.

Second, among low-spenders, the question of access to social policies represents an important criterion to distinguish broad from minimal-segmented welfare providers. Whilst both groups have allocated considerably less to welfare than their high-spending counterparts, broad welfare providers have ensured greater accessibility of their social policies and thereby managed to provide welfare more widely among their populations. This is particularly visible in the area of health care. In contrast to Morocco, Pahlavi Iran, and Jordan, Syria and Egypt have established a system of universal health care provision. Though lacking in terms of quality as a result of low spending, their public health care system has ensured free access for low-income groups, with sizeable impacts in their health outcomes. Child mortality rates dropped remarkably faster in Egypt and Syria than other low-spenders, which ranks them right in-between authoritarian welfare states and minimal provision regimes. The picture is similar for enrolment and literacy. And their social security systems exhibit higher coverage rates than all other low-spenders, except for Jordan. On closer inspection, Syria features significant regional discrepancies in welfare provision reflecting the communal nature of the regime coalition. Yet considering access restrictions in all areas of social protection in minimal providers, Egypt and Syria stand out as a distinctive type of broad welfare provision. Jordan stands out for its stark segmentation of social policies, separating regime insiders with access to fairly generous social policies from regime outsiders. This is a reflection of the historical communal cleavage structuring the regime's support coalition.

Third, despite the variability of social spending revealed by the spending plots, the chapter emphasizes persistence of welfare trajectories more than anything else. To be sure, high-spenders have at times weakened their effort in the face of adverse economic conditions; and low-spenders have at times boosted their social expenditures to levels characteristic of high-spenders, in particular when looking at education and health spending more specifically. However, it is important to note that spending has generally oscillated around long-term historical averages. By the mid-2000s, aggregate welfare expenditures in authoritarian welfare states were on average 15 per cent higher than in low-spenders. In the mid-1950s, this difference had stood at 20 per cent—a mere improvement of 5 percentage points for low-spenders over five decades. Moreover, if we take into consideration social insurance schemes and outcomes, the divergence becomes even more pronounced as none of the low-spenders has managed to catch up with the coverage and outcome performance of high-spenders. Granted, regimes like Jordan have established relatively generous systems of welfare provision for regime 'insiders'; yet this comes at the expense of the welfare provision to the population as a whole. In total, it is a story of long-term, persistent divergence that emerges from the foregoing analysis.

3

Divergent Paths

The Coalitional Origin of Authoritarian Welfare States

This chapter begins the empirical investigation of my argument. Macro-comparative in nature, it links the outlined theoretical framework and the variation of welfare provision with the historical evidence of patterns of regime formation in the MENA region. Analysing the genesis of regime coalitions in their specific geostrategic context, this chapter explores to what extent my theoretical framework captures the divergent patterns of regime formation and welfare efforts in labour-rich MENA countries. It demonstrates that foundational intra-elite crises that pitted rival elite groups against each other crucially affected the shape of regime coalitions and hence the incentives for elites to provide social welfare. Elites are thus the central actor in this chapter, whose struggle for power had tremendous and long-lasting consequences for the structure of the regimes they strove to build. Besides intra-elite conflict, this chapter emphasizes the formative impact of communal cleavages on the size of regime coalitions. Salient communal cleavages are found to undermine the formation of broad cross-class coalitions, prompting elites to give more weight to their communal base. It further demonstrates that the ability to hand out welfare goods effectively was conditioned by external threat and available resources. By establishing the moment of coalition formation as a moment of divergence placing the eight regimes on different trajectories, the analysis substantiates my theoretical argument about the coalitional origin of authoritarian welfare states.

The chapter is organized as a structured focused comparison of regime formation and its geostrategic context in my eight cases. Each case narrative systematically answers the same set of questions to assess whether my argument broadly holds in light of the empirical pattern. With regard to regime formation, I assess first whether the causal conditions were present and, secondly, whether there is evidence of the expected causal effect. Did intra-elite conflict occur, was it intense, and is there any evidence that it entailed a broadening of the initial coalitions? If elites managed to avoid major conflict, what were the sources of elite cohesion? Similarly, were there ethnic cleavages, were they salient, and did they affect coalition size in the expected manner? Importantly, I also seek to ascertain that coalitions were not broad prior to intra-elite conflict, which would confound my theoretical argument. Likewise, regarding the geostrategic context, I analyse

Social Dictatorships: The Political Economy of the Welfare State in the Middle East and North Africa. Ferdinand Eibl, Oxford University Press (2020). © Ferdinand Eibl. DOI: 10.1093/oso/9780198834274.001.0001

whether a severe external threat existed at the moment of regime formation, whether it was perceived as a threat to regime survival, and whether it had noticeable repercussions on government spending. Finally, the presence and effect of resource endowment is examined in the same way.

In the explanatory logic of this book, the chapter represents a necessary empirical hurdle the proposed argument has to clear. Certainly, it is not meant to substitute for a detailed analysis of the causal link between coalitions and welfare distribution, which will be the subject of later chapters. However, before delving into in-depth case studies, it seems appropriate to assess whether the theory broadly holds in view of the historical genesis of these eight regimes. Building on a broad range of secondary and some primary sources, the evidence presented in the following narrative is not entirely novel. Yet its reassessment in the light of my theory is.

The remainder of the chapter proceeds as follows. Section 3.1 demonstrates how intra-elite conflict and communal cleavages jointly shaped authoritarian regime coalitions. Section 3.2 analyses the geostrategic context in which these regimes emerged. Section 3.3 concludes this chapter.

3.1 Elite Conflict, Communal Cleavages, and the Formation of Regime Coalitions

This section demonstrates how elite conflict and communal cleavages critically affected the size of authoritarian regime coalitions. The variation of these conditions across my eight cases is such that all possible combinations are empirically observed, which makes the MENA sample an interesting ground for theory generation (see Table 3.1). Whilst maintaining the conceptual distinction between broad and narrow coalitions, analysing the eight cases along these two dimensions enables me to present a slightly refined pattern of regime formation.

Table 3.1 Coalition formation in labour-abundant MENA regimes

| | | Communal cleavages | |
		Salient	Not salient
Irreconcilable *and* irrepressible elite conflict	*Yes*	Syria	Tunisia Egypt Islamic Republic of Iran Algeria
	No	Jordan	The Pahlavi regime Morocco

narrow coalition
broad coalition

Tunisia, Egypt, the Islamic Republic of Iran, and Algeria all represent cases of a broad, cross-class coalition. As the following narratives set out to show, irreconcilable and irrepressible conflict among those vying for power gave elites in these regimes a strong impetus to the formation of a broad coalition in an attempt to outcompete their rivals. This process was unaffected by communal cleavages, which either were absent (Tunisia) or not salient (Algeria, Morocco), or the sidelined community was too small (Egypt) to trigger an ethnic narrowing of the coalition.

Morocco and the Pahlavi regime represent cases where intra-elite conflict was present but the distribution of coercive power between elite groups meant that the rival side could be repressed, rather than beaten by forming a larger coalition. Conflict was thus irreconcilable but repressible, leading to narrow regime coalitions. The regimes differed in their source of coercive power: while the Shah regime's status as a Western client state meant it could contract foreign support to beat its rivals, the Moroccan monarchy benefited from the fact that the military leaders of the Moroccan independence movement threw their weight behind the King. Neither of the regimes had engaged in extensive coalition building.

Finally, Syria and Jordan both underline the importance of communal cleavages for coalition formation. While intra-elite conflict encouraged Syrian elites to build a cross-class coalition, the salient communal cleavages in Syria meant that this coalition was 'under-sized' and lopsided in favour of minorities, most notably the Alawites. The specific pattern of regime formation explains why social policies in Syria exhibit elements of broad, universalist and minimal-segmented welfare provision at the same time. Jordan, on the other hand, represents a case of highly cohesive elites coupled with a salient communal cleavage between East Bankers and Palestinians. This incentive structure elucidates the particular pattern of social policies outlined earlier, consisting in segmented social policies targeting strategic groups of a specific community.

3.1.1 Rivalling elites in the absence of communal cleavages: broad cross-class coalitions

Tunisia

The Tunisian regime emerged on the back of a labour–middle class coalition that, unaffected by ethno-religious cleavages, included a large cross-section of the population and provided the regime with a strong incentive for welfare provision. Elite conflict is crucial to understanding the emergence of this coalition and the unfolding of the post-independence regime formation.

Intra-elite conflict in Tunisia was intense, irreconcilable, and irrepressible. When the two leaders of the Tunisian nationalist movement, Habib Bourguiba and Salah Ben Youssef, clashed during the second half of 1955 over the leadership of the country, Tunisia was brought to the brink of civil war.[1] More than 1,000 people lost their lives in the brutal intra-elite strife, representing more than twice as many victims as during the whole struggle for independence between 1953 and 1955.[2] In late 1955, the conflict turned into an armed rebellion launched by the supporters of Ben Youssef. In response, vigilante committees, set up by the Bourguibist camp, assaulted and tortured purported supporters of Ben Youssef.[3] Yet neither side could command a sufficiently strong coercive apparatus to force an end to the conflict. The French, who still controlled public security, were reluctant to carry out arrests of Youssefists and wanted to avoid being drawn into the conflict.[4] Contracting great power support in a client relationship was therefore not an option for either side.[5] Efforts by party members to reconcile both camps had equally failed. In sum, the end of the French protectorate was thus marked by 'a profound crisis among the elites that had fought for the liberation of the country'.[6]

At its heart, the antagonism between Bourguiba and Ben Youssef was driven by their ambition to become the sole leader of the national movement, represented by the Neo-Destour party. Given that the Neo-Destour clearly was a mass party,[7] it might be argued that a broad cross-class coalition already existed before the outbreak of elite conflict. To see that this was not the case, it is important to bear in mind the state of the Neo-Destour party on the eve of independence. On the one hand, recent historiographical research suggests that repeated French crackdowns had severely weakened the party since the late 1940s.[8] French intelligence reports noted a serious regression of the party's activities coupled with increasing conflict among its leadership following these crackdowns,[9] to the extent that the French expected an implosion of the Neo-Destour in 1949.[10] And the resistance groups (*fellaghas*), recruited from the rural poor in the south of Tunisia, were not under direct control of the party.[11] On the other hand, the depiction of the party as a broad cross-class movement needs to be qualified. Analysing the party's register of members, Kraïem estimates that about 70 per cent of the party's followers were small merchants and artisans.[12] Likewise, in April 1955 the upper echelons of the party were mainly composed of merchants, artisans, and small landowners.[13] Notably, the party's leadership comprised only one worker.[14] On the eve of independence, the party primarily represented Tunisia's *petit bourgeois*,

---

[1] Both historical protagonists, such as the former ministers Ahmed Ben Salah and Ahmed Mestiri, and academics have used the term 'civil war' to describe the conflict between Ben Youssef and Bourguiba. See Borsali 2008, p. 35; A. Mestiri 1999, p. 91; Alexander 2010, p. 34; and Rudebeck 1967, p. 37.

[2] Bessis and Belhassen 1988, pp. 170–1. See also Charfi 1989, p. 60.   [3] Sghaier 2011, p. 61.

[4] C. H. Moore 1965, p. 67.   [5] Yom 2016, p. 13.   [6] Kraïem 2011, p. 168.

[7] Estimates of the party's membership range from 200,000 to 325,000. See Oualdi 1999, pp. 70–1; and Kraïem 2011, p. 13.

[8] Borsali 2008, p. 19.   [9] Kraïem 2011, p. 21.   [10] Oualdi 1999, p. 31.

[11] Sghaier 2010, p. 58.   [12] Kraïem 2011, p. 29.   [13] Ibid., p. 28.   [14] Ibid., p. 28.

property-owning lower middle class. The situation Bourguiba and Ben Youssef thus found upon their return in summer 1955 was an enfeebled Neo-Destour with a considerably narrowed social base.

Regarding ethnic cleavages, Tunisia lacked a significant ethnic or linguistic divide,[15] and (pre-)colonial state formation had effectively weakened tribal organizations and thereby brought about the outlines of a stable national community with clearly recognized boundaries.[16] Compared to other countries in North Africa, a berberophone population was 'virtually non-existent',[17] which reinforced the sense of communal cohesion among the population. Bourguiba and Ben Youssef were therefore able to form their support coalitions in the absence of any salient communal cleavage.

As for the link between elite conflict and the broadening of coalitions, the strategic behaviour of both actors clearly demonstrates how they were looking for allies to outcompete each other. In this process, both protagonists built coalitions that reflected different socioeconomic constituencies of Tunisian society.[18] Ben Youssef pitched his rejection of autonomy offered by the French in a pan-Arab nationalist tone, which resonated well within large segments of society and the Neo-Destour.[19] French military intelligence estimated that 40 per cent of the party supported Ben Youssef, who could also claim the support of the biggest party federation in the country's capital city.[20] Hailing from a Djerban merchant background, Ben Youssef, furthermore, managed to secure the support of Tunisia's traditional economic elite, mostly merchants and large landowners whose business unions he had helped to set up in the 1940s.[21]

Pledging to preserve a constitutional monarchy after independence, he was also able to gain the favour of the Tunisian aristocracy, along with the country's traditional religious establishment represented by the Zaituna Mosque and its various satellite institutions.[22] The latter provided a particularly powerful network through which he could mobilize his supporters throughout the country.[23] Although predominantly upper class in nature, his coalition also comprised sectors of the rural, landless poor, mainly recruited from the *fellagha* movement, and a young urban lumpen-proletariat.[24] In a show of force, Ben Youssef gathered 20,000 supporters in the central stadium of Tunis prior to the Neo-Destour's national congress in November 1955, which underlines his popularity and organizational capacity alike.

In view of the extensive support enjoyed by Ben Youssef, Bourguiba seemed to be in the weaker position in autumn 1955. His core social base was predominantly

---

[15] C. H. Moore 1970, p. 324.   [16] Charrad 2001, p. 89.   [17] Ibid., p. 201.
[18] Anderson 1986, p. 233; and King 2010, p. 77.   [19] Alexander 2010, p. 33.
[20] SHAT nd; and Alexander 2010, p. 38.
[21] Erdle 2010, p. 60; Toumi 1989, p. 25; and Bessis and Belhassen 1988, p. 158.
[22] Kraïem 2011, p. 68.   [23] Sghaier 2010, p. 93.
[24] Micaud, L. C. Brown, and C. H. Moore 1964, p. 91.

lower middle class and consisted of *petit bourgeois* landowners and merchants from the Sahel region.[25] The leadership of the Neo-Destour supported Bourguiba, while the party's rank and file was deeply divided. Tunis, the capital city, was in the grip of the Youssefist camp. The arabophone press and most nationalist organizations affiliated with the Neo-Destour also backed Ben Youssef. Bourguiba thus 'desperately needed support'.[26] In this decisive moment, he turned to the *Union générale tunisienne du travail* (Tunisian General Labour Union; UGTT), the country's second most powerful organization, seeking to garner labour's support against Ben Youssef.

Labour was by no means a natural ally for Bourguiba. Within the UGTT, the choice of the 'right' camp was hotly debated. As the only political actor in the country the UGTT had outlined an extensive programme of social and economic reforms, and the union was discerning with whom it would be able to realize most of its socioeconomic goals.[27] What is more, Bourguiba had insinuated that he would opt for a liberal economic policy after independence, which ran counter to the UGTT's economic and social programme. Bourguiba was thus not considered particularly pro-labour and he himself worried that the UGTT would alienate Neo-Destour's liberal middle-class supporters.[28]

Why, then, an alliance with Bourguiba? Essentially, the UGTT brought itself to side with Bourguiba because of the strong pro-business constituency in Ben Youssef's camp. Ben Youssef's alliance with large landowners deeply antagonized the labour union. And although Bourguiba was not euphoric about the UGTT's left-wing ideas, an alliance with him appeared more promising for implementing social reforms.[29] Gaining the UGTT's support, in turn, afforded Bourguiba a much broader support coalition, bringing in scores of agricultural and industrial workers as well as civil servants, mostly teachers, who could be mobilized against Ben Youssef.

In sum, it was intense, irrepressible, and irreconcilable intra-elite conflict in the aftermath of independence that brought about a broad cross-class coalition and afforded labour the role of 'king-maker'.[30] Under the strong influence of the trade union, this coalition would be at the origin of the country's authoritarian welfare state.

Algeria

The Algerian regime coalition bears strong similarities to the Tunisian case. Cross-class in nature, the Algerian regime as it emerged in the post-independence period crucially relied on the support of labour and the lower middle classes. Likewise, the fact that independence was officially won by a national liberation front, the *Front de libération nationale* (National Liberation Front; FLN), should not obliterate the

---

[25] Anderson 1986, p. 232.   [26] Alexander 1996, pp. 83–4.   [27] Oualdi 1999, p. 38.
[28] Alexander 2010, pp. 38–9.   [29] Oualdi 1999, pp. 39–40.   [30] Bellin 2002, p. 91.

fact that a viable, broad coalition emerged only after independence, not prior to it. It was the inability of the country's elites to remain cohesive and divide power amongst themselves that made them reach out to large segments of the population. This inability can be explained by the divisive impact that the Algerian struggle for independence had on the country's elites—divisions that rendered intra-elite conflict irreconcilable.

Historically, the nationalist movement had emerged in different stages which brought about consecutive generations of nationalist elites with increasingly radical demands.[31] These differences in political socialization coupled with varying degrees of repression by the French authorities explain why the FLN, which led the military liberation from colonialism in 1954, was not a broad-based, cohesive movement.[32] Organized as a loose platform without a unitary organizational structure, the FLN's cohesion was further aggravated by the war of independence. Guerrilla warfare against the French army necessitated decentralized command structures divided into regional command centres (*wilayas*).[33] Militarily defeated on Algerian ground in 1958, the *Armée de libération nationale* (National Liberation Army; ALN) came to operate outside Algeria, on Moroccan and Tunisian territory.[34]

Furthermore, cleavages also emerged between the political and the military leadership within the FLN. As the general staff of the external army grew in influence, the *Gouvernement provisoire de la République algérienne* (Provisional Government of the Algerian Republic; GPRA)—the country's government in exile formed in 1958—was struggling to maintain its eroding authority in the face of military competitors.[35] Finally, a few months before granting Algeria independence, France released five historical leaders of the FLN, among them future President Ahmed Ben Bella, whom it had captured in 1956. Despite lacking a power base inside the country, these men, in particular Ben Bella, still claimed a leadership position in the FLN.

Four distinct groups were thus contending for power on the eve of Algerian independence: the internal *wilaya* fighters, the ALN's general staff, the GPRA, and the historical leaders, especially Ben Bella. Aligning himself with the general staff, the latter entered the country from Morocco and established the Tlemcen group, composed of himself, the general staff, and a group of former members of the GPRA. The GPRA entered the country in the East, formed the Tizi Ouzou group in the capital of Kabylia, and laid claim to the political leadership of the country. The ensuing conflict between the two groups was intense. The 'fratricidal struggle for power'[36] that emerged between the two groups claimed more than 1,000 lives.

---

[31] Quandt 1969.   [32] Ruedy 2005, p. 180; and Connelly 2002, p. 207.

[33] Charrad 2001, p. 174.

[34] Financially supported by Egypt under Nasser and tolerated by the Moroccan and Tunisian authorities, the ALN amassed by the end of the war about 32,000 soldiers outside Algerian territory.

[35] Quandt 1972, p. 294.   [36] Lowi 2009, p. 76.

In the capital Algiers, only the intervention of the war-weary population prevented further bloodshed.[37]

Regarding ethnic cleavages, the fact that the Tlemcen group was entirely Arab whilst the Tizi Ouzou group comprised large numbers of berberophone Kabyles has been interpreted by some authors as a sign of a salient communal cleavage.[38] However, the majority of the historiographical literature denies the presence of inter-communal strife in the aftermath of Algerian independence.[39] Berberist ideas played no role in the internal power struggle within the FLN, and Berberism as an issue never resonated with the post-independence political elite.[40] While my theoretical argument predicts serious collective action dilemmas in the presence of salient communal cleavages, Quandt notes that 'Berbers were no more likely to collaborate with one another than they were with the like-minded Arabs [and] fought one another almost as passionately as they fought Arab rivals for power.'[41] Therefore, it is safe to conclude that the existence of two ethno-linguistic communities did not undermine the building of a broad regime coalition in post-war Algeria.

Coalition building unfolded in two stages. In late 1962, the two ad-hoc coalitions represented by the Tlemcen and the Tizi Ouzou groups confronted each other in a series of military battles, which ended in the capitulation of the Tizi Ouzou group. This victory heralded another round of intra-elite conflict within the Tlemcen group, with Ahmed Ben Bella as its key protagonist. The link between intra-elite conflict and the enlargement of coalitions is particularly visible at this stage. Despite being one of the historic leaders of the Algerian nationalist movement, Ben Bella lacked an established support base within Algeria due to his long captivity in France (1956 until 1962). And even though he had sided with the ALN in 1962, the army's support was far from certain as its leader, Boumediene, seemed to harbour political ambitions himself. Ben Bella could thus not rely simply on repression to establish his leadership. Consequently, when Ben Bella became head of government in September 1962, he was clearly in need of supporters.

Similar to Bourguiba in Tunisia, Ben Bella turned first to labour, represented by the *Union générale des travailleurs algériens* (General Union of Algerian Workers; UGTA), to consolidate his position in power. During the power struggle between the Tlemcen and the Tizi Ouzou groups, the UGTA had stood on the sidelines, and with an estimated membership of 300,000 unionists, it was clearly a significant ally to win over.[42] It is important to note that this move was strategically and not ideologically motivated. Underlining the strategic aspects of this alliance with the

[37] Willis 2012, p. 57.   [38] Charrad 2001, p. 177; and Heggoy 1970, p. 21.
[39] See, amongst others, Quandt 1972; and Roberts 2001.   [40] Quandt 1972, p. 228.
[41] Ibid., p. 287.   [42] D. Ottaway and M. Ottaway 1970, p. 7.

working class, Alexander notes that the bargain with labour came about because 'the new government needed labor's support against internal rivals'.[43]

A key element of Ben Bella's strategy to win over labour was his support for the *autogestion* (self-management) movement that had emerged in the immediate aftermath of the war. In reaction to the rapid flight of European entrepreneurs and landowners, workers occupied vacant factories and agricultural estates and established self-management committees. As the movement lacked clear leadership,[44] Ben Bella seized the opportunity to release a series of decrees in March 1963 which aimed at regularizing and protecting the movement. Not coincidentally, Ben Bella issued the decrees at a moment when he was embroiled in an exacerbating struggle with Mohamed Khider, the head of the FLN.[45] Ben Bella's endorsement of the movement thus afforded him a surge in popularity and put him in a position to sideline Khider shortly after the enactment of the decrees.[46]

Having sidelined most competitors within the FLN, Ben Bella eventually took on the last remaining autonomous institution: the army. Seeking to undermine Boumediene, he gradually began to purge ministries and the general staff of Boumediene's supporters and thereby delimit their influence within government. When he threatened to dismiss Boumediene himself, the latter decided to depose Ben Bella forcefully in a coup that was carried out in June 1965. Suspending the constitution, Boumediene established a military government, the Council of the Revolution. He also relegated the ruling party, the FLN, to a position of political insignificance, dislodging, in essence, all newly created post-war institutions. Yet, despite his rather pragmatic approach to questions of economic and social policy, Boumediene did not dismantle the cross-class coalition inherited from Ben Bella. While he toned down leftist rhetoric, he was anxious not to alienate the working–middle-class coalition that had coalesced after independence.

In sum, the Algerian case demonstrates well the nexus between irreconcilable and irrepressible intra-elite competition and the coalitional dynamics that emerge from it. It shows that the broad post-independence coalition did not emerge during the struggle for independence; rather, it was forged during the struggle for leadership after independence. Regarding the effect of ethnic cleavages, it lends support to the claim that the cleavages need to be salient to have an effect, for the presence of two ethno-linguistic communities did not visibly undermine cross-ethnic collective action.

Egypt
Egypt represents the only case of a broad coalition that did not lead to the establishment of an authoritarian welfare state. While this deviation is due to the country's particular geostrategic context and, thus, its ability to provide social

---

[43] Alexander 1996, p. 99. See also Lowi 2009, p. 79.   [44] Francos and Séréni 1976, p. 140.
[45] Ruedy 2005, pp. 200–1.   [46] Ibid., p. 199.

welfare, the incentives to distribute were—like in Tunisia and Algeria—created by a cross-class coalition, including lower middle classes and labour. This coalition emerged out of intense intra-elite struggle during regime formation and was unaffected by ethnic cleavages. Though ethnic cleavages were salient, the sidelined community—the Copts—was too small to have a sizeable effect on the coalition.

Let us first ascertain the presence of intra-elite conflict and its irreconcilable and irrepressible nature. After the ouster of King Farouk at the hand of the Free Officers Movement (FOM) in July 1952, Egypt came to be ruled by a military junta, the Revolutionary Command Council (RCC). Conflict emerged from within the junta as General Naguib—a renowned war hero, chosen by FOM as a figurehead to represent the RCC publicly—came to develop his own personal ambitions, which put him on a direct collision course with Nasser, the leader of the FOM.[47] As both sides vied for political leadership, the loser was likely to face reprisal in the form of exile, imprisonment, or loss of life. With trust between both sides having broken down, this extremely high-stakes, zero-sum conflict made reconciliation virtually impossible. The conflict reached its height in spring 1954 after Naguib's resignation from the RCC, which sparked an immediate wave of protest against the RCC, with thousands of demonstrators turning out in the streets of Cairo demanding the reinstatement of Naguib and a return to parliamentary rule. Underlining the irrepressible nature of the conflict, the divisions between both camps also ran across the armed forces, which brought the country to the brink of civil war.[48]

Regarding ethnic cleavages, the political context of coalition formation was marked by heightened communal tensions between Egypt's Coptic minority and its Muslim majority. In addition to riots against them,[49] Copts were well represented in the country's political and economic elite and hence were disproportionately affected by the Free Officers' attempts to purge the political system of what they considered old, corrupt elites.[50] Moreover, there were clear signs of mistrust between both communities as Copts were systematically excluded from security-related positions in the public administration because their loyalty to the state was considered uncertain.[51] Underlining Lieberman's argument about the importance of relative group size for communal fragmentation,[52] the Copts were too small a minority to have a decisive impact on the size of the nascent regime coalition. Representing about 10 per cent of the population, exclusionary policies vis-à-vis the Copts—which at any rate only targeted the elite—did not undermine the building of a broad cross-class coalition.[53] There is also no evidence of collective action problems within the RCC as a result of communal cleavages.

---

[47] Hopwood 1993, p. 38; and Baker 1978, p. 32.   [48] Gordon 1992, p. 129.
[49] V. Ibrahim 2011, p. 159.   [50] S. E. Ibrahim 1996, p. 16.
[51] Ibid., p. 16.   [52] Lieberman 2009, p. 33.
[53] Pennington 1982, pp. 177–8 describes the relations at the popular level as 'usually close and harmonious'.

As the RCC could not rely on any political platform, the field for coalition formation was wide open. The sense of a political *tabula rasa* was reinforced by (i) the RCC's lack of a programme other than 'cleansing the nation of tyrants'[54] and putting an end to British colonialism;[55] and (ii) the abolition of existing political institutions, such as political parties and the monarchy, which were outlawed in January and June 1953 respectively, and the implementation of land reform to weaken the upper class.[56] Clearly, the RCC knew whom they feared, but not whom they stood for. Finding constituencies in their support was thus key for both rivals.

Building on his popularity as a war hero, Naguib started a public-relations campaign to promote the goals of the revolution, as the nascent political order came to be called, shortly after the Free Officers' coup in 1952.[57] Of Sudanese origin, he enjoyed a particularly high standing in the southern parts of the country where he travelled extensively.[58] Seeking to identify his own bases of support within society, Naguib gradually became the focal point of all those who had an interest in the return to a parliamentary system, first and foremost the Wafd party. Having dominated Egyptian politics under the monarchy, the Wafd was likely to be at the centre stage of any new parliamentary system. Another important player that initially turned toward Naguib was the Muslim Brotherhood (MB). Its extensive grass-roots network made it the 'the strongest political actor at the onset of the 1952 coup'.[59] Should the country return to democracy, the MB could reasonably expect to be one of the key players, especially after the weakening of the Wafd party.

Besides these two mass organizations, Naguib more generally managed to garner the support of Egypt's liberal upper middle class. This included the, at the time, relatively small number of university students, as well as Egypt's liberal professions: lawyers, doctors, and higher-ranking civil servants predominantly favoured Naguib.[60] Finally, owing to his military status, Naguib enjoyed widespread popularity among the army.[61]

Nasser lacked Naguib's status and was, initially, unknown to the public.[62] Conscious of this disadvantage, he endeavoured to counter Naguib's popularity. To this end, the Liberation Rally (LR) was set up in spring 1953 as a substitute for the outlawed political parties and a platform to muster popular support against Naguib's nascent coalition.[63] The LR failed, however, in one of its principal goals, which was to attract followers of the MB to Nasser's camp.[64]

With powerful organized groups on Naguib's side, it is surprising that Nasser initially made no particular effort to court labour. One reason is that Egypt's

---

[54] Cited in Hopwood 1993, p. 38.
[55] Bayat 2006, p. 137; Beinin and Lockman 1988, p. 437; Lenczowski 1966, p. 36; and Hinnebusch 1985, p. 14.
[56] Waterbury 1983, p. 423; and Beinin 1989, p. 72.   [57] Mohi El Din 1995, p. 157.
[58] Ibid., p. 157.   [59] Vatikiotis 1961, p. 77.   [60] Baker 1978, p. 34; and Brownlee 2007, p. 54.
[61] Gordon 1992, p. 125.   [62] Mohi El Din 1995, p. 160.   [63] Hopwood 1993, p. 39.
[64] Beattie 1994, p. 82.

working class, though numerous, was weakly organized, which is why Nasser first tried to gain the support of the MB. Another reason for this disinterest was that Nasser and the unions differed over the future socioeconomic order in Egypt as Nasser made a deliberate effort to court Egypt's capitalists to spark growth and investment.[65] Finally, the RCC had shown little tolerance for labour activism by violently suppressing a strike of textile workers in Kafr al-Dawwar and sentencing two strike leaders to death shortly after the coup.

It was the demonstrations in favour of Naguib's reinstatement in 1954 that proved crucial in shaping 'Nasser's own conception of the social bases of his support'.[66] He realized that his coalition lacked popular support and needed to be enlarged to confront Naguib effectively. Thus, to wrest the advantage of urban mobilization away from Naguib's camp, Nasser made the deliberate decision to reach out to labour unions, some of which had grown very concerned about the conservative elites' return to power.[67] The negotiations, in fact, resembled a genuine bargain in which the RCC offered immediate and more long-term material benefits in return for staging demonstrations against Naguib.[68]

On 26 March, worker demonstrations against a restoration of political parties and a return to democratic rule paralysed Cairo for two days, until the RCC announced an indefinite postponement of general elections. Taken by surprise, Naguib's camp failed to turn out into the street and Naguib was eventually put under house arrest in November 1954. For Nasser's regime coalition, the events of spring 1954 were crucial. Not only had labour's support proved decisive in defeating Naguib,[69] the events also 'crystallised Nasser's thoughts regarding real and prospective sources of regime support'.[70] Prompting the idea to develop labour and the lower middle classes fully as a pillar of his rule,[71] the events of 1954 thus stood at the origin of Egypt's broad-based regime coalition.

In sum, regime formation in Egypt was structured by the struggle between Nasser and Naguib and followed a similar logic of populist appeal to outcompete one's rival. Salient ethnic cleavages between the Muslim majority and the Copts did not undermine the formation of a broad, cross-class coalition as the Coptic community was too small to affect coalition formation.

The Islamic Republic of Iran

Like the three preceding cases, the regime coalition underpinning the Islamic Republic of Iran has spanned large parts of the country's working and middle classes, which formed the basis for Iran's extensive post-revolutionary welfare state. With the country's largest minority, the Azeris, well integrated in the

---

[65] S. Cook 2012, p. 45.   [66] Baker 1978, p. 34.   [67] Beinin and Lockman 1988, p. 439.
[68] Beinin and Lockman 1988, pp. 454–9. Details of this bargaining process will be the subject of Chapter 6.
[69] Ibid., p. 440.   [70] Beattie 1994, p. 98.   [71] Ibid., p. 98.

coalition, ethnic cleavages played a marginal role in the dynamics of coalition formation, despite salient cleavages with smaller minorities. Contrary to analyses emphasizing religion and ideology,[72] the following account demonstrates the importance of power politics and intensive conflict between political elites in explaining the emergence of the regime's support coalition.[73] As Harris points out, '[b]eginning from the first days, postrevolutionary power was consolidated by forming or commandeering parallel groups to outflank contenders'.[74]

To start with ethnic cleavages, it is important to note that despite Iran's multi-ethnic composition, intra-elite conflict did not crystallize around communal divides. Cross-ethnic in nature, the anti-Shah front was largely unaffected by local and ethnic centrifugal tendencies and cultural differences did not play an important role during the popular uprisings.[75] Most minorities initially welcomed the revolution.[76] This had certainly to do with the fact that the Azeris, the country's biggest minority representing about a quarter of the population, were not marginalized in Iranian society.[77] Azeri businessmen formed an important part of Iran's economic elite, in addition to being well represented in the military, political, and religious establishment.[78] At the height of the conflict, clashes occurred within the Azeri community, rather than between Azeris and the Persian-speaking community, which half of all Iranians at the time belonged to.[79] Notwithstanding widespread inter-ethnic cooperation during the revolution, communal conflicts occurred in the Kurdish and Arab provinces, which represented an estimated 7 and 3 per cent of the population, respectively.[80] However, like in Egypt, the minority communities that were discriminated against were too small effectively to undermine a broad regime coalition in Iran. And the only community with the potential to shift the power balance in the country, the Azeris, was well integrated into the regime coalition.

Turning to the causal mechanism, the role of elite conflict can only be understood when considering the multifarious nature of the 'rainbow coalition'[81] that unseated the Shah. Lacking a specific ideological programme other than regime change,[82] the revolutionaries comprised communist and Marxist groups, secular nationalists, religious liberals, segments of the industrial working class, the conservative bazaar *petit bourgeoisie*, and the Shiite clergy.[83] Owing to his long exile since 1963, the core of Khomeini's supporters was rather small and he mainly relied on the bazaaris and clerical actors, who had been alienated by the Shah's pro-Western secularism and were anxious about their dwindling economic

---

[72] Kippenberg 1981. For a dissenting argument, see Keddie 2003, p. 241.
[73] Maloney 2000; and K. Harris 2017, p. 82.   [74] Ibid., p. 86.
[75] Hourcade 1988, p. 161.   [76] Samii 2000, p. 130.   [77] Higgins 1984, p. 59.
[78] Elling 2013, p. 31.   [79] Higgins 1984, p. 60.
[80] L. Beck 1991, p. 209; Entessar 1984, pp. 926–7; and Samii 2000, p. 131.
[81] Amuzegar 1991, p. 14.   [82] Behdad 1996, p. 98.
[83] Keddie 2003, pp. 218–32; and Abrahamian 1982, p. 510.

status.[84] Whilst other actors, such as the opposition parties, had been able to build, at least, rudimentary institutions on the ground and had an idea about their supporters in society, Khomeini arrived in the midst of a revolutionary atmosphere, characterized by mass mobilization, without an institutionalized political platform at his disposal. Though recognized as the primary leader of the revolution, he did not have a viable coalition of supporters that would enable him to secure power. Moreover, the security apparatus of the Shah regime was disintegrating at a rapid pace and, as the principal organ of repression under the *ancien régime*, could not be trusted. Granted, Khomeini's camp quickly set up its own paramilitary force, the Revolutionary Guards, to fend off 'counter-revolutionary' forces. But this was partly counterbalanced by paramilitary forces of other revolutionary actors, such as the leftist *Mojahedin-e Khalq*, and the fact that many Revolutionary Guards were utilized at the front in the Iran–Iraq War. Outright repression to impose his leadership was thus not an option for Khomeini. In search for supportive constituencies in Iranian society, Khomeini faced two main challengers from within the anti-Shah front.[85]

Within Iran's clerical forces, Khomeini was far from being the uncontested leader and had to face serious opposition from within Iran's religious elite.[86] Parts of the religious establishment called into question his competence as a religious scholar and his main concept of the Guardianship of the Islamic Scholar (*Vilayat-e Faqih*) was rejected by a great number of scholars on the eve of the revolution.[87] Khomeini's most powerful opponent within the Iranian clergy was Grand Ayatollah Shariatmadari who was in 1979 head of the religious seminary in Qom, Iran's most important centre of religious learning. Being one of Iran's most influential Shiite scholars, Shariatmadari rejected Khomeini's idea of clerical rule,[88] and became increasingly critical of the repressive tactics used by Khomeini's camp.[89] His supporters, most numerous in the north-eastern Azeri provinces, were organized in the Muslim People's Republican Party (MPRP).[90] Given his prestige, Shariatmadari represented a serious threat to Khomeini from within the religious establishment.

Khomeini's position was also threatened by the representatives of the liberal middle class, religious and secular. Both trends were initially well represented in the immediate post-revolutionary landscape. Mehdi Barzargan, who was head of the Freedom Movement and stood for the secular segments of the Iranian middle class, became the first Prime Minister of the Provisional Revolutionary Cabinet (PRG). Abolhassan Bani-Sadr represented the left-leaning, religious middle class,

---

[84] Abrahamian 1982, p. 533.

[85] The provisional government under Shapour Bakhtiar, set up by the Shah a few days prior to his departure, did not constitute a major challenge for the revolutionary coalition and quickly disintegrated after Khomeini arrived.

[86] Moin 1999, p. 216.   [87] Keddie 2003, pp. 194–5.   [88] Ibid., p. 194.

[89] Moin 1999, p. 216.   [90] Amjad 1989, p. 133.

which was a sizeable constituency at the time.[91] In July 1980, he was elected Iranian President with 75 per cent of the vote, which was an impressive sign of his popularity.[92] Upon his election, Bani-Sadr also became head of the Iranian armed forces, and when his conflict with Khomeini broke out in the open in spring 1981, there were concerns in Khomeini's camp that he might attempt a military coup.[93] That said, the allegiance of the armed forces amidst the political turmoil in post-revolutionary Iran was not certain.

Crucial for the argument here, Iran's peasants, working class, and a 'lumpenproletariat' of the urban poor—all mobilized during the revolution—lacked a strong affiliation with any of the established political actors. Highly susceptible to the idea of redistributing the Shah's wealth, these constituencies saw themselves courted by Khomeini in the early stages of the revolution. Considering the rather right-wing, conservative profile of his core supporters, this move seems strategically, not ideologically motivated.

Benefiting from the liberal camp being divided over nationalizations and radical socioeconomic reforms, Khomeini cunningly organized the seizure of the Shah's wealth and began a massive programme of redistribution to gain the loyalty of the poor.[94] This programme was based on and executed by a number of revolutionary organizations, most notably the Foundation of the Dispossessed which had seized the fortunes of the Pahlavi foundations and other confiscated properties.[95] The so-called Reconstruction Jihad provided deprived rural areas with free housing, permitting some of the new occupants to keep seized urban and rural properties.[96] As the following quote from a former deputy minister of the Construction Jihad reveals, outcompeting leftist rivals was the primary motivation behind these distributive policies: '[R]ural reconstruction and development were secondary issues whereas the primary issue was preventing the People's Warriors (*Mojāhidīn-e Khalq*) [*sic*] and other communist groups from taking the lead and hijacking the revolution.'[97] Distributing 850,000 hectares of land to more than 220,000 peasant families, Khomeini's camp successfully ensured the allegiance of the country's rural areas.[98] As Keddie rightly points out, 'subsidies, price controls, redistribution of confiscated properties, and direct financial rewards [...] helped sustain the loyalty of the lower classes'.[99]

Whilst this programme ran counter to the ideological orientation of Iran's religious establishment,[100] the measures were crucial to broadening Khomeini's coalition. By tying the country's hitherto unaligned poor to the regime, Khomeini, in fact, created one of its most important constituencies. With Iran's liberal middle class migrating in great numbers, President Bani-Sadr was thus left with little

---

[91] Keddie 2003, p. 222.   [92] Bakhash 1990, p. 90.   [93] Moin 1999, p. 237.
[94] Moslem 2002, pp. 222–4.   [95] Maloney 2000, p. 153.   [96] Keddie 2003, p. 246.
[97] Lob 2017, p. 29.   [98] Abrahamian 2008, p. 180; and Amjad 1989, pp. 150–1.
[99] Keddie 2003, p. 256.   [100] Ibid., p. 256.

popular support to mobilize when Khomeini's Islamic Republican Party (IRP), based on its predominance in parliament, sought his ouster in spring 1981.

Taken together, the formation of Khomeini's regime coalition underlines the importance of intra-elite conflict as a key motivation in reaching out to the lower and middle classes. Since the profile and ideological outlook of his core supporters did not predispose Khomeini to such a coalition, the broadening of his support base can only be explained by the imperatives of power politics in post-revolutionary Iran.

Summary

The foregoing narratives all support the claim that coalition formation was critically influenced by the power politics of elites embroiled in irreconcilable and irrepressible conflict. While communal cleavages were found to be inconsequential, all four cases provide empirical evidence for a causal link between coalition size and intra-elite conflict. Moreover, the Iranian and Algerian narratives in particular underline a link between coalition building and social policies. In both cases, welfare distribution was used as an important tool to tie key social groups to the nascent regimes. In the case of Tunisia and Egypt, this nexus is analysed in greater detail in Chapters 5 and 6.

3.1.2 Repressible elite conflict in the absence of communal cleavages: narrow coalitions

Morocco

In contrast to the previous cases, the authoritarian regime that formed in Morocco after the country's independence in 1956 predominantly recruited the members of its support coalition from the country's traditional elites in the countryside.[101] Narrow in nature, the regime coalition was not shaped by major ethnic divides. Rather, its genesis resulted from the confluence of irreconcilable intra-elite conflict between the royal palace and the parties of the nationalist movement *and* a very unequal distribution of coercive capacity between the two rivalling camps. While King Mohamed V (1956–61) and his successor, Hassan II (1961–99), could rely on the Army of Liberation and the newly formed police force and military,[102] the nationalist parties were bereft of sufficient coercive power to counterbalance the monarchy. The monarchy was consequently not compelled to broaden its coalition and reach out to popular constituencies. Counterfactually speaking, the nascent regime would have rested upon a broad cross-class coalition if elite division had run across the security apparatus (as in Egypt) or in the absence of decisive means of coercion for either actor (as in Tunisia).

---

[101] Ba Mohammed 2001.   [102] Pennell 2000, p. 301.

Three main elite groups vied for power in Morocco in the aftermath of independence. The first one was the nationalist *Istiqlal* Party (Independence Party; PI)
which had published its first party manifesto in 1944. In it, the party demanded
complete independence from France in a constitutional monarchy under then
Sultan Mohammed VI. Sociologically, the party represented an amalgam of a
small but long-standing national-conservative bourgeoisie composed of merchant families and religious scholars, most notably from the city of Fes,[103] and
a nascent white-collar middle class composed of journalists, teachers, doctors,
and civil servants.[104] They were joined by a growing working-class movement
organized in the *Union Marocaine du Travail* (UMT), which according to Benseddik had 200,000 enrolled members on the eve of independence.[105] Both the
PI and the UMT were predominantly urban organizations,[106] with leaders who
for the most part had received modern education in the French protectorate.
Despite French repression, the PI had managed to establish a wide network of
cells and militants in the main urban centres with considerable mobilizational
capacity.

The second elite group were the traditional rural elites of Morocco's countryside,
composed of notables, tribal leaders, and heads of Sufi brotherhoods (*tariqas*).
Local aristocracies, these elite groups served as governors (*Pashas*) or local pre-
fects (*Caids*) in the colonial administration and formed the backbone of French
colonial rule in the countryside. In a system predicated on indirect rule, they
collected taxes, performed judiciary functions, maintained public order, and could
otherwise utilize their power to grow their fortune. Their offspring had access to
special schools for sons of notables (*écoles des fils des notables*) and frequently
joined the Moroccan colonial army as officers.[107] The French protectorate thus
afforded them unprecedented opportunities for wealth accumulation and social
mobility.

The third elite group was the Moroccan royal family. While historically the royal
court (*makhzen*) had had only very limited control of the Moroccan countryside,
the military subjugation of the country's restive rural areas by the French and
the modernization of the administrative apparatus placed the monarchy at the
centre of a renewed state apparatus with unprecedented powers.[108] Granted, the
French protectorate afforded the Sultan only a ceremonial role as power was kept
by French administrators, but the colonial period nonetheless established the royal
family as the symbol of the country's national sovereignty and thus made it one of
the key contenders for power in the postcolonial era.

The severity of the conflict which broke out between these three groups
following Morocco's independence reflected the irreconcilable nature of their

---

[103] Hence the term 'Fassi' bourgeoisie.   [104] Pennell 2000, p. 265; and Sater 2010, p. 22.
[105] Benseddik 1990, p. 497.   [106] Douglas Elliott Ashford 1961, p. 195.
[107] Sater 2010, p. 18.   [108] Willis 2012, p. 33.

post-independence interests. The PI sought to relegate the monarchy to a ceremonial role in a constitutional monarchy with the party as political hegemon. The monarchy was not ready to become a merely reigning monarchy and strove for a return to the *status quo ante* of a ruling monarchy.[109] Rural elites, in turn, were anxious to maintain the status acquired under the French protectorate. This constellation in principle predicated Morocco for a broad-coalition regime, but the uneven distribution of coercive power in this power struggle meant that the monarchy could forgo popular incorporation and instead build a system of repressive notable rule characterized by local authoritarianism exercised at the hands of traditional elites allied with the King.[110] Regime formation, which lasted from 1956 until the adoption of the country's first constitution in 1962, unfolded as follows.

In a context of heightened insecurity and lawlessness in the immediate aftermath of independence, with anti-French militias roaming the countryside and urban terrorist groups settling their scores out in the open,[111] the question of who would be able to re-establish public order and a monopoly of violence was of primary importance. The PI had made a first move in this direction by creating the *Shabab Nizam* (Youth of Order), a party militia which acted as unofficial police in urban areas where the PI was solidly implanted. The PI also claimed to be in control of the Army of Liberation, an amalgamation of tribal, often Berber, militias under the command of military leaders which had fought French troops in the countryside throughout 1955. The army comprised several thousand fighters in the wake of independence and was at this point 'the only organised military force in Moroccan hands'.[112] In reality, only two military leaders of the Army of Liberation, Mohammed Basri and Hassan El-Araj, openly supported the PI, while the allegiance of other military leaders was uncertain.[113] Nonetheless, the build-up of coercive capacity of the PI was of deep concern for the monarchy.[114]

In a decisive counter-move, the King created the Moroccan Royal Armed Forces (RAF) in May 1956 and named his son, Crown Prince Hassan, as its chief-of-staff. This critically altered the coercive power balance between both sides as the King was not only able to incorporate the vast majority of Moroccan officers who had served in the former French colonial army, but also absorbed large junks (about 10,000) of the troops in the Liberation Army into the newly created RAF.[115] While the legal power to issue decrees, which the French had bestowed upon the King before independence, legally enabled the King to do so—and prevented the PI from a similar move—the success of this strategy was rooted in the deep mistrust between the PI, on the one hand, and the military leaders of the Liberation Army and the former colonial army, on the other. From a class point of view, Pennell points out that the military leaders of the Liberation Army 'had little in common

---

[109] Willis 2012, pp. 41–2.   [110] Leveau 1970, p. 238.   [111] Pennell 2000, p. 300.
[112] Ibid., p. 300.   [113] Ibid., p. 301.   [114] Storm 2007, p. 15; and Monjib 1992, p. 32.
[115] Willis 2012, p. 43.

with the urban middle class Arab nationalists who dominated Istiqlal,[116] as they hailed and drew their support from the countryside, often Berber areas. The majority of Moroccan officers, in turn, belonged to notable families of rural *Caids*, and bore the stigma of collaborators with the French, which the PI did not fail to highlight.[117] It was thus the PI's inability to commit credibly to maintaining their elite status which drove them into the hands of the King. The establishment of an official police force, which was similarly recruited from the old colonial police forces, followed a similar pattern. The historically contingent nature in which the French had created the colonial security apparatus thus significantly disadvantaged the PI in its attempt to match the King's coercive power.

The same holds true for the local administration. Under the French protectorate, local notables, *Pashas* and *Caids*, had been key to ensuring control of the country-side, as they acted as guarantors of security and formed the extended arm of the Ministry of Interior in rural areas. For the PI, however, they represented former collaborators and anti-modern forces of feudalism and backwardness.[118] The PI therefore moved swiftly to (i) replace notables with party cadres across the country and (ii) set up a commission to investigate wealth accumulation by notables during the colonial period.[119] In addition, many local notables felt doubly vulnerable as about 40 per cent of them had supported the French in 1953 when they exiled Sultan Mohamed V and temporarily replaced him with rival Sultan, Ben Arafa.[120] Defeated and discredited, the rebellious local elites now all turned toward the King who, in the face of a very hostile *Istiqlal* movement willing to dismantle the traditional pre-colonial institutions, was their only chance to preserve at least some of their privileges.[121] This was compounded by the heavy-handedness with which the PI pursued its strategic goal of controlling the countryside. Rural rebellions ensued.[122] In 1957, for instance, the provincial governor of Tafilalet, Addi Ou Bihi, violently opposed the imposition of new administrative personnel, proclaiming that he was 'loyal to the monarchy alone'.[123]

A final issue that prevented the PI from matching the King's coercive capacity was internal rivalries within the party.[124] Similar to the Tunisian case, some of its historic founders, such as Allal Al-Fassi, had returned from long exile upon independence and found themselves competing with a new generation of party leaders. As a result, attempts to build rival coalitions characterized intra-party dynamics and led to a split in 1959 along generational and ideological lines (younger, middle-class leftists vs. older, merchant-bourgeois nationalists). The PI

---

[116] Pennell 2000, p. 303.   [117] Sater 2010, p. 24.
[118] Ibid., p. 24.   [119] Pennell 2000, p. 307.
[120] Sater 2010, pp. 22–3.
[121] Approximately 400 colonial *Caids* were disempowered, but the majority of them managed to transfer their privileged status onto their sons, who came to provide the bulk of local administrators in post-independence Morocco. See Leveau 1970, p. 215.
[122] Charrad 2001, p. 148.   [123] Sater 2010, pp. 24–5.   [124] Waterbury 1970, pp. 171–9.

also vehemently tried to undermine the smaller rival political parties, such as the Democratic Independence Party (*Parti démocratique de l'indépendance*, PDI), whose leader was assassinated in 1957.[125] These conflicts within the nationalist movements facilitated the gradual usurpation of the critical levers of power by the King.

It might seem natural to suggest salient communal cleavages as the main driver of coalition formation in postcolonial Morocco in view of the prominence of Berbers in the King's regime coalition. Morocco's Berber community constituted nearly half of the country's population, with the remainder being arabophone. Nonetheless, the overwhelming judgement of historians, both foreign and Moroccan, denies the existence of a distinctive Berber identity in the wake of independence as lower-level, tribal identities generally prevailed.[126] Moreover, colonial authorities could not 'prevent Berber-speakers from joining with their Arabophone compatriots in ejecting France from the Maghreb'.[127] Ethnic diversity did thus not impair inter-ethnic collective action. And when the remnants of the Liberation Army refused to lay down their arms in 1958, the monarchy did not have any qualms about violently dismantling the predominantly Berber troop, using the full force of its newly formed army.[128] Altogether, historical evidence suggests the existence of a rural–urban, rather than an inter-communal, cleavage.

With the traditional elites rallying around the monarchy and the security apparatus cohesively standing behind it, the King could eventually settle the conflict with the *Istiqlal* by repression, not the building of a broad coalition. The first signs of this appeared in 1959 when a number of PI newspapers were banned and its editors arrested, all while PI members were represented in government.[129] In January 1960, one of the key leaders of the nationalist movement, Mehdi Ben Barka, was forced into exile.[130] In the same year, the King made himself head of the executive by assuming the office of prime minister. The accession of Hassan II to the throne in 1961 further accelerated the repression, arrest, and torture of opposition forces. The 1962 constitution reflected this power balance by enshrining a ruling monarchy with very little democratic control into law. The concentration of power by the King culminated in a final abrogation of parliament and the declaration of a state of emergency in 1965. Urban riots in the same year were repressed at the cost of over 1,000 casualties.[131]

The Pahlavi regime

Qualified as 'sultanistic'[132] and lacking broad societal support,[133] the Pahlavi regime represents in many ways the epitome of a narrow coalition. Firmly

---

[125] Sater 2010, p. 26; and Pennell 2000, p. 303.   [126] Crawford 2002, p. 59.
[127] Willis 2012, p. 206.   [128] Pennell 2000, pp. 304–5.   [129] Ibid., p. 313.
[130] He was assassinated in Paris in 1965.   [131] Brouksy 2005.
[132] Katouzian 1998.   [133] B. Smith 2007, p. 118.

established after the violent overthrow of Prime Minister Mohamed Mosaddeq in 1953, the regime under Mohammad Reza Shah Pahlavi relied upon three main pillars.[134] First and foremost was the army, which owed its very existence to the Pahlavi dynasty and had been instrumental in the ouster of the Qajar dynasty at the hands of Mohammad's father, Reza Pahlavi.[135] The Pahlavi dynasty considered the army their private possession and anxiously guarded it from any civilian interference.[136] Orders were given directly to the officers and the Shah cultivated personal relationships of patronage and dependence with the officer corps. The second pillar was the upper echelon of the state bureaucracy, comprising between 500 and 750 high-ranking civil servants.[137] Interlinking the monarchy with the country's elites composed of rural notables and absentee landowners, aristocrats, religious and business elites, the court patronage system was the third pillar of the regime. Although dubbed 'a thousand families', these elite groups amounted to fewer than 100 families.[138]

The case bears a resemblance to Morocco in that the narrow coalition did not result from salient communal cleavages. The country's largest minority, the Azeris, had been politically and economically well integrated even before the Pahlavi era.[139] Likewise, the narrow coalition cannot be explained by the absence of elite conflict during the regime formation period as 'power was not concentrated in one place [but] hotly contested between the royal palace, the cabinet, the Majles, and the urban masses'.[140] The Iranian monarchy struggled with a broad-based nation-alist movement (National Front) led by the country's upper-middle-class elite. Similar to Morocco, the Iranian case demonstrates how the unequal distribution of coercive capacity between rival elite groups makes conflict repressible, resulting in a narrow coalition. Unlike the Moroccan case though, the Pahlavi monarchy was not able to overcome its rivals solely by relying on domestic sources of repression. Instead, as Yom has pointed out, it had to seek foreign support, thus instituting a long-term cliency relationship with the United States.[141]

The Pahlavi regime emerged out of the so-called interregnum period, which commenced with the joint Soviet–British invasion of Iran in 1941 and the forced abdication of the incumbent, Reza Shah, who allegedly harboured Nazi sympa-thies. This critically weakened the monarchy as the Shah, in return for retaining direct control of the army, had to restore property, estates, and religious endow-ments illegally expropriated by his father, which shattered the court patronage system.[142] The interregnum also saw the emergence of semi-competitive elections

---

[134] Abrahamian 2008, p. 123.   [135] Abrahamian 1982, p. 177.
[136] Abrahamian 2013, p. 137.   [137] Amuzegar 1991, p. 280.   [138] Abrahamian 2008, p. 26.
[139] Higgins 1984, p. 59. Notably, the Shah's narrow coalition included a number of important Azeri notables, such as Manucher Eqbal. Granted, the Shah regime after 1953 pursued an anti-tribe and anti-minority policy based on Iranian nationalism, which led to a concentration of investment in the Persian-speaking parts of the country. This, however, did not affect the dynamics of regime formation in the run-up to the 1953 critical juncture. See Elling 2013, p. 54; and Entessar 1984, p. 916.
[140] Abrahamian 2008, p. 99.   [141] Yom 2016, ch. 5.   [142] Abrahamian 1982, p. 178.

for parliament, the *Majles*, which before 1941 had been stuffed with Reza Shah's appointees.[143] Concomitantly, the *Majles* became the major forum in which Iran's landed elite and notables reasserted their influence.[144] While elite dominance of the parliament until the early 1950s prevented the *Majles* from becoming a source of overt opposition to the Shah, elites clearly sought to balance the power of the Shah and prevent a return to outright dictatorship. Since the 1907 constitution awarded the parliament significant potential power,[145] elites benefited from the forced return to constitutional government as a result of the 1941 invasion. Mohammed Reza Shah, though structurally empowered to defy constitutional provisions,[146] thus had to concentrate his efforts on re-establishing royal hegemony as the previous regime had clearly ended and a new one was yet to emerge.[147] The 1949 expansion of royal prerogatives was a first step in this direction, but it was only by 1955 and after the repression of the National Front that complete control over government was restored.[148] The dynamics of elite conflict during the critical juncture between Mosaddeq becoming Prime Minister in April 1951 and his ouster in August 1953 are key to understanding this process.

The National Front (NF) was not a conventional party but rather a network of like-minded associations and individuals built in the late 1940s around its leader Mosaddeq.[149] As the scion of a Qajar princess and a landowning former Minister of Finance, Mosaddeq was clearly part of Iran's elite. This was also the case with many leading figures in the Iran Party, which formed the NF's inner circle:[150] The Moazemi brothers, Abdollah and Seyfollah, who served as MPs and ministers under Mosaddeq, came from an upper-class, titled land-owning family. Sayyed Kazemi, later Mosaddeq's Foreign Minister, was son of a wealthy, titled notable. Shams Al-Din Amir-Alai, Iran Party MP and Mosaddeq's closest adviser, was the offspring of an aristocratic Qajar family. What they all had in common was foreign education in France and a profound conviction of the virtues of a reigning, not ruling, monarchy and national ownership of Iran's oil reserves.

They endeavoured to achieve these goals in an alliance with the nascent group of non-elite urban middle classes, which formed the second pillar of the NF's support. This included professional organizations, such as the Lawyers Guild, the University Professors' Association, and the Engineers' Association, as well as parts of Iran's *petit bourgeoisie* represented by bazaar merchants, exporters, and certain guilds (e.g. the restaurateur guild).[151] This alliance initially also included other political parties, such as Muzaffar Baqai's Toilers Party—an amalgam of university-educated Marxists and lower segments of the Tehran bazaar frequenting traditional wrestling clubs[152]—and Ayatollah Kashani's Society of Muslim Mojaheds,

---

[143] Keddie 2003, p. 106.   [144] Abrahamian 2008, p. 100.   [145] Yom 2016, p. 101.
[146] Azimi 2004, p. 33.   [147] Abrahamian 2008, p. 99.   [148] Amjad 1989, p. 65.
[149] Abrahamian 2013, p. 54.   [150] Ibid., p. 52.
[151] Azimi 2004, pp. 29–31; Katouzian 2004, p. 20; and Abrahamian 2013, p. 54.
[152] Abrahamian 2013, p. 55.

a religious movement recruiting from the pious *petit bourgeoisie* and seminary students. Both turned against the NF in late 1952. The communist *Tudeh* party, though banned in 1949, was equally sympathetic to the NF, although it mobilized its powerful organizational base—about 90 per cent of Iran's organized labour, 40,000 active members, and a clandestine military wing—only sporadically in support of Mosaddeq, whom it considered a representative of the bourgeoisie.[153]

When Mosaddeq was elected Prime Minister in April 1951 on the back of a massive strike in the country's oil industry denouncing the harsh working conditions imposed by the Anglo-Iranian Oil Company (AIOC), the Shah immediately perceived him as a potential threat and, at first, refused to ratify his appointment.[154] Not only was his nationalization policy anathema to the Shah's interest in maintaining cordial Anglo-Iranian relations, his insistence on a constitutional monarchy was diametrically opposed to the Shah's agenda of regaining political hegemony. Mosaddeq's ouster therefore became very quickly the monarchy's primary objective, which it pursued in a two-fold manner.

In line with the theoretical framework, the Shah first sought to broaden his own coalition by enlisting the support of pro-monarchy political parties. For example, three months after Mosaddeq's election the Shah encouraged veteran politician Seyyed Zia to revive his National Will Party and mobilize against the National Front.[155] The anti-communist Zolfaqar party also received instructions and funding from the court.[156] Yet these were organizations without a significant base and the Shah was hampered in his, somewhat half-hearted, attempts to build party support by his constitutional position and the legacy of his father's repression against organized political movements. When in late 1952 Kashani and Baqai fell out with Mosaddeq, they were successfully lured into supporting the Shah in return for influence in the future government.[157] Kashani had a well-organized 'street machine' in the capital,[158] but as Yom concludes the Shah was still not able to 'match the opposition's mobilizational capacity to incite collective action on the street'.[159] This was also due to the fact that, as theoretically expected, Mosaddeq responded by enlarging his own coalition, which is most visible in the referendum campaign to dissolve parliament shortly before the coup in August 1953. As Abrahamian puts it, '[t]he liberal aristocrat who had in the past appealed predominantly to the middle classes was now appealing to the general public. The moderate reformer who had at one time even proposed restricting suffrage to literates was now openly seeking the support of the downtrodden masses'.[160]

The second, ultimately successful strategy consisted of utilizing superior repressive capacity to get rid of the NF. As early as December 1951 the Shah started

---

[153] Yom 2016, p. 102; Behrooz 2004, p. 105; and Abrahamian 2013, pp. 58–9; 139.
[154] Yom 2016, p. 104.   [155] Rahnema 2015, p. 13.   [156] Ibid., p. 53.
[157] Abrahamian 2013, p. 155.   [158] Rahnema 2015, p. 49.   [159] Yom 2016, p. 106.
[160] Abrahamian 2013, p. 170.

talking about using a coup d'état in conversations with British and American diplomats.[161] A series of incidents made it clear, however, that domestic sources of coercive power would not be sufficient to unseat Mosaddeq. When Mosaddeq resigned in July 1952 after the Shah denied him the right to name the War Minister and control the officer corps, both the army and the police force were unable to quell the five days of pro-Mossadeq riots led by the NF and Tudeh:[162] 'The army was sent to disperse the demonstrators, but the junior officers and soldiers disregarded the order of their commanders to create a blood bath.'[163] Prison guards abandoned their uniforms and defected, leading to the release of hundreds of detained protesters.[164] Realizing the split running through the security apparatus, the Shah rejected the proposed strategy of the newly appointed Prime Minister Qavam to declare martial law, dissolve the *Majles*, and arrest the opposition.[165]

Measures taken by Mosaddeq after his reinstatement further exacerbated the Shah's predicament as they severed, for the first time, the link between the Pahlavi dynasty and the armed forces:[166] Mosaddeq named himself War Minister, cut military spending, retired 135 senior officers, named a loyalist as new chief-of-staff, and replaced the head of police, gendarmerie, and customs guards. All heads were instructed to report directly to the ministry, instead of their weekly habitual meetings with the Shah by-passing the government. The Shah's Imperial Guards were stripped of their heavy weaponry.[167] While these purges swelled the ranks of disgruntled officers and potential coup plotters, they also meant that '[f]or the first time in Iranian history [...] the shah could not count on tangible military support'.[168] The failure of what Rahnema calls a proto-coup in February 1953, largely carried out by domestic actors mobilized by the Shah's brother, Shahpur Ali-Reza Pahlavi, brought further curbs on the Shah's power and entailed a complete breakdown in the relationship with Mosaddeq, who subsequently refused any audiences.[169] More importantly, it exhausted options relying on domestic coercion only,[170] leaving the solicitation of foreign support as the only viable option.

Granted, the term 'solicitation' does not fully capture the eagerness with which the United States and the United Kingdom lent their support to the Shah. In fact, potential coup scenarios had been scripted since late 1951. Britain deemed justifiable any means to rid itself of Mosaddeq and reverse the AIOC's nationalization; the USA, fed by British intelligence, had grown wary of a potential communist threat to Iran.[171] Irrespective of the foreign motives, for the Shah the availability of a foreign patron with high coercive capacity meant that he could not only violently oust Mosaddeq; he, critically, could also rely on their support to fatally wipe out

---

[161] Rahnema 2015, p. 239. [162] Katouzian 2004, p. 11. [163] Amjad 1989, p. 61.
[164] Abrahamian 2013, p. 140. [165] Ibid., p. 140. [166] Abrahamian 2013, p. 141.
[167] Ibid., pp. 143–4; 182–3. [168] Azimi 2004, p. 86. [169] Ibid., pp. 79–81.
[170] Rahnema 2015, p. 239. [171] Ibid.

opposition in the aftermath of the coup, enabling him to continue his rule based on a narrow coalition.[172]

In terms of the coup, the instrumental role of the USA and UK has been amply recognized, not least by the Shah himself.[173] Britain could mobilize an urban network of rioters thanks to its long-standing relationship with the Rashidian brothers, who acted as the business godfathers of mob leaders in Tehran's south,[174] while the CIA funded anti-communist parties opposed to the NF.[175] More important was the military support of the coup operation. In April 1953, British intelligence actively participated in the kidnapping and killing of General Mahmoud Afshartous, Mosaddeq's police chief.[176] And both the CIA and MI6 vetted and recruited young colonels as coup plotters through their established relationship with high-ranking officers. This recruitment effort was supported with considerable financial resources.[177] Likewise, the entire logistics and planning of the coup was equally managed by MI6 and the CIA. Equally important was the support of the Shah's repressive campaign in the aftermath of the coup. Thanks to tremendous financial support from the USA—US aid surpassed oil revenues until 1957 and between 1953 and 1960 one billion USD were given to Iran, 450 million USD of which was military aid, amounting to 41 per cent of GDP annually—the Tudeh party was practically wiped out by 1955. The CIA was also instrumental in setting up SAVAK, Iran's domestic intelligence service, which became notorious for its brutal interrogation methods.[178] Narrow in nature, the emerging regime coalition gave the Shah no political incentive to engage in welfare distribution.

Summary

The cases of Morocco and Pahlavi Iran highlight the importance of coercive capacity in the dynamics of authoritarian regime formation. Both were in conflict with rival elites at the head of a broad-based nationalist movement which threatened to sideline or potentially end the monarchy. An excess of coercive power enabled the Allawi and the Pahlavi dynasty to end the conflict by using repression. In Morocco, the ability to do so resulted from the uneven way in which coercive capacity had been distributed when the anti-colonial coalition broke apart. In Iran, coercive capacity needed to be 'contracted' from a foreign power, entailing a long-term client relationship with the USA. This meant that intra-elite conflict in both countries did not entail the formation of a broad cross-class coalition, although the counterfactual contours of such a coalition were visible in the Istiqlal and the National Front.

---

[172] Yom 2016, p. 98. As the accounts by Abrahamian and Rahnema demonstrate, the coup's success was to a large extent the result of luck, which highlights the 'structured contingency' in regime formation. See Abrahamian 2013; and Rahnema 2015.

[173] Gasiorowski 2004, p. 259; Katouzian 2004, p. 16; and Rahnema 2015, p. 4.

[174] Rahnema 2015, p. 4; and Abrahamian 2013, p. 151.   [175] Gasiorowski 2004, p. 236.

[176] Abrahamian 2013, p. 179.   [177] Ibid., p. 151; and Rahnema 2015, p. 91.

[178] Yom 2016, pp. 113–15.

3.1.3 Elite conflict and communalism: ethnic cross-class coalitions

Syria

Established by a Ba'thist[179] coup d'état in March 1963 and consolidated after an internal, 'corrective' coup led by Hafez al-Asad in 1970, the Syrian regime is unique in that it combines intensive intra-elite struggle with highly salient ethnic cleavages during the moment of regime formation. The outcome of these confluent factors brought about a hybrid coalition, which was cross-class but 'undersized' and with a considerable communal bias. It 'indisputably incorporated a middle-lower class',[180] which, as I will detail below, was propelled by conflict within the coup coalition.[181] But significant communal cleavages led to minority, specifically Alawite domination in key areas of political decision making,[182] which incentivized communal favouritism. This domination was not absolute and the regime retained the support of important non-Alawite constituencies, not least because of its hybrid cross-class nature.[183] It should also be noted that intra-elite struggle consisted mostly of intra-military rivalries which entailed limited popular mobilization as, in the words of Rabinovich, 'the struggle was kept indoors'.[184] This further weakened the regime's incentive for welfare distribution.

Before analysing coalition formation, a short note on the ethnic background in Syria is in order. Syria's majority population, Sunni Arabs, represented approximately 58 per cent of the population in the early 1960s and constituted the country's dominant social class, populating urban centres along with Syria's Christian community (14 per cent).[185] About 12 per cent of all Syrians belonged to the Alawite sect,[186] the country's largest Shiite minority group. The two smaller Shiite minority groups are the Druzes and the Ismailis, representing 3 and 1.5 per cent of the population, respectively. Though numerically small, the three Shiite minorities came to play a pre-eminent role in post-independence Syria, as the French colonial authorities, to offset Sunni anti-colonial nationalism, had preferentially recruited minorities into the indigenous army, the *Troupes spéciales du Levant*. Alawis, Druzes, and Ismailis were therefore heavily over-represented in the Syrian armed forces after 1946.[187] Colonialism critically amplified the political salience of communal divides.[188]

It should also be kept in mind that the initial coup coalition was, indeed, rather small, as the Ba'th party barely comprised a membership of 6,000 members and thus lacked a wide support base.[189] The other pillar of the coup coalition were

---

[179] The Ba'th party was founded in 1940 by Michel Aflaq and Salah Al-Din Bitar with the aims of unifying Arab nations and socialist modernization.
[180] Hinnebusch 2002, p. 81.   [181] Van Dam 1996, p. 26.
[182] Perlmutter 1969, p. 828. See also Drysdale 1981b, p. 16; and Hinnebusch 1990, ch. 5.
[183] Hinnebusch 2015, p. 115.   [184] Rabinovich 1972, p. 136.   [185] Van Dam 1996, p. 1.
[186] Ibid., p. 1.   [187] Drysdale 1982, p. 53.   [188] M. Kerr 2015, p. 10.
[189] Rabinovich 1972, p. 49; Seale 1965, p. 176; and Hinnebusch 2002, p. 34.

Nasserist officers whom the Ba'th party had lured into the alliance by promising a revival of the defunct United Arab Republic—the previous union of Syria and Egypt under the leadership of Nasser. When internal strife convulsed this heterogeneous coalition soon after its rise to power, the combination of intra-elite conflict and communal cleavages had two countervailing effects: an outreach to Syria's working classes coupled with a narrowing of the coalition's communal composition. Let us look at each of them in turn.

Regarding intra-elite conflict, the struggle opposing Ba'thists and Nasserists in the initial coup coalition was critical for the widening of the coalition. Populist reforms during the UAR period had made Nasserism the strongest current among Syria's 80,000 unionized workers and the country's student population.[190] Immediately upon seizing power, Ba'thists were thus confronted with working-class mobilization in the form of pro-Nasser demonstrations. Demanding the reinstatement of the UAR, demonstrators were supported by Nasserist officers within the coup coalition who expected Ba'thists to make good on their promise. The conflict intensified in July 1963 when Nasserist officers attempted to sideline the Ba'th in an abortive coup which claimed more than 800 lives.[191] In response, Nasser's propaganda machinery incited workers to rise up against the 'separatist regime'.[192] Recognizing its own position of weakness, the Ba'th's leadership came to the conclusion that 'the only way open to the party was to launch massive social and economic reforms that would outdo those of Nasser and guarantee the regime its popular basis of support'.[193]

The party's 6th National Congress, held in October 1963, translated this strategy to enlist working-class support into concrete political resolutions. Stating the necessity to 'attract those sectors of workers who are still loyal to 'Abd-ul-Nasser'.[194] the congress decided on the establishment of free medical services and the establishment of university quotas for students from under-privileged backgrounds.[195] Denouncing past exploitation of the countryside at the hands of the urban bourgeoisie, the Ba'th also relaunched the project of land reform, expropriating, by 1969, 1.5 million hectares of land.[196] In October 1964, Ali Taljabani, a senior labour leader, was made Minister of Labour and Social Affairs.[197] Importantly though, this was a strategic response to a situation of intra-elite conflict from a position of weakness, not the enactment of Ba'thi political doctrine. In fact, before 1963, the theme of Arab unity had prevailed over programmatic positions on economic and social reforms, and amongst many of the Ba'thist older generation, such as Michel Aflaq, the leftist turn to outcompete Nasserism was supported only half-heartedly.[198]

---

[190] Hinnebusch 1982, p. 196; and Rabinovich 1972, p. 67.   [191] Hopwood 1988, p. 45.
[192] Rabinovich 1972, p. 66.   [193] Ibid., p. 92.   [194] Ibid., p. 92.   [195] Ibid., pp. 94.
[196] Perthes 1997, p. 81.   [197] Heydemann 1999, p. 198.   [198] Abu Jaber 1966, p. 147.

Parallel to the broadening of the regime's class base occurred a narrowing of its communal base. Propelled by intra-military rivalries following the 1963 coup, numerous purges led to a gradual predominance of the Alawite sect in the upper echelons of the regime.[199] Starting right after the coup, Sunni officers, who had been the main instigators of the 1961 secession from Egypt, were purged *en masse* from the army, whilst recruitment efforts favoured Shiite minorities in an unprecedented fashion.[200] As the Nasserist officers in the coup coalition were also predominantly Sunni, their ouster and the subsequent purges following the abortive coup in July 1963 further reduced Sunni presence in the officers corps. When Sunni President Amin al-Hafiz was ousted at the hands of an internal coup in February 1966, further anti-Sunni purges ensued.[201] In September 1966, a Druze-led abortive coup entailed the elimination of numerous Druze officers, such that by 1967 Alawite officers, most prominently Salah Jedid and Hafez al-Asad, outnumbered all other sects among the Ba'th party's powerful military command.[202]

At the same time, given that the Ba'th party had recruited its followers predominantly from neglected rural communities, which clustered in the Alawi Latakia and the Druze Dar'a region, both regions were significantly overrepresented in the regime's primary decision-making body, the Syrian Regional Command (RC).[203] Similarly, cabinet compositions equally reflected the predominance of elites from Latakia, the Alawis' home region. While between 1946 and 1958, Sunni elites from Damascus and Aleppo had held 66 per cent of all cabinet positions, their share declined to less than 30 per cent in the period from 1966 to 1976. Ministers from Latakia also remained in office on average one year longer. The picture is even more striking when considering key ministries only: that is, the Prime and Deputy Prime Minister, Defence, Interior, and Foreign Affairs. Between 1966 and 1976, 59 per cent of all these ministers were Latakian, compared to only 11 per cent from Damascus. Interior and/or Defence were always held by a minister from Latakia. Drysdale therefore concludes that '[t]here are also strong indications that while cabinets as a whole have been ethnically representative, most likely by design, Alawis have been overrepresented in key portfolios'.[204]

The reasons for this communal narrowing support the proposed theoretical mechanisms. Hinnebusch notes that 'intra-elite conflict reinforced sectarianism as it heightened the need to recruit from one's own sect in order to maximize loyalty and political security'.[205] Shared communal origin therefore translated into higher trust within minority communities and, as a result, 'empty posts tended to be staffed with trusted officers from their own sect'.[206] Van Dam equally

[199] Van Dam 1996, p. 30, 47.   [200] Hinnebusch 2002, p. 62.
[201] Van Dam 1978, p. 208.   [202] Ibid., p. 209.
[203] Drysdale 1981b, p. 8. All data on RC and cabinet composition are taken from the same source.
[204] Ibid., p. 13.   [205] Hinnebusch and Schmidt 2009, p. 7.
[206] Hinnebusch 2002, p. 5; and Hinnebusch 2015, p. 113.

emphasizes the mutual distrust between officers from different sects.[207] Finally, Batatu observes that within-community cooperation was stronger than coopera- tion across communities.[208] Taken together, these observations suggest that the transaction and monitoring costs in a predominantly cross-communal coalition would have been prohibitively high. With regard to expectations, Picard remarks that minorities in the periphery 'expected to be favoured by the new regime'.[209] A similar observation is made by Van Dam who notes that scores of young men from a minority background volunteered to join the public service after 1963 in expectation of a preferential treatment.[210]

Regarding welfare distribution, communal narrowing also had profound reper- cussions. As highlighted in Chapter 2, rural Alawi areas started to benefit dis- proportionally from the regime's populist policies. Education and health care in the Latakia region improved substantially and faster than in other regions,[211] and Alawis could expect to receive preferential treatment when applying for entry into the civil service.[212] Conversely, the urban Sunni communities, in particular Aleppo, and non-Alawi rural areas with the partial exception of Da'ra received relatively less welfare provision: 'It is noteworthy that al-Ladhiqlyah and Dar'a provinces have enjoyed disproportionate growth, possibly because of government favoritism.'[213]

In summary, the Syrian case illustrates in an exemplary way the countervailing effects of intra-elite conflict and ethnic cleavages. By forming a lopsided, com- munal cross-class coalition, the regime's incentive to provide social welfare was considerably weaker than in broad coalition types, such as in Tunisia or Egypt. This, in addition to the external context examined in the next section, underpinned Syria's particularly low welfare effort.

3.1.4 Cohesive elites and communal friction: narrow ethnic coalitions

Jordan

The Jordanian pattern of regime formation is also unique. It combines a highly cohesive elite, a 'tiny royal clique',[214] consisting of the officers corps, the upper echelons of the bureaucracy, as well as landowners and merchants.[215] The forma- tion of this elite coalition largely occurred during the mandate period, predating formal independence, and was steered and tightly supervised by British colonial authorities.[216] Importantly, this meant that Jordan reached independence with an intact regime in control of its security apparatus and, albeit rudimentary,

---

[207] Van Dam 1996, p. 113.   [208] Batatu 1981.   [209] Picard 1979, pp. 54–5.
[210] Van Dam 1996, p. 9.   [211] Drysdale 1981a.
[212] Zisser 1999, p. 138; Kienle 1991, pp. 218–19; and Van Dam 1996, p. 10.
[213] Drysdale 1981a, p. 109.   [214] Milton-Edwards and Hinchcliffe 2001, p. 26.
[215] Alon 2007, p. 155.   [216] Alon 2007; and Peters and P. Moore 2009.

bureaucracy. This contrasts with the cases of Morocco, Tunisia, and even Pahlavi Iran where political authority in the immediate post-independence/interregnum period was highly contested. Consequently, the threats the Jordanian regime faced from new middle-class, Arab nationalist parties post-independence were akin to bottom-up threats from a new political opposition force, rather than conflict within the regime's coalition itself or between elites seeking to build a regime that had yet to be established. In fact, as the following analysis demonstrates, it was the remarkable cohesion of Jordan's regime coalition in the face of these bottom-up threats that guaranteed its survival. That said, the post-independence period did add a distinctly communal dimension to the regime's support coalition as the Arab–Israeli War in 1948 and the resulting mass influx of Palestinians into Jordan heightened communal tensions between the Palestinian West Bankers and the Transjordanian East Bankers. This entailed a communal narrowing of the regime coalition in favour of its historical tribal support group, the East Bankers. The resulting narrow, communal coalition gave the regime very limited incentives to provide social welfare.

Regarding elite cohesion, the country's turbulent and protracted period of leadership succession following the assassination of the country's first King, Abdullah, in 1951 illustrates in an exemplary manner the elite's strong sense of loyalty and commitment toward the survival of the Hashemite Kingdom. When Nayif—one of Abdullah's sons and contenders for the throne—pondered the possibility of staging a coup against his brother Talal,[217] he was unable to find collaborators among the upper echelons of the court. As Talal's health subsequently deteriorated in spring 1952—he suffered from schizophrenia and alcoholism—the palace elite under the crucial leadership of al-Huda convinced parliament to depose Talal and in August 1952 his seventeen-year-old son, Hussein, was appointed new King of the Hashemite Kingdom. However, as Hussein was in the midst of his training at the British military academy in Sandhurst, a Crown Council was formed which oversaw the daily government business until the young monarch assumed power in May 1953. With Hussein absent abroad, it is remarkable that nobody within the inner core elite attempted to defect and form a rival coalition to seize power. The ouster of the Egyptian monarch at the hands of the Free Officers, which coincided with Talal's deposition in Jordan, could have served as a blueprint for regime change in Jordan. Yet, the inner circle of the country's elite valued the survival of the monarchy as an institution higher than potential personal gains from throwing in their lot with a potential contender.

The sources of this remarkable elite cohesion lay in 'the nature of the British-constructed state'.[218] Wary of the political ambitions of the local Transjordanian elite, Abdullah recruited the bulk of his civil servants from outside the country,

---

[217] Satloff 1994, p. 38.   [218] Robins 2004, p. 89. See also Satloff 1994, p. 174.

most notably from among Palestinian, Syrian, and Lebanese nationalist elites, some of whom had fought alongside his brother Faisal. Whilst being better educated than the local tribal notables, this elite had no historical roots in Transjordan and was thus bereft of an independent power base within the country.[219] Underlining the long-lasting effect of this strategy, Robert Satloof remarks:

> Central to Abdullah's thinking, delegating authority to expatriates – who, by definition lacked local political fiefdoms—kept power out of the hands of potential adversaries. In so doing, Abdullah built up a circle of non-Transjordanians who attained power and privilege solely because they had thrown in their lot with his. Loyalty to the monarchy was the only guarantee of their status; their vested interest in the survival and prosperity of Hashemite Jordan was almost as great as that of the Hashemites themselves.[220]

Numerically, the presence of expatriates in the bureaucracy was sizeable, with 32 per cent of non-native civil servants in 1936.[221] Moreover, the upper echelon of the administration was almost exclusively expatriate, which turned this elite group into an indispensable pillar of the regime following independence.

The second institution that guaranteed elite cohesion after the end of the mandate was the Jordanian army, the so-called Arab Legion, which was central in tying the local tribal population to the regime.[222] Absorbing the local tribesmen into the state without having to disarm them forcefully, the Arab Legion's officers corps became the main springboard for the aspiring sons of Transjordan's most influential tribes, such as the Huweitat, Beni Saqr, and Sirhan.[223] Tribal solidarities were thus gradually substituted by a sense of loyalty toward the new 'chief', the Emir and later King, and, over time, tribes began to vest their interests in the survival of the Hashemite dynasty.[224]

Cohesion was further reinforced by salient ethnic cleavages after the Palestine War in 1948–9. East Bankers henceforth only constituted a third of the country's population; two-thirds were Palestinian, of whom 458,000 came as refugees.[225] Moreover, the Palestinian community had a very different socioeconomic profile that distinguished them from the tribal East Bank population. In terms of class background, they were mostly urban middle class and on average better educated than East Bankers. Many of them had also been successful merchants and traders, and therefore brought not only cultural but also economic capital.[226] Finally, the Palestinian community lacked the sense of loyalty to the King that had developed over nearly three decades in the East Bank.[227]

---

[219] Aruri 1972, p. 34.   [220] Satloff 1994, p. 7.   [221] Robins 2004, p. 33.
[222] Vatikiotis 1967, p. 5.   [223] Day 1986, p. 80.   [224] Alon 2007, p. 1.
[225] Robins 2004, p. 82.   [226] Vatikiotis 1967, p. 109.   [227] Shwadran 1959, p. 300.

In the Jordanian case, it was the presence of strong communal expectations on the part of the East Bankers that triggered ethnic narrowing of the coalition. In fact, expecting the regime to maintain their privileges, many East Bankers were displeased by the massive influx of Palestinians.[228] Reiter therefore portrays both sides as 'two conflicting ethnic groups' after 1948.[229] Against the backdrop of heightened communal tensions, the nascent regime could not jeopardize the support of the East Bankers, who were considered more loyal to the regime and, in addition, formed the bulk of the Jordanian armed forces.[230] As a result, Jordanian authorities dealt with the Palestinians with great caution and distrust, discrimination at the hands of the authorities was widespread—particularly in the early years—and refugee camps in particular were subject to disruptive security measures.[231]

Economically, the continued hegemony of the East Bank was ensured by concentrating industrial projects almost exclusively in the East Bank and politically by granting the West and East Bank equal representation in parliament, which meant that, de facto, every Palestinian vote counted only half as much as a Transjordanian one.[232] When King Abdullah died at the hands of a Palestinian assassin in Jerusalem in July 1951, anti-Palestinian riots ensued. Summarizing their sense of exclusion, Pappé remarks that 'with the monarchy belonging to the Hashemites and the army to the Bedouins, the Palestinian majority felt as though it was living under the rule of a dictatorial minority'.[233]

These tensions were exacerbated by the fact that Palestinians formed the core of a new political opposition that emerged in the form of Arab nationalist parties organized under the umbrella of the Jordanian National Movement. The movement was strongly supported by the General Federation of Jordanian Trade Unions, the establishment of which was instigated by remnants of labour activists from the former Palestine mandate.[234] Nationalist opposition parties had achieved a resounding victory in the 1956 elections and thus left the King no choice but to appoint socialist Suleiman Nabulsi as Prime Minister, who packed the cabinet with his political allies.[235] The fact that the King was able to dismiss the Nabulsi cabinet after seven months, in April 1957, purge a small group of pro-Nasser officers from the army, and proceed with a 'violent counterattack [and] coercive restoration of authoritarianism'[236] involving mass arrests, the banning of all political parties and suspension of parliament, newspaper closures, a state of emergency dividing the country into seven military districts, and hundreds of arrests[237]—all of this without elite defections from his inner core and whilst maintaining full control of the security apparatus, with rank-and-file willing to carry out repression—is

---

[228] Tal 2002, p. 9.   [229] Reiter 2004, p. 72.   [230] Brand 1999, p. 283.
[231] Dann 1989, p. 14.   [232] Dann 1994, p. 20; Robins 2004, p. 87; and Nevo 2003, p. 190.
[233] Pappé 1994, p. 71.   [234] Yom 2016, p. 162.   [235] Robins 2004, p. 96.
[236] Yom 2016, p. 166.   [237] Ibid., pp. 165–6; and Robins 2004, pp. 100–2.

testimony to the high level of cohesion within the regime's support coalition. It also critically underlines the limits of bottom-up mobilization 'against a regime which maintains the cohesion, capacity, and disposition to apply repression'.[238]

Overall, the combination of cohesive elites and salient ethnic cleavages led to the formation of a narrow coalition coupled with pro-East Bank favouritism. The generosity towards the regime's key communal constituency—Transjordanian East Bankers—is reflected in the segmented nature of Jordan's welfare provision, which exhibits generosity towards 'insiders' with high levels of segmentation and barriers to access. Conversely, the regime had very little incentive to distribute social welfare broadly or universally, as it would then have reached a community whose political allegiance to the regime was more than uncertain.

3.2 Coalitions in Context: External Threats and Resource Endowment

This section analyses the geostrategic context in which regime formation took place. This step is important to assess a regime's ability to provide social welfare, which is a necessary condition for the emergence of an authoritarian welfare state. Since military defeat and territorial losses at the hand of a foreign power are highly destabilizing and can jeopardize regime survival, the existence of severe external threats considerably constrains a regime's distributive capacity. With resources channelled toward national defence to maintain an efficacious threat level vis-à-vis external forces, the regime's ability to provide social welfare is hampered, and only resource-abundant regimes are able to honour both their commitments to welfare and defence. This external dimension has been particularly important in the MENA region. Hosting 25 per cent of the world's armed conflicts since 1945, the region has been haunted by protracted military conflicts. The Arab–Israeli conflict alone has cost over 200,000 lives, left 3 million displaced, and caused material damage of more than 300 billion USD.[239] This conflict will thus play a particular role in this section.

To preview the case studies, Tunisia and Morocco represent cases of 'poor' states at peace. This means that their geostrategic environment was free from external threats to regime survival. While Tunisia was exempt from any military conflict during regime formation, Morocco had a minor border clash with Algeria which entailed an ongoing rivalry between both countries. Yet, as I show, this threat was minor, not perceived as endangering the survival of the regime, and thus inconsequential for the regime's ability to distribute welfare. Given similar abilities, the marked difference in social policies between Morocco and Tunisia directly points to incentives stemming from coalitions as the key explanatory factors.

---

[238] Guillermo and Schmitter 1986, p. 21.   [239] Ibrahim 1998, pp. 229–30.

Table 3.2 Geostrategic context of regime formation in labour-abundant MENA regimes

		External threat	
		High	Low
Resource endowment — High		Islamic Republic of Iran	Algeria The Pahlavi regime
			low abilities high abilities
Resource endowment — Low		Jordan Syria Egypt	Tunisia Morocco

Jordan, Syria, and Egypt represent cases of 'poor' states at war. In contrast to Tunisia and Morocco, their geostrategic environment constituted a vital challenge to regime survival, with considerable consequences for the countries' state budgets. While this was less consequential for Jordan and Syria, considering their low incentive to provide welfare, external threats coupled with a low resource endowment seriously affected social policies in Egypt and pushed the country onto its specific trajectory of broad, yet ungenerous welfare provision. The cases of Syria and Egypt also demonstrate well how threat perception changed during regime formation and the external environment gradually came to be perceived as a threat to regime survival.

Algeria and the Pahlavi regime are cases of 'rich' states at peace. While receiving ample fiscal surpluses from exportable resources, particularly oil, none of the regimes was exposed to an existential threat emanating from the external environment. Unconstrained by external forces, state expenditures thus reflected the incentives coming from the regime coalition, favouring welfare in Algeria in contrast to defence in the case of Iran.

Finally, the Islamic Republic of Iran represents the case of a 'rich' state at war. It, thus, represents the gateway case for my claim that abundant resources can alleviate the dilemma between 'butter or guns' and enable a regime to build a welfare state whilst deterring external threats.

3.2.1 Poor states at peace

Tunisia

In Tunisia, the incentives for broad welfare provision were not affected by the regional environment. In the absence of a severe external threat, the regime could fully commit its resources to building an authoritarian welfare state. Conversely, the country's meagre resource endowment did not impair its ability to provide welfare.

Remote from the epicentre of conflict in the Middle East, the Tunisian regime emerged in a comparatively unthreatening regional environment. During the period of regime formation, the country was spared from any major military conflict with neighbouring states and national security was a second-order concern for the country's leadership. Granted, its small size made it potentially vulnerable to interference from its two bigger neighbours, Algeria and Libya.[240] When conceiving the country's post-independence defence strategy, the Tunisian leadership therefore came to the conclusion that the country would be unable to defend itself alone in the event of a major foreign attack.[241] Military protection from a Western superpower, notably France, thus became the cornerstone of Tunisia's strategy of national defence.[242]

However, the country's small size was also a blessing since it meant that Tunisia was not regarded as a rival for regional hegemony, which in combination with a lack of extractable resources allowed it to remain 'under the radar'. Though endowed with oil and gas reserves, it would be wrong to characterize Tunisia as a resource-abundant state. In comparison, reserves were minor and income from natural resources represented a negligible proportion in the state budget before the oil boom in the early 1970s.[243] And even at the peak of the oil price, Tunisia's per capita revenues from resources were comparatively small, with three-quarters of all state revenues still coming from taxation.[244]

In line with its defence strategy, the country's own military forces were kept deliberately small—about 11,000 soldiers.[245] In the words of one of the country's first Ministers of Defence, Ahmed Mestiri, it would have been 'pointless to dedicate more than 10 per cent of the budget to the armed forces'.[246] In reality, defence spending has rarely exceeded 6 per cent since independence.[247] This meant that the Tunisian government was financially not encumbered by the burden of a heavy defence budget.

An unthreatening environment did not mean, though, that Tunisia's foreign relations were entirely free of conflict. In 1958, French warplanes bombarded the Tunisian town of Sakiet, an important base of the Algerian FLN. Moreover, French officials repeatedly alluded to the possibility of carrying out a 'blitz invasion' of Tunisia to wipe out Algerian resistance fighters.[248] Nonetheless, just a few years after decolonization, a permanent occupation of Tunisia by the former colonial

---

[240] Willis 2012, p. 87.   [241] Former Minister of Defence, A. Mestiri 1999, p. 199.
[242] Willis 2012, p. 87.
[243] It is not clear why Richards and Waterbury 2008, p. 196 speak of 'substantial revenue' in the case of Tunisia, which is situated in the lowest quartile in terms of oil rents.
[244] Decaluwé et al. 1990, p. 1054.   [245] Bourguiba 1976, p. 115.
[246] A. Mestiri 1999, p. 198.   [247] IMF 2011; and V. Lucas and Richter 2016.
[248] A. Mestiri 1999, p. 127.

power was considered inconceivable and, despite sporadic tensions, France had a clear interest in preserving the territorial integrity of Tunisia, which was the most pro-Western and also pro-French of all Maghrebi states.

In sum, the situation of a 'benign neglect' in regional rivalries meant that Tunisia could allocate resources to socioeconomic development, most notably social welfare, instead of national defence. Counterfactually, a severe external threat would have critically undermined the regime's welfare effort.

Morocco

Compared to Tunisia, the Moroccan regime was exposed to a more challenging external environment upon regime formation. Rivalling its neighbour Algeria over regional hegemony in the Arab Maghreb,[249] Morocco's foreign relations have witnessed periods of military conflict. However, it is safe to say that border disputes with Algeria were never perceived by the country's elites as a threat to the regime itself.

Considering the first outbreak of hostilities in the autumn of 1963, it is note-worthy that during August and September both governments were trying to de-escalate the situation and sought to attribute the hostilities to 'uncontrolled elements'.[250] Moreover, as Damis points out, the confrontation was short and small in scale, involving only a minimal level of casualties and no superpower intervention.[251] Nor did the 'War of Sands', as it came to be called, entail a sizeable expansion of military expenditures or an arms race on both sides. In fact, both countries reduced defence spending in the years following the conflict.[252] The potential threat was arguably higher for Algeria, considering the military superi-ority of the Moroccan armed forces at the time and Morocco's rather expansionist foreign policy.[253] Crucially, neither of the parties sought an overthrow of the other regime by military means and the conflict remained geographically confined. While relations remained tense throughout the 1960s, the conflict was, in all, too minor to influence the domestic political economy of spending in the long run.

As for the country's resource endowment, Morocco has had only a very limited amount of exportable resources at its disposal. Although hosting two-thirds of the world's phosphate reserves, non-tax revenues were negligible during the period of regime formation as a result of low world market prices.[254] Only when the international prices of phosphate tripled in 1974 did Morocco come to enjoy notable resource rents.[255] However, with prices plummeting in the late 1970s, the phosphate bonanza was short-lived and left conspicuous traces of a boom–bust

---

[249] Damis 1985, p. 142.   [250] Wild 1966, p. 24.   [251] Damis 1985, p. 141.
[252] IMF 2011; and V. Lucas and Richter 2016.
[253] At the time, Morocco laid claim to a number of territories outside its borders, such as current Mauritania, yet without very actively pursuing this agenda. See Douglas E. Ashford 1962, p. 644.
[254] IMF 2011; and V. Lucas and Richter 2016.
[255] Denoeux and Maghraoui 1998, p. 56.

cycle in the state budget.[256] Overall, it can be said that Morocco has depended to some extent on its income from exportable resources, without being resource abundant.

Summary

These two cases of poor states at peace underline the importance of domestic incentives to distribute welfare irrespective of the resource endowment. Whilst both countries have been resource poor and thus had the same ability to build a welfare state, the marked difference in their social policies points to different incentives coming from the regime coalition as the key explanatory factor.

3.2.2 Poor states at war

Egypt

Egypt is the showcase of a regime that, in the absence of abundant resources, was unable to honour its welfare commitments *and* build a strong army to deter external threats. Counterfactually speaking, Egypt would have arguably spent much more on social welfare if it had been located 2,000 kilometres more to the West. Besides, the Egyptian case also illustrates well how a series of events in the early stages of regime formation significantly changed the threat perception of the ruling elites who came to perceive the external environment as one of the biggest threats to the regime's survival.

This shift of perception and, by consequence, spending priorities happened in stages. When the Free Officers seized power in July 1952, the Arab–Israeli conflict did not figure among the key priorities of Egypt's new rulers. Granted, the humiliating defeat in the Palestine War (1948–9) in which about 4,000 Egyptian soldiers lost their lives had made the Free Officers aware of Egypt's military weakness and spotlighted Israel as a potential threat to the regime. However, in the Free Officers' assessment of the Palestine defeat, military inefficiency was considered an expression of more far-reaching domestic political problems, most notably a corrupted party system with a weak monarch at its top. Consequently, the new leadership exhibited a certain 'ambivalence' vis-à-vis the Arab–Israeli conflict and sought to avoid further escalation. In terms of foreign policy, its main priorities were the end of British military presence and the full establishment of national sovereignty over the Suez Canal. Domestically, the Free Officers believed that only economic development coupled with a functioning political system would allow Egypt to withstand potential external threats. The ruling Revolutionary Command Council (RCC) therefore initially agreed to keep the size of Egypt's

---

[256] Willis 2012, p. 234.

armed forces relatively limited and prioritize economic and social development, including welfare distribution.[257]

Israel, in turn, feared that an economically reinvigorated Egypt would, in the long run, constitute a much more dangerous military threat. While the monarchy had been viewed as weak and fragile, Nasserist Egypt was a 'red rag' for the Israeli leadership. As Avi Shlaim notes, 'Israeli rulers considered the toppling of Nasser and the defeat of his army as their primary aim.'[258] To this end, several operations were mounted to destabilize the Egyptian regime, which in combination significantly altered its perception of Israel. According to Barnett, the first change of perception came as a result of the so-called Lavon Affair in July 1954 when Israeli spies failed to execute a bomb plot against Egyptian and American cultural centres. The attack, which should have been imputed to Egyptian Muslim Brothers and communists, aimed to torpedo the ongoing Anglo-Egyptian negotiations about a British withdrawal from the canal zone.[259]

The second, more consequential, incident occurred in February 1955 when Israeli troops attacked an Egyptian army base in Gaza, which at the time was occupied by Egypt. Whilst human losses were limited, the attack significantly altered the regime's perception of external threat. As Khaled Mohi El Din, a Free Officer and member of the RCC, remarks in his autobiography, 'Israel did not begin to figure on the list until after the incidents of Gaza.'[260] Highlighting the profound impact of the Gaza raid, the historian Vatikiotis notes that 'after the Gaza raid he [Nasser] clearly came to perceive Israel as a serious threat'.[261] Another indicator of the change in perception is the spending shifts that occurred in the wake of the crisis. Defence spending increased by 75 per cent and, exasperated over US refusal to deliver weapons to Egypt, the regime turned to the Soviet Union to provide weapons in a historic arms deal, which was sealed in September 1955.[262]

The third event that consolidated Egypt's turn to a defence-centred spending policy was the Suez War of 1956. In particular, the defeat of the Egyptian army in Gaza and Sinai at the hand of the Israelis made the regime acutely aware of its vulnerability. The capital city, Cairo, had been affected by air raids and the damage inflicted on the Egyptian armed forces was substantial. Over 3,500 Egyptian soldiers died in the conflict. Port facilities and infrastructure along the canal area, which had been occupied by British and French forces, were largely destroyed. Moreover, Ben Gurion's initial refusal to withdraw from occupied Sinai and Gaza and his advocacy of a partial annexation of these territories reinforced the perceived threat to Egypt's territorial sovereignty and the survival

---

[257] Vatikiotis 1978, p. 254; and Barnett 1992, p. 48. Low defence spending also aimed at avoiding military coups.

[258] Shlaim 2007, p. 115.

[259] Barnett 1992, p. 84; in response, Nasser sponsored Palestinian guerrilla (*fedayeen*) attacks along the Israeli border.

[260] Mohi El Din 1995, p. 131.   [261] Vatikiotis 1978, p. 254.   [262] Barnett 1992, p. 88.

of the regime.[263] In combination, these three events led to a marked about-face in the regime's defence policy. The regime's leadership came to the conclusion that it needed a strong army capable of defending the country against external threats. This is reflected in the regime's defence spending. After an initial drop to 19 per cent of the budget, defence spending stood at nearly 30 per cent in the early 1960s.[264]

Regarding Egypt's resource endowment, as Barnett points out, 'Nasser was severely limited by the simple fact that Egypt was a resource-poor country [and thus] the never-ending concern was how to fund such escalating military costs while furthering the regime's other objectives of political stability.'[265] Apart from raising additional tax revenues, the regime had no exportable resources at its disposal.[266] It therefore crucially relied on the financial support of external donors in order to finance large development projects, such as the Aswan High Dam, which was built with the help of Soviet funding.[267] Aid, however, was insufficient to finance both extensive welfare and defence expenditures, which is shown by the country's steadily increasing budget deficits, in particular since the early 1960s.[268]

In summary, Egypt is the critical case to demonstrate how a lack of ability undermined the establishment of an authoritarian welfare state despite strong incentives to do so. As the external environment came to be perceived by the regime-building elites as a serious threat to regime survival, spending priorities shifted toward national defence. Egypt was pushed on a welfare trajectory of broad, yet not generous provision, characterized by 'cheap' social policies (see Chapter 6).

Syria

Syria's geostrategic environment was in many ways similar to Egypt's. According to Patrick Seale, there was an accute 'sense of limited resources and permanent siege' among the Syrian ruling elites.[269] It was this combination of a strong external threat and scarce resources that pushed the Syrian regime toward low social spending. However, compared to Egypt, the incentive to provide welfare was weaker and it is not clear whether the regime would have established an authoritarian welfare state, considering its lopsided communal coalition.

As in Egypt, the ruling elites gradually came to view their external environment as a danger for the survival of the regime. In the early stages of regime formation, Syria's leadership was well aware of the military imbalance with Israel,[270] without

---

[263] Perry 2004, p. 98.   [264] IMF 2011; and V. Lucas and Richter 2016.

[265] Barnett 1992, p. 85, 87.

[266] As a result, the regime adopted Defence Tax Law No. 277 of 1956, which increased direct taxes and excluded taxes on commercial profits in selected industrial and manufacturing activities. Revenue from oil and gas exports were negligible before the early 1970s. See ibid., p. 88; IMF 2011; and V. Lucas and Richter 2016.

[267] Barnett 1992, p. 119.   [268] IMF 2011; and V. Lucas and Richter 2016.

[269] Seale 1995, p. 494.   [270] Ibid., p. 118.

considering this threat as existential. Compared to the Israeli Defence Forces (IDF), the Syrian army was badly trained and ill-equipped with cheap Soviet weaponry, and its officer corps had been decimated by waves of purges as a result of intra-elite struggles.[271] Geographically, Syria's location made it liable to being outflanked through either Lebanon or Jordan in the case of an Israeli attack.[272] Finally, the Syrian leadership was aware that a growing lobby within the IDF advocated the provocation of border conflicts with Arab neighbours to expand Israeli borders and thus render them more defensible.[273] In view of this strategy and past clashes along the border, the new regime expected Israel 'to fight every year to weaken surrounding Arab states and improve border security'.[274]

Yet, importantly for the argument at hand, the crushing defeat in the 1967 Six-Day War permanently altered the regime elites' threat perception. This is particularly true of later President Asad, for whom the defeat was 'the decisive turning point'[275] in his life, persuading him that Israel was 'a concrete, existential threat to his regime, to Syria'.[276] The war had devastated the Syrian army, destroying the country's entire air force and killing about 2,500 soldiers. On a humanitarian level, thousands of refugees flocked to Damascus from the Golan Heights, which were now occupied by Israel. Strategically, the loss of Golan was a disaster as it lay bare the entire Damascus plain and left the capital city virtually without protection. The ambition of Israel's Prime Minister Eshkol 'to occupy Damascus, if necessary'[277] was thus not an idle, but a very real threat to the regime.

Beyond its immediate material damage, this defeat had a profound impact on the regime's policies and its national security strategy. While before the war Syria had pursued an active policy of socialist economic reforms, nationalizing and collectivizing the country's economy, in the hope of achieving strength through development, the regime's leadership and, in particular, Asad became convinced after the war that military strength was the only viable deterrence against Israel. For Asad, the notion of military parity was important and, as a result, the procurement of military equipment became one of his main concerns. Outlining his political priorities, he remarked that 'our prime efforts are [...] to strengthen our military force for the purpose of defending the homeland and withstand the cruel enemy [Israel]'.[278] Defence spending figures are illustrative of this strategic turn, rising from 6.6 per cent of GDP in 1967 to 15.1 per cent in 1973 and remaining in double digits until the late 1980s.[279]

Syria had to pursue this strategy of military deterrence under conditions of scarce resources. Oil production, which had started in 1958, only began to produce sufficient quantities for exportation in 1968 and, given the country's

[271] Zisser 2001, p. 103.   [272] D. Roberts 1987, p. 117.   [273] Seale 1995, p. 128.
[274] Seale 1995, p. 118.   [275] Ibid., p. 143.   [276] Zisser 2001, p. 103.
[277] Hopwood 1988, p. 48.   [278] Ma'oz 1988, p. 57.
[279] IMF 2011; and V. Lucas and Richter 2016.

modest reserves, remained limited even during the height of the oil boom in the 1970s.[280] Other resources, such as phosphate and gas, were too scarce to create important fiscal surpluses. Similar to Egypt, Syria had to rely primarily on deficit spending and economic assistance, which poured in at considerable levels with the onset of Egyptian–Israeli peace negotiations after 1973. Syria ran deficits in the vicinity of 15 per cent of GDP throughout the 1970s and of 20 per cent from the late 1970s until 1986.[281]

In the light of the massive defence burden, the regime decided to sacrifice most of its initial commitment to welfare provision that stemmed from the regime's, albeit communally narrowed, cross-class coalition. As Hinnebusch aptly summarizes, 'the central vulnerability of the Ba'thist political economy was that neither public sector accumulation nor taxation produced sufficient resources to finance the state's many commitments'.[282]

Jordan

The Jordanian case shares with Egypt and Syria an exposure to regime-threatening external threats and meagre financial resources. Externally derived income, mostly aid, could not substitute for large fiscal surpluses from exportable resources. Jordan is the classic case of a rent-dependent, not a rent-abundant regime. In contrast to Egypt and Syria, Jordan's narrow regime coalition meant that it could eschew the dilemma of having to arbitrate between welfare and defence spending. Nonetheless, the severity of the threat meant that even without a strong welfare commitment, the country struggled with the economic burden of war preparation and making. For example, defence spending amounted to 68 per cent of the budget in 1955, and at the height of the conflict with Israel in 1967, only three countries in the world outspent Jordan in terms of defence spending as a percentage of GDP.[283] Even after the 1994 peace treaty with Israel, levels of defence spending have remained high, which underlines the continuing importance of the Jordanian military in the regime coalition. In a 2004 report, the IMF lamented that there was 'limited [...] scope for a significant reduction in on-budget military outlays and military spending continues to exceed that in many other emerging market economies in more stable regions'.[284] The organization further remarked that '[m]ilitary and security-related outlays account for another 8½ percent of GDP or 22 percent of total spending, one of the highest levels by international and regional standards'.[285] Path dependency clearly affects welfare *and* defence spending alike.

Regarding threat perception, the Jordanian regime considered Israel an existential external threat from the moment of independence. Since its annexation of the West Bank following the Palestine War of 1948–9, Jordan had to defend a

---

[280] IMF 2011; and V. Lucas and Richter 2016.   [281] IMF 2011; and V. Lucas and Richter 2016.
[282] Hinnebusch and Schmidt 2009, p. 14.
[283] See Tal 2002, p. 18; IMF 2011; and V. Lucas and Richter 2016.   [284] IMF 2004b, p. 51.
[285] IMF 2004a, p. 16.

630-kilometre armistice line and, unlike Egypt and Syria, was not protected by a geographical buffer zone, such as the Sinai or the Golan Heights. Both capital cities were only 110 kilometres apart and the distance from the armistice line to Tel Aviv was a mere 25 kilometres. Aware of their military inferiority in terms of numbers and weapons, the Jordanian elites therefore concentrated on strengthening the country's defensive capacities whilst avoiding 'any provocation that would give Israel a pretext to attack'.[286] The regime's defence effort notwithstanding, the military balance remained highly unfavourable for Jordan. As a British official commented shortly before the Six-Day War, 'if Israel wanted, it could snatch the West Bank within hours'.[287] The challenging geostrategic context is precisely summarized by British Ambassador Charles Johnston who, analysing the Jordanian situation in retrospect, commented that 'not a single foreign observer in Amman [...] believed that, even with British and American help, the Jordanian monarchy had a chance of surviving'.[288]

In addition, Jordanian territory covered large areas that at least some in the Israeli leadership considered an essential part of Greater Israel, the annexation of which was a legitimate political goal.[289] The Jordanian elites therefore perceived Zionism as particularly expansionist[290]—a feeling which was reinforced by the official line of the Israeli government. For instance, when King Abdullah was assassinated in 1951, the Israeli Prime Minister, Ben Gurion, contemplated the possibility of attacking Jordan.[291] His public views on Jordan were not very reassuring either, as he stated that 'Jordan was not viable as an independent state and should therefore be divided.'[292] Finally, Israeli raids into Jordanian territory, some of which were provoked by operations of Palestinian resistance fighters against Israel, became very frequent after 1951.[293] In total, Jordan's geographical location and military weakness meant that Hussein was generally fearful of Israeli expansionism and therefore anxious to maintain as high a level of deterrence as possible.[294]

As for Jordan's resource endowment, the regime was bereft of notable exportable resources and had to rely on external donors to allay the financial burden of national defence. Foreign aid was of enormous importance for the Jordanian government and came to cover large parts of the regime's expenditure, mostly dedicated to the armed forces.[295] For instance, between 1957 and 1967, the USA paid annual economic and military aid of approximately 55 million USD.[296] Following the 1973 war, aid became the primary source of income for the regime, amounting

---

[286] Tal 2002, p. 36. See also Day 1986, p. 82.   [287] Tal 2002, p. 116.

[288] Peters and P. Moore 2009, p. 268.

[289] According to UN General Dag Hammarskjold, Israel would consider itself incomplete until moving its frontiers eastwards to the Jordan river. See Tal 2002, p. 78.

[290] Day 1986, p. 85.   [291] Shlaim 2007, p. 36.   [292] Ibid., p. 116.

[293] This includes an Israeli raid on the village of Qibya in 1953 and on Qalqiya in 1956. See Tal 2002, p. 6.

[294] Robins 2004, p. 122.   [295] Peters and P. Moore 2009, p. 209.   [296] Ibid., p. 269.

to 86 per cent of government revenue in 1979.[297] These figures notwithstanding, it would be wrong to depict the Jordanian regime as resourse- or rent-abundant. Rather, it was highly rent-dependent, having to rely on external streams of revenues to finance the state's most basic functions, such as security.[298] Moreover, high levels of foreign aid, particularly from Arab Gulf countries, were contingent upon there being a strong external threat—the primary cause of Jordan's fiscal woes.

Summary

The three cases of poor states at war illustrate in an exemplary way how a challenging geostrategic environment can (i) critically undermine a high welfare effort and impair generous social policies, as in the case of Egypt; (ii) negatively affect social policies when incentives to provide welfare are less pronounced, as in the case of Syria; and (iii) financially destabilize a regime even without any incentives for welfare provision, as in the case of Jordan.

3.2.3 Rich states at peace

Algeria

The geostrategic environment in which the Algerian regime emerged in the early 1960s mirrors the situation of Morocco in that external threats and confrontation were present, but they were not perceived as existential. This meant that, given the regime's broad support coalition, the Algerian regime had the incentives and the ability to provide social welfare, and made social spending the key fiscal priority after independence. Importantly, analysing the country's revenue streams in the decade after independence shows that Algeria was actually not resource-abundant when it laid the foundations for its welfare state and hiked up social spending in the decade after independence. Thus, the Algerian case further weakens claims that the regime 'only' provided social welfare because of its rich oil resources.

Regarding external threats, the Algerian ruling elites perceived Morocco as a threat to Algeria due to Morocco's military superiority.[299] This perception was reinforced by Morocco's expansionist foreign policy. Since 1958, the monarchy had officially endorsed claims put forward by the nationalist movement to restore the country's historic frontiers, including Western Sahara and Mauritania. As such an expansion would have increased Moroccan territory by 60 per cent, these claims certainly concerned the Algerian regime although, arguably, there was an understanding that Morocco's stance was more rhetoric than real policy given the Spanish and French position on the territories south of Morocco. Morocco's

---

[297] Ibid., p. 270.
[298] IMF 2011; and V. Lucas and Richter 2016.   [299] Damis 1985, p. 141.

and Algeria's clashing ambitions triggered an enduring rivalry between them but there is no evidence to suggest that either regime perceived this threat as existential. As mentioned earlier, both sides quickly sought to de-escalate in the wake of the 'War of Sands' and the limited scope of this rivalry meant that it was inconsequential for Algeria's budget making. In fact, the government took steps to reduce defence expenditures in the wake of independence. Having to maintain an army of 880,000 soldiers immediately after independence, security-related expenditures represented a considerable burden on the budget that the government was anxious to allay.[300] By the early 1970s, the share of defence in the budget had fallen from 15 to 8 per cent.[301]

These spending cuts were also a consequence of the regime's dire financial situation in the decade after independence, which stands in contrast to the usual portrayal of Algeria as a resource-rich country.[302] Certainly, after the discovery of oil in 1958, Algeria became one of the world's major oil and gas exporting nations. However, it is crucial to recognize that, until the early 1970s, most oil revenues did not accrue to the state budget but were captured by foreign, first and foremost French, companies. Owing to the legal arrangements in place—the Algerian government did not, in fact, own the country's national resources until their nationalization in 1971—Algeria earned in the early 1960s four to five times less than other oil exporters.[303] For instance, out of 4,800 million dinars (DZD) of net profits in 1963, the government only received 220 million, a mere 4.6 per cent.[304] As a percentage of total revenues, hydrocarbon taxes amounted to less than 10 per cent in the early 1960s and not more than 20 per cent until 1970.[305] Insufficient to cover even capital expenditures, most oil revenues had to be spent on the amortization of foreign investments in the oil industry after independence.[306]

It was only due to a policy of austerity and substantial French aid that the government was kept financially afloat in the first few years after independence.[307] For example, the French government agreed to pay the salaries of Algerian civil servants out of its own budget in the first two years after independence. It was not until the nationalization of oil in 1971 that the regime experienced a real oil bonanza, the effect of which was amplified by the concomitant spike in the world market prices. Between 1973 and 1974, the state budget effectively doubled. Could the anticipation of oil wealth have driven up welfare spending before the onset of large-scale oil rents? Given the evidence, this seems unlikely. Social spending reached 50 per cent of the budget in the last year of Ben Bella's rule in 1965, three years after independence. Ben Bella, however, had refused the idea of nationalizing oil as his main focus was the re-appropriation of land owned by the French

---

[300] Stora 2001, p. 137.   [301] IMF 2011; and V. Lucas and Richter 2016.
[302] See, for example, Lowi 2009.   [303] Francos and Séréni 1976, p. 234.
[304] Bennoune 1988, p. 99.   [305] Ageron 1991, p. 135.   [306] Aïssaoui 2001, p. 12.
[307] D. Ottaway and M. Ottaway 1970, p. 85.

colonists.[308] It is therefore unlikely that he made budgetary decisions based on the anticipation of massive oil revenue.

In summary, this means that the rapid expansion of social expenditures in the decade after independence cannot be imputed to any form of resource abundance as it occurred *before* rent streams inflated the state budget. Most remarkably, the expansion occurred in a general climate of austerity which affected all types of public expenditure save the realm of social welfare. This points to coalitional incentives as the key explanatory factor.

The Pahlavi regime

The geostrategic environment in which the Pahlavi regime was formed in the early 1950s was free of major external threats. As a matter of fact, Iran did not experience any major or even minor armed conflicts in the first decade after the Shah's restoration to power in 1953. By virtue of its size and substantial natural resources, Iran was a powerful regional actor and thus had to fear relatively little from its, mostly less developed, neighbours. Owing to its narrow support coalition, the regime lacked an incentive to provide extensive welfare and, instead, spent most of its resources on the country's army, which, as described in the foregoing section, was a key pillar of the Shah regime. By the late 1960s, Iran had 'the biggest and most modern army in the Persian Gulf'[309] and had replaced Britain as the new hegemon in the region.[310] The smaller sheikhdoms of the Gulf even considered Iran the region's new 'policeman'.[311]

This is not to suggest, though, that the regime's external relations were free of antagonism. Smaller in size but rich in resources, Iraq was certainly regarded as the primary challenger to Iranian hegemony in the region.[312] This rivalry was fuelled by a simmering border conflict along the Shatt al-Arab river. In theory, the dispute had been resolved by the Iranian–Iraqi Treaty of 1937, yet the Shah refused to recognize its terms fully. The antagonism was reinforced by the overthrow of the Iraqi King at the hands of Colonel Qasim in 1958, which the Shah regarded as sponsored by communism.[313] In 1960, an armed conflict between both countries was only averted at the very last minute.[314] Mindful of Russian occupations of Iran during both world wars, the regime also considered the bordering Soviet Union as a latent threat.[315] However, its adamant allegiance to the West and, most notably, the USA effectively shielded the Shah from potential Soviet expansionism.

Regional hegemony could only be achieved thanks to Iran's abundant oil reserves. Since the time of the Shah's father, Reza Pahlavi, Iran's most important

---

[308] Aïssaoui 2001, p. 74.   [309] Cottrell 1978, p. 418.
[310] Lenczowski 1978, xxii; and Halliday 1979, p. 251.   [311] Ansari 2007, p. 224.
[312] Cottrell 1978, p. 402.   [313] Ibid., p. 416.
[314] Ibid., p. 414.   [315] Griffith 1978, p. 387.

source of income has been oil.[316] During the Shah's rule, between 60 and 70 per cent of the country's foreign exchange earnings stemmed from resource exports, which gave him ample financial surpluses to finance his lavish defence budget.[317] Revenues had only dipped noticeably during the Mossadeq period immediately prior to the Shah's seizure of power as a result of the British oil boycott. Following Mossadeq's overthrow, the regime benefited from a rapid rise in oil income, supporting a rapid economic recovery from 1953 until 1958.[318] Oil revenues rose from 34 million USD in 1954 to 181 million USD in 1956 and to 358 million USD in 1960.[319] In total, rent flows increased 100 times between 1953 and 1975.[320]

Summary

The juxtaposition of two rich countries at peace underlines the insignificance of abundant resources for social spending in the absence of a political incentive. Whilst the financial situation, at least since the first oil boom in the early 1970s, left both regimes with ample fiscal surpluses to distribute, social policies differed markedly as the Algerian regime was catering to a broad coalition, including lower and middle classes, whilst the Shah used his oil income to become a military hegemon in the Persian Gulf and ruthlessly repress domestic opposition.

3.2.4 Rich states at war

The Islamic Republic of Iran

The case of the Islamic Republic of Iran is unique in its combination of a severe external threat, threatening the survival of the nascent regime, and significant fiscal surpluses from exportable resources, most notably oil. It is only this combination of circumstances that enabled the regime to expand social spending and commit large sums to the protracted war effort with its neighbour, Iraq. The Islamic Republic is thus the critical case to demonstrate the crucial importance of a resource endowment in adverse geostrategic contexts.

Considering external threats first, the Islamic Republic of Iran emerged in a hugely challenging geostrategic environment. The stake was clearly regime survival as Iraq's president, Saddam Hussein, had made clear that his goal was to overthrow the nascent Iranian regime.[321] In terms of material and humanitarian costs, the 'Iran-Iraq War from 1980 until 1988 was the greatest and most costly conflict in the Modern Middle East, and one of the longest interstate wars in the 20th century'.[322] Over 600,000 people lost their lives and more than 1,000,000 Iranians and Iraqis were displaced in the course of the conflict.[323] The total costs

---

[316] Katouzian 1981, p. 113.   [317] Abrahamian 2008, p. 169.   [318] Issawi 1978, p. 153.
[319] IMF 2011; and V. Lucas and Richter 2016.   [320] Stobauch 1978, p. 248.
[321] Arnold 2009, p. 49.   [322] Halliday 2005, p. 106.   [323] S. E. Ibrahim 1998, p. 230.

of the war amounted to over 300 billion USD, of which about 100 billion incurred to Iran.[324] These costs represented an enormous financial burden on the state budget, with war-related expenditures consuming between 33 and 40 per cent of the government budget.[325]

This notwithstanding, war making left social spending largely unaffected. On the contrary, the expansion of military expenditures occurred alongside a boost in welfare spending. Whilst social spending amounted to 29 per cent of the budget when the Shah left the country, it stood at 43 per cent by the end of the Iran–Iraq War.[326] Crucially, this twin expansion was financially only possible thanks to the country's abundant resources. As Amjad points out, oil revenues 'enabled the government to fund the development plans and the distribution of welfare among the poor and victims of the war, hence securing their support'.[327] Similarly, Abrahamian remarks that a constant influx of oil rents enabled the expansion of state spending after 1979.[328]

Oil was crucial to finance this double commitment. Responding to the funding constraints imposed by the outbreak of the war, Iran significantly increased its oil production between 1981 and 1983, scaling up oil revenues from 12 billion to 20 billion USD.[329] Income levels subsequently dropped, reaching a low of 6 billion USD in 1986, yet this contraction was partly offset by the vast foreign exchange reserves—over 13 billion USD—that the the previous regime had accumulated.[330] Harris equally highlights the crucial importance of oil, suggesting that until the 1986 price crash oil had made it possible for the regime 'to sustain both "guns and butter"'.[331] Unlike other regimes in the region, Iran's foreign debt was very small,[332] which, of course, can also be imputed to the country's abundant natural resources.

In sum, the Iranian case supports the notion of resource endowment as a gateway condition for an authoritarian welfare state. While economically the costs of the war provided a strong incentive to reduce the burden of non-war-related expenditures, politically the regime had a strong incentive to cater to its lower- and middle-class constituencies by providing extensive social welfare. Without the support of oil income, this expansion of welfare would have been highly unlikely and the regime would have struggled to eschew the dilemma of 'guns or butter'.

3.3 Conclusion

This chapter has shown that divergent welfare outcomes in labour-abundant MENA regimes are a corollary of (a) different coalitional incentives, shaped by elite

---

[324] Amuzegar 1993, pp. 304–5.   [325] Bakhash 1990, p. 245.
[326] IMF 2011; and V. Lucas and Richter 2016.   [327] Amjad 1989, p. 151.
[328] Abrahamian 2008, p. 169.   [329] Kanovsky 1987, p. 242.   [330] Bakhash 1990, p. 177.
[331] K. Harris 2017, p. 113.   [332] Bakhash 1990, p. 177.

rivalries and salient communal cleavages, and (b) the geostrategic environment of these coalitions conditioned by external threats and their resource endowment. Whilst the coalitional underpinnings of these regimes provide the necessary incentives to distribute social welfare broadly, the regimes' environment crucially influences their ability to do so. Confirming the presence of the causal conditions in a way consistent with my theoretical argument, the foregoing case narratives have also provided evidence of the causal mechanism linking intra-elite conflict and communal cleavages to coalitional outcomes. Linking these coalitions, in turn, to social policies and spending will be the subject of in-depth case studies in Chapters 5 and 6. The analysis has also shown how the perception of external threats as a danger to regime survival compelled regimes to boost their defence effort, which critically affected their ability to provide social welfare. As the case of the Islamic Republic of Iran demonstrates, only abundant resources make it possible to escape a dilemma between 'butter or guns'. The analysis has furthermore yielded a number of insights that are worth pointing out.

First, intra-elite conflict and communal cleavages often had their origins in antecedent conditions that preceded the period of regime formation.[333] Regarding intra-elite conflict, personal rivalries, frequently framed in ideological terms, played an important role. Yet not least important were the contingent processes of decolonization that most countries went through. Divisions as a result of a long-lasting war, such as in Algeria, or a harsh crackdown of colonial authorities on the nationalist movement, as happened in the case of Tunisia, laid the basis for virulent intra-elite strife once the colonial powers had left. Elite cohesion, on the other hand, mainly occurred whenever elites did not have a social base outside the regime coalition and thus feared being sidelined if they defected. The salience of communal cleavages was often the outcome of ethnic discrimination carried out at the hands of colonial authorities.

Second, it is striking that the aspiring elites did not systematically represent clearly delineated constituencies at the moment of regime formation. Rather, acting strategically in a context of heightened insecurity about effective support bases, elites chose or sometimes even came to create the constituencies of their support coalition. As much as Bourguiba was not a representative of labour, Khomeini did not represent the urban proletariat when he arrived in Tehran shortly after the ouster of the Shah. In other words, social policies in all high-spending regimes were instrumental in engendering societal groups in demand of the continuation of these policies, rather than elites representing these groups in the first place.

---

[333] Slater and E. Simmons 2010, p. 889, define antecedent conditions as 'factors or conditions preceding a critical juncture that combine with causal forces during a critical juncture to produce long-term divergence in outcomes'.

Third, given the highly strategic context of (post-independence) power struggles, ideological predilections, if present among elites, were most often set aside and gave way to the more urgent imperative of building a viable support coalition. A good case in point is the Islamic Republic where the clerical core constituency of Khomeini was not particularly fond of populist redistribution, yet the necessities of his power struggle with rivalling elite groups inside the revolutionary coalition induced Khomeini to overcome these ideological impediments.

4

Social Pacts over Time

This chapter uses quantitative data to analyse social spending in labour-rich MENA regimes between 1960 and 2005. Building on the insights of the previous chapter, it takes the explanation of divergent welfare trajectories one step further by bringing the dynamic variation of spending back into the analysis. The chapter does not seek to provide an alternative explanation of high welfare efforts in authoritarian regimes. Rather, the following analyses should be considered complementary to foregoing chapters. Mindful of Barbara Geddes' advice that it is often more persuasive to show multiple flawed tests of an argument than to aim for one perfect one,[1] the following statistical analyses set out to test observable implications of the proposed theoretical framework. If the theory were true, which patterns should we see in the variation of longitudinal spending data? This is the question this chapter sets out to answer.

The analytic shift to the dynamic aspects of welfare spending might come as a surprise given that I have argued at length that variation of spending over time has been outweighed by the persistent cross-regime differences in the MENA region. This still holds true. Alignments of societal actors and the formation of support coalitions during critical junctures gave authoritarian regimes varying incentives to provide social welfare and placed them on long-term spending trajectories that have conditioned the development of social policies in the last four decades. Yet the path-dependence of social pacts should not obliterate the marked socioeconomic changes and political challenges the region has gone through since the early 1960s. If support coalitions are as powerful a causal factor as I claim, they should have visible effects on the way different regimes deal with similar socioeconomic shocks and political events. In other words, responses to dynamic changes in the socioeconomic and political environment should be conditioned by the particular welfare trajectory of an authoritarian regime, which itself is underpinned by different types of coalition.

The chapter is divided into four sections. Section 4.1 examines whether there is a visible trade-off between social and defence spending and whether this trade-off is attenuated by the availability of abundant resource income. Section 4.2 focuses on the politics of retrenchment and analyses whether broad-based regime coalitions are less likely to carry out large social spending cuts. Section 4.3 scrutinizes

---

[1] Geddes 2003, p. 40.

Social Dictatorships: The Political Economy of the Welfare State in the Middle East and North Africa. Ferdinand Eibl, Oxford University Press (2020). © Ferdinand Eibl. DOI: 10.1093/oso/9780198834274.001.0001

how different regime coalitions deal with additional resource windfalls and to what extent these are channelled toward social welfare. Section 4.4 concludes the chapter.

4.1 'Butter or Guns': Is There a Trade-Off?

In line with the view that 'the budget [is] the skeleton of the state',[2] my theoretical argument has rested upon the assumption that political pressures and incentives will find their expression in the spending patterns of authoritarian regimes. This particularly concerns the areas of social and military spending and the interrelation between them. Whilst coalition types incentivize regimes to distribute in specific ways, external threats induce authoritarian rulers to channel resources toward national defence, and as Chapter 1 has argued, this takes precedence over counteracting incentives to maintain high levels of social spending. Only resource-abundant regimes are expected to escape this dilemma. We should therefore see a clear trade-off between 'butter or guns' in labour-abundant MENA regimes, alleviated by the presence of affluent resources.

Although its intuitive appeal might make this hypothesis look like an 'easy test', the global empirical evidence stands against it. While a number of studies have backed the idea of a defence-welfare trade-off—mostly in the context of the USA and Europe[3]—most empirical research has yielded mixed findings. Based on correlation models, Wilensky has argued that defence spending can retard but not stop welfare spending.[4] Likewise, Russet finds no association between defence and social spending in the USA between 1941 and 1979.[5] Hess and Mullan come to the same conclusion, analysing a large sample of developing countries.[6] In the MENA region, Richards and Waterbury find little empirical evidence for a negative effect of defence on welfare spending.[7] Summarizing the literature, Whitten and Williams declare that 'governments do not face a trade-off between "butter" or "guns"'.[8]

---

[2] Schumpeter 1990, p. 100.

[3] Griffin, Devine, and Wallace 1982 find a negative relationship between civilian and military spending in the post-war USA; Rasler and Thompson 1985 show that defence spending displaces other types of spending in four major powers of the Second World War (USA, UK, France, Japan); Barroso and Rodríguez 2009 provide evidence of a trade-off between welfare and defence in Spain from 1880 to 1960; J. Carter 2017 presents descriptive statistics suggesting a trade-off; M. Q. Islam 2000 implies a trade-off in the MENA region but provides no empirical evidence; and Karadam, Yildirim, and Öcal 2017 demonstrate a negative effect of military expenditures on MENA growth but not expenditures.

[4] Wilensky 1975, p. 79.   [5] Russet 1982.

[6] Hess and Mullan 1988. See also Hicks and Misra 1993; Narizny 2003; Palmer 1990; and Gupta et al. 2004.

[7] Richards and Waterbury 2008, p. 350.

[8] Whitten and Williams 2011, p. 117. Evidence of a positive effect of defence spending on welfare and growth is also weak. See Hooker and Knetter 2001; and Mintz and Stevenson 1995; but see Best and Connolly 1982 for supporting evidence.

At a theoretical level, the idea of a trade-off is also challenged by the state formation literature, which suggests—following Tilly's assertion that 'wars make states'[9]—that war making can entail a substantial growth and expansion of the state apparatus. In consequence, the additional need for revenue could be counterbalanced by the state's increased capacity to collect taxes, and Thies has shown that such an effect can be found outside the context of advanced industrialized economies.[10] In the Middle East, however, this state-building effect has arguably been undermined by (i) the prevalence of conventional warfare financed, to a large extent, through externally derived resources;[11] (ii) the interference of external powers, which has prevented the emergence of regional hegemons;[12] and (iii) the fact that wars in the region have been severe, chronic, and more frequent than elsewhere.[13]

Thus, although warfare is not expected to entail heightened income from improved tax collection, the presence of a clear displacement effect of military on welfare spending cannot be taken for granted in light of the literature. The following two hypotheses are therefore serious tests of the theoretical assumption underlying my argument:

H1a: All else being equal, increases in defence spending should entail lower social spending.

H1b: This trade-off should be attenuated by the presence of fiscal surpluses from natural resource exports.

4.1.1 Empirical analysis

Data and variables

To measure a regime's level of welfare spending, two main indicators are used.[14] *Welfare/GDP* measures welfare spending as a share of the country's GDP. *Welfare p.c. (log)* represents the logged per capita value of welfare spending in constant 2005 USD, adjusted for purchasing power.[15] Welfare spending comprises both current and capital expenditures in the following areas: education, health, housing, and social protection.[16] While the former measure captures the weight of a regime's welfare effort in the national economy, the latter indicator gives a more accurate impression of a regime's welfare output as received by the population. Since the above-mentioned hypotheses focus on a trade-off between two major

---

[9] Tilly 1985. In the European context, see also Rasler and Thompson 1985; and Ertman 1997.
[10] Thies 2004.   [11] Gongora 1997.   [12] Lustick 1997.   [13] Lu and Thies 2012.
[14] Table 2 in Appendix B provides a descriptive summary of the main variables.
[15] The variable is constructed by dividing the total welfare expenditures in local currency units (LCUs) by the nominal GDP in LCUs. This ratio is then multiplied by GDP per capita values taken from Heston, Summers, and Aten 2006.
[16] The latter item includes social assistance programmes and subsidies to social security programmes.

portfolios in the state budget, I also employ a third indicator in this section, *Welfare/budget*, which measures welfare spending as a share of the government's total expenditures.

As stated in Chapter 1, extending the available spending data back in time has been a particular concern of this study. To do so, the underlying data for the dependent variable are taken from two different sources, which, combined, yield a complete time series from 1960 until 2005.[17] Data from 1972 onwards are taken from the functional classification of the IMF Government Finance Statistics (GFS),[18] which has been a widely used data source in the comparative political economy literature. Earlier spending figures are taken from a new dataset on Global State Revenues and Expenditures (GSRE) in developing countries.[19] In contrast to the GFS, which is based on an annual survey sent to IMF member states, the GSRE is based on spending and revenue data from historical documents of the IMF, available in the IMF's archives in Washington, DC. Using statistics from the annual reports of the IMF's regional departments, the GSRE offers time-series data usually available from the year of a country's membership in the IMF.[20]

It is important to note that the statistical data contained in the annual reports are collected independently of the IMF's statistical department, which produces the GFS. This has potential disadvantages. One of the downsides is that accounting standards might vary between different regional departments, which could lead to cross-country inconsistencies in the measures. However, as all data used in this chapter are taken from the same regional department (Middle East and North Africa), the GSRE data should be free of cross-country distortions. Moreover, when correlated with the GFS data, the coefficients are generally very high across different measures of social spending.[21] Considering the increased analytical leverage from a decade of additional spending data, combining both sources in one time-series panel seems justifiable.

Regarding the right-hand side of the equation, two explanatory variables are of particular interest in this section. *Defence/GDP*, *Defence p.c. (log)*, and *Defence/budget* measure a regime's defence effort in a given country-year. To capture potential displacement effects between defence and welfare spending, all three variables match the unit of measurement of the dependent variable.[22] Data are taken from the combined GSRE and GFS. *Rents p.c. (log)* measure the level

---

[17] Regimes emerging after 1960 (e.g. Syria, Algeria) enter the regression from their moment of formation.

[18] IMF 2011.

[19] V. Lucas and Richter 2016. A small number of remaining missing values for individual country-years were taken from statistical yearbooks. See data note in Appendix A.

[20] The historical IMF documents were made available to researchers in the early 2000s, with the most recent documents being declassified after a period of five years.

[21] Correlation is between 0.8 and 0.9.

[22] Per capita values are derived in the same manner as described above for welfare spending.

of available income from oil and gas exports in 2009 USD per capita.[23] Using a per capita measure is preferable to measuring resource income as a share of a country's GDP or share of exports, because all of these measures are an expression of a country's resource dependence, rather than resource abundance.

As regards control variables, I seek to strike a balance between meeting the standards of the welfare state literature and employing measures that are available for the entire time period. The latter point is crucial as the effort to collect additional spending data would be undone if combined with data for much shorter time periods. All of the following controls—or a subset of these—are available from 1960 and will be used throughout this chapter. Regarding socioeconomic variables, the welfare state literature has highlighted a number of potential confounders affecting the level of a country's welfare spending. Following a 'logic of industrialism',[24] welfare spending could reflect the variation in a country's GDP per capita. The underlying logic is essentially needs-driven and assumes that with increasing wealth new needs for social protection emerge, and that citizens articulate these needs vis-à-vis a responsive government.[25] Another mechanism through which GDP per capita can affect social spending is Wagner's Law, which postulates that state spending increases with rising levels of wealth.[26] The variable *GDP p.c. (log)* captures both of these effects. Data for this variables are taken from the Penn World Tables.[27] Demand for social protection could also be driven by the share of the dependent population[28] and urbanization, which is associated with emerging middle classes, industrialization, and labour activity.[29] The variables *Dependency* and *Urbanisation*, taken from the World Bank,[30] control for these effects.

Considering the effects of globalization, quite some ink has been spilled on the potential effect of trade on social spending. Two causal stories, one based on compensation, the other on efficiency gains, have been put forward.[31] The compensation hypothesis argues that workers will demand heightened social protection in return for the increasing demands of competitiveness in an open economy.[32] In contrast, the efficiency hypothesis argues that welfare spending

---

[23] Ross 2013.

[24] C. Kerr 1964. See also Wilensky 1975; Lindert 1994; and Obinger and Wagschal 2010. For contrary evidence, see, amongst others, Flora and Alber 1981; Baqir 2002; and Huber and J. D. Stephens 2001; and Loewe 2010 for the MENA region.

[25] Myles 1984.   [26] Wagner 1883.   [27] Heston, Summers, and Aten 2006.

[28] This designates people younger than fourteen and older than sixty-five years.

[29] On dependency, see Wilensky 1975; D. S. Brown and Hunter 1999; and Rudra 2002. Gandhi 2008 finds no effect of dependency in a sample of autocracies. On urbanization, see Avelino, D. S. Brown, and Hunter 2005.

[30] World Bank 2017.

[31] This distinction is made by Garrett 2001. Using formal modelling, Adserà and Boix 2002 argue that both outcomes are possible depending on domestic political dynamics.

[32] See, for instance, Cameron 1978; Katzenstein 1985; and Rodrik 1998. Avelino, D. S. Brown, and Hunter 2005 provide supportive evidence in the context of Latin American economies. Nooruddin and J. W. Simmons 2009 find a compensation effect in the case of democracies. Rudra 2004 provides corroborating findings comparing developed and developing countries.

will come under pressure as a result of increased pressures from a competitive, globalized economy.[33] While this study is agnostic with regard to the direction of the effect, the importance of trade openness is recognized by including a variable *Trade* in the regression, measuring the sum of imports and exports as a share of a country's GDP. The Penn World Tables provide these data.[34] As social spending can also be affected by cyclical shocks in the pattern of imports and exports, which frequently entail liquidity problems,[35] I control for a country's *Current account balance*, with data provided by the World Bank.[36] A final set of socioeconomic variables controls for resource constraints.[37] Potentially alleviating financial constraints, *Foreign aid p.c. (log)* measures the amount of foreign aid per capita accrued to a regime using data from the World Bank.[38]

Alongside socioeconomic variables, the literature has also pointed to important political determinants of social spending. *Polity* captures a regime's level of democracy: more specifically, the degree to which the executive is subject to political control. The data source is Marshall and Jaggers.[39] In view of the literature, higher levels of democracy are expected to be associated with higher levels of social spending.[40] The binary variable *IMF* indicates whether a regime is carrying out an IMF adjustment programme in a given country-year. Frequently associated with prescriptive spending cuts, IMF programmes are expected to have a negative impact on welfare spending.[41] The data are taken from Vreeland, updated by Dreher and Gassebner.[42]

This list of control variables is far from exhaustive. While a number of additional variables are tested in robustness tests later on, other common controls are omitted on purpose. An indicator measuring the strength of labour[43] is excluded because labour has been found to be rather subdued in authoritarian contexts[44] and good indicators are hard to come by.[45] The non-democratic context in combination

---

[33] See, for instance, Wibbels 2006. Kaufman and Segura-Ubiergo 2001 and Segura-Ubiergo 2007 find a negative effect of trade openness on social spending in the context of Latin America. Rudra and Haggard 2005 provide evidence for an efficiency effect in the case of autocracies, whilst Gandhi 2008 finds no such effect.

[34] Heston, Summers, and Aten 2006.   [35] Nooruddin and J. W. Simmons 2009.

[36] World Bank 2017.

[37] Kaufman and Segura-Ubiergo 2001; and Segura-Ubiergo 2007 emphasize the importance of fiscal constraints.

[38] World Bank 2017.

[39] M. G. Marshall and Jaggers 2010.

[40] See, for instance, Haggard and Kaufman 2008.   [41] Nooruddin and J. W. Simmons 2006.

[42] J. R. Vreeland 2003; and Dreher and Gassebner 2012.

[43] On labour and the welfare state, see, amongst others, J. D. Stephens 1979; Esping-Andersen 1990; Hicks 1999; Hicks and Misra 1993; Hicks, Misra, and Ng 1995; Korpi 1974, 1983, 1985; Korpi, O'Connor and Olsen 1998; and Huber and J. D. Stephens 2001.

[44] Kim and Gandhi 2010.

[45] As a result of, oftentimes coercive, state corporatism, unionization rates do not adequately reflect the strength of labour. Alternative indicators, such as developed by Rudra 2002, overemphasize the importance of structural variables and fail to provide data for all regimes analysed in this study.

with bad data also leads me to exclude measures of unemployment,[46] inequality and poverty,[47] institutional veto players,[48] and different electoral systems and party affiliations.[49] Colonial legacies are time-invariant and thus captured by fixed effects.[50] Development strategies[51] are not controlled for because (i) they have historically been relatively similar across the region, relying on state-led growth and some form of import substitution;[52] (ii) development strategies affect the type of welfare spending, rather than its level; (iii) varying levels of openness associated with different development strategies are captured by the *Trade* variable. For similar reasons, the specific skills distribution within a regime is also not included.[53]

Estimation strategy and model

To estimate the potential trade-off between defence and welfare spending, I use an error correction model (ECM) with the following functional form:

$$\Delta Y_{it} = \alpha_0 + \alpha_1 Y_{it-1} + \beta_0 \Delta \text{ Defence spending} + \beta_1 \text{ Defence spending}_{t-1} \\ + \beta_2 \Delta X_{it} + \beta_3 X_{t-1} + N_i + \varepsilon_{it},$$

where ΔY_{it} represents the change in social spending, α_0 is a constant, Y_{it-1} is the one-period lag of the dependent variable, ΔX_{it} is a vector of first-differenced control variables, X_{t-1} is a vector of lagged controls, N_i are regime fixed effects, and ε_{it} represents the error term. As unobserved heterogeneity is assumed to exist between regimes in addition to heterogeneity across countries, regime fixed effects are used instead of the more common country fixed effects. ECM models have a great number of advantages: they describe a general equilibrium model in its most general form without imposing any model restrictions; they allow conveniently for the estimation of short-run and long-run effects of X on Y; and they are robust to potential problems of integrated time series.[54]

With added regime fixed effects, the model is conservative and focuses on the variation within each regime.[55] Having the lag of the dependent variable on the right-hand side purges the model of serial correlation.[56] Any remaining serial correlation is addressed using Driscoll–Kraay standard errors with a Newey West adjustment and a one-order lag length. Such standard errors are robust to general forms of spatial and temporal heteroskedasticity and contemporaneous

---

[46] On social spending and unemployment, see, for instance, Huber and J. D. Stephens 2001.
[47] See, for example, Moene and Wallerstein 2001.
[48] On veto players and welfare states, see Immergut 2010; and Huber, Ragin, and J. D. Stephens 1993.
[49] See, for example, Persson and Tabellini 2000; and Kaufman and Segura-Ubiergo 2001.
[50] See the following subsection. On colonial legacy and social welfare, see Barbone and Sanchez 1999; Flora and Alber 1981; and Bailey 2004.
[51] On the link between development strategies and the welfare state, see Frazier 2006; Wibbels and Ahlquist 2011; and Haggard and Kaufman 2008.
[52] Richards and Waterbury 2008, ch. 7.
[53] On skill formation and the welfare state, see Hall and Soskice 2001; and Iversen 2005.
[54] De Boef and Keele 2008; and N. L. Beck and Katz 2011.
[55] A Hausman test suggests the use of fixed effects.
[56] An Arellano—Bond test indicates that there is no remaining serial correlation of a higher order.

correlation.[57] The regression is estimated using ordinary least squares (OLS). I am aware that autoregressive models combined with unit fixed effects make the parameter estimates liable to bias.[58] However, given an average length of thirty-seven years per time series, the bias becomes very small ($\frac{1}{37} \approx 3\%$) and alternative estimators have been found to perform worse in the presence of long time series.[59]

Main findings

Assessing the existence of a trade-off between welfare and defence spending, Table 4.1 presents the results for hypothesis H1a. Each column represents one of the three measurements of social spending: that is, social spending as a share of the budget, as a share of GDP, and on a per capita level. Substantively, the results suggest that there is a significant displacement effect of defence spending on social welfare, operating through the long-run effect of defence spending as indicated by the significant coefficients for $Defence_{t-1}$.

Considering column (1), a one percentage point increase in defence spending has no instantaneous effect but a significant long-run effect on social spending, amounting to roughly a 0.5 per cent reduction (see Figure 4.1(a)). To underpin this with a historical example, when Egypt increased the share of defence spending in the budget from 16 to 50 per cent between 1960 and 1970, the model predicts this to be accompanied by a drop of social spending by 17 percentage points.[60] Nearly half of this effect unfolds in the first two years after defence spending is increased, with 75 per cent of the effect having dissipated after four years (see Figure 4.1(b)). The effect is similar for social spending measured as a percentage of GDP (column (2); Figure 4.2) and per capita (column (3); Figure 4.3). While the long-run effect in column (2) is only significant at the 90 per cent level, the effects on social spending per capita are highly significant—suggesting a clear 'butter or guns' trade-off.

This trade-off seems to be attenuated, however, by surpluses from natural resource exports. The presence of such a counter-effect is shown in Table 4.2. The models presented are identical to Table 4.1 below, with the exception that they now include an interaction term between defence spending and the measure of resource abundance, *Rents p.c. (log)*.[61] Following Warner,[62] the model equation includes interaction between differences, levels, and levels and differences of *Rents p.c. (log)* and *Defence spending*. As the effect of these complex interaction terms is only poorly visible by assessing the statistical significance of the constituent terms,[63] I immediately turn to the graphical illustration of the model in Figure 4.4.

[57] Panel-specific heteroskedasticity was detected using a modified Wald test.   [58] Nickell 1981.
[59] N. L. Beck and Katz 2011.
[60] The actual fall in Egypt was slightly lower, about 11 percentage points.
[61] Due to space constraints, the coefficients for the political variables, *Polity* and *IMF*, are omitted.
[62] Warner 2016.
[63] Brambor, Roberts Clark, and Golder 2005, p. 70 point out that the overall effect can be statistically significant for some values of the modifying variable even if all constituent terms are statistically insignificant.

Table 4.1 Trade-off between welfare and defence spending

	(1) Welfare/budget	(2) Welfare/GDP	(3) Welfare p.c. (log)
Welfare spending$_{t-1}$	−0.390***	−0.482***	−0.363***
	(0.045)	(0.071)	(0.044)
Δ Defence spending	0.004	−0.024	0.085
	(0.053)	(0.053)	(0.063)
Defence spending$_{t-1}$	−0.184***	−0.057	−0.056**
	(0.048)	(0.037)	(0.024)
Δ Rents p.c. (log)	−0.251	0.021	−0.014
	(0.694)	(0.186)	(0.018)
Rents p.c. (log)$_{t-1}$	−0.336	0.157	0.014
	(0.277)	(0.102)	(0.009)
Δ GDP p.c. (log)	−4.410	−1.790**	0.769***
	(3.890)	(0.857)	(0.116)
GDP p.c. (log)$_{t-1}$	−0.226	−0.134	0.430***
	(1.711)	(0.488)	(0.072)
Δ Foreign aid p.c. (log)	0.074	0.082	0.006
	(0.257)	(0.069)	(0.009)
Foreign aid p.c. (log)$_{t-1}$	0.494	0.092	0.014
	(0.348)	(0.080)	(0.010)
Δ Dependency	−0.895	−0.656**	−0.080***
	(1.174)	(0.323)	(0.030)
Dependency$_{t-1}$	0.188	−0.005	−0.003
	(0.128)	(0.041)	(0.005)
Δ Urbanization	−2.949*	−0.254	−0.039
	(1.739)	(0.396)	(0.037)
Urbanization$_{t-1}$	0.042	0.062**	0.002
	(0.111)	(0.024)	(0.003)
Δ Current account balance	−0.019	−0.151***	−0.017***
	(0.074)	(0.026)	(0.003)
Current account balance$_{t-1}$	0.092	−0.110***	−0.011***
	(0.078)	(0.032)	(0.003)
Δ Polity	0.233**	0.009	0.002
	(0.109)	(0.022)	(0.004)
Polity$_{t-1}$	0.316**	0.040	−0.006
	(0.147)	(0.045)	(0.005)
Δ IMF	−0.807	−0.021	0.008
	(0.645)	(0.176)	(0.026)
IMF$_{t-1}$	−0.443	0.236	0.023
	(0.722)	(0.196)	(0.021)
Δ Trade	0.035	0.003	0.001
	(0.036)	(0.009)	(0.001)
Trade$_{t-1}$	0.029	0.015**	0.002***
	(0.027)	(0.007)	(0.001)
Regime FEs	Yes	Yes	Yes
Observations	306	304	304

Note: Error correction model with regime fixed effects and Driscoll–Kraay standard errors in parentheses. Constant and FE coefficients omitted. *$p < 0.10$, **$p < 0.05$, ***$p < 0.01$

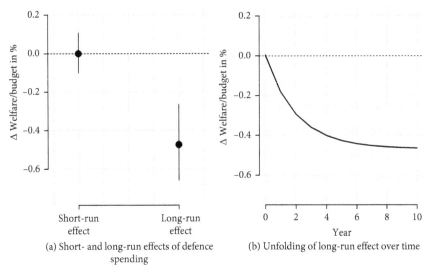

Figure 4.1 Effect of defence spending on social spending as a percentage of the budget

Note: Whiskers and shaded area indicates 95-percent confidence bounds.

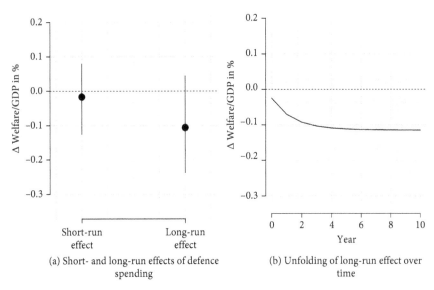

Figure 4.2 Effect of defence spending on social spending as a percentage of GDP

Note: Whiskers and shaded area indicates 95-percent confidence bounds.

Based on column (1) in Table 4.2, the graphs illustrate the short-run (Figure 4.4(a)) and long-run (Figure 4.4(b)) effects of defence spending on welfare for varying levels of resource rents. As before, defence spending has no instantaneous effect on social spending regardless of rents, as illustrated by the overlapping confidence bounds with the zero line in Figure 4.4(a). The long-run

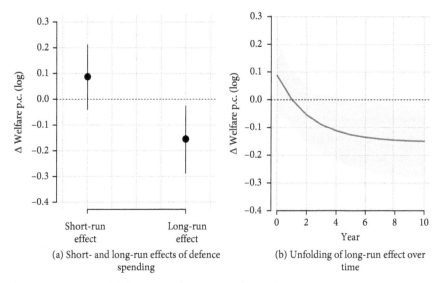

Figure 4.3 Effect of defence spending on social spending per capita
Note: Whiskers and shaded area indicates 95-percent confidence bounds.

effect, however, is significant and even stronger now that resource rents are taken into account. As Figure 4.4(b) shows, in regimes without any oil or gas rents, one percentage-point increase in defence spending reduces social spending by about 0.65 percentage points on average. Importantly, this effect gradually weakens the higher the levels of resource rents available to the regime until it finally becomes insignificant above rent levels of log 6.25. This corresponds to about 520 USD per capita in resource rents—levels comfortably reached by the resource-abundant regimes in my sample. The picture is similar when using *Welfare p.c. (log)* as the main indicator (Figure 4.6). In fact, using this indicator it seems that defence spending in resource-abundant regimes is accompanied by a significant *positive* effect on welfare in the short term (Figure 4.6(a)) and a *positive* average, albeit insignificant, long-term effect (Figure 4.6(b)). As before, the findings for *Welfare/GDP* are weaker and do not clearly support H1b (Figure 4.5). This notwithstanding, the results suggest that resource-abundant MENA regimes can engage in both welfare and warfare without facing significant trade-offs.

Robustness tests

To ascertain the robustness of my findings, I conduct a number of additional tests, the results of which are detailed in Appendix B. For hypothesis H1a, I test the sensitivity of the results to alternative or additional control variables. More specifically, I replace the variable *Trade* by two alternative measures of *Trade openness* and *Capital account openness*, taken from the CACAO dataset.[64] Both

---

[64] Martin 2005.

Table 4.2 Welfare, defence, and resource endowment

	(1) Welfare/budget	(2) Welfare/GDP	(3) Welfare p.c. (log)
Welfare spending$_{t-1}$	−0.403***	−0.489***	−0.392***
	(0.045)	(0.069)	(0.044)
Δ Defence spending	−0.006	0.032	−0.060
	(0.079)	(0.079)	(0.111)
Defence spending$_{t-1}$	−0.261***	−0.035	−0.138***
	(0.069)	(0.056)	(0.038)
Δ Rents p.c. (log)	0.197	0.169	0.067
	(1.290)	(0.438)	(0.088)
Rents p.c. (log)$_{t-1}$	−0.815***	0.204*	−0.090**
	(0.303)	(0.124)	(0.037)
Δ Defence spending*	0.008	−0.007	0.034
Rents p.c. (log)$_{t-1}$	(0.025)	(0.006)	(0.023)
Δ Rents p.c. (log)*	−0.021	−0.007	−0.016
Δ Defence spending	(0.048)	(0.016)	(0.018)
Δ Rents p.c. (log)*	−0.180*	−0.018	−0.073
Defence spending$_{t-1}$	(0.106)	(0.030)	(0.103)
Rents p.c. (log)$^*_{t-1}$	0.022*	−0.003	0.021***
Defence spending$_{t-1}$	(0.013)	(0.004)	(0.007)
Regime FEs	Yes	Yes	Yes
Standard controls	Yes	Yes	Yes
Observations	306	304	304

Note: Error correction model with regime fixed effects and Driscoll–Kraay standard errors in parentheses. Constant and FE coefficients omitted. *$p < 0.10$, **$p < 0.05$, ***$p < 0.01$

measures indicate the level of trade and capital restrictions on an ordinal scale ranging from 1 to 7 and 1 to 5 respectively. Secondly, I use an additional indicator for financial constraints, namely *Tax/GDP* taken from the combined GFS and GSRE datasets.[65] Finally, I add the variable *Output gap* which measures a country's deviation from its long-term growth pattern and unexpected economic shocks. The variable was constructed by applying a Hodrick—Prescott filter. I also test the sensitivity of the baseline model to using alternative Beck—Katz panel-corrected standard errors.[66] With regard to H1b, I use the variable *Resources p.c. (log)* as an alternative indicator for resource rents. Compiled by Haber and Menaldo,[67] the data capture resource income from *all* exportable resources, not simply oil and gas. This is relevant as some MENA countries have significant non-oil primary

[65] IMF 2011; and V. Lucas and Richter 2016.   [66] N. L. Beck and Katz 1995.
[67] Haber and Menaldo 2011.

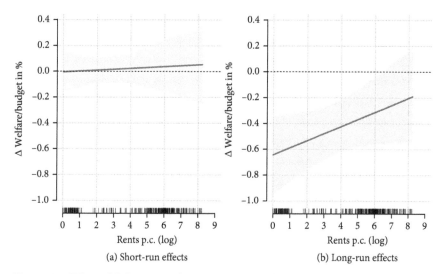

Figure 4.4 Effect of defence spending on social spending as a percentage of the budget by resource abundance

Note: Shaded area indicates 95 per cent confidence bounds.

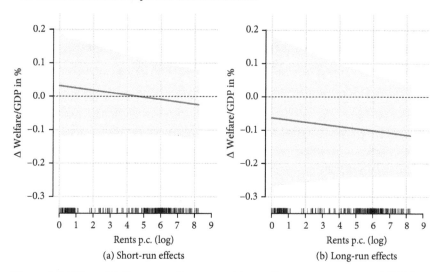

Figure 4.5 Effect of defence spending on social spending as a percentage of GDP by resource abundance

Note: Shaded area indicates 95 per cent confidence bounds.

commodities to export, such as phosphate. In addition, I probe the robustness of my findings to using the alternative Beck—Katz standard errors.[68] None of these tests alters the substantive findings of this section.

---

[68] The findings for H1b are robust to adding further control variables, such *Output gap* or *Tax/GDP*. Results are available upon request.

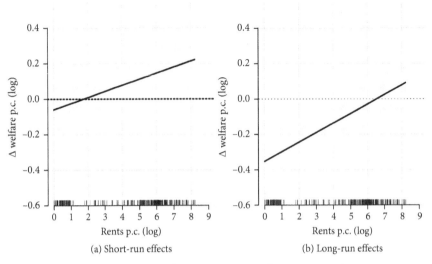

Figure 4.6 Effect of defence spending on social spending per capita by resource abundance

Note: Shaded area indicates 95 per cent confidence bounds.

4.2 Protecting Coalitions: Welfare Retrenchment across Coalition Types

In labour-abundant MENA regimes, the political incentives emanating from broad-based authoritarian support coalitions led to an expansion of welfare spending that, typically within the decade after the regime's formation and geostrategic circumstances permitting, set them apart from their narrow, elite-based counterparts. This expansion happened in a supportive geo-economic environment of post-Second World War reconstruction, low interest rates, and strong global growth rates. From the mid-1980s, the economic conditions of labour-abundant MENA economies worsened as state-led development strategies of all regimes came under pressure from a worsening macroeconomic outlook, coupled with rising unemployment, heightened fiscal constraints, and liquidity crises. This compelled all regimes to carry out economic adjustment policies which challenged domestic patterns of resource distribution and, thereby, the very foundation of the underlying coalitional structure. The predominant narrative in the MENA literature holds that this process ushered in a phase of post-populist authoritarianism in which all regimes retreated from their welfare responsibilities.[69]

---

[69] Hinnebusch 2006, p. 385. See also Bozarslan 2011; Hinnebusch 2010; and King 2010.

This general claim does not withstand empirical scrutiny. Looking at the end result of the process, social spending levels in the mid-2000s stood at levels similar to the heyday of the so-called populist era.[70] This is remarkable as, arguably, pressures to tighten budget constraints were even higher for high-spenders than for low-spenders. The reason why high-spenders avoided major welfare retrenchment lies, again, in the underpinning coalitional structure. As the literature on institutions teaches us, coalitions, as expressions of specific constellations of political power, will create institutions that maintain their power.[71] Thus 'storing' their power resources in institutions,[72] coalitions 'favor the reproduction of the political and allocational regime'.[73] Therefore, coalitions not only offer advantages to those included in times of spending expansion, they also offer better protection in times of spending compression.[74] In other words, coalitions regulate the distribution *and the protection* of power, and thus 'mediate how economic interests translate into adjustment policies'.[75]

As coalitional structures create positive feedback effects for those included,[76] the costs of switching coalitions and altering the patterns of domestic resource allocation become higher the longer coalitions are in power.[77] Lacking an institutionalized mechanism of coalition (re-)formation such as exists in democracies, the pillars of a support coalition are thus more difficult to substitute for autocratic rulers.[78] Moreover, welfare states have a tendency to create their own constituencies beyond their initial group of supporters as groups in society that were not initially targeted come to benefit from extensive, often universal social policies.[79] Given that all labour-abundant regimes were exposed to similar economic pressures to adjust, the varying protective power of different coalitional structures should be traceable in the patterns of social spending cuts over time. I thus advance the following hypothesis 2:

H2: The longer broad-based coalitions are in power, the less likely major welfare retrenchments become.

4.2.1 Empirical analysis

Identifying periods of retrenchment
While the welfare state literature has argued that the politics of retrenchment is a distinctive process,[80] there is no definitive conceptualization of what exactly constitutes a period of welfare retrenchment. Apart from case studies, comparative

---

[70] IMF 2011; and V. Lucas and Richter 2016.   [71] Ikenberry 1994; and Knight 1992.
[72] Korpi 1985.   [73] Pepinsky 2008a, p. 450.   [74] T. Cook 2002, p. 26.
[75] Pepinsky 2009, p. 9.   [76] Ritchie 2010, p. 18.   [77] Pepinsky 2009, p. 17.
[78] Martin 2005, p. 29.   [79] Pierson 1994, p. 2; and Thelen 2003, p. 216.   [80] Pierson 1994.

quantitative analyses of welfare cutbacks have pointed to a number of important challenges when identifying periods of retrenchment.[81] First, periods of retrenchment must be distinguished from momentary fluctuations in spending levels as a result of economic downturns in the business cycle or structural socioeconomic changes. The former point is mostly relevant for nations with extensive unemployment insurance which entails a countercyclical movement of social spending levels in periods of rising unemployment. More relevant in the context of developing nations are changes in the demographic structure, such as the maturation of the age pyramid, which are associated with declining demands for certain types of social spending. For instance, having pushed for full primary enrolment following independence, developing countries can reduce education spending at later stages without palpable side-effects for the population. The latter point is related to the second dimension of retrenchment, which is noticeability. For retrenchment to be a political process involving conflict and divergent interests, it must have an effect on, at least parts of, the population. In other words, retrenchment must be doubly painful, for politicians and the population alike.

Taking these two dimensions into account, I closely follow the coding proposed by Hicks and Zorn[82] and conceptualize welfare retrenchment as a combination of sustained and substantial cuts in per capita welfare spending. As per capita measures best capture the effect of spending as felt by the population, it is preferable to operationalizing retrenchments based on contractions in welfare effort (spending as share of GDP or the budget).[83] I use the following formula to identify periods of retrenchment:

$$\frac{\text{Social per capita spending}_{it+k} - \text{Social per capita spending}_{it}}{\text{Social per capita spending}_{it}} < c,$$

where k denotes the duration of the decline and c indicates the cut-off point below which a cutback is coded as retrenchment. Thus, larger values of k indicate more sustained periods of retrenchment, while larger values of c correspond to deeper spending cuts. Based on the variation in their spending data, Hicks and Zorn propose to focus on values of $k = 2$ and $k = 3$, and choose values of c between -0.04 and -0.06.[84] When examining all cut-backs in per capita welfare spending in my own data, it turns out that in labour-abundant MENA regimes spending cuts are rather deep whenever they occur. Considering spending cuts

[81] Three papers have studied welfare retrenchment using statistical tests, all of them exclusively in an OECD context. Korpi and Palme 2003 examine retrenchment between 1975 and 95 in eighteen OECD countries. Hicks and Zorn 2005 look at retrenchment periods from 1978 to 1994 in all OECD countries. Fernández 2012 studies retrenchments in pension policies in nineteen OECD countries from 1981 until 2004.

[82] Hicks and Zorn 2005, pp. 641–4.

[83] More refined data, such as net replacement rates used by Korpi and Palme 2003, are unfortunately not available.

[84] Hicks and Zorn 2005, p. 642.

Table 4.3 Incidences of welfare retrenchment in labour-abundant MENA regimes

Regime	Years	Event type
Algeria	1988–90	sustained retrenchment
	1995–6	retrenchment
	2004–5	retrenchment
Egypt	1961–2	retrenchment
	1973–4	retrenchment
	1977–8	retrenchment
	1995–7	sustained retrenchment
Shah Regime	1965–6	retrenchment
Islamic Republic of Iran	1980–1	retrenchment
	1984–7	sustained retrenchment
Jordan	1965–6	retrenchment
	1983–5	sustained retrenchment
	1989–92	sustained retrenchment
Morocco	1969–70	retrenchment
	1983–5	sustained retrenchment
	1995–7	sustained retrenchment
Syria	1977–8	retrenchment
	1984–90	sustained retrenchment
	2003–4	retrenchment
Tunisia	1972–3	retrenchment
	1987–8	retrenchment

occurring for a minimum of two subsequent years, reductions all exceeded 10 per cent, averaging 28 per cent for each retrenchment period. More interesting variation can be found with regard to the duration of spending cuts. Similar to the pattern noted by Hicks and Zorn in OECD countries, periods of retrenchment rarely exceeded three subsequent years in my sample; and cutbacks in a single year seem too ephemeral to consider them retrenchment events.

In the light of this pattern, I distinguish between two types of retrenchment: *Retrenchment* denotes periods of a minimum of two subsequent years of spending cuts; *Sustained retrenchment* denotes spending cuts of at least three subsequent years. Subsequent years of cutbacks are treated as one connected retrenchment event, with the first period of spending reduction treated as the event onset. Table 4.3 gives an overview of retrenchment periods in the sample. It should be noted that the coding of sustained retrenchment corresponds more closely to periods of economic adjustment and hardship highlighted in the MENA literature.

Estimation strategy and model

I analyse the occurrence of retrenchment events using a Cox proportional hazard model. The Cox model has been used as the standard model in the literature when it comes to analysing welfare retrenchment.[85] The model takes the following form:

$$h(t) = h_0(t) \exp^{X_{it}\beta},$$

where $h_0(t)$ is the baseline hazard and X_{it} denotes a vector of, possibly time-varying, covariates that affect the baseline hazard in a multiplicative form. In contrast to parametric survival models, the Cox model has the advantage that the overall shape of the hazard rate does not have to be specified prior to the analysis. This comes with the drawback that expected absolute durations cannot be modelled because the model only uses the partial likelihood function. The Cox model can thus only indicate relative changes in the likelihood of an event, rather than estimating the absolute probability of its occurrence.

As periods of retrenchment can occur multiple times within a country and prior periods of retrenchment are likely to have an impact on the probability of subsequent retrenchment, I use a stratified Cox model that estimates a separate baseline hazard for each event.[86] However, as stratification strains the degrees of freedom and reduces the number of possible control variables, I also report results without stratification. As the probability of an event might be heterogeneous across cross-sectional units—that is, regimes in my case—frailty models have been proposed to account for unobserved heterogeneity.[87] However, akin to conventional random effects regressions, these models require a certain minimum of cross-sectional units, which my sample of eight regimes unfortunately does not provide. Finally, it should be noted that all standard errors are robust and clustered by regime.

Data and variables

The key explanatory variable in this section is a count variable called *Broad coalition duration*, which accounts for each year a regime has been based on a broad-based support coalition. In the case of narrow coalitions, the variable takes the value of 0. Note that broad regime coalitions are not limited to authoritarian welfare states, but denote all regimes that have experienced initial intra-elite conflict in the absence of salient intra-communal cleavages.[88] Whilst not all broad-coalition regimes become high-spenders, it is still plausible to assume that, given their support base, they will seek to shield social spending from major cutbacks, regardless of the specific spending level.

As for control variables, limited degrees of freedom as a result of stratification allow only for the inclusion of a subset of the standard controls. Selection was based on theoretical grounds and considerations of model fit. If not stated otherwise, sources and coding of the variables are identical to the previous model. Adding *Output gap* to the regression, I control for positive and negative shocks from

[85] See Korpi and Palme 2003; Hicks and Zorn 2005; and Fernández 2012.
[86] Box-Steffensmeier and Zorn 2002.   [87] Box-Steffensmeier, De Boef, and Joyce 2007.
[88] These are Algeria, Egypt, the Islamic Republic of Iran, and Tunisia.

the long-term growth pattern of a regime. Taking into account both trend and deviations from it, the variable is better suited to capture the volatility of the macroeconomic environment than growth rates alone. I also add the variable *Debt service*, taken from the World Bank,[89] which accounts for the share of a country's GDP spent on the reimbursement of foreign debt. As social spending cutbacks have often been prescribed by the IMF, I also include the *IMF* dummy in the equation. Externally derived resources might also provide considerable respite in moments of financial pressure. I therefore include the variables *Resource p.c. (log)* and *Foreign aid p.c. (log)* in the regression. Finally, I control for structural changes in the socioeconomic environment, which could alter the demand for social spending. This is done by adding *Dependency* and *Urbanization* to the regression.

In the non-stratified model, I include a number of additional controls. *Defence spending*, measured on a logged per capita basis, accounts for potential effects of the external threat environment mediated through the defence budget. *Debt service* and *Current account balance* account for financial constraints stemming from the external economic environment. And considering potential efficiency pressures from increased openness to the world market, I also include *Trade* in the extended set of control variables.

Main findings

Table 4.4 presents the estimation results. Columns (1) and (2) report the coefficient for *Retrenchment* as dependent variable; columns (3) and (4) contain the results for *Sustained Retrenchment*. Positive coefficients increase the hazard rate and, by consequence, make retrenchment more likely. Conversely, negative coefficients can be be understood to decrease the likelihood of retrenchment. The results provide at least partial support for hypothesis H2. When periods of retrenchment and sustained retrenchment are combined in one dependent variable, the duration of a broad coalition does not seem to have an effect on the risk of retrenchment. In other words, broad coalitions fail to protect their support base from temporally more confined, yet possibly painful, periods of social spending cuts. However, broad coalitions appear to provide a powerful protection of social spending against longer, more sustained periods of spending adjustment. In both columns (3) and (4), the coefficient of *Broad coalition duration* is highly statistically signif-icant, meaning that every additional year under a broad coalition reduces the risk of major retrenchments.

As before, the substantive implications of the model are best explored graphi-cally. Figure 4.7 displays the percentage change of the risk of retrenchment asso-ciated with one more year under a broad coalition. To keep the number of graphs manageable, I use the stratified model only. The graph using the non-stratified

---

[89] World Bank 2017.

Table 4.4 Coalition type and welfare retrenchment

	(1) Retr.	(2) Retr.	(3) Sustained Retr.	(4) Sustained Retr.
Broad coalition duration	−0.00631	−0.00640	−0.114**	−0.221***
	(0.0162)	(0.0258)	(0.0473)	(0.0723)
Defence spending	0.959		1.178*	
	(0.845)		(0.657)	
Rents p.c. (log)	0.124	0.0292	−0.148*	−0.140
	(0.107)	(0.105)	(0.0843)	(0.286)
Dependency	0.0191	−0.0952	0.481	0.727*
	(0.101)	(0.107)	(0.328)	(0.395)
Urbanization	−0.0392	0.00293	0.187*	0.113**
	(0.0345)	(0.0340)	(0.100)	(0.0538)
Trade	−0.00171		−0.0582**	
	(0.0105)		(0.0256)	
Current account balance	−0.0238		−0.00360	
	(0.0355)		(0.116)	
Output gap	−5.782	−2.701	−3.530	−15.78**
	(4.214)	(2.646)	(2.419)	(7.330)
Debt service	0.0320		0.237***	
	(0.0520)		(0.0595)	
Foreign aid p.c. (log)	0.0942	0.0845	−1.362***	−1.001*
	(0.282)	(0.220)	(0.337)	(0.525)
IMF	1.232**	1.265**	1.046	2.998**
	(0.537)	(0.538)	(1.138)	(1.278)
Observations	296	305	296	305

Note: Non-stratified Cox model in columns (1) and (3). Stratified Cox model in columns (2) and (4). Standard errors robust and clustered by regime in parentheses. $^{*}p < 0.10$, $^{**}p < 0.05$, $^{***}p < 0.01$

model differs only marginally and is shown in Appendix B. The plot suggests a rather exponential reduction of risk, in which the risk of retrenchment declines rapidly after regime formation. For example, after five years only, the model suggests that the average risk of retrenchment is reduced by over 60 per cent. On the whole, the figure highlights the importance of coalition type for retrenchment. The longer a broad-based authoritarian support coalition is in power, the lower the risk that such a regime will carry out major social spending cuts.

Diagnostic tests

To better adjudicate between both models, I carry out a number of diagnostic tests probing the underlying assumptions of the model. One of these assumptions is that covariates will have a proportional and constant effect, invariant across time (proportional hazards, PH). If this is not the case (non-proportional hazards), it could mean that certain variables only have an effect until a certain point of time or that the strength of the effect varies over time. A test of the proportional

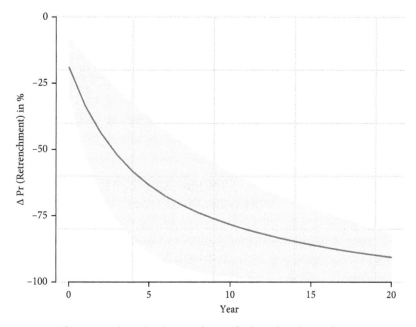

Figure 4.7 Changes in the risk of retrenchment by broad coalition duration

Note: Shaded area indicates 95 per cent confidence bounds. Graph based on the stratified model.

Table 4.5 Test of proportional hazard assumption

Variable	Prob. >χ^2 (non-stratified)	Prob. > χ^2 (stratified)
Broad coalition duration	0.5495	0.3795
Output gap	0.0288	0.4270
IMF	0.0288	0.1590
Rents p.c. (log)	0.6403	0.6080
Dependency	0.0480	0.1196
Urbanization	0.0402	0.9352
Foreign aid p.c. (log)	0.9140	0.1232
Defence spending	0.0667	
Debt service	0.0454	
Current account balance	0.0542	
Trade	0.0191	
Global test	0.4452	0.8950

hazard assumption, based on Schoenfeld residuals, is presented in Table 4.5. P-values below 0.10 indicate that the assumption is violated for a particular covariate. The comparative test shows that the results of the non-stratified model should be viewed with caution. As the risk of retrenchment seems to depend on previous retrenchment period—which is modelled by the stratification parameter—the non-stratified model results violate the PH assumption. Substantively, this corroborates my findings as the stratified model provides stronger support for hypothesis H2.

Another diagnostic test for Cox models uses the distribution of the Cox–Snell residuals. As the residuals should exhibit a unit exponential distribution, the Cox–Snell residuals can be considered a good indicator of model fit. In line with the previous test, the distribution of the residuals suggests that the stratified model more adequately fits the data.[90]

4.3 Distributing to Coalitions: Sharing Windfalls across Coalition Types

If coalitions condition the way in which resources are preserved in periods of macroeconomic readjustment, they should also have an impact on how windfalls are distributed in periods of economic expansion. The early literature on rentier states in the Middle East adopted a rather mechanistic view on this issue as oil rents were quasi-automatically associated with public policies of welfare distribution. To compensate for their lack of political legitimacy, Arab rentier states were assumed to use their resource income for the subsidization of large parts of their population.[91] This argument was extended to other forms of rents, such as strategic or locational rents,[92] which were attributed the same welfare effect as resource income.[93] More recently, the MENA literature has come to challenge this allocational determinism of rents. Yom, for instance, supports a 'revisionist' theory of rentierism that views rents as an intervening variable, the political impact of which is mediated by further conditions.[94] In the same vein, Herb points out that 'oil does not mechanically predict outcomes, even when oil arrives in similar quantities in similar situations'.[95] Comparative work outside the MENA region has also contributed to a more nuanced view of rents that pays greater attention to the interests of rulers under various political conditions.[96]

In line with the revisionist work on the rentier state, I hold that the distribution of windfalls from resources and other forms of rents critically hinges on the type of underlying authoritarian support coalition. Providing incentives to distribute either broadly or to a narrow elitist clientele, coalitions structure the political economy of resource allocation in authoritarian regimes. Given that, it can be expected

---

[90] Figures are available upon request.   [91] See Beblawi 1987; and also Schlumberger 2008b.
[92] For an overview of different types of rent, see Knowles 2005, p. 5.   [93] M. Beck 2007a.
[94] Yom 2009, p. 219. See also Peters and P. Moore 2009.
[95] Herb 2009, p. 391. For other, more nuanced approaches to rents, see Crystal 1989; Herb 1999; Richter 2007; and Hertog 2010.
[96] B. Smith 2007. See also Dunning 2008; and Richter 2012b.

that broad-based coalitions channel additional resources derived from resource windfalls toward social spending; coalitions based on a narrow constituency, by contrast, experience a lesser need for extensive side-payments and, considering their core supporters, are likely to prefer other types of spending to hand out favours and spoils. I primarily focus on windfalls from oil and gas because they are politically unconstrained: that is, they have not been levied from a group in society that expects some form of services in return. Furthermore, taking into account that patterns of distribution have a tendency to become institutionalized and create positive feedback effects for the group of beneficiaries, I expect the constraining effect of coalitions to grow over time. This finds expression in hypothesis H3:

H3: The longer broad-based coalitions are in power, the more windfalls from oil and gas should be channelled toward social spending. This should set them apart from narrow support coalitions.

4.3.1 Empirical analysis

Data, variables, and estimation strategy

I use *Welfare/GDP* as independent variable in this section as it most adequately reflects how resources are channelled to different sectors in the national economy.[97] To capture income from oil and gas, I use the same *Rents p.c. (log)* variable as in previous regressions. The variable uses data from Ross.[98] To measure the duration of support coalitions, I use a count variable *Coalition duration* which captures the duration of broad and narrow coalitions respectively. As for my control variables, I use the set of standard socioeconomic and political variables as described abvoe. Given that the effect of windfalls is expected to be contingent upon the duration of support coalitions, I employ the same ECM interaction model as in section 4.1. I run two sets of regressions interacting, respectively, the duration of broad and narrow coalition with the *Rents p.c. (log)* variable.

Main findings

Results are displayed in Table 4.6. To improve the clarity of the regression output, coefficients for all control variables are omitted from the table. As stated before, it is difficult to interpret this interaction model substantively purely by inspecting the sign and significance of the coefficients. To assess the interactive effect of both variables, I turn again to the simulation of meaningful quantities of interest, using graphical support to illustrate the findings.

---

[97] If not stated otherwise, the data sources and coding of all variables are as described in section 4.1.
[98] Ross 2013.

Table 4.6 Resource windfalls, coalition type, and welfare spending

	(1) Broad coalition	(2) Narrow coalition
Welfare spending$_{t-1}$	−0.470***	−0.462***
	(0.063)	(0.064)
Δ Rents p.c. (log)	0.128	−0.177
	(0.221)	(0.415)
Rents p.c. (log)$_{t-1}$	0.237*	0.046
	(0.126	(0.099)
Δ Coalition duration	4.320***	0.340
	(1.008)	(1.337)
Coalition duration$_{t-1}$	−0.009	−0.018
	(0.038)	(0.018)
Δ Rents p.c. (log)* Coalition duration$_{t-1}$	−0.015	0.005
	(0.022)	(0.009)
Rents p.c. (log)$^{*}_{t-1}$Δ Coalition duration	−0.358**	−0.048
	(0.145)	(0.162)
Δ Rents p.c. (log)*Δ Coalition duration	−0.087	0.218
	(0.544)	(0.504)
Rents p.c. (log)$^{*}_{t-1}$ Coalition duration$_{t-1}$	0.008	0.006
	(0.005)	(0.004)
Regime FEs	Yes	Yes
Standard controls	Yes	Yes
Observations	304	304

Note: Error correction model with regime fixed effects and Driscoll–Kraay standard errors in parentheses. The independent variable is *Welfare/GDP* in %. Constant and FE coefficients omitted. *$p < 0.10$, **$p < 0.05$, ***$p < 0.01$

This is done in Figure 4.8. The graphs depict the short- and long-run effects of resource windfalls on welfare spending at varying levels of coalition duration. Figures 4.8(a) and 4.8(b) demonstrate the effect in broad coalitions; Figures 4.8(c) and 4.8(d) show the marginal effect of resource windfalls depending on duration of narrow coalitions. Substantively, two main findings stand out. First, resource rents do not have a significant short-term effect on social spending in either broad or narrow coalitions. Second, regarding long-term effects only broad coalitions seem to convert the higher revenues from resource windfalls into increased welfare expenditures. What is more, they only seem to do so after the coalition has been in place for several years—the lower confidence bound in Figure 4.8(b) only crosses the zero line after about five years. Finally, the average effect of resource windfalls increases the length of time that broad coalitions are in place, which supports the assumption underpinning H3 that distributive commitments to broad coalitions tend to grow and become more constraining over time.

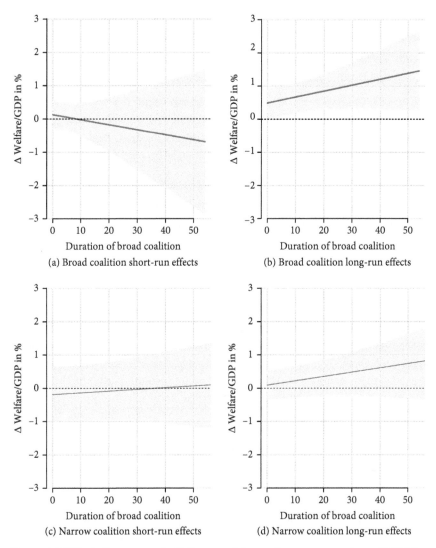

Figure 4.8 Effect of resource windfalls on social spending as a percentage of GDP by coalition type and duration

Note: Shaded area indicates 95-percent confidence bounds.

Robustness tests

To assess the robustness of these findings, I carry out a number of sensitivity tests. Specifically, I use an alternative indicator of resource windfalls based on Haber and

Menaldo,[99] and I employ Beck–Katz panel-corrected instead of Driscoll–Kraay standard errors (see Appendix B).[100] Reassuringly, the main findings of the model remain unchanged.

4.4 Conclusion

This chapter has derived a number of observable implications from my theoretical framework and tested them empirically, using social spending data from 1960 until 2005. All tests were guided by the overarching question of whether the variation in spending over time would be consistent with the predictions derived from my theory. The chapter has sought to highlight implicit theoretical assumptions and, by subjecting them to empirical scrutiny, aimed to gain additional leverage for my theoretical argument. The above tests could have seriously challenged my argument in the absence of supportive empirical findings.

The first assumption tested was that defence spending tends to displace social spending and, as a result of this crowding-out effect, confronts autocratic rulers with a dilemma of 'butter or guns'. The second assumption is that different social pacts, embedded in broad or narrow regime coalitions, not only played a critical role for the initial divergence of social spending, but also critically shaped its subsequent evolution over more than four decades. This is because, as I have argued earlier, coalitions are the central structure both underpinning the political economy of distribution and securing the overall political stability of authoritarian regimes. Moreover, these coalitions are self-reinforcing in the sense that, once formed, they engender institutions that maintain and protect the power position of those included. Given that, they should be *the* crucial driving force of social spending.

Turning to the individual sections, a number of key findings stand out. First, section 4.1 has demonstrated the detrimental effect of military spending on social welfare in labour-abundant regimes. Long-term effects of sustained periods of high defence outlays have been shown to be fatal for social expenditure in the context of limited resources. By contrast, provided that ample resource income is available, the dilemma of 'butter or guns' can be avoided or, at least, significantly alleviated. In other words, resource abundance gives regimes crucial respite if the external environment is threatening and pushes for high military outlays. Given the centrality of this trade-off in the overall argument, these findings significantly increase the empirical plausibility of my theory and its validity in the context of labour-abundant MENA regimes. The section also represents to my knowledge the

---

[99] Haber and Menaldo 2011.
[100] The findings for H3 remain unchanged when adding further controls, such as *Tax/GDP*. Results are available upon request.

first systematic empirical test of the 'butter or guns' dilemma in the Middle East and, by providing robust evidence in its favour, challenges the emerging consensus in the literature disputing the existence of such a trade-off.

Sections 4.2 and 4.3 have highlighted the protective and distributive effect of coalition types. The sections provide evidence that the difference between broad and narrow coalitions critically affects autocrats' incentives (a) to cut back social spending, and (b) to share the spoils of rents with large segments of the population. Regarding spending cuts, I found that broad coalitions shield their population from sustained periods of welfare retrenchment. As for rents, broad coalitions seem to channel additional resources to a greater extent toward social welfare than narrow coalitions. This provides further support to a revisionist version of the rentier state theory. In line with my theoretical argument, these patterns become more accentuated with the duration of authoritarian support coalitions as networks of patronage and distribution become institutionalized over time.

5

Tunisia

An Authoritarian Welfare State

Previous chapters have focused on the macro-level from a comparative perspective. I have established an association between patterns of regime formation and subsequent welfare provision, and demonstrated the effect of regime coalitions on spending over time using statistical analysis. This case study draws attention to the underlying causal mechanisms of these patterns. By analysing the Tunisian authoritarian welfare state as a case study, this chapter has a dual purpose.

On the one hand, I seek to substantiate the proposed association between early intra-elite conflict and welfare provision by retracing the foundation of the Tunisian welfare state. To do so, I use a broad array of sources, including official documents from the Tunisian National Archives; archived correspondences between the Tunisian government and the IMF; and the Tunisian press. The analysis is further informed by interviews with some of the 'founding fathers' of Tunisian social policies, including former ministers and trade unionists. Moving to the micro-level enables me to tackle rival hypotheses that cannot be refuted by macro-level analysis. These mainly concern the role of the authoritarian ruler and his ideas in shaping social policies, which, as detractors might claim, could have been the driver of welfare provision. Finally, parts of the analysis should be read as a comparison to the Egyptian case, following in the next chapter. I therefore include cross-references where appropriate. To foreshadow, my argument regarding the foundation of the Tunisian welfare state can be summarized as follows. First, Bourguiba was sceptical about extensive welfare provision and it would be wrong to ascribe to him the sole authorship of Tunisia's social policies. Second, the Tunisian labour union, UGTT, was the trailblazer of the country's welfare state, yet its privileged position in the regime coalition and the imposition of its programmatic ideas on the ruling party could only happen as a result of intra-elite conflict. Elite factionalism was thus instrumental in bringing about a powerful pro-welfare coalition.

On the other hand, this chapter seeks to elucidate the mechanisms of path dependence that have prevented the Tunisian welfare trajectory from 'steering off track'. As outlined in Chapter 1, path dependence was the outcome of, first, societal groups being able to mobilize successfully against welfare cuts. In so doing, these groups could capitalize on initial advantages achieved in the early stages of welfare development which had a positive impact on their capacity to mobilize. In line

Social Dictatorships: The Political Economy of the Welfare State in the Middle East and North Africa. Ferdinand Eibl, Oxford University Press (2020). © Ferdinand Eibl. DOI: 10.1093/oso/9780198834274.001.0001

with analyses of welfare dynamics elsewhere, my account demonstrates that some of these pro-welfare constituencies were in fact a product of the welfare state itself. I illustrate this mechanism using two major episodes of attempted spending cuts and reform in the area of education and social security. The second mechanism of path dependence highlights the role of unintended beneficiaries: that is, groups in society who inadvertently came to benefit from social policies. Taking the example of food and energy subsidies, I can show that well-connected business actors have become major beneficiaries from these policies and, thereby, turned into an important stakeholder in the status quo. Alongside a narrative account, I also use simple regression techniques to make this case.

The chapter proceeds as follows. Section 5.1 presents my analytic narrative of the foundation of the Tunisian welfare state. Section 5.2 illustrates the mechanisms of path dependence, using the examples mentioned above. A final section concludes the chapter.

5.1 The Founding of the Tunisian Welfare State

This section retraces the historical origin of the Tunisian welfare state, in particular in the fields of labour market policies, education, health, and social security. The aim is not, however, to provide a detailed description of the country's social policies. My goal is rather to examine the claimed association between Tunisia's early intra-elite conflict and welfare provision using a range of primary and secondary sources. By analysing in greater detail Bourguiba's own stance toward welfare provision, I seek to corroborate my claim that Tunisia would not have embarked on its welfare trajectory without the foundational moment of elite conflict. Likewise, my account of early Tunisian social policies focuses on conflictual episodes which highlight Bourguiba's reluctance to make, what were in his view, too extensive welfare commitments. Finally, my analysis highlights the role of the Tunisian labour union, UGTT, in the establishment of the Tunisian welfare state, which was equally conditioned by early elite factionalism.

5.1.1 Bourguiba's position in the ideological battlefield for a postcolonial order

Bearing in mind the pivotal role that Bourguiba played in the struggle of national liberation and the one-party state established after independence, it is understandable that accounts of Tunisian post-independence politics have often narrowed down to a study of the leader's mindset and character. Brown, for instance, suggests that historians turn to Bourguiba's records to explain the country's postcolonial political trajectory.[1] In a similar vein, Willis attributes Tunisia's remarkable development record to Bourguiba's altruism, which 'was genuine rather than a convenient rhetorical cover'.[2] This ruler-centric narrative of Bourguiba as the 'mover and shaker' contrasts with a style of governing that his former ministers have described as 'non-interventionist' and 'governing from above'.[3] According to former Minister of Social Affairs, Mohamed Ennaceur, Bourguiba refrained from micro-managing his ministers and mostly intervened in the context of conflict of interests.[4] Likewise, Ahmed Mestiri, who held various ministerial positions under Bourguiba, states that Bourguiba gave his collaborators 'large freedom of manoeuvre'.[5] Far from being a lone decider, Bourguiba relied considerably on his entourage in the policy-making process.[6] In fact, his deteriorating health from the early 1970s forced him to spend, at times extended, periods abroad during which the business of government was left to the Prime Minister and his cabinet. Hence, to state that 'Bourguiba's ideological convictions cannot be separated from those of his entourage'[7] seems a rather accurate depiction and suggests that Bourguiba was open to and influenced by political currents around him.

This is all the more important considering that Bourguiba lacked a firm ideological framework that could have guided his socioeconomic policies.[8] On social issues, his discourse was dominated by general notions of equality and fraternity, and he rarely broached concrete socioeconomic problems.[9] In September 1956, he prided himself at the general conference of the Tunisian labour union federation, UGTT, on not having any ideology: 'I loudly proclaim that I am an adversary of all ideology. [...] Because I'm not prisoner of any political doctrine, I have complete freedom of manoeuvre.'[10] Fundamentally pragmatic and dreading the idea of 'noxious class struggle' that could disrupt national unity, Bourguiba repeatedly voiced his apprehension of UGTT-advocated 'socialism' in the run-up to independence.[11]

---

[1] L. C. Brown 2001, p. 47.   [2] Willis 2012, p. 52.

[3] Personal interview with Driss Guiga, Hammamet, 17 June 2013. Guiga was Minister of Social Affairs and Public Health (1969–73), Education (1973–6), and Interior (1980–4) under Bourguiba.

[4] Personal interview, Tunis, 21 May 2013. Ennaceur was Minister of Social Affairs (1974–7, 1979–85) under Bourguiba.

[5] Personal interview, Tunis, 11 June 2013. Mestiri was Minister of Justice (1956–8), Finance and Commerce (1958–60), Defence (1966–8), and Interior (1970–1).

[6] Personal interview with Mohamed Sayah, Tunis, 16 May 2013. Being a leading figure of the Neo-Destour party, Sayah held several ministerial positions, amongst others Public Works (1971–3) and Housing (1980–3).

[7] Personal interview with Ahmed Ben Salah, Gabes, 27 April 2013. Ben Salah was Minister of Health (1957–61) and Social Affairs (1958–61) before becoming 'super-minister' of Finance, Planning, Economic Affairs (1961-69), and Education (1968–9). He was ousted in September 1969.

[8] Hopwood 1992, p. 85. Mansour Moalla, a former Minister of Finance under Bourguiba, also reports that Bourguiba had, in general, only a limited interest in economics. See Moalla 2011, p. 177.

[9] Temimi et al. 2000, p. 145.   [10] Bourguiba 1974b, p. 185.

[11] Interview with Mohamed Ennaceur, Tunis, 21 May 2013.

As former minister and political companion, Driss Guiga, puts it, Bourguiba's true ideology was development and his primary aim was for Tunisia to join the league of developed nations.[12] In this regard, far from his being left wing, the concrete evidence we have regarding Bourguiba's ideas on how to achieve development portends a pro-business strategy. Prior to independence, he proposed in a letter to his party companion Hédi Nouira, later Minister of Finance, to rely on large landowners and big businesses—most of which collaborated with the French—for post-independence modernization.[13] Accordingly, Bourguiba expressed his support for economic liberalism soon after independence, proclaiming: 'Our political programme is liberal. We have to give capital full freedom of circulation.'[14] Similarly, his statement that 'every consumer who does not produce is a parasite'[15] casts doubt on his commitment to welfare provision. Thus, from what we know about Bourguiba's personal preferences, it seems inaccurate to extrapolate a strong desire to build an extensive welfare state. A notable exception in this respect is the field of education, for which Bourguiba's interest has been well documented.[16] Having had the privilege of studying at the best schools in Tunisia and France, Bourguiba viewed the eradication of illiteracy and the expansion of basic education to the masses as an invaluable prerequisite for developing Tunisia and instilling a strong sense of unity in the young nation.[17]

Party supporters from Bourguiba's home base, the Sahel, were equally wary of massive state-led welfare distribution. Mainly consisting of *petit bourgeois* landowners and merchants,[18] Neo-Destour members from the Sahel were anxious to prevent political measures that would significantly increase their tax burden. At the national level, recent estimates suggest that up to 70 per cent of the party's membership consisted of small merchants and artisans in the urban areas, and subsistence farmers in rural Tunisia[19]—all of whom shared the same concern about an exuberant tax burden after independence. Regarding large capital-owners, the Neo-Destour party had established important business ties prior to independence, and entrepreneurs, such as the founder of the first Tunisian bank, Mohamed Chenik, were important funders of the party.[20] In all, merchants, landowners, and entrepreneurs represented important constituencies within the party.[21]

Unlike Bourguiba, whose own ideas about a socioeconomic postcolonial order remained vague, these business constituencies, organized in the *Union tunisienne de l'artisanat et du commerce* (Tunisian Union of Craft and Commerce; UTAC) and the *Union générale des agriculteurs tunisiens* (General Union of Tunisian Agriculturalists; UGAT), developed an adamantly liberal, pro-capital programme

---

[12] Personal interview, Hammamet, 17 June 2013.   [13] Quoted in Hermassi 1972, p. 118.
[14] B. Mestiri 1983, p. 205.   [15] Bourguiba 1974c, p. 315.
[16] Hopwood 1992, p. 83; and Allman 1979, p. 59.
[17] Perkins 1997, pp. 57–8.   [18] Anderson 1986, p. 232.
[19] Bechri and Naccache 2003, pp. 10–11; and Kraïem 2011, p. 29.
[20] C. H. Moore 1965, p. 34.   [21] Alexander 2010, p. 69.

for post-independence Tunisia, for which they lobbied within the party and vis-à-vis the last Tunisian government under the protectorate.[22] Documents from the Tunisian National Archives reveal the extent to which the business community was worried about post-independence taxation and an expansion of the state apparatus. In a political motion addressed to the Council of Ministers from September 1955, the UTAC denounced the—in hindsight rather minimalist— bureaucracy of the protectorate as 'too costly' and a major source of the country's financial difficulties.[23] In the same vein, the 'exorbitantly large budget of the state' exceeded, in the UTAC's view, the contributive capacity of Tunisian businesses. Significantly, the same motion called for a five-year moratorium on any new recruitment in the public sector. Reflecting the pro-capital programme advocated by the Tunisian business community, the motion thus called for a minimalist state, based on low taxation and minimal state interference.

At the opposite end of the ideological spectrum, the Tunisian labour union federation, the UGTT, had also been working, since its inception in 1946, on a detailed socioeconomic programme for the post-independence period. Under the aegis of left-leaning union intellectuals such as Mahmoud Messadi and Ahmed Ben Salah, and inspired by the Scandinavian model of the welfare state,[24] this programme attributed a primary importance to the question of social policies and welfare provision.[25] For example, in March 1951 the secretary general of the UGTT, Farhat Hachet,[26] declared at the UGTT's Fourth National Congress: 'Social security is one of our central demands, [alongside] the fight against unemploy- ment, redundancy payments for workers, [...] free health care for workers and their families, [...] and the establishment of a pension system for elderly workers to protect them from starving and misery.'[27] Like the business associations, the UGTT carried out extensive political lobbying to make itself heard in government circles. Based on the motions addressed to the government preserved in the Tunisian National Archives, the union's post-independence programme appeared to be on full collision course with the business community. For instance, in August 1955, the UGTT called upon the government to hasten and intensify the recruitment of teachers to guarantee the enrolment of all children, and to establish a fully fledged social security system for the public and private sectors, including small businesses and agriculture.[28] By independence in March 1956, the UGTT

---

[22] Led by the head of the Tunisian Camber of Agriculture, Tahar Ben Ammar, between August 1954 and April 1956, this government comprised independent Tunisian ministers alongside Neo-Destour members and trade unionists. Until August 1955, the portfolios of Finance, Public Works, Education, and Interior were controlled by the French.

[23] Tunisian National Archives 1955a.

[24] Garas 1956. These ideas came to the UGTT mainly through its representatives in the International Confederation of Free Trade Unions (ICFTU), which was dominated by Scandinavian unions.

[25] Eqbal 1967, p. 89.

[26] Hachet was assassinated one year later by extremist French colonialists.

[27] Aicha 1989, p. 89.   [28] Tunisian National Archives 1955b.

had developed the programmatic profile of a social-democratic party, which was at loggerheads with the liberal economic programme advocated by the UTAC and the UGAT.[29]

A number of important points emerge from this cursory overview. First, Bourguiba was not a lone decider; rather, he was influenced to a considerable extent by his entourage, which opened the door to interest politics and political lobbying. Second, while Bourguiba cared profoundly about education, he otherwise lacked a coherent framework of ideas that could have guided his post-independence social policies. Third, Bourguiba's preferences for Tunisia's socioeconomic future accorded with the majority of the Neo-Destour membership in favouring economic liberalism, driven by private-sector initiative and supported by pro-business policies. This means that the Tunisian welfare trajectory cannot be explained merely by reference to Bourguiba. Fourth, both business and labour had developed diametrically opposed programmes with regard to post-war development. They fundamentally differed on questions regarding the role of the state in the economy, public employment, and taxation.

When discussing the formation of the labour–middle class regime coalition in the following subsection, it is therefore important to keep in mind that a mobilized constituency against extensive welfare provision existed prior to independence and that Bourguiba's own preferences sympathized with their socioeconomic programme. It thus seems reasonable to entertain the counterfactual that, had a different regime coalition formed after independence, it is unlikely that Tunisia would have embarked on a path of extensive and costly welfare provision. In addition, it is important to consider that Bourguiba's ideas of educational expansion might have clashed with and possibly been scaled down by a pro-business development programme, supported by the right-wing constituencies within the Neo-Destour.

5.1.2 Intra-elite conflict and labour's foothold in power

In view of Bourguiba's apprehension of labour's socioeconomic programme, it is understandable that Bourguiba first sought to resolve the conflict with his competitor, Salah Ben Youssef, internally, rather than risking an alliance with an 'uneasy bedfellow' such as the UGTT. To recall, the conflict between Bourguiba as president of the Neo-Destour party and his secretary general, Salah Ben Youssef, formally revolved around the issue of independence. Whilst Bourguiba accepted the French offer of partial independence, arguing that this represented an intermediate step, Salah Ben Youssef fervently insisted on immediate complete independence from the former colonial power. In reality, the conflict between the

---

[29] Kraïem 2011, p. 25.

two represented a struggle between two ambitious leaders who both laid claim to power in the emerging postcolonial state. Despite their seemingly irreconcilable differences, Bourguiba still made an attempt to appease Ben Youssef in order to prevent a rift within the party. Preferring co-optation over conflict, Bourguiba offered him leadership of the next government in return for his approval of the French offer.[30]

Yet Ben Salah refused and instead chose to rally Tunisia's conservative and business constituencies with the clear aim of outbidding Bourguiba. His coalition included the Tunisian *haute bourgeoisie* organized in the Neo-Destour's elitist predecessor party, the Old Destour,[31] as well as the royal family of the Bey, who were promised by Ben Youssef a preservation of their financial status.[32] Frightened by the UGTT's ideas about land reform and a break-up of the large estates, the landed elite and rural notables, represented by the Agricultural Union, UGAT, also rallied behind Ben Youssef.[33] Similarly, Tunisia's merchant class, especially those from Ben Youssef's home region Djerba, feared the new tariff agreements included in the proposed Franco-Tunisian agreement and were thus susceptible to Ben Youssef's call.[34] His radical pan-Arabic and religious discourse also attracted the majority of Tunisia's old religious elite and its main institution, the Zitouna mosque, as well as urban youths, in particular in the capital, Tunis.[35] Overall, the French secret services estimated at the time that 40 per cent of the Neo-Destour's members supported Ben Youssef.[36]

In contrast to an imploding Neo-Destour party, labour could mount this struggle from a position of strength. The UGTT's membership was concentrated in strategic sectors, such as mining, and the urban centres.[37] In addition, its considerable size—the union claimed 180,000 members at independence[38]—made the UGTT the only organization that could rival the Neo-Destour in terms of organizational capacity. Its options in this conflict were thus manifold: it could conceivably launch its own political party, seek an equal share of government responsibility with the Neo-Destour, or become a strong pressure group without any political affiliation.[39] In any event, a victory of Ben Youssef's coalition needed to be averted as this would have been detrimental to the union's interests.[40] Conversely, the UGTT's leadership, in particular its secretary general, Ahmed Ben Salah, clearly grasped the opportunity that the rift within the Neo-Destour presented to labour as it would enable the union to secure its political influence in the post-independence period.[41] In this regard, Ben Salah was convinced that the union was best served if

---

[30] Allani 1999, p. 140.   [31] Julien 1976, p. 1516.   [32] Oualdi 1999, p. 54.
[33] Sghaier 2011, pp. 28–9.   [34] Oualdi 1999, p. 54.   [35] C. H. Moore 1965, p. 63.
[36] Cited in Oualdi 1999, p. 67.   [37] Eqbal 1967, p. 144.   [38] Bellin 2002, p. 93.
[39] Eqbal 1967, p. 144   [40] Ibid., pp. 146–7.   [41] Hermessi 1990, p. 134.

it directly oversaw the execution of its socioeconomic programme and participated in government.[42] Ultimately, by imposing its socioeconomic reform programme onto a battered Neo-Destour party, the UGTT hoped to form an 'organic union' with the party and transform it along the lines of the British Labour Party.[43]

For Bourguiba, forming an alliance with the UGTT and embracing its socioeconomic programme was a tactical response to the aggravating conflict within the Neo-Destour—an assessment which is shared both by academics[44] and protagonists of the time, such as former minister Tahar Belkhodja[45] and, importantly, by labour activists, such as Ben Salah himself.[46] Prior to independence, Bourguiba had expressed his disapproval of the UGTT's programmatic ideas on many occasions,[47] and had agreed with Ben Youssef on implementing a liberal economic order before their conflict fully broke out.[48] The alliance thus 'reflected shared interests more than a shared philosophy'.[49]

To seal the deal with the UGTT, Bourguiba offered to adopt the union leadership's socioeconomic programme as the Neo-Destour's official doctrine. In return, the UGTT would host the party's conference in the mining town of Sfax since Bourguiba was unable to ensure a safe place to run the party congress.[50] Tunis, the capital, was under the tight control of the Youssefist camp. This agreement between the UGTT and Bourguiba constituted a first major victory for the union. While the conference, held in November 1955, finalized the exclusion of Ben Youssef from the Neo-Destour party, the UGTT, under the auspices of Mustapha Filali, was given the chairmanship of the party's social and economic affairs committee, which was responsible for drafting the Neo-Destour's socioeconomic programme. Its report, which was approved by the party's plenary assembly, represented an amalgamation of the UGTT's various ideas about post-independence development. Concerning economic policy, the report called for interventionist policies in favour of the country's poor, including a tighter control of large foreign companies, fiscal reform, the redistribution of large estates to poor peasants, and the establishment of agricultural cooperatives.[51] As for social policies, the report urged a massive expansion of the public sector, particularly in the areas of health and education, and called for a public works programme to attenuate unemployment.[52] When the UGTT refined the report and turned it into a fully fledged programme at its Sixth National Congress, held in 1956, it also contained admonishing lines toward private businesses, warning them 'not to interfere in the political affairs of the country'.[53]

---

[42] Eqbal 1967, p. 154.   [43] Bechri and Naccache 2003, p. 10; and Toumi 1989, p. 43.
[44] Amongst others, Guelmami 1996, p. 259; and Haddad 2011, p. 70.
[45] Belkhodja 1998, p. 76.   [46] Interview with Ahmed Ben Salah in Borsali 2008, p. 35.
[47] Bechri and Naccache 2003, pp. 10–11.   [48] Borsali 2008, p. 34.
[49] Alexander 2010, pp. 38–9.   [50] Haddad 2011, p. 44.
[51] Oualdi 1999, pp. 39–40; and Eqbal 1967, p. 162.   [52] Tunisian National Archives 1956a.
[53] Tunisian National Archives 1956c.

For the Neo-Destour, this step was troublesome. Adopting the UGTT's programme had pushed the Neo-Destour far to the left of the Tunisian political spectrum and the new-born labour–party alliance could not belie its inherent contradictions. For instance, whilst the socioeconomic programme of the party called for increased taxation of businesses, the congress also passed a motion encouraging the state to lower taxes for the productive sector.[54] Moreover, when Bourguiba was presented with the full version of the UGTT's programme, he reportedly tore it apart and threatened Ahmed Ben Salah: 'This is communism, Ahmed! I won't let you do that.'[55] In an attempt to attenuate the UGTT's radical programme and to prevent a further drifting of the party to the left, Bourguiba therefore sought to back-pedal. This mainly concerned the area of economic policy. For instance, upon forming his first government, Bourguiba reassured capital owners of his respect for private property and sought to encourage private investment by improving the business climate and giving businesses fiscal advantages. He also, until 1960, resisted calls for a state-led investment plan and the imposition of capital controls demanded by the UGTT.[56] To rein in the critical labour union—the UGTT had heavily criticized Bourguiba's first budget for 'following a capitalist logic [of balancing] revenue and expenditures'[57]— Bourguiba further instigated a split within the UGTT in order to enforce Ahmed Ben Salah's resignation.[58] The outcome of this struggle over economic policies was, for the first four years after independence, a moderately liberal economic policy based on private sector initiative.

Importantly, however, Bourguiba's attempt to renege on his commitments was only partially successful as 'his authority remained limited by the obligation to preserve the socio-political coalition that had allowed him to take power'.[59] On the one hand, he still needed the UGTT to put down the Youssefist guerrilla uprisings that flared up in southern Tunisia following Ben Youssef's ouster.[60] On the other hand, the UGTT also used the window of opportunity to get a strong foothold in the executive. Not only was Ahmed Ben Salah brought back as Minister of Health only shortly after his toppling as UGTT secretary general in 1956, the labour union also managed to occupy a vast array of key positions in the administration. At the governmental level, the first all-Tunisian cabinet that was formed in September 1955 included three ministers from the UGTT.[61] The first cabinet under Bourguiba, formed in April 1956, included four members of the UGTT,[62] and in 1957 and 1958, two former leaders of the UGTT joined the

---

[54] Le Parti Neo-Destour 1955.
[55] Borsali 2008, p. 31; see also A. Mestiri 1999, p. 208; and Zribi 2011, p. 110.
[56] Moalla 1992, p. 259.   [57] UGTT 1956, p. 8.   [58] Bessis and Belhassen 1989, p. 45.
[59] Khiari and Lamloum 2000, p. 378.   [60] Liauzu 1996, pp. 211–12.
[61] These were Ezzeddine Abbasi (Public Works), Fathi Zouhir (Social Affairs), and Chadly Rhaiem (Post and Telegraph).
[62] Ministers from the UGTT were Mustapha Filali (Agriculture), Ezzeddine Affasi (Public Works), Mahmoud Khiari (Post and Telegraph), and Lamine Chebbi (Education).

government: Ahmend Ben Salah and Mahmoud Messadi respectively.[63] Henceforth, all Ministers of Social Affairs would either be from the UGTT or have close ties to it.[64] At the party level, the UGTT saw two of its Executive Bureau members included in the Neo-Destour's Political Bureau, whilst the newly formed business association, the *Union tunisienne de l'industrie, du commerce, et de l'artisanat* (Tunisian Union of Industry, Commerce, and Crafts; UTICA) could file only one member. The old business associations, UTAC and UGAT, had been dissolved because of their support for Ben Youssef.[65] And when the party enlarged its Political Bureau in 1964, the UGTT could increase the number of representatives to eight, whereas the UTICA was still only represented by its president. At the level of the presidency, the director of the presidential cabinet (Abdullah Farhat) was also a union member until his replacement in 1963 by Bourguiba's son. At the legislative level, three out of five Vice-Presidents of the Constituent Assembly were unionists, in addition to thirty-five deputies out of ninety-eight. In Tunisia's first parliament (1959–63), the UGTT further took control of the influential Financial, Economic, and Social Affairs Commission, representing twenty-three out of thirty members. Rachid Sfar, who was Director of General Taxation in the Ministry of Finance after independence and later became Prime Minister, thus described the relationship of the government with the UGTT at the time as one of 'permanent consultation'.[66] On balance, the outcome of this struggle between the UGTT and Bourguiba was an implicit compromise whereby, until Bourguiba's espousal of the UGTT's ideas of planned economic development in 1960, economic policies followed a liberal trajectory while the UGTT was given a nearly free hand in the realm of social policies, as we will see in the next section.

In summary, the intra-elite conflict between Bourguiba and Ben Youssef enabled the UGTT to expand its influence in a manner that would have been unthinkable with a united Neo-Destour party. Bearing in mind the ideological orientation of Bourguiba and the party at large, the UGTT could never have imposed its socioeconomic programme onto a Neo-Destour in better order.[67] As Bourguiba's subsequent attempts to alter the deal demonstrate, the alliance with labour was born out of the necessity to outcompete the Youssefist camp. Seizing the opportunity, the UGTT used its clout to make itself indispensable in the emerging state institutions and managed to manoeuvre itself into a position where, in the words of former minister Driss Guiga, 'the Neo-Destour was permanently obliged to accommodate the union [and] no reform was made without consulting

---

[63] Former UGTT secretary general Ahmed Ben Salah first joined as Minister of Health in 1957 before adding the Ministry of Social Affairs in 1959. From 1961 until 1969, he was 'super-minister' of Finance, Economic Affairs, and Planning. Mahmoud Messadi was former head of the influential teachers union and joined as Minister of Education.

[64] Charfi 1989, p. 87.   [65] Debbasch and Camau 1974, p. 49.

[66] Personal interview, Tunis, 30 June 2013. After holding a number of administrative and ministerial positions, Sfar was Prime Minister from July 1986 until October 1987.

[67] Hermessi 1990, pp. 134–5; and Belhadi 2011, p. 643.

them'.[68] Moreover, as the old business associations were dissolved and the newly formed UTICA kept a very low profile,[69] the UGTT was left with no major business counterpart to wrangle over reforms. As the following subsection will show, this compromise laid the foundation for the Tunisian welfare state.

5.1.3   Intra-elite conflict and welfare provision

This subsection specifically traces the effect of elite factionalism on social policies and welfare expenditures after independence. In this regard, it is important to distinguish the *direct effects* of the intra-elite conflict on social policies from the *indirect effects*. While the former represent an immediate response of the government to the factional infighting in the form of social spending, the latter are the result of the UGTT's predominance in the field of social policies which was made possible by intra-elite conflict.

Direct effects

The most notable social policy measure that can directly be attributed to the conflict between Bourguiba and Ben Youssef was the establishment of the *Caisse nationale du centre et du sud* (National Fund for the Centre and the South), set up by decree in November 1956. Representing the first large-scale public investment project of Bourguiba's newly formed government, the fund's primary aim was to invest in social and infrastructural projects in the inner regions of Tunisia, such as the building of health centres and hospitals, the improvement of sanitation, and schools. Stricken by poverty and long neglected by the colonial authorities, these regions had become a stronghold of the Youssefist movement and constituted an important area of retreat for Ben Youssef's guerrilla fighters, the *fellaghas*. The government allocated 300 million francs to the fund—the equivalent of Tunisia's entire housing budget for the financial year 1956/7.[70]

The government's intentions with regard to the fund are clearly expressed in the administrative note, called 'synopsis of motives', preserved in the Tunisian National Archives.[71] The note gives a clear reference to the Youssefist uprising and is worth quoting at length:

> The Southern regions represent a favourable terrain for the hostile propaganda against the government. [...] Only a forceful intervention on the part of the state can quickly allay this dangerous distortion between North Tunisia and the Centre and the South. The psychological impact that the Fund will have on the

---

[68]   Personal interview, Hammamet, 17 June 2013.   [69]   Oualdi 1999, pp. 107–8.
[70]   Spending figures for the period 1955–7 are taken from Tunisian National Archives 1957a.
[71]   Tunisian National Archives 1956b.

populations benefiting from it will certainly put paid to the pernicious actions of the government's enemies amongst the populations of the South.[72]

Whilst it is difficult to ascertain whether the desired effect was achieved, the creation of the fund underlines the government's concern to regain popularity amongst Ben Youssef's supporters and the strategic role social policies played in this respect.

Indirect effects

The more consequential effects of the intra-elite conflict on welfare policies were indirect. By propelling the UGTT into a position of power from where it could implement its social policy agenda, the intra-elite conflict not only allowed for the implementation of a vast array of social policies and the increase of welfare expenditures, but also—as we will see later in this chapter—created a powerful constituency that would fight for a continuation of these policies in the long run. Specifically with regard to social policies, protagonists of the time unequivocally acknowledge the formative impact of the UGTT on the Tunisian welfare state. According to former Minister of Social Affairs, Mohamed Ennaceur, 'the social reforms would not have happened without the support of the UGTT'.[73] Similarly, Ahmed Mestiri states that 'the social legislation was implemented thanks to the UGTT'.[74]

The forceful role that the labour union played in the field of social policies crucially relied on its socioeconomic programme. While its implementation was initially hampered in the field of economic policy, the UGTT ministers in power freely used the union's socioeconomic programme as a template for their social policy reforms.[75] As representatives of the UGTT in government, these ministers made sure that the union's demands were heard, but compared to other ministers, they could also be easily held accountable by the union's rank and file, which put them under particular pressure to deliver. Ben Salah's speech at the 1956 UGTT congress is exemplary in this respect, stating that '*Our* ministers hold to their credit important achievements concordant with *our* programme'.[76]

Delivering in the field of social policy was all the more important because the union explicitly avoided making wage demands in the first decade after independence.[77] Conscious of the inflationary cycle that wage demands might entail, the labour union was seeking an alternative way to have workers partake in the benefits

---

[72] Tunisian National Archives 1956b.

[73] Personal interview, Tunis, 21 May 2013. Ennaceur was secretary of state in the Ministry of Health and, later, Social Affairs under Ahmed Ben Salah. He later became Minister of Social Affairs himself.

[74] Ahmed Mestiri, Tunis, 11 June 2013. Mestiri held various ministerial positions after independence, amongst others, Finance and Defence.

[75] Guelmami 1996, p. 269; Nerfin 1974, p. 45; and Tunisian National Archives 1957b.

[76] Tunisian National Archives 1957b, emphasis added.   [77] Ben Salah 2008, p. 44.

of development.[78] In this regard, the final report of the UGTT's 1956 congress states that 'due to the limited resources available [. . .], an immediate improvement of the living standard is not possible. Therefore, the UGTT recommends measures that make it possible for the workers to have a share in the growing national revenue, by, amongst others, a generalization of education and social security.'[79] It is thus important to realize that, for the UGTT, increasing social expenditures were viewed as a compensation for the compression of wages. Regarding welfare expenditure more specifically, the UGTT represented the driving force behind the expansion of the welfare budget. According to Mohamed Sayah, who was head of the Student Union at the time and in 1964 joined the Neo-Destour's Political Bureau, 'the UGTT exerted constant pressure to increase social spending'[80]— financed primarily from higher taxes.[81] Major fields of legislative activity and spending expansion were labour market policies and labour laws, education, health, and social security, which shall be scrutinized in turn.

Labour laws and labour market policies
Improving the conditions of agricultural workers had long been a particular concern for the UGTT, not least to gain a foothold in the agricultural sector. Under the protectorate, the union had therefore elaborated a number of proposals aiming at the regulation of a sector that had hitherto escaped the oversight of the state:[82] wages were entirely unregulated, lay-offs were arbitrary and exempt from any form of redundancy payment, and day labouring was the predominant form of employment. Unsurprisingly, proposals to regulate the sector had met with staunch resistance from a vociferous farmers' association, the UGAT, prior to independence. Bourguiba himself was sceptical and initially insisted that the rules should only be applied to workers who had been continuously in employment for some time.[83] With the UGAT dissolved in 1956 and the union at the helm of the Ministry of Social Affairs, however, the way was now clear for a new labour code for agricultural workers. Enacted by two decrees in 1956, the code introduced a minimum wage, established a number of bonuses, such as for dangerous work, limited the hours of work, and obliged employers to pay redundancy money. Equally important was a new code for government employees that came into force in the same year. Whilst introducing an improved pay scheme for civil servants,[84] the code heralded a wave of recruitment into the civil service. Underlining the importance of public sector expansion for labour, the UGTT's secretary general thus boasted in January 1957 to 'have recruited 4,000 civil servants to replace the French officials. These are now 4,000 families out of misery. [And] there are still many vacant positions.'[85]

---

[78] Eqbal 1967, p. 258.   [79] UGTT 1956.
[80] Personal interview with Mohamed Sayah, Tunis, 16 May 2013.   [81] IMF 1959, p. 1.
[82] Eqbal 1967, p. 161.   [83] Bourguiba 1974a, pp. 63–4.   [84] Eqbal 1967, p. 179.
[85] Tunisian National Archives 1957b.

Another area in which the union's imprint became clearly visible was active labour market policies. Since the end of the Second World War, unemployment had become a widespread phenomenon, in particular across the country's inner regions. In response to this, the UGTT had since 1946 called upon the state to intervene actively in the labour market to combat unemployment.[86] Yet, to achieve this aim, the UGTT had to overcome Bourguiba's apprehension that a government-run employment programme might too easily transform into public alimentation of the unemployed, with little incentive for production.[87] Besides, giving work to all unemployed was considered way too costly in view of the government's limited resources. To accommodate these points, the UGTT-led Ministry of Public Works developed a food-for-work programme, which gave the unemployed general interest jobs in return for a basic meal and a minimal salary. Initially equipped with relatively modest resources, the programme rapidly expanded in scope given persistent unemployment and, according to an IMF report from 1962, had by the early 1960s 'become a considerable burden on the Treasury'.[88]

Education

There was a widespread consensus in the regime coalition that education should be a major priority of reform after independence. As a result, educational policies were much less conflictual than other areas of social policy. In fact, in the run-up to independence, Bourguiba and the UGTT Federation of Teachers had reached a preliminary agreement regarding the broad outline of the new educational system.[89] Yet, despite widespread agreement, the role of the UGTT was still crucial both in moulding the shape of the new educational system and in accelerating the pace of expansion.

Regarding the nature of the new educational system, it is important to note that Bourguiba did not have a thought-out idea of what a postcolonial education system could look like. He had a strong interest in education, but lacked a concrete plan of reform. The UGTT, by contrast, had been elaborating a detailed plan of educational reform since the late 1940s. At its second congress in 1949, the union voiced its first concrete demands in the field of education, calling for a generalization of education to all Tunisians and the abrogation of all school fees.[90] Later in the same year, the UGTT's Federation of Teachers under the leadership of Mahmoud Messadi presented the French authorities with a detailed plan of educational reform.[91] The reform proposal was structured around four major principles: a unification of the educational system, which was, at the time, fragmented into

---

[86] Eqbal 1967, p. 243.   [87] Personal interview with Mohamed Ennaceur, Tunis, 21 May 2013.
[88] IMF 1962b, pp. 1–2. Unfortunately, I was unable to obtain detailed annual spending figures for the programme.
[89] C. H. Moore 1965, pp. 53–4.   [90] Haddad 2011, p. 59; and Al-'Usbua 1949.
[91] Temimi et al. 2000, p. 158.

French-only, mixed, and Tunisian-only streams and heavily skewed in favour of the former; free access to education without charge; expansion of education to all social classes; and Arabic to replace French as the primary language of instruction.[92] With regard to Arabic, it is important to note that this proposal was more than just a nationalist demand to restore Tunisian national identity. It also served a very practical purpose, for by making Arabic the main language of instruction, teaching positions would be much more accessible for Tunisians, in particular UGTT members. In October 1955, the Secondary Teachers' Union reiterated labour's demand for educational reform by submitting another detailed report to the first Tunisian Minister of Education, Jallouli Farès, in which it also called for the creation of a Tunisian university and explicitly demanded free secondary education.

Considering the preliminary work that the UGTT had done, Bourguiba called upon unionists from the Federation of Teachers to head the Ministry of Education when he formed his first cabinet in April 1956. Two former heads of the teachers' union held the position from 1956 until 1968: Lamine Chebbi (1956–8) and Mahmoud Messadi (1958–68). Both had worked very closely within the UGTT on the union's educational reform project and drafted considerable parts of it. UGTT members also represented the majority in the technical commissions that forged the details of the reform.[93] As a result, the UGTT's draft proposal and the final law were nearly identical documents.[94] The reform unified all co-existing educational institutions in a national system, which included the previous French-only section as well as religious schools previously run by the Zitouna mosque.[95] Compulsory for all, primary education was to take six years, at the end of which pupils could obtain a certificate conditional upon passing a test. The system further established a three-year lower-secondary stream, which had a vocational character, and secondary education which could lead to higher education. To enter middle-school or secondary education, pupils had to pass an entrance examination.[96] Following the continental European model, the system was highly stratified with a number of dead-ends and increasing selection after primary education. Regarding Arabization, it should be noted that the UGTT was much keener on this point than Bourguiba himself, who was anxious not to sever the links with the former colonial power.[97] It thus represented a 'concession' of Bourguiba to the union.[98]

---

[92] Sraïeb 1968; and personal interview with Mustapha Filali, Gabes, 19 June 2013. Filali was member of the Federation of Teachers and co-author of the draft.

[93] Ayachi 2000, p. 63.   [94] Temimi et al. 2000, p. 158.   [95] Duwaji 1967, p. 74.

[96] For an overview, see Sraïeb 1968.

[97] Mohamed Mzali cited in Slim et al. 2010, p. 194. Mzali was head of Chebbi's cabinet in the Ministry of Education and later Prime Minister from 1980 until 1986.

[98] Eqbal 1967, pp. 163–4.

As for the expansion of spending, the role of labour was equally important. First, in coordination with the UGTT, the student union, *Union générale des étudiants tunisiens* (General Union of Tunisian Students; UGET), launched an assault on all remaining school and tuition fees in 1956.[99] This explicitly included secondary education fees, not only higher education, and thus overlapped with a demand that the UGTT Secondary Teachers' Federation had voiced in October 1955. The ensuing student strikes profoundly angered Bourguiba as he was unwilling to give in to their demands.[100] Yet, in the face of a combined UGET and UGTT campaign, he eventually gave in and by the end of 1956, tution fees for secondary education had been abolished.[101] Second, the union managed to couple the educational reform with a substantial pay rise for teachers, which was in line with the above-mentioned new code for public servants. It satisfied a concrete demand on the part of schoolteachers who had vociferously expressed their discontent with their remuneration.[102]

Third, and most importantly, the UGTT successfully pressured for a much more rapid expansion of the educational system, based on a massive recruitment drive for teachers and a sustained construction campaign for new schools. To fully appreciate the union's contribution in this regard, it is important to note that—though being in favour of educational reform—Bourguiba had opted for a liberal economic policy. In budgetary matters, this meant that Bourguiba, in collaboration with his Minister of Finance, Hédi Nouira, insisted on having a balanced budget. In line with this strategy, Nouira declared in January 1956 that the Tunisian state was living above its means and, therefore, a policy of austerity was required.[103] This policy of fiscal discipline was on a direct collision course with the UGTT. In fact, at its 1956 congress, the union called for a rapid expansion of enrolment, the immediate hiring of 1,700 teachers, and the building of the same number of schools.[104] In the medium term, its plan envisaged complete primary enrolment within nine years, starting in 1957, involving the recruitment of 16,000 teachers between 1957 and 1964 and the construction of 16,000 classrooms. The plan targeted a share for education of 25 per cent of the budget.[105] Thus, the union and Bourguiba disagreed on the speed at which expansion should occur, whilst agreeing on the objective.

This disagreement resulted in fierce bargaining within the government, in which Bourguiba sought to contain the UGTT's pressure for fiscal expansion.[106] This hesitation as to how fast to expand education is also reflected in education spending, which in the period from 1956 to 1960 fluctuated between 12 and 19 per cent, with the low point being reached in 1960. In fact, the massive expansion of educational expenditure to levels of up to 30 per cent by 1972 only started

---

[99] Le Petit Matin 1956.   [100] Ayachi 2003, p. 72.   [101] Ibid., p. 72.
[102] C. H. Moore 1965, p. 170.   [103] Tunisian National Archives 1957a.
[104] UGTT 1956.   [105] Ibid.   [106] A. Mestiri 1999, pp. 132–3.

after Bourguiba had abandoned his cautious fiscal policy and given the UGTT the 'green light' to devise a ten-year public investment plan starting in 1961. While it is impossible to ascertain whether Bourguiba would have been willing to boost public investment in education to these levels without the UGTT, his hesitation until 1960 and his concerns for macroeconomic stability suggest that the spending levels might have been more moderate.

Health and social security

The Tunisian social security system has been a distinct feature of the Tunisian welfare state, exceeding coverage rates of 80 per cent in the mid-2000s.[107] The origin of this system can be clearly traced back to the UGTT's influence on social policies after independence. To begin with, the establishment of a comprehensive social security system, including health insurance and pensions, had been one of the union's core demands, as visible in the resolutions of its 1949 congress.[108] While public sector workers had, on the eve of independence, a relatively comprehensive health insurance and pension scheme,[109] the UGTT's demand mainly targeted private sector workers, who at the time only benefited from family allowances and a minimal workmen's compensation scheme for accidents.[110] To improve their condition, the union proposed at its 1956 conference the establishment of a comprehensive social security institution for all workers—including the agricultural sector—which would cover work accidents, health, family allowances, housing benefits, as well as pensions. In addition, the union called for the creation of a national health service to cover those without health insurance.[111]

Since social security represented a contentious issue for parts of the Neo-Destour party and employers, the UGTT had to implement this programme gradually over the period from 1956 until 1971. The first step consisted in granting a sectoral pension fund to mining workers, a key constituency of the UGTT, and establishing an insurance-based compensation system for work-related accidents and illnesses in 1957.[112] Both measures had been part of the initial agreement with Bourguiba in the run-up to the Sfax conference and hence met with no significant political opposition. The next step consisted in extending the existing social insurance system of the private sector to include new benefits, most notably health, pensions, and life insurance benefits. To this end, Ahmed Ben Salah, Minister of Health and Social Affairs since May 1958 and former secretary general of the UGTT, elaborated an extensive draft proposal that he presented to the

---

[107] See Chapter 2.   [108] Guelmami 1996, p. 268.
[109] In 1898, the French authorities had introduced the *Société de prévoyance des fonctionnaires*, covering pensions, maternity, and sick leave. The system was completed by a health insurance scheme in 1951.
[110] Family allowances, introduced in 1918, granted a lump-sum benefit for every child. The workmen's compensation scheme was created in 1921.
[111] Tunisian National Archives 1957b.
[112] Ben Romdhane 2006, p. 36; and Eqbal 1967, pp. 163–4.

cabinet in early 1959.[113]   In cabinet, however, the draft law got a rather cold reception from Bourguiba, who was concerned that it would overburden Tunisian employers. Questioning whether it was actually the right moment to introduce this piece of legislation,[114] Bourguiba made it clear that he would not agree to a social security system that included either pensions or invalidity benefits in the scheme.[115] Opposition to the law also formed within the business community. In the eyes of the country's business association, the UTICA, Tunisia could not afford the luxury of social insurance. In particular, small shopkeepers and artisans would be unable to carry the financial burden, in addition to the disruptions caused by the law's regulatory aspects, such as paid holidays and sick leave.[116] Again, Bourguiba expressed his sympathies for the employers' position, stating that the draft law was 'not appropriate for this kind of activities [small businesses and crafts]' and would therefore 'deal a deathblow to Tunisian crafts, which are already struggling'.[117]

Despite the resistance, Ben Salah was able to use the UGTT's leverage to pass a trimmed-down draft law without pensions and life insurance benefits through cabinet and submit it to parliament in October 1960. There, the law was subject to another round of fierce negotiations between business representatives and the UGTT in the chamber's finance commission. In a compromise with the UTICA, the UGTT abandoned its demand to pay child benefits up to the age of twenty-one instead of twenty and, for the time being, excluded the agricultural sector from the scheme. The business sector also managed to negotiate a reduction of the employer's contribution in the mining and building sectors to 15 per cent from 27.5 and 22.5 per cent respectively.[118] To compensate for the loss, the UGTT effected a 5 per cent salary increase across all sectors and made employers pay all contributions—both their own and those of employees—for a transitional period.[119] Most importantly, the union ensured that the scheme would cover not only the insured person, but also all dependent persons, normally children and the spouse. On the whole, the social insurance law passed in 1960 represented a major victory for the UGTT over both the UTICA and, to a certain extent, Bourguiba.

Having overcome the initial resistance and laid the legislative foundations for social security, the UGTT found it easier to improve and expand the system in the course of the 1960s. In 1963, benefits increased substantially and students were allowed to join the scheme free of charge in 1965.[120] From labour's viewpoint, two major shortcomings persisted: the exclusion of the agricultural sector and the exclusion of pension benefits. Accordingly, the Executive Committee issued a report in 1964 urging the government to extend the coverage of social security and to include old-age pensions.[121] The reasons for the government's hesitation were financial. Including pensioners would add a group of claimants to the regime who

[113] C. H. Moore 1965, p. 192.   [114] Borsali 2008, p. 68.   [115] C. H. Moore 1965, p. 192.
[116] Ibid., p. 193.   [117] Bourguiba 1974d, p. 165.   [118] Eqbal 1967, pp. 239–40.
[119] La Presse 1960, 1961.   [120] Al-Amal, 1963.   [121] Haddad 2011, p. 139.

had only paid into the scheme for a short period, if at all, and extension would thus require assistance out of the general budget. Similarly, adding agricultural workers, in addition to the logistical problems, would add a group that was more liable to work accidents and was more likely to claim health insurance benefits. The union thus had to wait for the right moment to push its demand. Eventually, the strong growth performance in the late 1960s allowed it to put the issue back on the table and, after negotiations in a joint UGTT–UTICA commission formed in 1967, the government incorporated employed agricultural workers permanently in 1970 and added pension benefits in 1971.[122] The measures cost the Tunisian treasury about 2.3 million dinars, equivalent to a 1.1 per cent increase in the social spending budget.

The expansion of public health care was intimately related to the social security dossier. As described above, the union had in 1956 encouraged the establishment of a tax-based public health care system for those without social security coverage. This meant that expenditure on public health was to rise until the social security system had fully expanded. In this regard, it was again key for the UGTT to have access to the budget-making process. The union therefore invested considerable effort in building an extensive network within the public health care organization. According to Driss Guiga, who was head of the Budget Office in the Ministry of Health at the time, the union was heavily involved in the drafting of the budgets as it 'had the best information about what was going on on the ground'.[123] Its influence was reflected in the rapid increase of health expenditures.

A comparative note with regard to Egypt: defence and 'cheap social policies'

As described in Chapter 3, Tunisia's geographic location and size prevented it from being drawn into the geopolitical conflicts pervading the Middle East. Hence, the country's leadership felt no need to invest extensively in the country's armed forces. As Bourguiba himself stated, Tunisia only needed 'a tiny army [...] to satisfy national prestige'.[124] Interestingly, the UGTT's 1956 conference had also warned that the army should not take too big a part of the national budget as this would have complicated the union's plans in the realm of social welfare.[125] In the early 1960s, the UGTT needed to reinforce this position by steering Bourguiba away from joining the US-led CENTO defence alliance, also known as 'Baghdad Pact', which the USA urged Tunisia to do. According to Ahmed Ben Salah, 'super-minister' at the time, joining CENTO would have been very detrimental to the government's welfare effort, which is why the UGTT dissuaded Bourguiba from doing so.[126] This stands in contrast to Egypt where—as we will see—the perceived necessity to bolster defence crowded out welfare, not the other way around.

---

[122] Adam 1970; and Monastiri 1971.   [123] Guiga 2013, p. 31.
[124] Bourguiba 1976, p. 176.   [125] UGTT 1956.
[126] Personal interview, Gabes, 27 April 2013.

Another important difference from Egypt was the absence of what I have called 'cheap social policies' in Tunisia. This is particularly visible in the area of social security. While in Egypt—as we will see in the next chapter—social security was established with the aim of increasing national saving, which could then be utilized to finance the country's development and defence effort, the Tunisian social security system had in comparison a purely social character. Several pieces of evidence support this claim. Firstly, in a note from the Council of Ministers discussing the future strategy to improve Tunisia's borrowing capacity, social security is not mentioned at all.[127] Secondly, the Tunisian government established a number of saving funds parallel to the social security system, the unique purpose of which was to boost the available income for investment. In 1956, the *Caisse nationale d'épargne* (National Savings Fund) was established, which by the end of 1972 had amassed savings worth 5 per cent of the government budget.[128] In 1959, the government created the *Société nationale d'investissement* (National Investment Organization; SNI), a public equity company with shares held by Tunisian nationals, public sector institutions, and foreign investors.[129] The surplus of the social security system was out of direct government control and invested in bonds of banks and the post.[130] The investment of social security funds in public development projects was made possible only in 1973,[131] in sharp contrast to Egypt which immediately channelled the social security surplus toward its development programme upon the inception of the scheme in 1955. This suggests that in Tunisia new groups were not included as a remedy for cash crises.

5.1.4 Summary

This section has sought to substantiate one of the central claims of this study, which is the link between intra-elite conflict and social spending. To summarize the key points of this section, I showed in a first step that it would be erroneous to attribute the rapid expansion of welfare distribution in post-independence Tunisia solely to Bourguiba. Against the background provided by the foregoing, it is safe to say that Bourguiba was ideologically not predisposed to massive welfare distribution and, as a result, turned out to be an impediment to welfare state expansion that needed to be overcome. Second, and related to the previous point, I argued that the UGTT would have never been able to impose its social policy agenda onto the Neo-Destour party, had the party not been shattered by the intra-elite conflict between Ben Youssef and Bourguiba. Third, despite Bourguiba's attempts to renege on his commitments to labour, the UGTT successfully managed to seize the opportunity presented by the intra-elite conflict to gain a foothold in the state

---

[127] Tunisian National Archives 1957c.   [128] IMF 1972, p. 78.   [129] Ibid., p. 29.
[130] Guelmami 1996, pp. 555–6.   [131] Ibid., p. 706.

Table 5.1 Foundational social policy reforms in Tunisia (1956–1971)

UGTT-led post-independence welfare reforms	
Measure	*Spending implication*
New code for agricultural workers	None
New code for government employees	Substantial increase in remuneration, including for employees in the fields of education and health
Establishment of public works programme	Substantial increase in outlays for active labour market policies
Educational reform	Accelerated hiring of teachers and school building, and pay increases for teachers
Expansion of public health care organizations	Substantial expansion of health expenditures
Social security legislation	Though system based on payroll taxes, successive additions of new groups of beneficiaries were partly financed through the state; long-term implications once the budget started to run deficits in the 1980s
Introduction of retirement benefits for mine workers	Until establishment of public pension scheme in 1970, costs shouldered by the state
Housing cooperatives for workers	Government grant of 300 million francs

institutions, which enabled it to implement its social policy agenda and thereby laid the foundations of the Tunisian welfare state. As Table 5.1 shows, the UGTT left its mark on nearly all fields of social policy after independence, with notable repercussions on the country's long-term social expenditure. Against arguments about 'labour aristocracy' and insider dynamics,[132] the UGTT was also keen to expand social, in particular social security, benefits to hitherto excluded groups in the agricultural sector as this was seen as a way to gain a strong foothold and expand the membership amongst these constituencies. After analysing the foundational moment of Tunisia's welfare trajectory in this section, I will next illustrate the mechanisms that have allowed the country to stay 'on track'.

5.2 Staying on Track: Mechanisms of Path Dependence in the Tunisian Welfare State

This section seeks to illustrate the mechanisms of path dependence that have contributed to the perpetuation of the Tunisian welfare trajectory beyond its founding moment. As outlined in Chapter 1, I emphasize two mechanisms to explain the persistence of high welfare distribution in Tunisia.

---

[132] Bellin 2000; and Hertog 2016.

On the one hand, the establishment of generous social policies conferred an initial advantage on a number of societal actors which has increased over time as the size of these groups has grown. This initial advantage has taken different forms. Some groups, such as pupils and students, have been major recipients of state resources. Other actors, such as the labour union, have established themselves as the privileged interlocutor of the state when it comes to social policies, giving them an advantage in terms of voice and access. Finally, new constituencies, such as teachers and public health care workers, were in fact created by the welfare state itself and, similar to target groups of social policies, have become stakeholders of the welfare state. Being part of the regime's support coalition, these actors have seen their power resources reinforced with the expansion of the welfare state and have been able to mobilize these resources in the face of potential divergence from the welfare trajectory, such as large spending cuts and structural reforms.

On the other hand, the Tunisian welfare state has brought about a number of completely unintended beneficiaries, who are neither target groups of social policies nor welfare providers, such as teachers and health service workers. Rather, these groups have tapped into what could be called 'regulatory rents' generated by the welfare state: that is, financial advantages stemming from market regulations that have been implemented to facilitate welfare provision. As we will see, the subsidization of food items and energy products has involved massive regulatory interventions on the part of the state in order to control domestic prices, which, in turn, has generated lucrative opportunities for business. This effect has been reinforced by the fact that politically connected entrepreneurs have found it much easier to access these rent streams and, utilizing their access to political decision making, to guarantee their continuation.

5.2.1 Protecting the status quo and pushing for expansion: education and social insurance reform

The mobilization of constituencies against path divergence and in favour of expansion of social policies has occurred repeatedly since the foundation of the country's welfare system. The following two episodes represent examples of what I consider to be important moments of potential divergence from the country's welfare trajectory. To give an impression of the range of pro-welfare constituencies involved, I focus on two different policy areas, which are education and social security.

Educational expansion and reform
Following a decade of educational expansion since the 1958 reform, there was growing discontent with the country's educational system in government circles by the late 1960s. Rapidly increasing enrolment rates had pushed educational

expenditures to what, in the eyes of the government, was financially unsustainable.[133] In 1968, educational spending reached 8.2 per cent of GDP, which was one of the highest rates in world.[134] Accordingly, Minister of Finance Hédi Nouira pointed to the 'considerable pressure on the [financial] possibilities of Tunisia'[135] as a result of the elevated education budget. In addition, expansion had not necessarily been accompanied by high completion rates as a considerable number of pupils dropped out of education before graduation.[136] Finally, the rising number of Tunisians with primary education had created considerable knock-on effects as an increasing number of pupils sought to continue their education at the secondary and tertiary levels.

Seeking a solution to the engulfing education bill, the government formed an inter-ministerial commission in November 1969 to elaborate a set of concrete proposals.[137] The timing seemed propitious as Bourguiba had just ousted Ahmed Ben Salah and reverted Tunisia's development paradigm away from state-led planning back to private sector growth. Two main themes dominated the recommendations made by the commission, published in May 1970. First, whilst primary education was considered to be a right, secondary and tertiary education were deemed a privilege which only a limited number of Tunisians should have access to.[138] This was in line with an earlier statement by Bourguiba that the generalization of secondary education was financially not possible.[139] Second, the commission emphasized the need for savings in the education budget and improvements in its financial efficiency. In terms of concrete proposals, it was therefore envisaged to (a) decrease the number of secondary pupils by 1976; (b) increase selection into and within secondary education; (c) rein in the costs at the level of tertiary education by excluding students who took longer than three years to obtain a degree, reducing the growth rate of university students to 5.4 per cent by 1979, and reducing the number of scholarships, considered 'too generous and comprehensive'.[140] In addition, it was also envisaged to reduced the success rates of higher education students by 5 to 10 per cent, from levels ranging between 28 and 48 per cent.[141]

Shortly after their announcement, these measures met with significant resistance. Mobilized by the Tunisian Student Union, UGET, students started to turn out in numbers against the proposals at the beginning of the 1970/1 academic year, launching the biggest student protest since independence.[142] As the UGET was also open to secondary students, the union was able to mobilize considerable numbers and maintain protests throughout 1971 and 1972. Whilst their ire

---

[133] Monastiri 1974, p. 525.   [134] Sraïeb 1971, p. 410.   [135] Monastiri 1971, p. 424.
[136] For example, the cumulative drop-out rate for primary education amounted to 40 per cent in 1971. See UNESCO 2015.
[137] Sraïeb 1971, p. 401.   [138] Al-Bakoush 2010, p. 90.   [139] CDN 1970, p. 14.
[140] Sraïeb 1971, pp. 400–14.   [141] Bouqra 2012, pp. 71–2.
[142] See, amongst others, Monastiri 1971 and for a description of the events.

was directed at the concrete measures which they rejected, more fundamentally students feared, in the words of historian Abdel-Jelil Bouqra, that the proposals constituted a first step toward a reversal of 'the project of 1958'—that is, the democratization of education.[143] Rejecting the government's idea of guaranteeing Tunisians only primary education, the UGET declared that secondary and higher education should also be considered a right for all Tunisians.[144]

According to Driss Guiga, who was Minister of Health until 1973 before taking charge of the Ministry of Education until 1976, the government was quite impressed with the vehemence of the students' response.[145] As ad hoc measures to appease the students—such as reintegrating 594 out of 817 students who had been suspended from university for taking longer than three years[146]—had only little effect, the government discreetly decided to suspend the application of these measures and look for alternative saving options, without officially repealing them.[147] As a result, none of the announced reduction targets of the government were met. Regarding the intake of secondary students, numbers in fact rose from 190,000 in 1971 to 250,197 in 1979.[148] Similarly, the percentage of repeaters at the secondary level only dropped from 29 to 22 per cent in the same period. And instead of reducing the growth rate of tertiary education, the number of university students rose dramatically from 10,347 in 1971 to 28,971 by the end of the decade, representing annual growth rates well above the targeted 5.4 per cent.

More discreet, yet no less effective, resistance against the reform also emerged from teaching staff organized by the UGTT.[149] The union had two main concerns. First, it feared that too abrupt a reduction in the hiring rates of teachers, or even its cessation, would have a negative effect on both the working conditions of existing teachers, who were suffering under the burden of high student numbers, and those of aspiring teachers, who had anticipated joining the civil service.[150] The union therefore lobbied for a smooth continuation of the hiring process—with success. As a matter of fact, growth rates of the teachers corps exceeded the growth rate of students in the period from 1971 until 1979. At the secondary level, the number of teachers increased by 67 per cent (from 7,361 to 12,262) compared to a student growth rate of 31 per cent. At the tertiary level, the contrast was even starker with the number of teaching staff increasing by 500 per cent (from 600 to 3,646) compared to a student increase of 179 per cent. The bulk of the savings in the educational budget which occurred over the period came from a sharp reduction in capital expenditures.[151]

---

[143] Bouqra 2012, p. 70.   [144] Al-Bakoush 2010, p. 90.
[145] Personal interview, Hammamet, 17 June 2013.   [146] Sraïeb 1971, p. 413.
[147] Personal interview with Driss Guiga, Hammamet, 17 June 2013.
[148] Unless stated otherwise, the following figures are all taken from UNESCO 2015.
[149] Personal interview with Driss Guiga, Hammamet, 17 June 2013.   [150] Ibid.
[151] Ibid.

The second major concern of the union was related to the status of low-skilled primary teachers, the *moniteurs*. Given the lack of personnel after independence, these teachers had been hired on a provisional basis pending the availability of more qualified native teaching staff. Being low-skilled—many *moniteurs* had only completed lower-secondary education—these teachers received a very low salary and, not fully integrated in the civil service, had no access to the social security system. Their status was precarious and the UGTT had unsuccessfully lobbied for their full integration in the civil service in the early 1960s when the government had revised the legal code for primary school teachers.[152] Countervailing the government's attempt to reduce spending, the UGTT decided to renew this demand in the early 1970s and put considerable pressure on the Minister of Education, Driss Guiga, to regularize their situation.[153] In terms of numbers, the 4,200 *moniteurs* represented about a fifth of the total primary teaching staff and giving them full status would entail considerable costs, including a substantial salary rise in addition to the state's contribution to social security. It is noteworthy that this demand was pushed in a general context of saving and cost reduction. When the government showed reluctance, the UGTT remained steadfast and threatened with strikes, should the government not give in to its demand.[154] Given the volatile situation at universities, the government eventually decided to satisfy the union's request and *moniteurs* were upgraded to full teacher status in 1975.

In the broader context of path dependence, the episodes represent illustrative examples of how the Tunisian welfare trajectory was prevented from going 'off track'. In the case of the student protest, it was the mobilization of beneficiaries that averted a considerable curtailing of access to secondary and higher education. Against Bourguiba's exhortation that universal secondary education would overstretch the country's resources, expansion of secondary education continued unabated and, in the year of Bourguiba's ouster in 1987, secondary enrolment stood at 40 per cent.[155] Similarly, in the case of the UGTT, it was stakeholders in the status quo that mobilized for the continuation of spending. When mobilizing against spending reductions, the UGTT certainly benefited from its privileged access to decision making. It could thus capitalize on an initial advantage it had gained in the early stages of the Tunisian welfare state.

The 2004 universal health care reform

Tunisia's 2004 overhaul of its health insurance system represents another good example to illuminate the mechanisms of path dependence in the Tunisian welfare system. Passed in August 2004, the reform merged the health insurance of civil servants, the *Caisse nationale de retraites et de prévoyance sociale* (National Pension and Social Welfare Fund; CNRPS), and private sector employees, the

---

[152] La Dépêche 1961.   [153] Slim et al. 2010, p. 190.
[154] Personal interview with Driss Guiga, Hammamet, 17 June 2013.   [155] UNESCO 2015.

Caisse nationale de sécurité sociale (National Social Security Fund; CNSS), into the new *Caisse nationale d'assurance maladie* (National Health Insurance Fund; CNAM). Unifying the country's two biggest social security funds with millions of beneficiaries, the reform constituted without any doubt the biggest social policy reform since the introduction of the country's social security system in 1960. Launched in 1996 and stretching over a period of eight years, negotiations about the reform involved the UGTT, the employers' association UTICA, as well as representatives of the private health care sector. The duration and long-winded character of the law's elaboration gives an impression of the economic and political stakes that were at play. For my purposes here, the reform represents an exemplary case where stakeholders in the status quo—in this case, the UGTT—fundamentally transformed the nature of the reform to their advantage and thus averted systemic change in the Tunisian health care system by preserving its public, distributive character.

To fully understand the positions of the involved actors, it is important to briefly situate the CNAM in the context of previous reform attempts. In fact, the 2004 reform was not the first attempt to unify Tunisia's private and public sector insurance system. In 1986, the Tunisian government had passed a law providing for a unified pension fund covering all employees in the public and the private sectors. The reasons for the reform were economic. While the private sector scheme exhibited large surpluses, the more generous public sector scheme had started to operate at a deficit in the mid-1980s. It was therefore hoped that by merging both funds, the deficit would be wiped out and the new fund would stand on a more sustainable financial footing. This would have entailed an alignment of the more generous public sector scheme on to the private sector fund.[156] However, the reform encountered severe resistance on the part of public sector workers, who opposed the benefit cuts that would have followed the 'downgrading' of their scheme.[157] Led by the UGTT's section for financial sector workers, public sector employees launched a strike lasting for three months and, as a result, achieved the effective shelving of the reform.[158] This, of course, did not solve the problem that the public sector scheme continued to exhibit a deficit, biting into its savings, and that different regimes with unequal benefit structures continued to coexist alongside each other. By the mid-1990s, the situation was such that, in the words of Naceur El Gharbi, 'everybody was discontent'.[159]

In February 1996, the government therefore launched a second attempt to merge the public and private sector schemes, this time in the area of health

---

[156] Personal interview with Mohamed Ennaceur, Tunis, 21 May 2013. Ennaceur was Minister of Social Affairs from 1974 to 1977, and again from 1979 until 1985. The attempted reform was prepared by his successor.
[157] Vittas 1997, p. 6.   [158] Ben Dhiaf 1986, p. 883.
[159] Personal interview, Tunis, 2 July 2013. Naceur El Gharbi was the first CEO of the CNAM from 2004 until 2009. He was a key figure in the negotiations leading to the CNAM's creation.

care. The roadmap adopted by the Council of Ministers envisaged the progressive fusion of both schemes, the coverage of all essential costs by the merged insurance fund, and the outsourcing of additional costs beyond the basic coverage to complementary private insurances.[160] At this point, it is very important to understand the context and the motives of the government when the reform was first launched in order to fully appreciate the subsequent transformation that the reform project underwent. The first motive was clearly to reduce the escalating costs of the system, which required increasing financial support out of the general budget. This objective had already been spelled out in Tunisia's 7th Development Plan (1987–91), which had called for more private participation in the health care costs to preserve the financial balance of the social security funds.[161] In the early 1990s, Tunisia had just completed an IMF-led structural adjustment programme and the years between 1992 and 1995 showed a meagre growth record, which reinforced the government's willingness to reduce the costs. The second motive, which is visible in the government's above-mentioned roadmap, was to restructure the public health care system, such that the state would provide a basic coverage which could then be topped up by private insurance. In other words, the reform initially aimed at a greater privatization of the system. The third motive was to guarantee the long-term financial stability of the system. This was to be achieved by negotiating an increase in the monthly payroll contributions to ensure the financial viability of the new system.

Yet, from the very beginning these economic motives of reform coexisted with, and contradicted, the political objective to turn this reform into a political success for the regime. By introducing universal health insurance for all Tunisians, the relatively new leadership—Ben Ali had taken over in 1987—sought to sharpen its social policy profile.[162] Ben Ali also had a strong interest in coming to peace with the UGTT—after a very conflictual relationship at the end of Bourguiba's tenure—and endeavoured to turn the UGTT into a support constituency of his regime.[163] When comparing these initial objectives with the final outcome presented below, it becomes clear that the economic motives gradually gave way to the political imperative not to alienate a core constituency of the regime.

The reason for this shift was the labour union's leverage in the negotiation process. This is not only the assessment of the UGTT itself,[164] but also of the government representatives[165] and the private health care representatives whom

---

[160] Kasmi 2008a, p. 14.   [161] Republic of Tunisia 1987, pp. 336–7.

[162] Personal interview with Ridha Kechrid, Tunis, 12 June 2013. Kechrid was Minister of Health from 2004 to 2007 and closely involved in the negotiations about the CNAM.

[163] Personal interview with Moncer Rouissi, Tunis, 22 May 2013. Roussi held various ministerial portfolios, amongst others Social Affairs (1989–91) and Employment (1992–2001), and was a personal adviser of former President Ben Ali.

[164] Personal interview with Ali Ben Romdhane, Tunis, 2 May 2013. Romdhane was deputy secretary general during the negotiation period.

[165] See personal interviews with Ridha Kechrid and Naceur El Gharbi above.

I interviewed in Tunis.[166] According to Ali Jebira, the reform's purpose gradually became to 'please the UGTT',[167] and the union managed to introduce a number of 'populist measures', while successfully marking out its 'red lines' which the government was not supposed to cross.[168] Although the bargaining involved occasional public threats of strikes, such as in January 2005,[169] the UGTT mostly relied on its political weight, its ties with the respective ministries, its accumulated expertise in the area—the UGTT elaborated several reports and expert notes along the way—and its experience in negotiating with the government.[170] It certainly also benefited from a change in the overall economic climate, which by the early 2000s was much more favourable and gave the government more distributive leeway. The initial reform proposal was gradually transformed in the following way.

First, in contrast to the 1986 reform, the UGTT averted an alignment of the more generous public sector scheme on to the private sector one. Whilst the government had not been explicit on this point in the initial 1996 roadmap, its position in the negotiations was to achieve a compromise which would have entailed some upgrading of the private sector scheme coupled with some benefit reductions for public sector employees.[171] Yet, the UGTT rejected this position as a 'race to the bottom'[172] and made it clear that no reform could be made at the expense of past achievements in the area of health care and coverage.[173] When asked by the author whether the government feared a widespread strike within the public sector, one of the chief negotiators of the government responded: 'There are 45,000 civil servants on a very generous scheme. We had to let them continue.'[174] Aligning the private sector employees with the more generous public sector benefits structure, the reform thus entailed a substantial upgrading of the private sector scheme. Similarly, the union obtained the maintenance of a number of special regimes within the public sector, such as for works doctors or employees of insurance funds.[175]

Second, the union made sure that the reform would be accompanied by a substantial improvement of the public health care system in the form of a public investment programme. This measure aimed to alleviate the UGTT's concerns that the reform would be carried out at the expense of the public health care sector.[176] Since one of the objectives of the reform was to make the private health sector accessible to those covered by the CNAM, the UGTT feared that the public health sector would be exposed to disloyal competition from a much

---

[166] Personal interview with Ali Jebira, Tunis, 3 July 2013. Jebira is head of the *Syndicat tunisien des médecins spécialistes libéraux* (Syndicate of the Independent Specialist Doctors; STMSL) and, in this function, participated in the negotiations.

[167] Ibid.   [168] Ibid.   [169] Al-Sabah 2005.

[170] Personal interview with Ali Ben Romdhane, Tunis, 2 May 2013.   [171] Ibid.

[172] Ibid.   [173] Al-Sh'ab 2006b.

[174] Personal interview with Naceur El Gharbi, Tunis, 2 July 2013.   [175] Le Quotidien 2008a.

[176] Personal interview with Ridha Kechrid, Tunis, 12 June 2013.

better equipped private sector. Ultimately, the public sector would be obliged to introduce fees for its services to keep up, which would lead to the establishment of a 'two-class health care system'.[177] Throughout the negotiations, the UGTT was adamant about this point, declaring that 'the improvement of the public health care sector is an absolute priority, without which there won't be any reform'.[178] Concretely, the labour union demanded a modernization of public hospitals, new medical equipment, especially for the country's A & E departments, and more personnel.[179] Obviously, these demands went completely against the initial objective of cost reductions. Eventually, the government agreed to invest 2 billion dinars for the modernization of public health care. Given that, in 2005, total state expenditure amounted to about 10 billion dinar, the volume of the programme was substantial and the government was only able to finance the programme with the support of a financial grant from the EU.[180]

Third, while the UGTT had to concede higher payroll contributions for civil servants, private sector employees, and pensioners, it successfully cushioned the financial impact of the increase. On the one hand, the union made sure that increases were introduced gradually over a three- to five-year period and were not be revised for five years once the agreed level was attained.[181] On the other hand, contributions rose only moderately and in greater proportions for employers than employees. For instance, for civil servants, the previous contributions of 1 per cent of monthly salaries went up to 2.75 per cent, whilst the state's contribution increased from 1 to 4 per cent.[182] These moderate rates could only be achieved because the fees that private doctors could charge to the CNAM were set at levels below the Tunisian market rates. Voicing their discontent, private doctors thus complained that they had to 'give up about a third of their income in "an effort of solidarity"'.[183] While this statement seems slightly exaggerated, it is true that the moderate contributions could only be achieved because the costs were partly shifted onto the private health care providers.

Fourth, in relation to the private health care sector, the unions were insisting on the need for a third-party payment system.[184] This meant that if policy holders decided to use a private sector provider, the patient would not be obliged to pay in cash; rather, the provider would have to invoice the CNAM and claim back its expenses. In the words of the UGTT's chief negotiator, Ridha Bouzriba, a third-party system would represent a 'tranquility premium' for patients, allowing them to use the private health sector without having to advance the costs and

[177] Le Quotidien 2008b.   [178] Deputy SG Bouzriba cited in Le Temps 2006.
[179] Le Temps 2008; Al-Sh'ab 2006b; and Al-Sh'ab 2006a.
[180] Personal interview with Ridha Kechrid, Tunis, 12 June 2013.
[181] Personal interviews with Ridha Kechrid and Naceur El Gharbi, Tunis, 12 June and 2 July 2013.
[182] World Bank n.d., p. 85. It is noteworthy that, as of 2013, the CNAM was already running deficits.
[183] Femmes 2007.   [184] Personal interview with Naceur El Gharbi, Tunis, 2 July 2013.

being financially overburdened.[185] Private doctors, on the other hand, feared that they would be stuck with costs if the CNAM refused full reimbursement. Despite publicly expressing their concern about this system,[186] their bargaining power was not strong enough to overcome this 'red line' in the negotiations.[187] For the UGTT, the introduction of third-party payment represented an important achievement as it could take credit for having opened the private health care sector to low- and middle-income employees.

In sum, the 2004 reform was a major victory for Tunisia's trade union. Using its bargaining power and supported by propitious economic conditions, the UGTT managed to reverse nearly all of the initial reform objectives. An increasing privatization of the Tunisian health care system was averted; financial charges for employees were kept low; costs of reform were outsourced to private sector providers; and the public health care system was given a financial boost. This meant that the fundamental character of the Tunisian health care system with the state as the major provider and funder of health care was successfully kept in place. In comparison to private health care providers for whom the CNAM reform often meant financial losses, the UGTT could also draw on its past experience in striking deals with the government and its privileged access to power, which itself was partly a consequence of Tunisia's particular welfare trajectory.

5.2.2 Intended and unintended beneficiaries: the subsidy conundrum

Thus far, examples of mobilization against spending cuts and systemic reforms have mostly involved the target groups of social policies, such as students or workers benefiting from social security. Resistance against spending cuts has also involved providers of social welfare, such as teachers, who are an integral part of the welfare state. This section draws attention to a further mechanism of path dependence involving groups that were neither initially targeted by social policies, nor are welfare providers. To the extent that these groups can become major beneficiaries from social policies and have an interest in their continuation, these spill-over effects are an important additional mechanism that contributes to the perpetuation patterns of distribution over time.

Less conspicuous, networks of unintended beneficiaries and their association with welfare policies are often ignored.[188] However, their discreet nature should not deceive us over their political influence. Especially when regime insiders—that is, actors with a privileged access to the centre of political decision making—are able to tap into resource streams generated by social policies, they can become

---

[185] Le Temps 2007.   [186] Le Temps 2005.
[187] Personal interview with Ali Jebira, Tunis, 3 July 2013.
[188] Blatter and Buzzell 2013, pp. 4–5.

major veto players able to fend off attempts to change the status quo. This dynamic is particularly visible with regard to food and energy subsidies in Tunisia.[189] As it is argued in this section, the particular combination of target groups hostile to reform and insider capture of subsidy streams has undermined major reforms.

The Tunisian subsidy system: a brief overview

Like most other MENA countries, Tunisia entertains an extensive system of food and energy subsidies.[190] Regarding food products, price controls for basic food items, such as bread and sugar, were first introduced in June 1959 in an attempt to keep wages stable and secure the provision of affordable food to low-income groups.[191] To put the food subsidy system on a more solid financial basis, the Tunisian government created a special subsidy fund in May 1970, the *Caisse générale de compensation* (General Compensation Fund; CGC), which today subsidizes four main groups of products: wheat and derivative products, such as flour, bread, pasta, and couscous; vegetable oils; milk; and sugar. In terms of their relative weight, wheat derivatives have since the 1980s represented the bulk of Tunisia's food subsidy bill, ranging between 50 and 75 per cent of the total.[192] At its inception, the CGC was deliberately designed as a mechanism of redistribution because it was financed through taxes on 'luxury goods', such as alcohol.[193] In reality, the distributional effect of food subsidies has often been regressive as high-income groups disproportionately consume subsidized goods and the income generated from luxury taxes does not cover the costs.[194]

Whilst the technical details of the compensation system are complex, the CGC basically fixes prices of basic food items below the world market price and then compensates local producers for the difference between the local and the world market price.[195] In case local production is not sufficient to satisfy domestic demand, the CGC compensates either for the import of the final consumption good, such as sugar, or for the import of inputs, such as wheat, which are then distributed to local producers. Though the importation of food products has been liberalized since the mid-1990s, the quasi-totality of these imports is made through public and para-statal institutions, such as the *Office des céréales* (Wheat office; OC) and the *Office du commerce de Tunisie* (Tunisian Office of Commerce; OCT), which controls all sugar imports into Tunisia. Para-statal organizations are also involved in the local collection and distribution of subsidized goods. It is important to note that, with the exception of sugar, food items are in principle only subsidized if they are destined for final consumption. However, substantial leakages occur along the production and distribution chain as producers and

---

[189] Woertz 2013 finds a similar dynamic in the context of Saudi Arabia.

[190] For an overview of food security regimes in MENA, see Woertz 2014.

[191] IMF 1962b, pp. 7–8.   [192] CRES 2013, p. 12.   [193] Khaldi 1995, p. 346.

[194] World Bank 2012a, p. 45; and IMF 2014, p. 91.

[195] For a good overview, see World Bank 2006b.

sellers divert subsidies toward non-subsidized products or sell them on the black market.[196]

In terms of their financial weight in the budget, between 1970 and 2010 food subsidies amounted to 2 per cent of Tunisia's GDP, or 6.3 per cent of the country's budget, on average. This broadly represents Tunisia's total outlays for health care in the same period. However, as Tunisia has never been food self-sufficient and has had to rely to a large extent on imports, outlays for food subsidies have exhibited considerable fluctuation, reflecting the volatility in international food prices (see Figure 5.1). It should also be noted that the CGC has been running deficits since 1974 because the earmarked taxes on 'luxury' goods have not proved sufficient to finance Tunisia's food subsidy bill[197]—despite the introduction of new 'luxury' taxes. An important part of the subsidy bill has therefore been financed through the general budget.

In addition to food subsidies, Tunisia has also established a system of extensive energy subsidies in the form of cheap electricity, gas, and petrol. Since the state has acted as a quasi-monopolist in the production and provision of energy, energy subsidies take the form of monopolist price setting by the state, with prices generously below the level of the world market. In contrast to food subsidies,

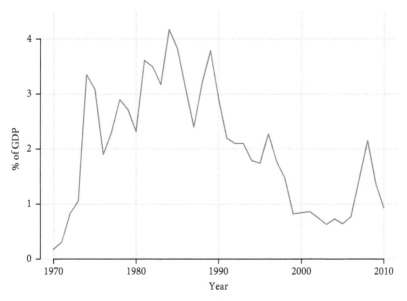

Figure 5.1 Expenditure on food subsidies as a percentage of GDP in Tunisia (1970–2010)

Source: Adaab and Elloumi 1997; and Banque Centrale de Tunisie 2015.

---

[196] IMF 1997, p. 31.   [197] Ben Dhiaf 1982, p. 590.

however, Tunisia was a net energy exporter from the early 1970s until the late 1990s and was able to provide cheap energy from its own domestic resources in this period. With falling production levels and increasing consumption, the country turned into a net importer of energy in the late 1990s, having to import about 17 per cent of its energy needs between 2000 and 2010.[198] Coupled with a general increase in world energy prices during the 2000s, the Tunisian government had to spend an increasing amount on the subsidization of energy, amounting to about 1 per cent of GDP between 2004 and 2010 (see Figure 5.2). In response, the authorities introduced an automatic indexing mechanism of local energy prices to the world market price in 2009,[199] which was repealed shortly after the uprisings in 2011. Similar to food subsides, energy subsidies are primarily regressive in terms of their distributional impact, with the bulk of subsidies being reaped by high-income households and energy-intensive industries.[200]

In comparison with other social policies, the subsidization of food and energy has been the most problematic of all. First, while food and energy subsidies have used up a considerable part of Tunisia's resources, their distributional impact has

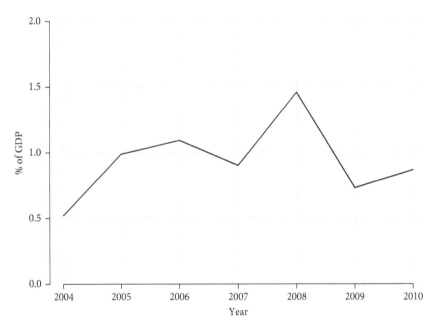

Figure 5.2 Expenditure on energy subsidies as a percentage of GDP in Tunisia (2004–2010)

Source: Republic of Tunisia 2013.

[198] World Bank 2012b.   [199] Fattouh and El-Katiri 2012, p. 20.
[200] IMF 2014, p. 18; and Blatter and Buzzell 2013.

been regressive as better-off citizens benefit disproportionately from the system. Second, having to rely on the world market to satisfy the local demand for cheap food and energy, subsidy expenditures have proven to be highly volatile and have put considerable pressure on fiscal resources during periods of rapid price inflation. Yet, reforming the system has proven politically risky due to the resistance of intended and unintended beneficiaries. Let us look at both groups in turn.

The told story: mobilized beneficiaries

Similar to other countries,[201] food riots in response to subsidy cuts forced the Tunisian government to repeal reform measures and, by setting a historical precedent, have left an enduring political legacy that has complicated further attempts at reform. The Tunisian food riots lasted from December 1983 until January 1984. Representing 'the worst violence since independence',[202] protests left about 100 people dead and caused considerable devastation as a result of rioting and plundering.[203] The background to the protests were government measures announced in mid-December 1983 to increase the prices of subsidized goods. In view of rapid price hikes on the international market, subsidization had become very costly in the early 1980s, representing over 4 per cent of GDP (see Figure 5.1). As a result, the government was looking for a way to alleviate the costs incurred from the subsidy bill. Initially, the cabinet envisaged gradually increasing prices over a period of ten years in order to reach parity with world market prices by the early 1990s. At this point, the CGC was supposed to be abolished.[204] Yet, according to Mohamed Ennaceur, who was Minister of Social Affairs at the time,[205] adjustment measures were sped up under the pressure of Prime Minister Mohamed Mzali, who sought to impress President Bourguiba by demonstrating his ability to achieve rapid and effective reforms.[206] The price increases announced in December 1983 were therefore considerably larger than initially envisaged, on average between 70 and 90 per cent.[207] For bread, prices more than doubled.[208] In haste, the government also made the mistake of launching the compensation measures consisting of wage increases and targeted social transfers *after* the implementation of the price increases.[209] There was no clear communication strategy to prepare the public.[210]

Shortly after the measures were announced, riots erupted in poor neighbourhoods of southern Tunisia and rapidly spilled over to the country's industrial centres of Sfax, Gafsa, and the capital, Tunis.[211] It is important to note that these riots generally had a spontaneous character and were driven by what could be called

---

[201] Walton and Seddon 1994.   [202] World Bank 1996, p. 28.   [203] Ibid., p. 28.
[204] Moalla 2011, p. 380.   [205] Personal interview, Tunis, 21 May 2013.
[206] Note that this occurred against the backdrop of a looming succession to Bourguiba.
[207] Kraïem 2011, p. 441.   [208] Bechri and Naccache 2003, p. 30.   [209] Ibid., p. 30.
[210] Blatter and Buzzell 2013, p. 16.   [211] World Bank 1996, p. 28.

labour market outsiders living in the poor urban quarters: small shopkeepers, seasonal workers, students, and young unemployed teenagers.[212] The latter group in particular resented the measure as they relied almost exclusively on food subsidies.[213] In view of the public discontent, Bourguiba first announced a reduction in the price increase by 50 per cent, before scrapping the measure entirely a few days later. The episode left a profound mark on the regime's collective memory which has made it difficult to tackle subsidies ever since. For example, Monceur Rouissi, former minister and personal adviser to President Ben Ali, described the subsidy issue as a 'nightmare for all successive governments, too sensitive to be reformed'.[214] Recently declassified IMF documents also reveal the impact of food riots on the government. Therein, the government justifies its hesitation with regard to subsidies by their 'marked social sensitivity [that was] now apparent'.[215]

Having negotiated a substantial wage increase for its members in compensation for subsidy cuts, the UGTT had remained on the sideline during the food riots. This does not mean, however, that the union would be a neutral actor in future attempts to reform. On the contrary, following the riots, the union immediately tightened its stance vis-à-vis future price increases. In August 1984, it called upon the government to 'stop its policy of price liberalization and impose stricter control on prices'.[216] In a similar vein, the former deputy secretary general of the UGTT, Ali Ben Romdhane, stated in a personal interview with the author that the subsidy system was a 'red line' that the government should not attempt to cross.[217] The former head of the employers' association, Hédi Jilani, also highlights the UGTT's role as a veto player. When asked whether any government would ever attempt to abolish the CGC, he replied: 'Never! The UGTT is adamant to keep it and constantly lobbies for its maintenance. Also, there would be riots across the country. No government would ever dare do that.'[218]

The combination of a legacy of violent unrest instigated by Tunisia's urban poor, and a strong labour union ready to defend the subsidy system has impeded successive governments in carrying out comprehensive reform. In consequence, changes to the existing system—such as the introduction of a self-targeting system[219]— have been discrete and left the fundamental architecture of the system intact.

The untold story: unintended beneficiaries and political connections
Yet the subsidy system has not only persisted because successive governments have feared the ire of ordinary citizens. Subsidies have also come to benefit a number of politically well-connected entrepreneurs, who have turned into an influential lobby in favour of the current system. To understand their role in the subsidy

---

[212] Ibid., p. 28.   [213] Kraïem 2011, p. 441.
[214] Personal interview, Tunis, 22 May 2013.   [215] IMF 1987a, p. 30.
[216] Réalités 1984.   [217] Personal interview, Tunis, 2 May 2013.
[218] Personal interview, Tunis, 13 June 2013.   [219] World Bank 1996.

system, it is important to explain briefly how manufacturers and merchants benefit from the system in place.[220]

Regarding energy, first and foremost it is the energy-intensive sectors that reap an important part of the energy subsidies. These include, on the one hand, energy-intensive manufacturing sectors, such as cement, textiles, and chemical products. On the other hand, energy subsidies disproportionately benefit companies in the transport and logistics sector, which heavily rely on subsidized fuel.[221] As regards food subsidies, two mechanisms make the system particularly profitable for insider firms. First, the food subsidy market is highly regulated and companies wanting to operate in the sector have to apply for government licences.[222] Whilst obtaining such a licence is difficult and generally requires political connections,[223] once companies have made it into the market, they face relatively little domestic competition as Tunisian authorities have been quite restrictive about access and international competitors are disadvantaged as a result of Tunisia's high tariffs on food imports. The low number of operating companies is testament to this restrictive access policy.[224] The licensing policy also applies to service providers along the distribution chain, such as the collectors of wheat.

Second, and related to the first point, companies operating in a subsidy-related sector have a guaranteed profit based on the allocated government quotas. In fact, firms have no pressure to operate cost effectively as the government pays the producers a fixed profit margin above the unit cost. Mark-ups are generally given out rather generously and profit margins in the region of 15 per cent are not uncommon.[225] Regarding the sugar sector, the business sector also benefits from the subsidization of sugar as an input, which means that biscuit, chocolate, and soft drink manufacturers receive one of their main ingredients at a rate subsidized by the Treasury. According to a business insider, about 80 per cent of all sugar is used for industrial purposes, not for final consumption.[226] The number of firms operating in the sector is relatively low, comprising twelve biscuit and seven chocolate factories.[227] Benefits are thus derived from the combination of state-licensed oligopolies and guaranteed prices.

Regarding the political clout of these business actors, it is difficult to gauge and document their influence exactly. Unlike the lobbying of the UGTT which frequently involves communication with its members and the public at large, business lobbying operates exclusively behind close doors. Actors privy to the government–business interaction confirm, however, that companies do indeed have significant lobbying potential. According to Moncer Rouissi, who was a member of the

---

[220] See also Eibl 2017.   [221] Blatter and Buzzell 2013, p. 29.
[222] The following description is based on World Bank 2006b; World Bank 1996; and IMF 1997.
[223] Personal interview with Maher Kallel, Tunis, 18 June 2013. Kallel is a board member of the Poulina Group, one of Tunisia's biggest conglomerates with various subsidiaries in the food industry.
[224] APII 2014.   [225] World Bank 1996, pp. 5–6.
[226] Personal interview with Maher Kallel, Tunis, 18 June 2013.   [227] APII 2014.

ruling party's Central Committee from 2003 until its dissolution in March 2011, business actors are 'an important lobby, difficult to keep in check'.[228] Maher Kallel portrays the subsidy-related sectors as 'being pervaded by businessmen with strong connections to the centre of power'.[229] While this anecdotal evidence provides preliminary support, my case would be considerably strengthened if I could demonstrate that actors with *well-known* political connections were more likely to operate in the subsidy sector. If true, this could be interpreted as implicit evidence for their interest in the subsidy system and, by extension, its continuation. Both qualitative and quantitative evidence supports this claim.

Qualitative evidence
Table 5.2 summarizes the activities of politically connected businessmen in sectors related to food subsidies before the ouster of President Ben Ali in January 2011. To identify actors with political connections to the regime, I used three different sources: internal documents of the market research company German Trade Invest;[230] an internal report of the German–Tunisian Chamber of Commerce;[231] and the reports published by the Tunisian Ministry of Finance on confiscated companies after the Tunisian Revolution.[232] Company-related information is taken from the Orbis database.[233] In combination, these sources yield a rather complete picture of the extensive networks that existed between certain businessmen and the presidential palace. The documents also reveal the different ways in which entrepreneurs established connections to the regime. Kinship relations by virtue of being part of the presidential families, Ben Ali and Trabelsi, or established through intermarriage played an important role. Other actors co-invested with the presidential family and made their inroads into the political centre of power as business associates. Finally, membership in the ruling party's influential Central Committee represented a third route through which political connections were established.[234]

Their presence in subsidy-related sectors can be described as pervasive. In the milk sector, eight out of ten milk factories in the country were in the hands of business cronies with political connections. Hamdi Medded, for example, was a major business partner of Ben Ali's son-in-law, Sakher El Materi, and shareholder in his Zitouna Bank. He had jointly purchased 25 per cent of Tunisia's mobile phone provider Tunisiana with El Materi. Similarly, five of the thirteen refineries producing vegetable oil were in the hands of politically connected entrepreneurs. The sector is particularly interesting as all three types of connections are present: the Ben Ayed family was represented by Abdelwahab Ben Ayed in the RCD's

---

[228] Personal interview, Tunis, 22 May 2013.   [229] Personal interview, Tunis, 18 June 2013.
[230] German Trade Invest 2011.   [231] German–Tunisian Chamber of Commerce 2011.
[232] Republic of Tunisia 2015.   [233] Bureau van Dijk 2013.
[234] For more detail on the cronyism dataset, see Eibl and Malik 2016; and Malik and Eibl forthcoming.

Table 5.2 Politically connected actors in sectors related to food subsidies: Tunisia

Actor	Company	Type of political connection	Sector
Sofiane Ben Ali	Fermes laitières	Kin: ruling Family	Milk
Belhassen Trabelsi	Ste UTIQUE pour la promotion agricole Al Baraka; Tunisie Sucre	Kin: Family of Leila Ben Ali, Ben Ali's second wife; part of ruling family	Milk and sugar
Ben Jemaa family	Elbene industrie; Ste régionale des industries laitieres; Ste tunisienne dengrais chimiques	Party: late Mohamed Ben Jemaa was member of the RCD Central Committee	Milk, sweets, and wheat collection
Hamdi Medded	Centrale laitiere de Cap Bon; Centrale laitiere du Nord SA; Centrale laitiere Sidi Bouzid, subsidiaries of Delice SA; Ste tunisienne des industries alimentaires; Ste des boissons du cap bon SA, subsidiary of Delice SA	Associate: business partner of Sakher Materi, son-in-law of President Ben Ali	Milk and soft drinks
Ben Ayed family	Med Oil Company; Ste des industries alimentaires et meunieres SIAM II; Générale industrielle des produits alimentaires GIPA SA	Party: Abelwahab Ben Ayed, CEO of the Poulina group, was member of the RCD Central Committee	Vegetable oil, flour, couscous, pasta, and sweets
Boujbel family	Ste des huiles Borges Tunisie SA	Associate: business partners of Trabelsi family	Vegetable oil
Hachicha family	Ste Cristal-Tunisie; Ste meuniere tunisienne	Associate: business partners of Maroune Mabrouk, Ben Ali's former son-in-law	Vegetable oil, flour, couscous, and pasta

Continued

Table 5.2 *Continued*

Actor	Company	Type of political connection	Sector
Imed Trabelsi	Agrimed	Kin: family of Leila Ben Ali, Ben Ali's second wife; part of ruling family	Vegetable oil
Taoufik Chaibi	Les Grands Moulins de Gabes, subsidiary of UTIC group; Biscuiterie Méditerranénne, subsidiary of UTIC	Kin: uncle of Slim Zarrouk, husband of one of Leila Ben Ali's relatives	Flour, couscous, pasta and sweets
Moncef Mzabi	Ste minoterie de la Soukra	Associate and party: business partner of Sakher Materi, son-in-law of President Ben Ali; Mzabi was also member of the RCD Central Committee	Flour, couscous, and pasta
Ben Ghorbal family	Compagnie africaine des pates alimentaires	Associate: business partner of Sakher Materi, son-in-law of President Ben Ali	Flour, couscous, and pasta
Marouane Mabrouk	Ste tunisienne de biscuiterie, Ste tunisienne de chocolaterie et de confiserie SA, Ste Sotuchoc	Kin: Ben Ali's former son-in-law, ex-husband of Cyrine Ben Ali	Sweets
Ben Yedder family	Grande fabrique de confiserie orientale, subsidiary of Amen group	Associate and party: business partners of Ben Ali and Trabelsi family; Rachid Ben Yedder was also member of the RCD Central Committee	Sweets
Ben Gaied family	Société de produits industriels de patisserie et alimentaires	Kin: Mehdi Ben Ghaid is Ben Ali's son in law, married to Halima Ben Ali	Sweets

Note: Politically connected actors are identified based on German Trade Invest 2011; German–Tunisian Chamber of Commerce 2011; and Republic of Tunisia 2015. Business information is taken from Bureau van Dijk 2013 and online research.

Central Committee; the Boujbel and Hachicha families were important business partners of the Trabelsi family; and Imed Trabelsi was Ben Ali's next of kin. In the sugar sector, Belhassen Trabelsi, brother of Ben Ali's wife, Leila, obtained the permission to build Tunisia's second only sugar factory, which effectively undermined the state's monopoly of sugar production. And sugar as a subsidized input also benefited businesses in the sweets sector, the majority of which was in the hands of connected businessmen.

The picture is similar as regards energy subsidies. Using UNIDO's classification of energy-intensive industries,[235] I was able to identify nine crony actors in energy-intensive sectors. A number of them, such as Hédi Jilani and Maroune Mabrouk, operated in Tunisia's long-standing textile sector. Another particularly telling example is the Carthago cement factory established by Belhassen Trabelsi. Not only did Trabelsi acquire the land for his factory for a ludicrously cheap amount, he also had 15 kilometres of railway built straight to his factory—at the expense of the public Treasury.[236] 'The family' was also active in Tunisia's transport and logistic sector, running, amongst others, a private airline and a water carriage company. On the whole, it appears that politically connected actors had a solid grip on sectors benefiting from Tunisia's food and energy subsidy system.

Quantitative evidence
To test the robustness of the link between subsidies and crony activity, I also ran a number of simple logistic regressions. This was to ascertain that cronies were indeed over-represented in subsidy-related sectors as opposed to other sectors of the economy and that their presence in these sectors was not due to an unobserved confounder, such as high tariff rates. The dependent variable, *Crony activity*, measures whether a politically connected actor is present in a given sector of the Tunisian economy. The binary variable is taken from a new dataset on crony activity in pre-revolutionary Tunisia by Eibl and Malik,[237] which measures crony activity in all manufacturing sectors based on the above-mentioned sources. The level of aggregation is the four-digit level of the UNCTAD ISIC 3.1 classification and thus relatively detailed, distinguishing 168 manufacturing sectors. The variable is time-invariant and codes the presence of cronies for the last decade under President Ben Ali. To capture the effect of energy subsidies, I use a binary variable, *Low intensity*, which takes the value of 1 if energy intensity in a sector is low, and 0 otherwise. The classification of sectors by energy intensity is provided by UNIDO.[238] With regard to food subsidies, I use two dummy variables. The first one, *Direct food*, measures whether a sector is directly involved in the provision

[235] UNIDO 2010.   [236] Jeune Afrique 2012.   [237] Eibl and Malik 2015.
[238] UNIDO 2010.

Table 5.3 Politically connected actors in energy-intensive sectors: Tunisia

Actor	Company	Type of political connection	Sector
Taoufik Chaibi	Cartonnerie Tunisie, Ste tunisienne des emballages modernes SA, subsidiaries of UTIC group	Kin: uncle of Slim Zarrouk, husband of one of Leila Ben Ali's relatives	Paper
Moez Trabelsi	Confection moderne	Kin: family of Leila Ben Ali, Ben Ali's second wife, ruling family	Textiles
Hédi Jilani	Groupe Hédi Jilani	Kin and party: father of Zohra Jilani, married to Belhassen Trabelsi; Jilani was also member of the RCD Central Committee	Textiles
Marouane Mabrouk	Tuntex	Kin: Ben Ali's former son-in-law, ex-husband of Cyrine Ben Ali	Textiles
Moncef El Materi	Adwya	Kin: two sons of Moncef El Materi married daughters of Ben Ali	Chemical products
Belhassen Trabelsi	Carthago Cement Company	Kin: family of Leila Ben Ali, Ben Ali's second wife, ruling family	Cement
Mourad Trabelsi	Med Sea	Kin: family of Leila Ben Ali, Ben Ali's second wife, ruling family	Transport and logistics
Imed Trabelsi	Med Business Holding	Kin: family of Leila Ben Ali, Ben Ali's second wife, ruling family	Transport and logistics
Slim Zarrouk	Opat, Ste MAS	Kin: husband of one of Leila Ben Ali's relatives	Transport and logistics

Note: Politically connected actors are identified based on German Trade Invest 2011; German–Tunisian Chamber of Commerce 2011; and Republic of Tunisia 2015. Business information is taken from Bureau van Dijk 2013 and online research. Classification of energy-intensive industries taken from UNIDO 2010.

of subsidized food items. The second variable, *All food*, includes all sectors in the previous variable plus those sectors that benefit from subsidized food inputs.[239]

To control for potential confounders, I include a couple of control variables.[240] *Tariff average*, taken from the WITS database,[241] measures the average most-favoured nation tariff in a given sector in the last decade of Ben Ali. The variable captures the level of protection of a sector from international competition. *Imports* indicates the value of total imports in current USD as import penetration might also deter cronies from entering. The variable is taken from UNIDO's Indstat database.[242] Both variables are available for the years of 2003, 2004, 2005, and 2008. The model is a pooled cross-sectional logistic regression with standard errors clustered at the four-digit sector level.

The results presented in Table 5.4 confirm the impression gained from the qualitative evidence that Tunisian crony capitalists have made considerable inroads into subsidy-related sectors. In view of columns (1)–(3), it appears that cronies are significantly more likely to be present in sectors with medium–high energy intensity; sectors involved in subsidized production; and sectors that additionally benefit from subsidized inputs. The finding remains robust when controlling simultaneously for energy intensity and food subsidies, as shown in the full model in column (4). To illustrate the strength of the subsidy effect on cronies, Figure 5.3 presents the predicted probability of crony presence by energy intensity and a sector's involvement in food subsidies. Notably, the average probability of cronies

Table 5.4 Crony presence and subsidies in Tunisia

	(1)	(2)	(3)	(4)
Low intensity	−3.370***			−3.373***
	(0.517)			(0.522)
Direct food		1.491**		
		(0.683)		
All food			1.491**	1.317*
			(0.683)	(0.732)
Tariff average	0.0148	0.0207	0.0207	0.00289
	(0.0137)	(0.0203)	(0.0203)	(0.0158)
Imports (log)	0.332**	0.0615	0.0615	0.371**
	(0.168)	(0.125)	(0.125)	(0.180)
Observations	172	172	172	172

Note: Logit model with robust standard errors in parentheses; constant omitted.
$^*p < 0.10, ^{**}p < 0.05, ^{***}p < 0.01$

---

[239] A summary of these sectors is available in Appendix C.
[240] The number of available control variables is limited by the scarcity of data at the sectoral level. The results should thus been viewed as merely descriptive of an empirical pattern.
[241] World Bank 2013.   [242] UNIDO 2013.

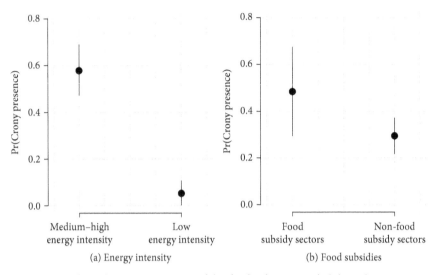

Figure 5.3 Effect of energy intensity and food subsidies on probability of crony presence in Tunisia

Note: Whiskers indicate 95 per cent confidence bounds. Marginal effects based on the full model presented in column (4) of Table 5.4. All variables were set to their observed values.

being present in sectors with medium–high energy intensity is about ten times higher than for low-intensity sectors. As for food subsidies, the average probability of crony presence nearly doubles when a sector is related to food subsidies. In combination, these findings present strong evidence that politically connected actors do indeed reap substantial benefits from the Tunisian subsidy system and, by extension, have a solid interest in its continuation.

5.2.3 Summary

This section has demonstrated the mechanisms of path dependence that have kept the Tunisian welfare state on its post-independence trajectory. They have involved a number of different actors (see Figure 5.4). On the one hand, we have seen the beneficiaries of social policies rallying against government attempts to cut spending, as in the case of the 1970s student protests, or attempts at structural reform which would have affected the level of welfare provision, as in the case of the 2004 health insurance reform. These pro-welfare constituencies were partly a product of the Tunisian welfare trajectory itself, which validates the claim made elsewhere that welfare states indeed create their own constituencies.[243] This partly

---

[243] Pierson 1994.

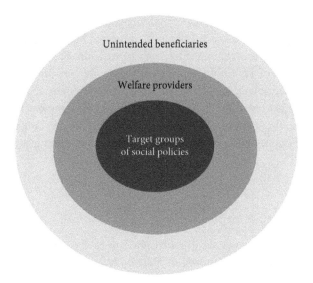

Figure 5.4 Welfare constituencies in Tunisia

applies to the student protests and, most certainly, to the teachers' union lobbying for an upgrade of low-level teaching staff.

Regarding labour more specifically, I have been able to show that the UGTT was not only the key actor in the foundation of Tunisia's authoritarian welfare state, but has also represented an important veto player against spending cuts and structural reforms. In this respect, the union could capitalize on early advantages gained from its privileged position in the political system, as well as its far reach into the state apparatus. The combination of these factors explains why, as El-Said and Harrigan point out, social expenditures have been shielded rather effectively from structural adjustment.[244]

The 2004 health insurance reform also demonstrates the continuous attempt of the Ben Ali regime to use social policy to garner legitimacy and sharpen its social profile. According to a former minister, Ben Ali regularly asked ministers of social portfolios to come up with new reform ideas—frequently in the run-up to the May labour day.[245] Their reforms included not only the 2004 health care reform, but also the extension of social security to self-employed and/or irregularly employed workers throughout the 2000s. In addition to boosting its legitimacy, the regime introduced such measures to counteract the influence of the UGTT amongst the Tunisian working class and widen the regime's social base *independent* of the UGTT.[246] In that sense, the duality between the UGTT and the regime partly substituted for the lack of party competition.

---

[244] El-Said and Harrigan 2014.
[245] Personal interview with Naceur El Gharbi, Tunis, 2 July 2013.   [246] Ibid.

On the other hand, mechanisms of path dependence have also involved unintended beneficiaries, more specifically well-connected businessmen who came to tap into resource streams generated by welfare provision. The evidence presented suggests that some of Tunisia's most powerful entrepreneurs, including the presidential family themselves, benefited from the country's extensive subsidy system. And although it is more difficult to document exactly how these actors prevented divergence from the status quo, their access to decision making coupled with their interest in the continuation of subsidies certainly made them a powerful lobby group.

5.3 Conclusion

This chapter pursued two goals. The first one was to give an analytic account of the foundation of the Tunisian welfare state by focusing specifically on the link between early elite conflict and welfare provision. In line with my theoretical claim, intra-elite conflict was indeed instrumental in Tunisia embarking on a path of extensive welfare provision. This conclusion rests on four key findings from my process tracing exercise. One, Bourguiba was not naturally inclined toward welfare provision and, as a result, would have preferred to form a regime coalition which economically would have leaned to the right of the political spectrum. Two, the conflict with his opponent Ben Youssef compelled him to look for an ally, which he found in the Tunisian labour union. Three, the union could use this window of opportunity to get a solid foothold in power which it later used to expand welfare provision. Four, Bourguiba's unsuccessful attempts to renege on his commitments suggest that another outcome, less favourable for welfare provision, would have been the outcome had the leadership of Tunisia's ruling party remained cohesive on the eve of independence. Granted, Tunisia's labour union perhaps represents a special case of workers' capacity to organize in the Middle East. However, the foregoing analysis strongly suggests that it would not have been able to impose its programme without the window of opportunity provided by divided elites. In the broader explanatory logic of this thesis, these findings provide important insights into the causal mechanisms underpinning the observed covariation of early intra-elite conflict and welfare provision, and thus lend credibility to the overall argument.

The second goal of this chapter was to provide illustrative evidence of the causal mechanisms that underpin the marked path dependence of Tunisia's welfare trajectory. In this regard, my account highlights the ability of actors who have benefited from welfare provision to avert divergence. Their capacity for collective action, in turn, built on an accumulated advantages these groups had gained from early welfare state development. In the case of labour, the UGTT had preserved significant routes to access the centre of political decision making, and its experience in the area of social policies and bargaining with the state gave it an advantage over other actors. This is particularly visible in the 2004 CNAM reform where the UGTT managed to outsource costs of the reform to private sector health care providers. My analysis has also demonstrated the importance of unintended beneficiaries who inadvertently came to benefit from social policies. Specifically, using both qualitative and quantitative evidence, I have shown that crony capitalists gained major stakes in the country's subsidy system and thus turned into an important gatekeeper standing in the way of reform. Taken together, both mechanisms underline a central tenet in the literature: welfare states indeed create their own, intended *and* unintended, constituencies.

6

Egypt: Between Warfare and Welfare

This chapter analyses the origin's of Egypt's welfare trajectory and demonstrates the causes of its path dependence. The focus is on teasing out the causal mechanisms underlying the macro-level variation and, by the same token, examining the validity of the causal claims developed in the theoretical framework. In many ways, this chapter represents a structured focused comparison[1] with the preceding Tunisia case study.

On the one hand, as in Tunisia, the combination of intra-elite conflict and the absence of salient communal cleavages prompted regime elites to broaden their coalition and heightened the regime's incentives to provide social welfare. With most historical actors of this time period having passed, I substantiate this causal mechanism by relying on the memoirs of members of the initial ruling circle, which give us a unique insight into the motives of the regime-building elites. Demonstrating the ideological ambiguity of the ruling elite, in particular Nasser, I also rule out ideology as a pertinent explanation of Egypt's social policy trajectory.

On the other hand, in comparison to Tunisia, the nascent regime in Egypt emerged in a much more hostile geostrategic environment where threats to regime survival emanated the outside. Consequent changes in the regime's threat perception undermined a sustained high welfare effort as, in the absence of resource rents, considerable funds needed to be allocated to national defence. Using primary and secondary sources, I show the shift in the regime elites' threat perception and, based on cabinet minutes from the National Archives, present a 'smoking gun' test[2] of the suggested trade-off between defence and welfare.

Finally, I provide evidence that the resulting social policies primarily relied on 'cheap' social policies, which are characterized by underfunding, the prominence of 'free' social policies, the use of windfalls, and a design which turns social policies into a source of revenue. To do so, I rely on qualitative evidence, in part stemming from archival material, and a number of simple regressions that test observable implications of my 'cheap' social policies argument.

Regarding mechanisms of path dependence, the analysis highlights important similarities with Tunisia but also emphasizes the effect of different welfare and regime formation legacies on processes of path dependence. While I find that

---

[1] George and Bennett 2005; see also Slater and Ziblatt 2013.
[2] Van Evera 1997; and Mahoney and Goertz 2006.

Social Dictatorships: The Political Economy of the Welfare State in the Middle East and North Africa. Ferdinand Eibl, Oxford University Press (2020). © Ferdinand Eibl. DOI: 10.1093/oso/9780198834274.001.0001

welfare constituencies have successfully averted attempts at retrenchment, using the example of health care and subsidy reforms, they have lacked the political impetus to shift Egypt on to a high-spending trajectory since the 1979 peace treaty with Israel. This lack of a path-changing peace dividend is also imputable to the legacies of war and a defence policy which has turned the Egyptian military into a major political veto player. As in Tunisia, I further show the importance of unintended beneficiaries of social policies for explaining path dependence. In this area, too, the legacies of Egypt's geostrategic environment have shaped the nature of unintended beneficiaries, with the army being a major one of these.

The chapter proceeds as follows. Section 6.1 presents an analytical narrative of the origin of Egypt's welfare trajectory, demonstrating the causal effects of intra-elite conflict and external threat and the resulting 'cheap' social policies. Section 6.2 elucidates mechanisms of path dependence which have prevented major changes of welfare spending in either direction. Section 6.3 concludes the chapter.

6.1 Too Many Commitments: The Origin of Egypt's Welfare Trajectory

This section consists of three main subsections. In the first, I demonstrate the ideological ambiguity of the regime-building elites by pointing out their ideological diversity, the lack of a clear political programme, the reliance on a 'trial and error' strategy, and their scepticism toward left-wing policies which translated into markedly pro-business policies in the aftermath of the coup. Second, I process trace the link between intra-elite conflict and welfare spending, relying on a range of primary and secondary sources. Third, I focus on the effects of Egypt's strong external threats on welfare spending by showing how a change in the regime elites' threat perception led to higher spending on national defence. I also provide qualitative and quantitative evidence suggesting that, to 'square the circle', the regime predominantly relied on 'cheap' social policies.

6.1.1 The Free Officers' Ideological Ambiguity

Much has been written about Nasser's role in shaping Egypt's political and socioeconomic order after the July 1952 coup at the hand of the Free Officers Movement (FOM). His pivotal role has found expression in the term *Nasserism*,[3] which—akin to socialism, liberalism, or Marxism—suggests a coherent body of ideas inspiring a plan of action to transform and modernize society. Naturally, Nasserism should then provide the explanation for Egypt's particular welfare trajectory.

[3] See, amongst others, Abdel-Fadil 1980; Craissati 1989; and Awad 1975.

While I do not question the tremendous importance of Nasser, I would submit that Nasserism, in a sense, *is* the Egyptian welfare trajectory and thus cannot sufficiently explain the nature of welfare distribution in Egypt. To support this claim, I highlight a number of elements that undermine an explanation based on ideology and ideas.

First, it is important to note that the FOM—comprising about 300 members before the coup[4]—was ideologically highly diverse. Its leadership, which formed the Revolutionary Command Council (RCC) after the coup, comprised members of the Muslim Brotherhood, such as Abdel Moneim Adel Rauf and Rashad Mehanna,[5] members of the communist organization HADETO, such as Uthman Fawzi and Ahmad Hamrush,[6] Marxists, such as Khaled Mohi Eddin, and members of the right-wing nationalist Young Egypt Party.[7] Nasser himself had joined the Muslim Brotherhood but left in 1949 as a result of a growing divide between nationalists and Islamists.[8] Including 'partisans of existing civilian parties and advocates of military rule, socialists and free traders, admirers of the West and violent anti-imperialist',[9] the FOM was thus characterized by notorious ideological eclecticism, born out of the necessity to prevent rifts within the movement.[10]

Second, resulting from its ideological diversity and the precipitancy in the run-up to the coup, the FOM lacked a clear political, let alone socioeconomic, programme apart from the operational plans for the coup itself.[11] In fact, when Khaled Mohi Eddin drafted a programme for the movement in September 1951, Nasser was most reluctant. He particularly resented the formulation of nationalist demands in leftist, anti-imperialist terms which, in his view, might discredit the FOM in the eyes of the British and Americans and trigger a military intervention, should the FOM take power.[12] In consequence, the movement had rather minimalist objectives when it seized power in July 1952: ending the British military presence in the Suez canal zone; purging the bureaucracy and political parties, notably the ruling nationalist Wafd party, of corruption; removing the King's agents from within the military; and implementing a land reform which would cut back the political power of the rural notability, which was rightly viewed as an impediment to development.[13] Having achieved these goals, the plan was, according to RCC member Kamal Eddin Hussein, to return to the barracks and allow parliamentary politics to resume.[14] On balance, the FOM was certainly

---

[4] Aclimandos 2001, p. 8.   [5] Vatikiotis 1978, p. 85.   [6] Aclimandos 2004, p. 510.
[7] Perry 2004, p. 91.   [8] Aclimandos 2001, p. 7.
[9] Sadowski 1991, p. 55. See also Tignor 1992, p. 293.
[10] Kandil 2012b, p. 198; and Beattie 1994, p. 68.
[11] Bayat 2006, p. 135; Beinin and Lockman 1988, p. 437; and Waterbury 1983, p. 49.
[12] Aclimandos 2004, pp. 653–4.   [13] Ibid., p. 509, 700, 1054; and R. Stephens 1971, p. 118.
[14] Cited in Jawhar 1975, p. 14.

guided by a desire for full national independence and modernization,[15] yet there was no plan to carry out a transformative, welfarist socioeconomic programme.[16]

Third, and related to the foregoing, in the aftermath of the coup the RCC acted mostly based on the principle of 'trial and error'.[17] This is best summarized by Nasser himself who, in 1962, declared that in the first ten years they had followed a practice predominantly based on experimentation.[18] Similarly, Nasser admitted that the Free Officers had 'extracted [their] ideologies from the details of the events [they] passed through'.[19] Their adaptability is visible, for instance, in their attitude toward the monarchy, the abolition of which was only pursued once they sensed the popularity of the measure.[20] Likewise, Nasser is reported to have offered the government to the Wafd party and restoration of pre-coup parliamentary life if they accepted land reform and removed certain politicians.[21] It is thus important to understand that post-coup politics opened the door wide to strategic political interaction and tactical alliances, taking primacy over ideology.

Fourth, Nasser and the RCC more generally were, at least initially, highly sceptical of left-wing ideologies and, as a result, their economic policies were largely pro-business, underpinned by a certain apprehension of organized labour. Regarding their scepticism to leftist ideas, it is important to note that the concept of socialism did not feature at all in the early documents published by the Free Officers after the coup, such as Nasser's *Philosophy of the Revolution* or Sadat's *Revolt on the Nile*.[22] Only by 1958 had the regime begun to appropriate the notion of socialism to legitimize its policies.[23] Nasser only gradually came to perceive himself as leftist while his initial stance is probably best described as nationalist.[24]

In economic matters, the RCC adopted a liberal, pro-businesss strategy following the coup. As RCC member and Minister of of National Guidance, Gamal Salem, put it: 'We are not Socialists. I think our economy can only prosper under free enterprise'.[25] Accordingly, the nascent regime adopted a number of measures to bolster private sector investment: repealing a law restricting foreign ownership of Egyptian companies to 49 per cent; lowering business taxes and exempting foreign companies from business and export taxes; rescheduling business debts; raising tariffs; and declaring a general amnesty for all tax evasion committed since 1947 if the capital was repatriated.[26] Egyptian industrialists were also encouraged to advise the government in the newly founded National Development Council.[27]

---

[15] Rodinson 1968, p. 87.   [16] Kandil 2012b, p. 281.
[17] Ramadan 1975, p. 80; and Vatikiotis 1978, p. 126.   [18] Cited in Aclimandos 2004, p. 1275.
[19] Cited in Be'eri 1970, p. 392.   [20] Aclimandos 2004, p. 835.
[21] R. Stephens 1971, p. 118. See also Aclimandos 2004, p. 1001.
[22] Nasser 1956; and El Sadat 1957.   [23] Lenczowski 1966, p. 36. See also Nordlinger 1977, p. 188.
[24] Beattie 1994, p. 159; and Bayat 2006, pp. 143–4.   [25] Quoted in O'Brien 1966, p. 68.
[26] Aclimandos 2004, p. 1286; Posusney 1997, pp. 42–3; S. Cook 2012, p. 45; and Owen and Şevket 1998, pp. 128–9.
[27] Sabhi 2002, p. 152.

These policies were backed by influential actors in government and the RCC, such as Sayyid Marei, Minister of Agriculture, and RCC member Abdel Moneim Amin, who supervised the Ministry of Social Affairs. In their view, Egypt should follow the route of economically conservative developmentalism, allowing for rapid industrialization based on a cheap workforce. Organized labour was not to play a major role in this strategy. In fact, the repression of left-wing labour unions was deemed an essential part of this strategy. A strike of textile workers in August 1952 was violently repressed and two of its ringleaders were executed. In a similar vein, Sayyid Marei argued that agricultural workers should not be given the right to join unions.[28] And Amin openly advocated the establishment of an 'industrial' dictatorship supervised by the military.[29] The draft labour law, which was prepared under his supervision, echoed this stance by outlawing any right to strike and facilitating lay-offs. The draft law was agreed upon in a joint session of the cabinet and the RCC in March 1953. Nasser had voted in favour, with only one dissenting voice from Khaled Mohi Eddin. When the latter threatened to resign from the RCC, Nasser gave in and the law was amended to forbid arbitrary dismissals because of union activity.[30] Unlikely to have been motivated by concern for workers, the primary reason for Nasser's about-face was to avoid splits within the RCC. Unsurprisingly, being courted by accommodating economic policies, the initial response of capitalists to the coup was positive, albeit cautious, welcoming tight control over labour and the sidelining of the land-owning notability.[31]

These liberal economic policies after the coup represented more than a policy orientation. Rather, they should be viewed as a first attempt at coalition formation. By distributing favours to industrial capitalists and sectors of the old bourgeoisie, it seems that Nasser sought to enlist the backing of capital and to transform it into an important pillar of his nascent regime.[32] Industrialization, not extensive welfarism, was thus the primary goal of the RCC as it seized power.[33] The September 1952 land reform, which is often used as evidence for a latent left-wing position of the RCC, does not alter this assessment. The adopted reform was very modest compared to previous proposals and the RCC had originally favoured the taxation of land in lieu of redistribution.[34] The amount of arable land redistributed was also low, with estimates ranging between 8.5 and 12.5 per cent.[35] Finally, the implementation of the law was such that proprietors were given various possibilities to evade redistribution: for instance, by selling off land to family members.[36] The reform's main goal was thus political: that is, to eliminate the landed aristocracy—whose

---

[28] Beinin 1989, p. 79.   [29] As recorded in Mohi El Din, 1995, 139–40.
[30] This episode is reported in two autobiographies of RCC members: Hamrush 1983, p. 151; and Mohi El Din 1995, pp. 139–42.
[31] Kandil 2012b, p. 195.   [32] Craissati 1989, p. 60. See also Tignor 1992.
[33] Wahba 1994, p. 76.   [34] Sabhi 2002, p. 149; and Ramadan 1976, pp. 16–17.
[35] Aclimandos 2004, pp. 1277–8; and Matzke 2008, p. 45.   [36] Sadowski 1991, p. 63.

opposition the RCC was certain of—as a powerful political actor in Egypt.[37] With ideology as a doubtful cause of Egypt's welfare trajectory, strategic interaction and elite factionalism provide a more pertinent explanation as we will see in the following account.

6.1.2 In Search for a constituency: intra-elite conflict, coalition building, and welfare provision

To understand the critical importance of intra-elite conflict for Nasser's decision to build a lower–middle cross-class coalition and the role of welfare provision in this process, it is important to recall the circumstances of the split that disunited the RCC following the coup. The conflict revolved around a personal rivalry between the nominal head of the RCC and, since June 1953, President of the new-born Republic, Muhammad Naguib, and the de facto leader of the RCC and FOM, Gamal Abdel Nasser. Major General Naguib was widely known as a war hero from the 1948 Palestine War and was chosen by the FOM as a figurehead to lend the coup plotters increased legitimacy. Not contenting himself with his ceremonial role, Naguib soon began to broaden his support by reaching out to various societal groups—to the great displeasure of the RCC. As RCC member Kamal Eddin Hussein put it, 'all he [Naguib] had to do was to drive from his home to his office, surrounded by motorcycles, under the applause of the bystanders [...] He visited hospitals, charities, distributed money [...] And we were toiling long and hard under tons of work and no one knew about it.'[38]

In his attempt to enlist political and popular support, Naguib had a number of advantages. First, he was much better known to the population which 'considered him the leader of the Revolution and their saviour [...] The people didn't know yet the members of the RCC and their service for the country.'[39] Second, being of Sudanese origin, Naguib enjoyed a particular high popularity in Sudan, which at the time was part of Egypt and which the RCC was keen to retain. 'Do not forget Sudan and the influence Naguib has with the Sudanese, with whom he is very popular,' Nasser was told by a Sudanese officer. 'Any exclusion of Naguib would lead to Sudan's secession from Egypt.'[40]

Alongside his attempt to court 'the masses', Naguib targeted a number of specific societal actors to build his power base. These included the Muslim Brotherhood,

---

[37] Barnett 1992, p. 83. At this point, it should also be noted that a number of social policies are often wrongly ascribed to the Nasser regime. Compulsory education from the age of seven to twelve (adopted in 1923), free primary education (in 1944), and free secondary education (in 1950) were all implemented before the Free Officers took power. See Ayubi 1978; Faksh 1973; Mabro 1974; and Albertus 2015a.

[38] Cited in Aclimandos 2004, p. 1079.

[39] RCC member Abdelatif Baghdadi in his memoirs. See Baghdadi 1977, p. 80.

[40] Episode recorded in the memoirs of RCC member Khaled Mohi Eddin. See Mohi El Din 1995, p. 184.

with whom Naguib entered into extensive contacts in December 1953 to 'liquidate' the RCC.[41] Representing the most effective civil society organization at the time,[42] the Brotherhood was vital to provide 'foot soldiers' for urban mobilization. A second pillar of his coalition represented the old political parties, first and foremost the Wafd party, which were lured into the coalition by the promise to restore an electoral system.[43] By the same token, he managed to bring on his side the majority of Egypt's middle-class professionals, notably the lawyers and press syndicates, as well as students.[44] Finally, and most importantly, Naguib commanded the loyalty of significant parts of the armed forces, which stood ready at his defence.[45]

The conflict came to a head in early 1954, culminating in the notorious March Crisis, which heralded the victory of the RCC and Nasser over Naguib. This episode highlights the magnitude of the rift that divided the military junta and the stakes for the actors involved. Two aspects are particularly noteworthy here. The first was massive demonstrations, led by the Muslim Brotherhood and joined by other actors of the Naguib camp, following the announcement of Naguib's resignation on 25 February 1954 in protest at the RCC's undermining of his presidential powers.[46] According to RCC member Salah Salem, 'the country [was] on the brink of explosion'[47] at this point, and Salem urged Nasser that he 'must notify them to announce Naguib's return, otherwise the country will rise in revolt against us!'[48]

The second aspect was the important split within the armed forces that became visible immediately after Naguib's announcement and which pushed the country to the brink of a civil war, which would have made 'Black Saturday, the burning of Cairo in January 1952, look like "child's play."'[49] As armoured vehicles and truckloads of soldiers took position around Naguib's house to protect him, the cavalry and armoured officers—whose headquarters were a stone's throw away from the RCC—demanded the immediate reinstatement of Naguib, and the All-Sudanese Frontier Force threatened to mutiny. Meanwhile, units loyal to the RCC encircled the cavalry in a climactic military stand-off.[50] Given considerable coercive power on both sides, the conflict could clearly not be repressed by force.

Naguib was reinstated as President a couple of days after his resignation, but the denouement of this crisis only came in late March. By that point, the RCC had tightened its grip on the army and persuaded the Muslim Brotherhood to remain temporarily on the sidelines. Mirror-imaging the February incident, the RCC announced its dissolution and a return of Egypt to the previous electoral

---

[41] Aclimandos 2004, p. 1091.   [42] Beattie 1994, p. 58.   [43] Aclimandos 2004, p. 1173.
[44] Gordon 1992, p. 125.   [45] Aclimandos 2004, p. 1162.   [46] Gordon 1992, p. 127.
[47] Cited in Aclimandos 2004, p. 1154.   [48] Quoted in Mohi El Din 1995, p. 204.
[49] Ihsan Abdel Quddous, the editor-in-chief of the *Al-Ahram* newspaper at the time, reporting to the US embassy as quoted in Gordon 1992, p. 152.
[50] Vatikiotis 1985, p. 381; and Aclimandos 2004, pp. 1130–55.

system. This was followed by a three-day general strike of labour unions, which paralysed the country from 26 to 29 March and paved the way for the RCC's return to power. Taken by surprise and diminished in size, Naguib's coalition remained immobilized at this point and left the way open for the RCC to finally sideline Naguib. As the Egyptian historian Tawfiq Aclimandos points out, the three-day strike was the crucial turning point in this struggle for power and it was the alliance with the working class that brought 'salvation' for Nasser and the RCC.[51]

Tracing the mechanism: intra-elite conflict and welfare provision

In this subsection, I provide evidence for a causal link between intra-elite conflict and social spending—a central mechanism of my argument. The repercussions of intra-elite conflict on welfare spending were extensive in Egypt and represented the key driver behind the nascent regime's early social policies up until the mid- to late 1950s. Unfolding in two subsequent stages, social policy measures comprised a first stage of mainly pro-active social spending to counter Naguib and a second stage in which the regime sealed a social policy bargain with labour unions. Since all the key actors of this period have passed away, I crucially rely on the autobiographies and memoirs of RCC members to unveil the motivation behind the regime's early welfare effort.

Regarding the first stage of pro-active spending, two RCC members—Khaled Mohi Eddin and Abdelatif Baghdadi—have written extensively on the motives driving the RCC's social policy strategy and highlighted the important role of intra-elite conflict in this context. One particularly insightful passage in Mohi Eddin's memoirs is worth quoting at length:

> The Revolutionary Command Council began to consider ways and means to gain popularity with the masses to counter Nagib's popularity and to meet any domestic or foreign conspiracy. One move was to confiscate the possessions of the Muhammad Ali dynasty and transferring that enormous wealth to a council called the Services Council. The funds were allocated to building schools and health clinics in the various villages. That project was of vital importance. It was a tremendous step for Egypt, for within the period of a few years there was a school and a clinic in almost every village.[52]

Redistributing the fortune of the former royal family among the Egyptian population, the Council for Social Services (CSS) represented the regime's major social policy initiative in the 1950s. Its aim was clear: building a popular constituency for the RCC and undermining Naguib. The CSS's competences were quite large. Charged with the overall planning of the regime's social policies, it drew up health, educational, and social projects, provided the funding, and supervised

---

[51] Ibid., p. 1171.   [52] Mohi El Din 1995, p. 168. See also Baghdadi 1977, pp. 79–89.

their execution.[53] Aiming to build one school every day, the CSS's main activity consisted in the establishment of Combined Centres (*al-wahdat al-mugammaʿa*) offering, social, medical, health, and educational facilities.[54] The council also funded a vast array of public housing projects.

Whilst being 'cheap' from the regime's perspective as the money was appropriated rather than acquired through costly taxation,[55] the CSS brought welfare expenditures in Egypt to an hitherto unprecedented level. To understand the extent of the spending boost, it is important to bear in mind the total value of the King's fortune. While estimates in published sources vary between 50 and 75 million Egyptian pounds (EGP),[56] recently disclosed cabinet minutes reveal that the volume of transferred property was in fact much larger. In a session especially dedicated to the confiscated royal properties,[57] the money—transferred in two tranches into the state budget—was estimated at 68.4 and 61.1 million EGP. This was the equivalent of 62 per cent of Egypt's *total* government expenditures in the financial year 1952/3 or 13.7 per cent of the country's entire GDP. The availability of these vast financial resources was reflected in the country's welfare budget, which increased by over 60 per cent from 57 million EGP in 1951—the country's last pre-coup budget—to 91.9 million EGP in 1953. In sum, the CSS represented a major shift in Egypt's social spending trajectory. What is more, it constituted the first major attempt to extend social services to the Egyptian countryside, which was reflected in the regime's success in increasing primary school enrolment from 45 per cent (1950) to 65 per cent (1960) within a decade.[58]

The CSS was assisted in its efforts by a second organization established by the RCC, the Liberation Rally. This political platform, which was set up following the banning of all political parties in 1953, has often been portrayed in the literature as a political failure for its inability to provide the regime with a ruling party.[59] This assessment overlooks the fact that the primary aim of the Rally was not the fostering of political activity, which the regime feared, but the distribution of social services. And in that respect, the organization represented an effective second pillar of the RCC's social policy strategy alongside the CSS. Pursuing the same goal of undermining Naguib,[60] the Rally targeted in particular the urban working class by providing worker health centres, a number of hospitals uniquely available to workers, and a Republican Workers Bank which provided cheap housing loans.[61] In addition, the Rally launched a first attempt at a workers' health insurance scheme.[62] Finally, the Rally was also vital in establishing a relationship

---

[53] IMF 1956, pp. 23–4.   [54] Vatikiotis 1961, p. 131.
[55] There is more on the regime's strategy of 'cheap social policies' in the next section.
[56] See Neguib 1955, p. 271; and IMF 1956, pp. 23–4.
[57] The session was held on 14 October 1953. See Egyptian National Archives 1953b.
[58] Faksh 1973, p. 239.   [59] Hopwood 1993, p. 89.   [60] Dekmejian 1971, p. 30.
[61] Personal memoirs of Ahmad Tu'aymah, the first head of the Rally. See Tu'aymah 1999, pp. 70–3.
[62] Ibid., pp. 70–3.

with the country's labour unions and paved the way for the RCC's bargain with labour in 1954.

This bargain constituted the second important element in the RCC's strategy to outbid Naguib. Just like the Liberation Rally, this bargain has at times been mis-represented as a simple manoeuvre on the part of Nasser to bribe the leadership of Egypt's transport unions into staging a paralysing three-day general strike.[63] This depiction of the 1954 events is inaccurate. Individual workers were not paid to participate in the demonstrations and the financial support extended to the unions was used to facilitate the logistics of the strike, not as a bribe.[64] Moreover, portraying the March 1954 strikes as a simple short-term manoeuvre belies the important social policy components that were included in the deal between the RCC and workers. As Aclimandos points out, 'having weighed the different "offers" made by both sides, the group (and at its head political entrepreneurs) that had the most sufficient resources at this point in time—that is, the workers who, thanks to their strategic position, could paralyse the country—chose a camp and made it triumph'.[65]

It is interesting to note that both sides—Naguib and Nasser—extended offers to the labour unions in March 1954. Naguib's camp offered the unions a labour party, with a leadership position for the head of the transport union, Al-Sawi. This party would allocate the workers a favourable share of the 'booty', meaning material compensation.[66] In the eyes of the workers, Naguib's offer had two major drawbacks: Naguib's camp included a number of actors—most notably the old Wafd party—that the unions considered reactionary and inimical to their interests, *and* the offer was subjected to the vagaries of electoral democracy which Naguib's camp campaigned for.[67] By contrast, with the RCC vouching for a continuation of the 'revolution' and against a return to democracy, workers were more confident about the RCC's capacity to actually deliver. As one of the participants in the negotiations with the RCC points out, workers 'were all convinced that the Revolution would improve the standard of living of workers and satisfy their demands'.[68] Retrospectively, this assessment turned out to be correct. As union leader Al-Sawi pointedly put it in a later interview, the regime 'made laws that protected workers' rights and insured their lives'.[69]

In terms of concrete concessions to labour, the RCC's offer comprised three main elements.[70] First, public sector employees received more generous bonuses, wage hikes, and a reformed recruitment and promotion system. Second, the RCC

---

[63] According to an oft-cited anecdote, Nasser apparently boasted about his success in having 'bought' the workers for 4,000 EGP. See, for instance, Mohi El Din 1995, p. 228.

[64] See a comprehensive discussion of this point in Aclimandos 2004, p. 1190.   [65] Ibid., p. 191.

[66] Ramadan 1975, pp. 118–19; and Aclimandos 2004, p. 1188. Unfortunately, I was unable to uncover the specific content of these material incentives.

[67] Ibid., p. 1191.   [68] Cited in Ramadan 1976, p. 213.   [69] Ramadan 1975, p. 119.

[70] This information is taken from the memoirs of RCC member Abdeltatif Baghdadi 1977, p. 172. See also Beattie 1994, p. 98; and Posusney 1997, p. 56.

ensured the increased provision of social services, in particular health services which were highly popular in rural areas, and a special building fund for public schools. Further measures included earmarked spending for housing in poor neighbourhoods, as well as a housing loan scheme in which the government guaranteed to take over interest rate payments for low-income workers.[71] Third, and most importantly, the RCC promised to introduce a comprehensive social insurance scheme for workers, including a pension scheme and health insurance. Introduced in 1955 and discussed in greater detail in the following section, this scheme and its extensions in the late 1950s and early 1960s constitutes one of the most important legacies of the Nasser regime in the realm of social legislation.

In sum, as the foregoing analysis has made clear, workers joined Nasser's ranks only under certain conditions[72]—conditions that would shape the country's social policy trajectory in the years to come. What is more, the repercussions of the March 1954 crisis proved to be long lasting as it 'helped shape Nasser's own conception of the social bases of his support'.[73] Whilst the RCC had been courting different societal groups since its seizure of power in July 1952, it lacked a clear understanding of its key constituencies in society before March 1954. In this respect, the crisis represented an important moment of learning for the regime elite as—in the words of RCC member Gamal Salim—it allowed the RCC to identify 'friend and foe'.[74] In a context of urban mobilization, quite clearly, capitalists turned out to be a rather ineffective coalition partner. With the Egyptian entrepreneurial bourgeoisie remaining quietly on the sidelines or openly supporting Naguib, the RCC realized that it needed a more effective pillar of support to remain in power. Nasser's conclusions from the March 1954 crisis were therefore clear: the revolution had come back 'on the shoulders of the workers',[75] and the regime needed populist redistributive measures to keep the coalition with workers and peasants in place.[76] Having been seeking a class to represent,[77] Nasser had found 'his' class in March 1954.

6.1.3 Squaring the circle: external threat and welfare distribution

Having demonstrated the link between elite factionalism and social spending, this subsection traces the second important causal mechanism of my argument: the trade-off between welfare and defence. While findings from previous chapters have demonstrated a strong negative correlation between welfare and defence, this subsection provides evidence that this trade-off was indeed perceived as such by the regime's leadership. Based on cabinet minutes from the Egyptian National

---

[71] IMF 1954, p. 35, 38.   [72] Salim 1976, p. 102.   [73] Baker 1978, p. 34.
[74] Salim 1976, p. 50.   [75] Ramadan 1976, p. 220.   [76] Hinnebusch 1985, p. 23.
[77] Abdel-Fadil 1980, p. 109.

Archives, the following analysis elucidates the reasons why the regime privileged defence over welfare. In a second step, I illustrate how the particular combination of a severe external threat and a strong incentive to distribute has led to what I call 'cheap social policies' in the absence of fiscal surpluses from resource rents.

Butter versus guns: tracing the mechanism

To demonstrate how the trade-off between 'butter or guns' worked out in the Egyptian case, it is, in a first step, important to establish how changes in the external environment—specifically increasing hostility between Egypt and Israel—changed the regime's threat perception and created a heightened incentive to invest in national defence. In this respect, it should be recalled that Israel did not figure prominently among the RCC's concerns when it seized power in 1952. Interviewed by a fellow Free Officer in 1983, Muhammad Naguib points out that Egypt and the Free Officers were keen on getting rid of the British, whereas Israel was initially not important.[78] In fact, wanting neither peace nor war, the Free Officers exhibited a certain ambivalence vis-à-vis Israel,[79] and their major focus was domestic, not foreign politics. A key indicator of this low level of threat perception was the 'heavy cuts in expenditure on defence'[80] carried out between 1952 and 1954.

Two key events fundamentally altered the threat perception of the regime: the Gaza raid in February 1955 and the Suez Crisis in late 1956. The former was a surprise attack carried out by the Israeli army against an Egyptian military base in the Gaza strip—then under the control of the Egyptian authorities—in which thirty-eight Egyptian soldiers were killed. The latter represented a tripartite attack on Egypt at the hands of France, Britain, and Israel starting in October 1956, which led to the temporary occupation of the Suez Canal zone and the Sinai peninsula. While the former represented a military provocation, the latter was a clear attempt to topple the Nasser regime, for immediately after the beginning of the first air raids, British Radio Cyprus called upon Egyptians to rise against the regime.[81] In combination, both events signalled to the regime that a serious threat to its survival would come from the outside.

This change of perception is reflected in statements from the regime's leadership. For example, Abdelatif Baghdadi, who was part of the regime's inner circle, states in his memoirs that the Gaza raid pushed the RCC to increase armament and defence spending.[82] And Nasser himself declared to a British journalist in April 1957 that 'the Gaza raid changed this idea [of low defence spending] in one night' as he realized that Egypt needed weapons to defend its territory.[83] Accordingly, defence expenditure experienced a rapid expansion, amounting to 116 per cent between 1955 and 1960 in absolute terms, whereas social expenditure only rose by

---

[78] Hamrush 1983, p. 436.   [79] Aclimandos 2004, p. 1346; and Barnett 1992, p. 84.
[80] IMF 1954, p. 15.   [81] Dawisha 2003, p. 179.
[82] Baghdadi 1977, p. 171. See also Mohi El Din 1995, p. 131.   [83] Al-Bahrani 2010, p. 145.

39 per cent in the same period.[84] Putting these outlays into broader perspective, defence expenditure consumed yearly about two-thirds of what was spent in the first five-year plan.[85] Beginning in 1962, Egypt's military intervention in Yemen in support of a socialist uprising further increased the upward pressure on defence outlays, such that on the eve of the 1967 war, defence expenditure amounted to nearly 12 per cent of the country's GNP.[86] To alleviate the burden on the budget, the regime was compelled to introduce an additional defence tax on direct income and business taxes.[87] Yet, the mounting defence burden could only be shouldered by forsaking other commitments of the regime, which brings me to the heart of the 'butter and guns' mechanism.

The inside perspective: closed-door discussions of welfare and defence
Micro-level evidence of the defence–welfare trade-off is not abundant, but it exists. Closed-door discussions documented in cabinet minutes represent such a 'smoking gun' test of the causal mechanism and, in the following, I rely on minutes from cabinet meetings held between 14 and 15 July 1959 to demonstrate the regime's inside perspective on this trade-off.[88] As mentioned before, existing evidence is patchy due to the secretive nature of these documents and the poor state of archives more generally. Having said this, the very nature of a 'smoking gun' test makes a single piece of evidence highly valuable. To avoid confusion, I should add that the chosen cabinet meeting occurred in the context of the United Arab Republic (UAR)—the merger of Egypt and Syria between 1958 and 1961—and therefore included Syrian ministers and references to Syria.

For our purposes, the relevant passages in the minutes revolved around an argument between the Chief of Staff of the Army, Abdel Hakim Amer, and Nasser on the one hand, and civilian ministers, mainly from the Syrian side, on the other. A central issue in this discussion was the size of the army and defence expenditure relative to the government's welfare effort. Akram al-Hourani, the Syrian Vice President of the UAR at the time, noted that the defence budget constituted more than half of the total and that it had not been reduced as previously agreed: 'The budget for domestic and external security represent 58 per cent of the budget, whereas the budget of the the Ministry of Education represents 20 per cent. This means that for all other Ministries there is only 20 per cent of the budget left'.[89]

Following al-Hourani's remarks, the Minister of Health, Bashir al-Azma, launched another scathing critique of the proposed budget. His statements are particularly indicative of the perceived trade-off between welfare and defence and are thus worth being quoted at length:

[84] Calculations based on my own data.   [85] Al-Jiritli 1974, p. 42.   [86] Waterbury 1983, p. 95.
[87] Barnett 1992, p. 88.
[88] All citations and references are taken from Egyptian National Archives 1959a.   [89] Ibid., p. 11.

I think that the expenditures for the army will have [negative] repercussions on the street. If the money was spent to improve healthcare, the social situation and culture, both the army and the people will benefit. But the man on the street doesn't understand the increasing expenditure for weapons. Why don't we evaluate the budgetary allocation for the armament of the army according to its needs? [...] In many areas there are no [social] services at all, except for Damascus and Aleppo. There are vast areas where there is not even an ambulance. The people desire an improvement of their conditions, so that it is possible to keep the internal front cohesive.[90]

On the opposite side of the argument stood the Chief of Staff of the Armed Forces, Abdel Hakim Amer. Representative of the regime's security concerns, his response to the foregoing criticism reveals that—whilst being cognizant of the strains high defence expenditures imposed on the general population—the regime essentially considered the external threat to survival greater than the internal one. Interrupting al-Azma, Amer stated: 'The army needed new weapons. I know that the deployment along the borders is costly. However, the external front is more important than the internal one. If we do not keep our defence up high, we might be overrun and there will not be any internal front to worry about. The people will have to understand the sacrifices they have to make in this situation.'[91]

Interestingly, Nasser had not intervened in the discussion until this point and had left it to Amer to fend off the ministers' criticism. Yet, upon further insistence from al-Azma, Nasser decided to put his foot down and end the discussion, but not without revealing an interesting second motive driving the UAR's defence spending: 'Enough! What you are saying might be tenable if we were going to increase defence spending, but the situation was already like that before the union. And, anyway, how could we deprive the army so quickly of its privileges?'[92] This suggests that defence spending was, at least partly, motivated by a strategy to pamper the army, probably with a view to avoiding coups. In any event, the statement underlines the difficulty of reducing defence expenditure—a point I will return to later in this chapter.

Taken as a whole, this episode in the cabinet meeting, albeit brief, provides important evidence in favour of the mechanism underpinning the negative correlation between defence and welfare. Whilst it is clear that the spending focus on the army was politically controversial within the regime's leadership and an alternative strategy relying on social spending to bolster domestic legitimacy was discussed, external threats to survival were perceived as more pressing and hence priority was given to defence.

---

[90] Ibid., p. 13.   [91] Ibid., p. 14.   [92] Ibid.

Cheap social policies

Facing conflicting spending incentives since the mid-1950s and lacking important resource rents, the regime had to 'square the circle' in order to meet both the expectations emanating from its domestic support base and the perceived necessity to keep the security budget at high levels. As I have argued earlier, this combination of circumstances resulted in the implementation of 'cheap' social policies. Such policies feature four main characteristics: insufficient financial commitment; a strong reliance on 'free' social policies distributing rent-generating statutory rights to lower and middle classes; the use of windfalls to finance social expenditure; and devising social policies that alleviate the regime's shortage of resources.[93] I now demonstrate each of these characteristics in the case of Egypt.

Insufficient financial commitment

Underfunded social policies are a necessary but insufficient criterion to identify 'cheap' social policies as low spending levels can also occur because there is no incentive to spend. As Egypt's spending trajectory was analysed in Chapter 2, I simple recall the major points here.

Regarding aggregate welfare expenditure, it is important to note that, following a period of rapid expansion, the share of social spending in the budget started to decline visibly with the change in the regime's threat perception in 1955 (see Figure 6.1). On the eve of the 1967 war, welfare spending amounted to barely a fifth of total expenditure, whereas it had reached nearly 45 per cent in 1954—a level characteristic of high-spenders. Regarding specific social policies, another way to gauge the extent of insufficient funding is to look at the discrepancy between targeted and actual social spending in Egypt's development plan. In the field of education, a reform commission set up in 1957 had recommended the building of 225 schools every year to achieve full enrolment within a thirty-year time frame. With 100 schools built on average between 1957 and 1987, actual construction activity lagged way behind the target goal as result of fiscal shortfalls.[94] Funding shortages also became an increasing problem in the area of higher education in the late 1950s, as underlined by the Minister of Education, Kamal Eddin Hussein, who, in a debate on the country's draft budget for 1960, underlined the state's 'serious financial problems to finance higher education'.[95]

Similar discrepancies can be found with regard to Egypt's health care policies. Of the 194 health care units to be built under the first five-year plan, only twenty

---

[93] The selective application of rule enforcement (forbearance) as described in Holland 2015 could be another instrument to achieve 'cheap social policies', but given the difficulty of collecting historical evidence on this policy aspect, forbearance is not analysed here.

[94] Figures are taken from Ratib 1998, p. 168. See also Al-Fiqi 1966, p. 242; Faksh 1973, p. 239; and R. Assaad 1997, p. 87.

[95] Cited in Qindil 1991, p. 386.

Figure 6.1 Expenditures on social welfare as a percentage of the budget in Egypt (1950–1967)

Source: IMF 2011; and V. Lucas and Richter 2016.

units were opened, amounting to 10 per cent of the target. Overall, the regime had envisaged operating 2,550 health care units across the country by 1965. Yet, again, actual numbers fell considerably short of the target. By 1965, 581 units had been built, revealing a 77 per cent shortfall.[96] Importantly, it was not administrative bottlenecks that held back implementation. As Baker notes, 'lack of funds [...] necessitated a drastic scaling down of the expansion plans'.[97]

'Free' social policies
Another prevalent feature of the regime's social policies was what I call 'free' social policies. Instead of distributing material resources, these social policies generate regulatory rents by conferring statutory rights on workers. Underpinned by extensive public interventions in the real estate and labour markets, these policies generally entail no or only very limited financial commitments for the state. Instead, the costs of these fringe benefits are outsourced to third parties, such as private sector employers and property owners, which makes them highly attractive for a regime struggling with severe resource constraints. To be sure, fringe benefits are by no means unique to Egypt and can also be found in the case of high-spenders, such as Tunisia. That said, the intensity and frequency of rent-generating market interventions in Egypt, in the absence of high spending

[96] Pawelka 1985, p. 206.   [97] Baker 1978, p. 221.

levels, makes them a distinct feature of 'cheap' social policies. It should also be noted that the bulk of social policies associated with the Nasser era consists of this type of 'free' social policies, which sets Egypt apart from the policy trajectory of high-spending welfare states.

Looking at the summary of policies shown in Table 6.1, extensive market interventions occurred in two areas. On the one hand, the regime implemented a series of laws which heavily regulated the property market and imposed strict controls on landlords.[98] Enacted in 1952 shortly after the RCC came to power, rent controls became a popular policy instrument that the regime used with increasing frequency as resources for social spending became scarcer. Underpinned by a strong populist undertone emphasizing the need for 'fair rents',[99] these policies conferred considerable benefits on the growing number of urbanites in search of affordable housing. Importantly for the regime, these measures did not necessitate

Table 6.1 'Free' social policies in Egypt (1952–1972)

Rent reduction and control	
Law 199/1952	15 per cent rent reduction for buildings constructed between 1944 and 1952
Law 55/1958	20 per cent rent reduction for buildings constructed after 1952
Law 168/1961	20 per cent rent reduction extended to buildings constructed after 1958
Law 46/1962	Establishment of Rent Assessment Committees to regulate property rents
Law 83/1965	30 per cent rent reduction for properties constructed after 1962

Fringe benefits and labour market policies	
Decree of 1952	Introduction of paid holidays and sick pay
1959 Unified Labour Code	Reduction of probationary period; extension of number of public holidays; introduction of redundancy money; increase in paid sick leave up to 180 days; reduction of working hours
'Socialist' Decrees of 1961	Reduction of working hours; limitation of right to work overtime; increase in paid holidays, sick pay, and redundancy money; extension of number of public holidays; establishment of workers' councils representing employees on company boards
Law of 1972	Improvement of sick leave provisions and introduction of bonus pay for hazardous work

[98] Rent controls were also enacted in Tunisia but, unlike Egypt, their coverage and enforcement was limited. See Malpezzi and Ball 1993.

[99] Abdel-Fadil 1980, p. 123.

any additional outlays as the costs were passed on to private landlords who, at that time, represented the bulk of property owners in the country. The establishment of Rent Assessment Committees in 1962 further prevented rents from being adjusted for inflation as these committees were heavily skewed in favour of tenants. As a result, Egypt did not witness the rapid rise in urban rents which usually accompanies phases of accelerated urbanization. This came as a huge advantage for the growing number of urban workers and civil servants, but to the detriment of property owners who saw the returns on property drastically reduced.[100]

The second area for 'free' social policies was the labour market. Similar to rent controls, many of the labour market regulations that the regime introduced were fiscally neutral but proved to be highly popular. For instance, the regime introduced paid holidays for private sector employees for the first time in 1952, granting fourteen days per year after one year's employment and twenty-one days for employees with more than ten years of employment.[101] In parallel, the regime gradually extended the number of national holidays from five in 1952, to seven in 1959, and finally to fourteen in 1961.[102] In the same vein, statutory sick pay was increased sixfold from 30 days at 50 per cent of wages introduced in 1952, to 180 days with nearly full wages by 1961. Labour market reforms further restricted the number of legal working hours, introducing a 42-hour week in 1961 without loss of pay.[103] The Unified Labour Code of 1959 significantly improved employment security by lowering the probationary period to three months, increasing the hurdles for lay-offs, and introducing redundancy payments for both voluntary and involuntary termination of employment.[104] It needs to be said that—to the extent that an increasing part of urban formal sector employment was taken on by the state, in particular after the large-scale nationalizations of 1961—the costs of these labour market regulations could only be partly outsourced to the private sector. That said, the majority of these measures, such as the reduction of working hours, did not entail higher public spending and where they did, as in the case of sick pay, the outlays were partly offset by the improved ability to tax public sector employees.[105] It is also important to note that these measures disproportionately benefited urban employees in the formal sector, whereas working conditions in the rural and informal sector did not improve at a similar rate.

The use of windfalls

The third component in the regime's strategy of 'cheap' social policies was the extensive use of windfalls to finance social expenditure. As compared to funds raised through taxation, reaping windfalls is economically less costly and

---

[100] Harik 1997, p. 176.   [101] Abdel-Fadil 1980, p. 30.
[102] Mabro and Radwan 1976, p. 136.   [103] O'Brien 1966, p. 136.
[104] Issawi 1963, p. 56; and Mabro 1974, p. 154.
[105] O'Brien 1966, p. 188.

politically expedient in that the government can freely use this non-tax revenue to appease societal demands and bolster its domestic legitimacy without having to jeopardize national defence.[106] Two main mechanisms for generating windfalls have been prominent in the case of Egypt.

The first mechanism consisted of large-scale confiscations which occurred in two waves. The first wave, carried out in 1953, confiscated the fortune of the Egyptian royal family by transferring the family's assets as tax revenue into the state budget. In total, the measure expropriated the riches of 407 royal family members and brought twenty-four royal palaces, 48,000 farms, yachts, and bank deposits under the control of the state.[107] As stated above, their equivalent value was estimated at 13.7 per cent of Egypt's GDP. The second wave occurred in the wake of the 1956 Suez Crisis. In reaction to the tripartite military attack by Britain, France, and Israel, the Egyptian government confiscated properties owned by British and French nationals as well as the country's Jewish population.[108] In terms of its scope, the measure represented a hitherto unprecedented appropriation of property by the state. More than 15,000 establishments were expropriated, including all British and French banks and insurance companies, such as Barclays Bank, in addition to a large number of industrial and commercial companies, such as the Egyptian assets of Shell.[109] Tignor estimates the total value of expropriated assets at 1 billion USD, the equivalent of 2.89 billion EGP.[110] This value amounts to 250 per cent of Egypt's GDP and nine times its total government expenditure in 1956. Relative to the annual revenue from the nationalization of the Suez Canal (22.2 million EGP),[111] this transfer of wealth can only be described as enormous.

The second mechanism consisted of nationalizations of domestic industrial assets, carried out in several waves between February 1960 and March 1964. In so doing, the regime nationalized the country's entire cotton trade, all banks and insurance companies owned by nationals, and the majority of Egypt's industrial and commercial property, including timber, cement, copper, and electricity production as well as transport.[112] The most important asset that the government appropriated was the Bank Misr, the deposits of which exceeded 1 billion EGP.[113] Bank Misr was one of Egypt's biggest industrial and commerical holding companies, whose affiliated companies accounted for 20 per cent of the country's industrial output.[114] According to former Minister of Finance, Abdel-Aziz Hegazy, who was a consultant for the Ministry of Finance at the time, the nationalizations flooded the fisc with much-need resources and, furthermore, facilitated the collection of taxes and the appropriation of profits.[115] Taken

---

[106] Morrison 2009.   [107] Essam El-Din 2002.
[108] For a good summary of the events, see Tignor 1992.
[109] Vatikiotis 1985, p. 393; and Owen 1991, p. 367.
[110] Tignor 1992, p. 276. I applied the official exchange rate to the US dollar to derive this value.
[111] Owen 1991, p. 365.   [112] Craissati 1989, p. 70.   [113] Abdel-Malik 1968, p. 140.
[114] O'Brien 1966, p. 125.   [115] Personal interview, Cairo, 28 January 2013.

together, 'these nationalisations substantially alleviated the government's present fiscal problems.'[116]

While the importance of these expropriations for Egypt's industrial development has been recognized,[117] their importance in the field of social policies has largely been overlooked. Yet combined qualitative and quantitative evidence presented below suggests that windfall money was an integral part of the regime's strategy to finance social policies. Regarding qualitative evidence, there are a number of archival documents highlighting the role of expropriations in supporting the regime's welfare effort. Most importantly, these unveil the importance of the King's fortune in funding social projects, as described above. Alongside these large-scale projects, cabinet minutes from the Egyptian National Archives also document the frequent resort to expropriations for smaller-scale projects. Table 6.2 summarizes all confiscations carried out for social purposes in 1953–54. The table is illustrative of a widespread practice by which the government used expropriations of land and real estate to expedite the expansion of Egypt's educational system. Importantly, this overview only represents a snapshot of the total amount of expropriations carried out and, though patchy, cabinet minutes throughout the 1950s contain references to confiscations such as the ones described herein.[118] Whilst it is unclear from the documents whether the owners of these properties received

Table 6.2 Confiscation measures for social purposes in Egypt (1953–1954)

Cabinet session	Expropriation measure
2 September 1953	Confiscation of three empty buildings in Cairo after the owner refused to rent them out to the Ministry of Education
8 September 1953	Confiscation of seven other buildings and land by the Ministry of Education
13 September 1953	Confiscation of one empty building and land by the Ministry of Education
18 October 1953	Confiscation of one building and land for educational purpuses
4 November 1953	Confiscation of land by the Ministry of Social Affairs
11 November 1953	Confiscation of land for educational purposes
2 December 1953	Expropriation of two buildings and land by the Ministry of Education
23 December 1953	Confiscation of land for educational purposes
20 January 1954	Confiscation of a building and land to construct a school after the owner's refusal to extend the tenancy contract with the Ministry of education
30 June 1954	Confiscation of a building for educational purposes

[116] Barnett 1992, p. 98.   [117] G. Amin and Nawwar 2006, p. 88.
[118] See, for example, Egyptian National Archives 1955b; Egyptian National Archives 1958; and Egyptian National Archives 1959b.

compensation, it is safe to assume that these measures helped alleviate the fiscal pressures weighing on the government.

Based on this qualitative evidence, I carry out a simple regression analysis to investigate the link between expropriations and social policies in Egypt more systematically. My analysis is guided by the following intuition: if indeed the regime deliberately used windfalls to finance additional outlays for social welfare, we should find, *ceteris paribus*, a positive association between instances of expropriation and social expenditure. These spending hikes in the wake of expropriations are expected to be short term, considering their highly discretionary, one-off nature.

To test this claim, I run a simple error correction model (ECMs), using Egypt's welfare expenditures as a share of GDP as the dependent variable.[119] To cover all expropriation events of the Nasser period, I use a long time series from 1952 until 2010. A nice feature of ECMs is that they allow me to distinguish between the short-run and long-run effects of expropriation events and thus align with my theoretical interest. Another advantage of ECMs is that they are fully general dynamic models and hence do not impose any potentially invalid parameter restrictions.[120] To facilitate comparison across models, I use the same set of control variables as in Chapter 4 and all variables are taken from the same sources.[121] The only addition to previous models is the *Expropriation act* variable. The variable is taken from Hajzler, who in turn extended the datasets compiled by Kobrin and Minor.[122] An expropriation act is defined as 'the involuntary divestment of assets of any number of direct investment firms, within a given 3-digit industry and in a given year'.[123] In its current form, Hajzler's expropriation dataset comprises all events between 1960 and 2006, which means that I needed to extend the data forwards and backwards to cover the full time period under investigation. To do so, I used the above-cited secondary sources, in particular Tignor, Owen, Abdel-Malik, and Essam El-Din.[124]

The regression results are presented in Table 6.3 below. Column (1) presents a baseline model with a restricted set of core controls. Columns (2)–(4) then successively add *Foreign aid p.c.*, *Dependency* and *Urbanization*, *Polity*, and *IMF* as additional controls. Typically for an ECM, all covariates are added in lagged and first-differenced form. While the former represents the longer term effect of a variable, the first difference gives an impression of the variable's short-term effect.

[119] Findings are similar when using social spending as a share of the budget. Results are available upon request.

[120] De Boef and Keele 2008.

[121] I refrain from logging the GDP per capita, aid, and rent income variables. Given that this is a one-country analysis, there was no need to correct for skewness, which I ascertained using histograms. Also the R-squared of models with non-logged variables was about 12 per cent higher, indicating a better model fit.

[122] Hajzler 2011; Minor 1994; and Kobrin 1980.   [123] Hajzler 2011, p. 122.

[124] Tignor 1992; Owen 1991; Abdel-Malik 1968; and Essam El-Din 2002. I also experimented with an alternative variable accounting for the number of expropriated firms. Results are similar but due to expected high measurement error, the findings are noisier.

Table 6.3 Expropriation and welfare spending as a percentage of GDP in Egypt

	(1) Welfare/GDP	(2) Welfare/GDP	(3) Welfare/GDP	(4) Welfare/GDP
Welfare spending$_{t-1}$	−0.617***	−0.624***	−0.591***	−0.549***
	(0.130)	(0.130)	(0.108)	(0.111)
Δ Expropriation act	0.492**	0.531**	0.414***	0.443***
	(0.197)	(0.220)	(0.148)	(0.171)
Expropriation act$_{t-1}$	−0.309	−0.272	−0.330	−0.272
	(0.282)	(0.302)	(0.239)	(0.270)
Δ Defence spending	−0.101	−0.114	−0.055	−0.083
	(0.067)	(0.070)	(0.054)	(0.052)
Defence spending$_{t-1}$	0.023	0.019	0.157**	0.055
	(0.044)	(0.054)	(0.068)	(0.078)
Δ Rents p.c.	−0.259	−0.233	0.827*	0.676
	(0.517)	(0.500)	(0.454)	(0.471)
Rents p.c.$_{t-1}$	1.234***	1.242***	2.606***	2.518***
	(0.447)	(0.445)	(0.501)	(0.593)
Δ GDP p.c.	−1.192	−1.108	−5.103	−3.166
	(4.818)	(4.833)	(3.503)	(4.029)
GDP p.c.$_{t-1}$	−1.875**	−1.880**	−0.971	−0.892
	(0.848)	(0.892)	(1.056)	(0.970)
Δ Foreign aid p.c.		0.140	−0.339**	−0.234
		(0.246)	(0.135)	(0.158)
Foreign aid p.c.$_{t-1}$		0.016	−0.425**	−0.227
		(0.200)	(0.205)	(0.249)
Δ Dependency			−1.377	−1.436
			(1.185)	(1.346)
Dependency$_{t-1}$			0.369**	0.335*
			(0.188)	(0.198)
Δ Urbanization			−0.866	−0.697
			(0.569)	(0.676)
Urbanization$_{t-1}$			−0.765***	−0.449
			(0.261)	(0.344)
Δ Polity				0.026
				(0.203)
Polity$_{t-1}$				−1.557
				(1.225)
Δ IMF				−0.271
				(0.457)
IMF$_{t-1}$				−0.353
				(0.621)
Observations	51	51	51	51

Note: Error correction model with Driscoll–Kraay standard errors in parentheses. Constant omitted.
*$p < 0.10$, **$p < 0.05$, ***$p < 0.01$

Note that the model also includes the lag of the dependent variable to capture spending inertia and control for autocorrelation. As in previous analyses, I use panel-corrected standard errors.[125]

Turning our attention to the variable of interest, *Expropriation act*, the findings support my prior. As expected, the occurrence of an expropriation event is strongly and positively associated with an increase in welfare expenditures. More specifically, the model suggests that a change in the *Expropriation act* variable increases social spending by 0.45 per cent of GDP on average (see Figure 6.2). Given that average social spending change in Egypt amounts to 0.11 per cent of GDP, an increase of this magnitude represents a considerable boost in welfare expenditure. This becomes even more apparent when we consider that more than one expropriation act can occur in any given year, which multiplies the effect. For example, the maximal number of acts empirically observed in Egypt is four, which corresponds to a 1.8 percentage point increase in total. Considering Egypt's mean social spending level of around 10 per cent of GDP, this increase does indeed represent a considerable spending bonanza. The results further indicate that, in line with my initial intuition, the effect of expropriation acts is not long lasting as the coefficient of the lagged *Expropriation act* variable is insignificant throughout.

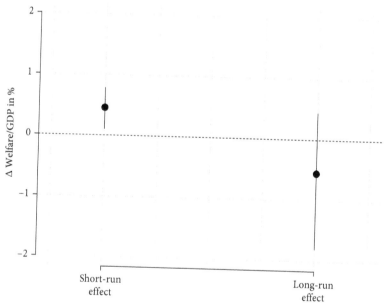

Figure 6.2 Effect of expropriation acts on welfare spending in Egypt
Note: Whiskers indicate 95 per cent confidence bounds.

---

[125] N. L. Beck and Katz 1995.

This is shown graphically in Figure 6.2 where the error bar of the long-run effect crosses the zero line. In other words, none of the initial spending boost is carried over into the next period. Finally, since expropriation events became increasingly rare, with the last one taking place in 1995, the findings are chiefly driven by the high number of expropriations in the 1950s and 1960s.

On the whole, the combination of qualitative and quantitative evidence presented in the foregoing illustrates the important role of windfalls for social policies in Egypt. In view of the findings, it seems that the regime followed a deliberate strategy of using windfalls in order to boost its popularity by increasing social spending. With threat levels and defence spending unchanged, however, these spending hikes only had a short-term effect as they were unable to alter fundamentally the structural constraints of the regime.

Alleviating shortage of resources

The last defining feature of 'cheap' social policies is the designing of social policies such that they alleviate the shortage of resources and support the regime's defence and development effort. Arguably, this turns the logic of distributive social policies on its head as social policies devised in this way become a mechanism of resource generation instead of resource distribution. Given conditions of resource scarcity and the need to cater to a large support base, these social policies become extremely advantageous since they enable the generation of additional revenue whilst, at the same time, bolstering domestic legitimacy. They are thus much more attractive than equivalent resource generation via taxation. In the case of Egypt, social policies of this kind occurred in two main areas.

The first area was labour market policies, more specifically, profit-sharing arrangements for workers. As part of Nasser's 'socialist decrees' implemented in 1961, the regime obliged large private and public sector firms to allocate 25 per cent of their profits to their employees in proportion to their salaries. Yet, what seemed to be a populist measure in the interest of the working classes was in fact an ill-disguised mechanism to generate more resources for welfare provision. Of the 25 per cent promised to workers, 5 per cent was to be retained by the company itself to provide social services and housing at the factory level. Another 10 per cent was recouped by the state as payment for 'central and social services'[126]—in other words, to finance social policies. Only 10 per cent was to be paid out directly in cash to workers and only after allowing the firms to build up reserves and deduct for depreciations. Moreover, the payment was capped at 50 EGP per worker per annum, a sum which was not adjusted for inflation and thus quickly depreciated in value.[127]

The second area where revenue-generating social policies were implemented was social insurance. To be sure, the financial contribution of social insurance

---

[126] Wahba 1994, pp. 85–6.   [127] Be'eri 1970, p. 417.

surpluses to Egypt's economic development has been pointed out. Abdel-Fadil, for instance, notes that the social insurance scheme has 'led to large accumulations of investible funds that have been utilised to finance development projects'.[128] Yet, the argument presented herein goes beyond making a general claim about the role of social insurance funds. Based on archival material, I show below that the generation of additional resources was, from the onset, at the heart of Egypt's social insurance legislation, rather than being a mere by-product of social legislation. I also illustrate the extent to which social insurance funds contributed to financing public expenditure, including on social welfare. And, finally, I show that, given its revenue-generating nature, the extension of social insurance to new groups of beneficiaries has been associated with deteriorations of Egypt's current account balance.

Egypt's social insurance system took shape in several stages between 1952 and 1964 and has remained unchanged in its basic architecture since then. The system was first established by Law 316 of 1952, which set up a pension and savings fund for civil servants. For the first three years, the fund was rather rudimentary and existed in parallel to corporate insurance schemes for particular groups of civil servants, such as teachers and judges. It was not accessible for all public sector employees. This changed in 1955 with the adoption of Law 416 which established a comprehensive public social insurance scheme comprising pensions, disability insurance, work accident insurance, which had previously been privately organized, and a widow's and orphans' pension, for all public sector employees. Moreover, the law laid the foundation for social security in the private sector by setting up a provident and insurance fund providing pensions, disability, and work accident insurance. This provident fund was transformed into a fully fledged social insurance scheme for private sector employees in the wake of the 1961 reforms, which also raised employers' contributions significantly from 7 to 17 per cent. In 1959, the Public Organization for Social Insurance was created, which added unemployment insurance for public sector employees. Finally, Law 63 of 1964 created the Health Insurance Organization (HIO) and added health insurance coverage for public and private sector workers.[129] Established during the 'golden era' of left-wing Nasserism, the social insurance scheme, without any doubt, represented a cornerstone of the regime's welfare effort.

For the argument I am trying to make, the question is whether increasing saving and thereby enhancing the financial capacity of the regime was a strategy or a by-product of social insurance legislation. A first indication that saving was indeed a pressing issue for the regime can be found in a study by the Egyptian historian Ramadan, who in 1997 published previously classified minutes of leadership

---

[128] Abdel-Fadil 1980, p. 119. See also O'Brien 1966, p. 188; and Barnett 1992, p. 119.
[129] For a good overview, see Abdel-Fadil 1980, pp. 117–19.

meetings with Nasser.[130] Therein, Nasser is quoted as saying that workers needed to understand the importance of saving: 'If voluntary saving does not work, then saving needs to be imposed by the government'.[131] A second, more detailed reference to the regime's motives can be found in the correspondence between the Ministry of Social Affairs and the Council of Ministers in the preparation of the social security legislation, preserved in the National Archives. Specifically, the explanatory notes accompanying the draft laws are particularly insightful as they uncover the regime's motives. Unfortunately, only the correspondence related to the 1952 and 1955 social insurance laws has been accessible, so the analysis comes with a caveat. That said, in the absence of any other 'smoking gun' evidence to the contrary, these archival documents carry a particular causal weight.

Regarding the 1952 law, the objective of increasing revenues features prominently in the explanatory notes. When presenting the draft law to the Council of Ministers in November 1952, the Minister of Finance pointed to the 'copious resources' that the funds would make available to the government and the extent to which this would support the national economy.[132] Significantly, the explanatory note contains no reference at all to any social motives whatsoever. In a second note, dating from June 1953, the Ministry of Finance and Economics urged the Council of Ministers to extend social insurance to all new state employees.[133] Underlining the 'present conditions of austerity'—recall the conservative economic policies after the FOM seized power—the minister highlighted the 'vast funding opportunities'[134] that would become available if social insurance were to be extended. This would help the government finance its development projects.

The same arguments for social legislation appear again in the context of the 1955 law, which extended social insurance to the private sector and considerably broadened its coverage. Note that this law was part of the bargain with labour described above, so my point is certainly not that the law was entirely motivated by an economic rationale. However, the archival notes strongly suggest that economic reasons played a major role in the government's motivation to pass the law.[135] Particularly insightful is an explanatory note from the Ministry of Social Affairs to the Council of Ministers from July 1955 laying out two key motives behind the draft law. First, social insurance was meant to 'calm down' workers and to make them more productive, so social considerations, albeit in a rather paternalistic sense, did motivate the adoption of the 1955 law. Second, and important for my argument, the generation of resources was again a key motivating factor in favour of the law: 'Given the enormous amount of money that the social

---

[130] Specifically, the minutes are from meetings of the Arab Socialist Union's (ASU) General Secretariat. The ASU, founded in 1962, was the regime's second attempt to establish a ruling party.
[131] Ramadan 1997, p. 137, 139.
[132] See note from 26 November 1952 in Egyptian National Archives 1953a.   [134] Ibid.
[133] Egyptian National Archives 1953a.
[135] All references are taken from Egyptian National Archives 1955a.

insurance system will accumulate after a while, the social insurance fund will become a powerful source of money that the government can rely on to finance social reforms and economic development projects'.[136] Taken together, both notes demonstrate that the idea of implementing social policies to fund social policies and development projects was not something the regime 'discovered' along the way. On the contrary, the generation of resources was a key motivation behind the social insurance legislation.

A further piece of evidence to support this claim is the ad hoc borrowings from the social security funds shown in Table 6.4. Starting almost immediately after the social insurance scheme came into operation, the loans taken from social insurance savings all occurred in the context of social policies, most notably school construction. A particularly telling example was the decision to increase pensions for public servants in May 1953. Technically, the entire measure amounted to a reallocation of deposits from one saving scheme to another, whilst declaring the transferred deposits additional revenue, which could then be paid out to existing pensioners.

Moving to the period from the run-up to the 1967 war until the aftermath of the 1973 war when resources were particularly scarce, Table 6.5 reveals the extent to which social insurance funds helped finance public expenditure. Based on IMF archival material,[137] the table shows that a quarter of Egypt's first five-year plan and an average of 44.6 per cent of all financing needs in the 1963 to 1976 budgets were provided by social insurance funds. In the inter-war period between 1967 and 1973, transfers from social security to the budget were particularly heavy,

Table 6.4 Ad hoc borrowing from social insurance in Egypt (1953–1954)

Cabinet session	Measure
22 April 1953	Ministry of Rural Affairs used surplus from social insurance to finance irrigation project
29 April 1953	1 million EGP borrowed from the savings fund for teachers to finance school buildings
6 May 1953	Exceptional increase in pensions was financed by declaring some deposits in the pension scheme additional revenue
20 September 1953	School Construction Administration was allowed to borrow 3 million EGP from the Social Insurance Fund to build schools
15 December 1954	School Construction Administration borrowed 2.5 million EGP from newly founded Pensions and Savings Fund

[136] Ibid.

[137] Detailed figures for later years are unfortunately not available. However, there are ample secondary sources documenting the use of social insurance funds from the 1980s onwards. See, for instance, Helmy 2004; Roll 2010, pp. 147–51; and Soliman 2011, p. 106.

Table 6.5 Social insurance funds and public spending in Egypt (1960–1976)

Spending programme	Amount(in million EGP)	Size of contribution (as a % of total financing needs)	Source
Five-Year Plan 60/1–65/6*	385	24	IMF 1962a
State Budget 1963/4	69.8	35	IMF 1966
State Budget 1964/5	100.1	44.8	IMF 1966
State Budget 1965/6	131.7	25.6	IMF 1967
State Budget 1966/7	148.8	36.4	IMF 1967
State Budget 1967/8	173.4	47.4	IMF 1967
State Budget 1968/9	161.5	40.3	IMF 1969
State Budget 1969/70	172	31.8	IMF 1970
State Budget 1970/1	188	65.5	IMF 1973
State Budget 1971/2	202	69.4	IMF 1973
State Budget 1973	229	52.5	IMF 1973
State Budget 1974	256.6	49.5	IMF 1974
State Budget 1975	376	50.6	IMF 1975
State Budget 1976	290	21.8	IMF 1976

* The National Planning Act of January 1957 created a new National Planning Committee (NPC) with the mandate to draft a comprehensive Five-Year Plan for the fiscal years 1960/1–1964/5. See Craissati 1989, p. 63.

amounting to nearly 70 per cent of financing in the 1971/2 budget. Technically loans, these transfers were amortized with a 6 per cent interest rate. Yet according to former Minister of Finance, Ali Lufti, interest payments were made irregularly,[138] and with inflation in two-digit figures for most of the 1970s through to the early 1990s, these transfers amounted to a hidden taxation of deposits.

Based on the foregoing, I resort to quantitative methods to test whether the extension of social security coverage in Egypt systematically correlates with difficulties in the country's current account. The intuition here is the following: if the regime systematically used the social insurance mechanism to counterbalance balance of payments problems by increasing domestic saving, we should expect drops in Egypt's currency reserves to be associated with coverage extensions in the social security scheme. To test this conjecture, I use a simple logit regression with a binary indicator, *Extension*, accounting for any extension of legal social insurance coverage in the public or private sector between 1952 and 2010. In the absence of any readily available dataset for this variable, I coded it myself using secondary sources.[139]

On the right-hand side, the key variable of interest is *Reserves*, taken from the IMF International Financial Statistics (IFS),[140] which measures the percentage

[138] Personal interview, Cairo, 26 February 2013.
[139] My main sources were Abdel-Fadil 1980; IDSC 2006; World Bank 1991; and Selwaness 2012.
[140] IMF 2015.

change in Egypt's foreign currency reserves relative to the previous period. In light of my priors, I expect falling reserves to be associated with a higher probability of coverage extensions and vice versa. Regarding control variables, the selection of appropriate controls is complicated by the fact that coverage extensions are poorly theorized and, hence, the choice of an appropriate set of control variables is unclear. In the absence of strong theory, I opt for a similar set of socioeconomic and political controls as in previous spending regressions. Following Carter and Signorino,[141] I add time polynomials to account for dynamic time effects. Finally, I use robust standard errors and lag all right-hand side variables by one time period to alleviate endogeneity concerns.

The findings are reported in Table 6.6. As before, column (1) presents a restricted model with a set of core variables, while columns (2)–(5) add further controls. Focusing on the negative and highly significant coefficient of the *Reserves* variable, the results are in line with my expectations. They suggest that as reserves increase, the adoption of legislation extending social security coverage becomes less likely. Conversely, with diminishing reserves, the extension of coverage becomes more likely. Notably, the *Reserves* variable is the only covariate that systematically correlates with coverage extensions, other than the effect of previous extensions.

To gauge the magnitude of the effect, I plot the predicted probabilities of coverage extensions by percentage changes of currency reserves shown in Figure 6.3. Whilst the range of percentage changes—from −100 to +150 per cent—seems large, reserve swings of this magnitude have empirically been observed in Egypt. Substantively, the graph highlights the growing likelihood of coverage extension as reserves start to shrink, which is indicated by the increasing slope of the graph left of the zero change line. At the mean level of reserve changes, which lies at 5 per cent, the probability of extensions amounts to about 17 per cent. Two standard deviations to the left, at −80 per cent, the average probability doubles to 70 per cent. Whilst these values should be approached with caution in view of the spreading confidence interval, the results suggest that the extension of social insurance coverage was used by the regime to allay current account pressures—a finding in line with my argument about 'cheap' social policies.

A note on public employment

Despite cumulative evidence that the regime relied on a strategy of 'cheap' social policies, detractors might still object that Nasser implemented a costly public employment programme for young graduates, which seems to contradict the argument made here. Indeed, the government initiated an employment guarantee scheme in 1961, formalized by law in 1964, which guaranteed every university graduate and, since 1964, secondary-level graduates a guaranteed job in the

---

[141] D. B. Carter and Signorino 2010.

Table 6.6 Current account crises and social insurance extensions in Egypt

	(1)	(2)	(3)	(4)	(5)
Reserves$_{t-1}$	−3.396**	−3.837***	−4.627***	−4.904***	−4.597***
	(1.336)	(1.322)	(1.643)	(1.563)	(1.573)
GDP p.c. (log)$_{t-1}$	−0.212	−0.288	−0.487	−0.499	−0.495
	(0.336)	(0.355)	(0.487)	(0.463)	(0.459)
Rents p.c. (log)$_{t-1}$	−0.264	−0.010	1.566	1.457	1.825
	(1.311)	(1.389)	(2.671)	(2.644)	(2.749)
Foreign aid p.c. (log)$_{t-1}$	0.956	1.160	0.965	0.912	0.847
	(0.743)	(0.862)	(0.856)	(0.836)	(0.899)
Dependency$_{t-1}$		−0.562**	−0.354	−0.382	−0.399
		(0.279)	(0.312)	(0.383)	(0.380)
Urbanization$_{t-1}$			−0.852	−0.930	−0.976
			(0.935)	(0.922)	(0.893)
IMF$_{t-1}$				0.857	1.077
				(1.710)	(1.922)
Polity$_{t-1}$					−0.907
					(2.540)
Previous extensions$_{t-1}$	−0.604	−1.099**	−1.178**	−1.165**	−1.168**
	(0.394)	(0.549)	(0.593)	(0.566)	(0.562)
Years since extension	1.508	1.400	1.571	1.452	1.402
	(1.206)	(1.234)	(1.187)	(1.162)	(1.227)
Years since extension^2	−0.322	−0.308	−0.320	−0.279	−0.273
	(0.224)	(0.229)	(0.237)	(0.233)	(0.243)
Years since extension^3	0.019*	0.020*	0.020	0.018	0.017
	(0.011)	(0.012)	(0.012)	(0.012)	(0.013)
Observations	52	52	52	52	52

Note: Logit model with robust standard errors in parentheses. Constant omitted. *$p < 0.10$, **$p < 0.05$, ***$p < 0.01$

public sector. This is reflected in Figure 6.4, which plots the evolution of public employment and investment in Egypt between 1953 and 2003.[142] Notwithstanding the visible rise in public employment, particularly under Nasser, the argument about 'cheap' social policies should not be easily dismissed for the following reasons.

First, to reiterate a point made in Chapter 1, to the extent that public employment increased in the area of social welfare, the expansion has in fact been accounted for by the social spending figures presented. As for Egypt, the combined sectors of health and education accounted for over 60 per cent of public employment in the early 1970s[143]—the overlap between the spending and employment figures is thus considerable. Second, the employment guarantee was rather short-lived and faded out from 1978 onwards as the government began to

[142] Note that some data points, especially for public investment, had to be linearly imputed, such that the graph should only be viewed as an illustration of the broad trend.
[143] Handoussa and El Oraby 2004, p. 2.

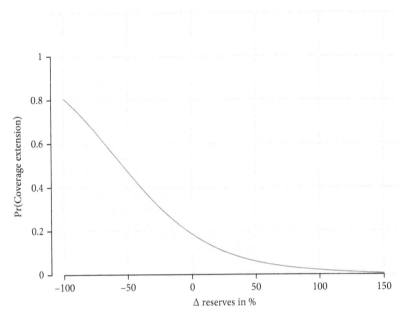

Figure 6.3 Predicted probability of extension of social insurance coverage in Egypt

Note: Shaded area indicates 95 per cent confidence bounds.

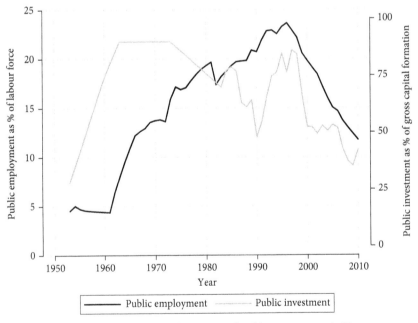

Figure 6.4 Evolution of public employment and public investment in Egypt (1953–2003)

Note: Data are taken from IMF 2011; V. Lucas and Richter 2016; and El-Issawy 1984. Missing data linearly imputed.

exempt public enterprises from the scheme and gradually increased the waiting period for public sector jobs, which had reached more than five years by the late 1980s.[144] Even before, then the government had sought to limit the annual intake of graduates by attempting to restrict university enrolments to 35,000 a year.[145]

Third, while the growth of public employment from 5 to 15 per cent under Nasser was indeed remarkable, it should be noted that Egypt started from comparatively very low levels of public employment prior to the 1960s. What is more, one should bear in mind that by far the largest increase in public employment resulted from the nationalization of nearly all industry and commerce in the early 1960s. This is reflected in the notably high levels of public investment, approximating 90 per cent in 1963. Importantly for my argument about 'cheap' social policies, it is safe to assume that, on balance, the nationalizations initially brought in more resources, be it in the form of appropriated profits or as a result of a better ability to tax the public sector.[146]

6.1.4 Summary

This section has made a number of key claims regarding the origins of Egypt's welfare trajectory. First, having eliminated ideology as a credible explanation, I established a link between intra-elite conflict and the regime's incentive for welfare provision. Based on autobiographical accounts by the main protagonists of the era, my analysis showed that the Free Officers' shift to welfare distribution was driven by growing conflict within the Revolutionary Command Council. Second, I demonstrated how this shift coincided with a simultaneous change in the regime's threat perception, which, as a result, burdened the regime with a double commitment to welfare and defence that was difficult to bear. The resulting trade-off between 'butter or guns' was process-traced at the micro-level using cabinet minutes from the Egyptian National Archives. Third, I provided both qualitative and quantitative evidence showing that this particular combination of circumstances led to the implementation of 'cheap' social policies, consisting of low funding, costless regulatory market interventions, a significant reliance on windfalls, and a strategy of using social policies to generate resources, rather than distributing them. In the next section, I explain why Egypt's welfare trajectory remained largely unchanged, even after the 1978 peace treaty with Israel.

---

[144] Binzel 2011, p. 8.   [145] Mabro 1974, p. 157.
[146] O'Brien 1966, p. 188. Note that I am not making any claims about the potential effects on productivity and growth in the long run, which were most probably negative.

6.2 Remaining Stuck: Mechanisms of Path Dependence in Egypt's Welfare Trajectory

This section draws attention to the mechanisms of path dependence that have maintained Egypt on its welfare trajectory following the Camp David Accords in 1978. Given a noticeable change in the regime's geostrategic environment, one could have expected a shift toward high welfare spending driven by a persistent incentive to cater to a low–middle class support coalition. In the absence of such a shift, this section turns to processes of path dependence as a possible explanation.

First, I demonstrate how the legacies of war making and external threat have turned the army into an important veto player in the budget-making process and narrowed the regime's fiscal margin of manoeuvre. Second, I use the examples of a failed attempt to overhaul Egypt's health insurance in the 2000s and the subsidy system to make the case that constituencies in favour of welfare provision were only able to defend past achievements, not to enforce a higher level of welfare spending. The example of the health care reform is particularly informative as it coincides in its timing and ambition with the health insurance reform in Tunisia and thus provides an interesting case for comparison. With regard to subsidies, my findings are very similar to Tunisia in that intended and unintended beneficiaries have become powerful stakeholders in the current system and have successfully mobilized against systemic changes.

6.2.1 No remarkable peace dividend: the reasons

Before discussing the peace dividend of the 1978 Camp David Accords, it is important to clarify the expected effect of a peace dividend on social spending. Given a changed threat perception and a persistent incentive to distribute to a broad-based coalition, we would expect defence spending to decrease and welfare spending to rise after a peace agreement. In Egypt, however, what happened was that defence spending only decreased with great difficulty and social spending failed to pick up. To the extent that a peace dividend existed, it was entirely consumed by the service of debt accumulated between the 1967 and the 1973 wars.

Military entrenchment and continuation of defence spending

There has been considerable disagreement in the literature about whether or not defence spending has decreased since the end of the 1973 war.[147] This is partly due to the secrecy around the military in Egypt, but also reflects different reference

---

[147] Compare, for instance, Kandil 2012a and Ayubi 1991, p. 256.

points in comparing pre- and post-war spending. Based on my own original data (see Figure 6.5), I offer a middle-ground position, which partly reconciles the different accounts in the literature. To begin with, defence expenditure dropped from its absolute peak of nearly 20 per cent of GDP in 1975 to about 7.2 per cent in 1978, the year of the Camp David Accords. In the period between the 1967 and the 1973 wars, defence spending had amounted to 43 per cent of public expenditure. The reduction was partly imputable to the shedding of military personnel from highs of 900,000 after hostilities had ceased.[148] While this account seems supportive of the idea that there was a substantial peace dividend,[149] two points need to be made here.

First, the levels of defence expenditure between 1967 and 1975 were economically absolutely unsustainable and brought the economy to the brink of collapse by the mid-1970s.[150] It therefore seems more sensible to compare defence spending to the levels prior to the 1967 war—7 per cent of GDP on average—when military spending was already crowding out social welfare. Using this benchmark, Egypt's defence expenditure remained high until the late 1980s and only began to drop below the 7 per cent threshold from 1987 onwards. Second, relative to levels of welfare high-spenders, such as Algeria and Tunisia, defence spending after the initial cutback remained high. From 1978 to 2005, defence spending as a percentage of GDP amounted to 2.1 and 2.9 per cent in Tunisia and Algeria respectively, compared to 4.4 per cent in Egypt—that is, respectively 110 and 52 per cent higher.[151] Even in Iran, which fought an eight-year war with Iraq in that period, average defence outlays stood at 3.1 per cent of GDP.

The reasons for this clearly lay in the military's substantial entrenchment in the state. Dominating Egypt's political elite, the army had by 1967 ' "extended its tentacles" into the various administrative, economic and political domains, as well as into the security apparatus'.[152] Kandil even goes so far as to talk about a 'shadow state' run by the military.[153] By 1970, almost every other position in the upper echelons of the administration was occupied by the military, which gave it important political leverage on the decision-making process.[154] Furthermore, Nasser's successor Sadat, though keen on demilitarizing Egyptian politics, had a strong interest in keeping the army complacent as he lacked a solid power base within the regime when he took over after Nasser's unexpected death in 1970.[155] Shortly before his assassination, Sadat appointed Field Marshal Abu

---

[148] This in line with the accounts of Kandil 2012a; Springborg 1989; and Owen 2004.

[149] See Cordesman 2004, p. 3.

[150] See Barnett's 1992 striking account of the post-war period; also Baker 1978, p. 136.

[151] IMF 2011; and V. Lucas and Richter 2016. Note that this period includes the civil war years in Algeria, which considerably hiked up spending.

[152] El-Sherif 1995, p. 15.   [153] Kandil 2012b.   [154] El-Sherif 1995, pp. 86–7.

[155] Barnett 1992, p. 131.

Ghazala as Minister of Defence and Chief of Staff, and he would become a serious competitor for Sadat's successor, Hosni Mubarak, and an ardent defender of the army's corporate interests.[156] In 1986, Abu Ghazala declared the armed forces budget immune from any spending cuts.[157] The army thus remained a key political veto player after the Camp David agreement, eager to preserve its political and economic interests.

As a result, reducing the defence budget beyond the immediate cutbacks after the end of hostilities proved difficult. This point is illustrated by a quote from the former Minister of Economy, Abdel-Latif El-Sayed, who in 1977 ruled out the possibility of further cuts in the defence budget: 'There are four major things in the budget: military, investment, subsidies and debt service. Should we cut back on our military? You can't do that. You cannot let defence go.'[158] The veto power of the army was also confirmed by three former ministers of Finance, Abdel-Aziz Hegazy, Ali Lutfi, and Medhat Hassanein, who respectively served as head of the Treasury under all three Egyptian presidents, Nasser, Sadat, and Mubarak.[159] They describe a practice whereby the military prevents a detailed discussion of the defence budget within the cabinet and instead makes direct contact with the presidency, by-passing the Prime Minister and the Ministry of Finance. Lutfi also stated that his resignation was prompted by pressure from the military as they were unhappy about proposed further cuts.

Given this distribution of power, it is little surprise that defence spending continued to hover at about 7 per cent of GDP until the late 1980s, after which it witnessed a gradual decline.[160] To compensate for destruction of equipment during the war, the army successfully lobbied for a replacement of the mostly Soviet weaponry with Western equipment, which proved to be much more expensive.[161] To illustrate, in only six years (1975–81) the military spent three times more on arms imports than in the previous twenty years.[162] Continued upward pressure also resulted from a resurgence of military recruitment, as a result of which the army increased from 298,000 in 1985, to 460,000 in 1980, to 680,000 by the end of the 1990s.[163]

Shift to security expenditures as coup-proofing strategy

The army's continuing clout had a further knock-on effect on public spending patterns which undermined a reallocation of resources to social welfare. Considering

---

[156] Springborg 1989, p. 98; Ayubi 1995, p. 256; and Kandil 2012b, p. 3970.
[157] Abul-Magd 2018, p. 104.   [158] New York Times 1977.
[159] Personal interview, Cairo, 28 January, 26 and 24 February respectively. Hegazy was Minister of Finance from 1968 to 1974, Lufti from 1978 to 1980, and Hassanein from 1999 to 2004.
[160] Note that these figures only include military spending financed through the state budget and not the two billion USD in military aid granted after Camp David as only budgetary defence spending has a crowding out effect on welfare.
[161] Butter 1989, p. 127; and Beattie 2000, p. 214.   [162] Barnett 1992, p. 130.
[163] Ayubi 1995, p. 255.

the new president's precarious position after his succession to Nasser, coupled with his eagerness to temper the army's political influence, Sadat opted for a deliberate strategy of building up the Ministry of Interior and its security apparatus to countervail the army. Staffing the security apparatus became even more vital for Sadat after he had thwarted preparations for a military coup against him in 1971.[164]

In financial terms, this bolstering of the regime's security apparatus absorbed an increasing share of the state budget.[165] Between 1977 and 1985, the budget of the Interior Ministry witnessed a nearly fourfold increase from 91 million EGP in 1977 to 348 million EGP in 1985.[166] This spending shift was accompanied by a rapid increase in size of Egypt's police force. According to figures from Kandil, the number of policemen swelled from 150,00 in 1974 to over 2 million by the early 2000s.[167] This is illustrated in Figure 6.5. From the early 1990s onwards, the decline in defence spending is nearly completely compensated for by a growing security budget.

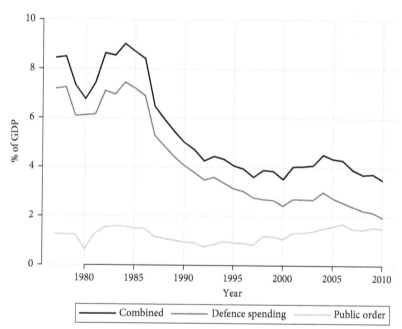

Figure 6.5 Defence and security spending as a percentage of GDP in Egypt (1980–2010)

Source: IMF 2011; and V. Lucas and Richter 2016.

[164] Hinnebusch 1985, p. 40.   [165] See also Diwan and Akin 2015, p. 21.
[166] Springborg 1989, p. 143.   [167] Kandil 2012b, pp. 4368–9. See also Soliman 2011, p. 54.

The rising burden of debt service

Increasing service of the debt that had been accumulated throughout the period between 1967 and 1973 further undermined a change in Egypt's spending pattern, since resources released from defence spending cuts were not freely available for the regime to invest in social welfare. As Wahid rightly points out, one of the primary reasons why the peace dividend did not trickle through was the growing burden of debt service weighing on the budget.[168] The overflowing debt service needs to be seen in Egypt's geostrategic context and is thus, at least indirectly, attributable to past external threats. Aggravating the destruction of two wars within a period of six years was the fact that hostilities had led to an occupation of the Sinai, which dealt a devastating blow to Egypt's three main sources of income: the Suez Canal, the Sinai oil fields, and tourism.[169] Lacking sufficient tax revenue to compensate for the losses, the regime had to rely on domestic and, more importantly, international loans to finance its deficit. This was reflected in public debt ratios hovering between 100 and 140 per cent of GDP between 1979 and 1992 (see Figure 6.6). Only one of the world's largest debt reliefs in the wake of the 1990–1 Gulf War brought Egypt's debt down to more sustainable levels.

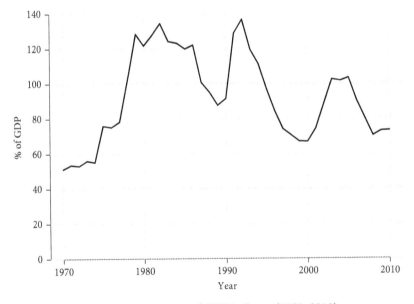

Figure 6.6 Public debt as a percentage of GDP in Egypt (1970–2010)
Source: Abbas et al. 2010.

---

[168] Wahid 2009, pp. 136–7.   [169] Barnett 1992, p. 129.

In sum, knock-on effects stemming from the legacies of the regime's past exposure to external threat undermined a diffusion of the peace dividend into social welfare. Nearly two decades of a security-focused spending strategy had conferred initial advantages upon the military relative to other social actors, which it converted into veto power in the political process. Moreover, considering the disastrous constitution of the Egyptian economy after a decade of war preparation and destruction, constituencies in favour of an expansion of social welfare had to take a defensive posture as existing social policies came under attack from austerity-oriented governments. Looking at the mechanisms of path dependence from the perspective of welfare constituencies, the following subsection demonstrates how the mobilization of intended and unintended beneficiaries of social policies foiled a dismantling of the existing structures of welfare distribution and, though unable to effect an expansion of welfare, forced the regime—both of Sadat and Mubarak—'to contend with the legacies of Nasserism and its commitment to the masses' welfare'.[170]

6.2.2 Too weak to push, too strong to withdraw: welfare constituencies defending the status quo

This subsection analyses the beneficiaries of social policies as an explanatory factor for the persistence of the Egyptian welfare trajectory after 1978. Two mechanisms are particularly important in this context. First, whilst lacking the political resources to push the regime onto a high-spending trajectory, welfare constituencies have successfully managed to fend off attempts at welfare retrenchment. Second, social policies have not only benefited the groups initially targeted as past welfare provision has engendered a powerful group of unintended beneficiaries who have come to play an important role as veto players standing in the way of any meaningful reform of the current status quo. I demonstrate these mechanisms using the example of a failed attempt to implement a major reform of the Egyptian health insurance system in the 2000s, and by analysing the Egyptian subsidy system. The latter case is particularly insightful for uncovering the influence of unintended beneficiaries, which include the public sector, the army, and politically connected business elites. The following analysis can also be read in comparative perspective to Tunisia and I highlight commonalities and differences in the summary of this section.

Health insurance reform in the 2000s
The attempted reform of Egypt's public health insurance system represented the single biggest reform attempt since the inception of the Egyptian Health Insurance

---

[170] Barnett 1992, p. 148.

Organization (HIO) in 1964. Seeking to combine elements of cost reduction and partial privatization with the ambition to universalize health insurance, the reform failed for two reasons: the mobilization of beneficiaries in favour of the status quo and the inability of the regime to muster the financial resources to fund a large-scale extension of coverage to low-income segments of the Egyptian population. We can thus see elements of constituency mobilization and 'cheap' social policies in the reform process.

Regarding the objectives of the reform, it is important to note that it had economic and political motives which, to some degree, stood in contradiction with each other. At the economic level, the reform was prompted by the realization that the current health insurance scheme was financially unsustainable. To start with, the existing benefit package has been generous, comprising costly surgeries such as transplants, plastic surgery, and treatment abroad. What is more, benefits have been limited neither by quantity nor by costs.[171] This has resulted in increasingly high deficits. For instance, the difference between average premium and costs for government employees has reached 207 per cent; for pensioners, it is even higher, amounting to 336 per cent.[172] Making losses since the early 2000s, the scheme had reached a deficit of 12 billion EGP shortly after Mubarak's ouster, whilst the total budget of the HIO amounted to 4 billion EGP.[173]

At the political level, the reform was viewed by the regime as an important asset in Mubarak's 2005 re-election bid, in what would be the first competitive presidential elections in the country's history.[174] By universalizing health insurance, the regime was hoping to address two principal deficiencies in the health care system: high out-of-pocket expenditures (72 per cent) which have been driven by uninsured Egyptians opting for private health care instead of using the free-of-charge facilities provided by the Ministry of Health, the quality of which is considered very low;[175] and the fact that the health care insurance system exclusively insureds the policy-holder and not any dependants. Taken as a whole, the measure was intended to raise the social profile of the National Democratic Party (NDP)—Egypt's ruling party.

Addressing the twin deficiencies of the existing system, the proposed reform included measures of cost reduction and coverage extension.[176] The former failed to overcome resistance from existing vested interest groups; the latter failed because the pro-welfare constituencies inside and outside the government were

---

[171] WHO 2005, p. 34.   [172] World Bank 2015a, p. 44.   [173] Al-Masry Al-Youm 2011.

[174] Personal interview with Awad Tag Eddin, Cairo, 19 February 2013. Tag Eddin was Minister of Health between 2002 and 2005.

[175] World Bank 2015a, p. 43; and Clark 2004a, p. 47. Note that these free-of-charge facilities exist in parallel to the health care facilities owned and run by the Egyptian Health Insurance Organization. The latter are only available to Egyptians with health insurance coverage.

[176] A first draft was launched and then withdrawn in 2000. The second draft, proposed in 2002, was then discussed throughout the 2000s until Mubarak's ouster, without having been put to a parliamentary vote.

too weak to muster the necessary financial resources. Regarding cost reduction, the draft reform included three main components. First, existing benefits should be restructured into a basic benefits package, comprising a number of major diseases, such as cancer, diabetes, and hepatitis. Similar to initial reform proposals in Tunisia, other diseases should be insured by contracting complementary private insurances.[177] Second, the reform envisaged a private out-of-pocket contribution of up to 30 per cent for all policy-holders depending on income, a demand which was pushed in particular by the ruling NDP.[178] Third, the reform aimed for a gradual privatization of health care facilities owned by the HIO. To this effect, the NDP sought to split off the HIO's role as a health care provider from its function as an insurer. The idea was then to sublet 74 per cent of HIO facilities to private providers as a first step toward full privatization.[179] Particularly after the appointment of Hatim al-Gibaly as Minister of Health in 2005—al-Gibaly was the CEO of one of the biggest private hospitals in Egypt[180]—privatization became a major priority of the reform project. Under his aegis, the HIO was transformed into a publicly listed holding company in 2007, with the idea of making it more profitable, opening it to non-HIO members and private investors, and ultimately privatizing it.[181]

These propositions met with serious resistance on the part of stakeholders in the current system.[182] Whilst opposition to the law occasionally took the form of public protests—such as in December 2009 when 500 pensioners demonstrated in front of parliament demanding a withdrawal of the law[183]—most of it was voiced in closed-door negotiations with the ministries in charge. The first interest group to express their concern were employers who opposed the reform for its plans to increase employers' contributions to the new insurance system.[184] This concern was partly shared by the government itself, in particular the Ministry of Finance, because, as Egypt's largest employer, the state would have had to shoulder the financial costs of higher contributions as well. To address these concerns, the government offered to offset higher contributions by reductions in the contributions to work accident insurance and shifting the costs of sick leave to the HIO instead of employers.[185] The government later back-pedalled even further, offering reductions in the employers' contributions which were to be offset by higher income taxes.[186]

---

[177] Clément 2007, p. 306; and IHS 2010.   [178] Khalil 2006, p. 93.
[179] Clément 2007, p. 322.   [180] Fintz 2006.
[181] Clément 2007, p. 308. Since the 2011 uprisings, all privatization attempts have come to a halt.
[182] The following assessment is informed by interviews with Awad Tag Eddin, Minster of Health until 2005, and Kamel Maait, Deputy Minister of Finance responsible for social insurance at the time. The interviews were conducted in Cairo on 19 February 2013 and 14 November 2012 respectively.
[183] American Embassy in Cairo 2009.
[184] Personal interview with Kamel Maait, Deputy Minister of Finance in charge of social security, Cairo, 14 November 2012.
[185] Clément 2007, p. 317.
[186] Personal interview with Kamel Maait, Cairo, 14 November 2012. See also IHS 2010.

Considerable opposition also emerged from policy-holders, in particular within the public sector. Organized in the Egyptian Trade Union Federation (ETUF), public sector workers expressed strong resistance to almost all aspects of the proposed law[187]—unsurprisingly, considering that the new insurance scheme would be much less generous than the old one. Out-of-pocket contributions, for instance, had last been negotiated in 1991 and were generally very low.[188] An increase of up to 30 per cent of the treatment costs was simply unacceptable. A second point government employees took exception to was the proposed increase in contributions, which they argued would be primarily used to reduce the government's budget deficit, as had happened with social insurance reserves in the past.[189] More importantly, they opposed the government's idea of unifying the contribution system, which would have meant that the full salary of government employees was used as a basis to calculate the contribution, rather than just the basic salary.[190] The full salary comprises a number of supplementary payments and bonuses, which in some administrations can amount to 83 per cent of the basic salary.[191] In essence, the new calculation system would have entailed a substantial increase in employees' contributions.

Finally, current policy-holders represented by ETUF and other civil society associations objected to the inclusion of new sectors under the umbrella of the HIO without adequate funding, while refusing to provide a major contribution to increasing funding. The following quote pointedly summarizes this insider logic: 'More than 90 per cent of private, public companies and associations have their own health insurance systems [...] So why, then, deprive them of this privilege and force citizens to join a system forcing them to pay extra money in return for a lesser health service?'[192] To alleviate opposition to the reform, the government first resorted to co-optation by making a representative of ETUF head of the newly founded HIO holding company. Yet, according to both Kamel Maait and Awad Tag Eddin, the government remained fearful that higher contributions would lead to strikes within the public sector and the HIO itself, in particular in a context of growing labour unrest after 2008.[193]

Regarding the second objective, coverage extension, the government's aim was to insure the 54 per cent of the Egyptian population without any health insurance coverage and to introduce a family-based insurance system with free insurance for dependants. In view of the high poverty level within the country, the government predicted that it would have to subsidize the premiums of up to 40 per cent of the Egyptian population, which meant that about two-thirds of the planned coverage

---

[187] Personal interview with Awad Tag Eddin, Cairo, 19 February 2013.
[188] Clément 2007, p. 317.   [189] Clément 2007, p. 318.
[190] Personal interview with Kamel Maait, Cairo, 14 November 2012.
[191] Handoussa and El Oraby 2004, p. 7.
[192] National Council of Women (NCW) representative, quoted in Reem 2010.
[193] Personal interviews, Cairo, 14 November 2012 and 19 February 2013.

extension would have to be funded entirely by the state.[194] Estimates of the exact cost varied but it seemed clear that at least 17 billion EGP of additional spending would be needed. This is almost twice as much as the entire health budget, which at the end of the Mubarak era stood at 10 billion EGP.[195]

It was unclear where this money should come from as increased business taxes were unpopular with employers, and employees remained adamant about contributions. Even with increased taxation, an increase of the health budget by nearly 100 per cent could only have been financed by spending reallocations within the government budget, for which the Ministry of Health lacked the political clout within the cabinet. This point is made clear by former Minister of Health, Tag Eddin: 'Money was the key issue in the failure of the health insurance reform [...] Our budget was never enough and our spending lower than needed. [...] In the drafting of the budget, the Ministry of Finance would only ever give us the "leftovers".[196] The faint influence of the pro-welfare constituency within the cabinet is also illustrated by a 60 per cent spending cut in the budget of the Ministry of Health in 2005—right at the height of negotiations about the health insurance reform.[197] Outside government, increased funding for health care was backed by the labour federation, the proposals of which were very similar to the Tunisian UGTT's proposition for an 'upgrading' of the public sector system: higher contributions for employers, construction of more hospitals, higher salaries for healthcare workers, and a boost in hiring.[198] Yet, unlike the UGTT, ETUF lacked the political power to push these demands through and, in the event, resigned itself to defending a beneficial status quo. The reform remained unfinished in the Mubarak period.[199]

Intended and unintended beneficiaries: the food and energy subsidy system

Food and energy subsidies represent another policy area where the influence of stakeholders in the status quo is particularly visible. This system of subsidization has spawned intended and unintended beneficiaries who have a vested interest in the continuation of the subsidies. The following analysis brings to light important parallels between Egypt and Tunisia regarding the political dynamics underpinning the subsidy system: food riots have left a deep imprint on the regime, making elites reluctant to engage in profound reforms; and beneficiaries in the production chain of subsidies have over time grown into a second pillar of support for the status quo.

---

[194] Personal interview with Kamel Maait, Cairo, 14 November 2012.
[195] IHS 2010. Youmna El Hamaki, former member of the NDP General Secretariat, estimates the additional costs at 40 billion EGP. Personal interview, Cairo, 23 January 2013.
[196] Personal interview, Cairo, 19 February 2013.   [197] Fintz 2006, p. 8.
[198] Clément 2007, p. 320.
[199] See Loewe and Westemeier 2018 for an analysis of the revived health insurance reform under President Sisi.

The Egyptian subsidy system: a brief overview

The subsidization of food and energy products has been a major component of Egypt's social policies.[200] As regards food products, subsidies were first introduced in the aftermath of the First World War in an attempt to temper food price inflation, especially in urban areas.[201] Expanded by Nasser in the mid-1960s,[202] food subsidies are provided in two different ways. First, cheap 'baladi' bread is available to all Egyptians at a subsidized price.[203] It is consumed by 90 per cent of all Egyptian households on a daily basis, with 60 per cent relying predominantly on subsidized bread.[204] Second, ration cards offer a quota of basic food items for a maximum of four persons per card.[205] In the past, ration cards provided up to twenty food items,[206] yet gradual reforms since the 1980s have restricted quotas to five goods: tea, sugar, vegetable oil, pasta, and rice.[207] In return, the number of card holders has grown considerably, in particular after the government decided in 2008 to reopen registration for children born after 1989.[208] As of 2008, nine out of ten Egyptians (69.2 million) benefited from a ration card.[209] In terms of proportions, at 66 per cent 'baladi' bread represents the bulk of food subsidies.[210] Distributively, food subsidies are highly regressive, with most benefits reaped by middle- and high-income groups.[211] Politically, food subsidies favour large urban communities at the expense of rural areas as, in the words of former Minister of Supply, Ali Moselhi: 'If you control Cairo, you control the whole of Egypt'.[212]

While the technical aspects of the subsidy system resemble the Tunisian case, it is important to note that, after significant liberalization in the trade of food commodities, both the state and private traders operate in the procurement of wheat and rice to produce the subsidized items.[213] About two-thirds of the grain is purchased by the state, represented by the General Authority for Supply Commodities (GASC), with the remainder being procured by private traders.[214] The grain is then distributed at a subsidized price to licensed public and private mills and, in the case of wheat, bakeries purchase the resulting 'baladi' flour from the mills. The price bakeries pay for 'baladi' flour is fixed and ensures a guaranteed profit for mills. Finally, bakeries sell the 'baladi' bread at a fixed rate of 5 piastres

---

[200] The following description does not account for subsidy reforms post-2011 as they fall outside the scope of this study.

[201] Omar 2012, p. 47; and Ahmed et al. 2001, p. 5. Thomson 2017 notes a general urban bias in food subsidies.

[202] Sadowski 1991, p. 159; and Omar 2012, p. 48.

[203] There is also a partly subsidized bread produced from higher-quality 76 per cent extraction flour.

[204] IDSC 2010, p. 3.   [205] World Bank 2010a, p. i.   [206] Omar 2012, p. 42.

[207] World Bank 2010a, p. 3. In 1981, the government introduced two categories of ration cards: fully subsidized (green) and partially subsidized (red) cards.

[208] World Food Programme 2008a, p. 22.   [209] ECES 2010, p. 7.

[210] IDSC 2010, p. 2.   [211] IDSC 2005, p. 12; and Aboulenein et al. 2010, p. 10.

[212] Personal interview, Cairo, 13 January 2013. Moselhi served as minister from 2005 until 2011.

[213] For a good overview, see Ghoneim 2012.   [214] World Bank 2010b, p. 4.

(less than 1 US cent), with the GASC compensating the bakeries for the difference between production costs and market price. Given the huge difference between the market and subsidized price of flour, bakers have a strong incentive to sell flour on the black market. They also sell subsidized bread as animal feed which is more expensive than 'baladi' bread. Up to a third of all subsidized flour and bread is leaked in this manner.[215]

In budgetary terms, food subsidies represented on average 3 per cent of GDP between 1953 and 2009. However, this average masks the enormous fluctuations of the subsidy bill over time (see Figure 6.7). While under Nasser expenditure on subsidies decreased gradually and was thus considered neither a political nor an economic problem,[216] the subsidy bill increased more than ten-fold following the 1973 war as a consequence of rising global commodity prices. Coinciding with Egypt's post-war reconstruction, this upsurge put additional pressure on a regime scrabbling for money. From their peak at 10.5 per cent of GDP in 1982, food subsidies have since declined but the vulnerability to price shocks from the world market has continued, visible in rising expenditure as a result of global food price inflation in the late 2000s.

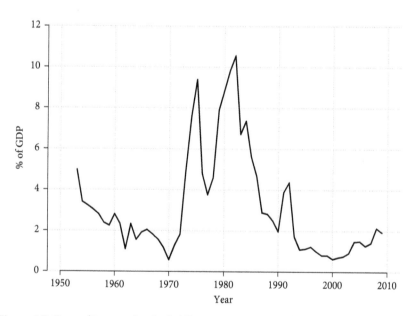

Figure 6.7 Expenditure on food subsidies as a percentage of GDP in Egypt (1953–2009)

Source: IMF 2011; and V. Lucas and Richter 2016.

---

[215] Ibid., p. 2; and World Food Programme 2008b.   [216] Sadowski 1991, p. 159.

Alongside food subsidies, Egypt has maintained an extensive system of energy subsidies, which offers energy products, such as petrol, gas, and electricity, at favourable rates below the world market price. Whilst oil and gas exports from Egypt have been declining, the country was a net exporter of energy until the Arab Spring, which makes the calculation of energy subsidies slightly more complicated. Available estimates from the late 2000s (see Figure 6.8) show that, since the rapid increase in world energy prices since the early 2000s, the cost of energy subsidies has outweighed the cost of subsidized food. In terms of their distributive impact, energy subsidies disproportionately benefit the highest quintile of income groups, who reap 33 per cent compared to 3.8 per cent captured by the lowest quintile,[217] and energy-intensive industries, such as transport and communications.[218]

Overall, like in Tunisia, food and energy subsidies are suboptimal social policies, failing to reach groups in need and pushing up expenditure and consumption. While Egyptian governments have been fully cognizant of these facts, subsidy reform has proven difficult, if not impossible, in the face of intended and unintended beneficiaries eager to maintain the status quo. Both groups shall now be scrutinized in turn.

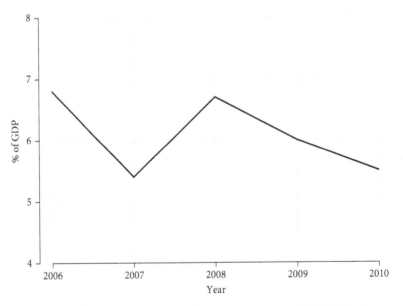

Figure 6.8 Expenditure on energy subsidies as a percentage of GDP in Egypt (2006–2010)

Source: Vagliasindi 2012, p. 205.

[217] Fattouh and El-Katiri 2012, p. 38.   [218] ECES 2010, p. 4.

The told story: food riots and mobilized beneficiaries

As in Tunisia, past food riots have left a lasting effect on the regime's willingness to reform the subsidy system. The major event in Egypt dates back to 18 January 1977 when President Sadat announced price increases for a number of subsidized food items, such as rice, tea, and gas cylinders for households. Notably, the main subsidy for 'baladi' bread was left untouched,[219] which did not spare the regime from popular unrest.

Demonstrations against the measures first broke out in Egypt's centre of steel production, Helwan, and quickly spread to the urban centres of Cairo, Alexandria, and other big cities, mobilizing industrial workers, students, state employees, and, to a lesser extent, the urban poor along the way.[220] As demonstrations rapidly turned violent, with administration buildings and consumer centres being attacked and burnt, a countrywide state of emergency was declared and the regime deployed the army for the first time since 1952 to quell the unrest. Rioting only stopped after Sadat repealed the measures on 20 January.[221] The army had to be called upon a second time when minor increases in the price of bread prompted rioting in the textile centre of Kafr al-Dawwar in 1984.[222]

In both incidents, the groups rallying against subsidy reductions did not primarily hail from the ranks of marginalized urban poor. On the contrary, they represented core constituencies of the regime's lower–middle class coalition, such as industrial workers and public sector employees.[223] While the short-term response consisted of repeal and spending increases,[224] the long-term legacy of key support groups rising up against price increases was a realization among political elites that 'the bread subsidy cannot be touched except at the peril of the regime'.[225] This legacy is conspicuous both in archival documents and in interviews.

References to the food riots are paramount in the correspondence between the Egyptian government and the IMF, which was declassified in the early 2000s.[226] For example, in 1987 the Egyptian government rejected the IMF's demand for faster subsidy reductions, referring to 'the delicate political and social fabric of the country' which would necessitate gradual adjustment.[227] Two years later, the Egyptian Ministry of Finance again turned down an IMF demand for reductions, stating that 'the resultant price increases would [...] exceed the absorptive capacity of the population, thereby endangering social and political stability'.[228] Evoking the legacy of past riots, the Egyptian government repeatedly insisted that 'the pace of reform had to be geared to the likely public reaction'.[229]

The same concern not to repeat the 1977 riots also emerges from interviews with former policy-makers. According to former Minister of Finance,

---

[219] Ahmed et al. 2001, p. 7.   [220] Walton and Seddon 1994, pp. 196–7.

[221] Sadowski 1991, p. 156.   [222] Ayubi 1991, p. 229.   [223] Ahmed et al. 2001, p. 7.

[224] Sadowski 1991, p. 160.   [225] Waterbury 1983, p. 230.

[226] See IMF 1978; IMF 1980; IMF 1982; IMF 1987b; IMF 1988; and IMF 1989.

[227] IMF 1987b, p. 5.   [228] IMF 1989, p. 12.   [229] See, for example, IMF 1988, p. 19.

Medhat Hassanein, food subsidies are 'politically way too sensitive to change them'.[230] Former Minister of Supply, Ali Moselhi, describes 'a real fear' of the government to touch the subsidy issue.[231] Moselhi had repeatedly suggested a reduction of subsidies to President Mubarak, but, according to Alia El Mahdy, a former member of the NDP Policies Committee, was told to 'find another way' and not 'to repeat 1977'.[232]

The untold story: unintended beneficiaries in the public and private sectors
Fear of consumer unrest is the predominant narrative to explain the persistence of subsidization in Egypt. Though important, this narrative is incomplete without giving due attention to unintended beneficiaries from subsidies in the public and private sectors. In Egypt, the untold story of the political economy of subsidy reform revolves around four key actors: public sector workers in the milling industry, commodity traders, business cronies, and the army.[233]

Given continuing state dominance in the Egyptian milling sector,[234] public milling workers have two major stakes tied to the continuation of the subsidy system: jobs and pensions. Producing daily 22,000 tons of flour and 70 per cent of all subsidized flour,[235] Egypt's public milling sector is one of the biggest industrial employers in the country, with an estimated 60,000 workers employed in the production and delivery of subsidized flour.[236] Similar to other state-owned enterprises, employment in public mills is characterized by a high degree of overstaffing. According to estimates of the World Food Programme, Egyptian public sector mills employ about 4.5 times the required workforce,[237] which has a negative impact on their cost structure and competitiveness. For instance, whilst private mills have costs of about 49 EGP per ton of flour, the costs of public mills are about 36 per cent higher (75 EGP/ton).[238] Thus, many public sector workers would be expected to lose their job if the system allowed for increased competition.[239]

Related to this, a second major concern of public sector workers is corporate pension schemes which are tied to the public milling sector. To understand this point, it is crucial to note that public sector workers are stakeholders in the public milling sector. As the milling sector was transformed into public holdings in the early 1990s, minority shares ranging between 5 and 15 per cent were ceded to

[230] Personal interview, Cairo, 24 February 2013.
[231] Personal interview, Cairo, 13 January 2013.
[232] Personal interview, Cairo, 18 January 2013.   [233] For a similar argument, see Kamal 2015.
[234] Though the milling industry was liberalized in the early 1990s and three big mills were ceded to private investors, the milling sector remains dominated by state-owned enterprises (SOEs). Organized in two publicly listed holding companies, the Holding Company for Rice and Wheat Mills (HCRWM) and the Holding Company for Food Industries (HCFI), the public milling industry consists of 126 mills, 109 of which produce the subsidized 'baladi' flour. See Kherallah et al. 2000, p. 90; and Mansour 2012, p. 4.
[235] World Bank 2010b, p. 5.   [236] Al-Masry Al-Youm 2009a.
[237] World Food Programme 2008a, p. 17.   [238] World Bank 2010b, p. 5.
[239] World Food Programme 2008a, p. 5.

labour unions and public sector insurance funds, as shown in Table 6.7. These shares not only guarantee that workers benefit from the companies' profits through dividends, but also, more importantly, form the basis of corporate pension funds offered to unionized workers, which represent an attractive supplement to the public pension scheme. A restructuring of the subsidy system would thus have

Table 6.7 Egyptian workers' stakes in the food subsidy system

Company	Shareholder	Share	Number of employees
General Company for Silos and Storage (GSSC)	Union Workers Shareholders	10%	2,875
Middleand West Delta Flour Mills (WCDF)	Union Workers Shareholders	10%	4,555
	Insurance Fund of Suez Canal Authority Employees; Social Insurance Fund for Governmental Sector Employees; Social Insurance Fund for Public and Private Sector Employees	n/a	
South Cairo and Giza Flour Mills and Bakeries (SCFM)	UnionWorkers Shareholders	10%	2,631
Alexandria Flour Mills (AFMC)	UnionWorkers Shareholders	10%	2,278
East Delta Flour Mills (EDFM)	UnionWorkers Shareholders	10%	3,880
Upper Egypt Flour Mills (UEFM)	UnionWorkers Shareholders	15%	n/a
	Insurance Fund of the Workers of Upper Egypt Flour Mills Co.	5%	n/a
North Cairo Flour Mills (MILS)	UnionWorkers Shareholders	6%	3,352
Middle Egypt Flour Mills (CEFM)	UnionWorkers Shareholders	6%	3,365
Extracted Oil & Derivatives Company SAE	UnionWorkers Shareholders	5%	2,202
	Employee Shareholders Union	n/a	

Note: Business information is taken from Bureau van Dijk, 2013.

negative repercussions on jobs and pensions, which is why public sector workers have opposed reform.

Opposition to reform was particularly visible in the late 2000s when the public milling sector successfully derailed further liberalization of the flour market proposed by Minister of Supply, Ali Moselhi. Seeking to replace the fixed flour quotas with a tender mechanism in which private and public mills entered into competition, the reform immediately met with resistance from mill workers who feared being outcompeted by the private sector. When a first trial of the mechanism was launched in one governorate in May 2007, workers at the Middle Egypt Mill staged a strike after they had been outbid by a private company. Eager to avoid disruptions in the bread supply, the government quickly gave in and allocated the mill the usual quota.[240] When the government decided to test the mechanism on a larger scale in November 2008, labour leaders accused the Ministry of Supply of trying to 'destroy the public milling sector and put at risk jobs'.[241] Underlining their political leverage, mill workers not only threatened to stage a general strike, which would have disrupted food production, but also alarmed consumers about an 'inevitable increase in the price of subsidised bread' should the tendering mechanism be introduced.[242] Whilst their argument might be doubtful, workers indeed managed to stir the fear of urban consumers, who became increasingly hostile toward the reform and joined mill workers in a number of minor walkouts.[243] Mill workers also managed to mobilize opposition within the government against the reform, co-drafting a warning letter which the Ministry of Investment addressed to the Prime Minister.[244] In response, the government pledged to compensate public mills unable to obtain a tender and further promised investments to make the sector more competitive—all in an effort to attenuate workers' protests.[245] Yet, in the face of producers, consumers, and parts of the government all rallying against the reform, the Ministry of Supply lost Mubarak's backing and was consequently forced to back down.[246] The idea of a tendering system was scrapped.

As regards the second group of unintended beneficiaries—local wheat and rice traders—it is important to understand that the government and a small set of traders compete in the procurement of local wheat and rice, which results in exaggerated price levels and considerable profits for the traders.[247] In the case of wheat, the GASC and traders freely compete in the purchase of grain from local farmers. In the interest of encouraging domestic wheat production, the GASC further guarantees a domestic price above the world market price. Nonetheless, many farmers have preferred to sell to private traders as (a) until 2008 they guaranteed a marginally higher price than the GASC; (b) they collect wheat directly from the farm whereas farmers need to ensure delivery to the

[240] Al-Ishtiraki 2007.   [241] Al-Masry Al-Youm 2008.   [242] Al-Masry Al-Youm 2009a.
[243] Personal interview with Ali Moselhi, Cairo, 13 January 2013.
[244] Al-Masry Al-Youm 2009b.   [245] Al-Masry Al-Youm 2009c.
[246] Personal interview with Ali Moselhi, Cairo, 13 January 2013.
[247] World Food Programme 2008a, p. 3; and Mitchell 2002, pp. 259–61.

GASC; and (c) unlike the government, they provide cheap loans for inputs, such as fertilizers.[248] Having successfully outcompeted the GASC in the procurement of domestic wheat, private traders then sell the wheat back to the GASC which has the monopoly of wheat distribution for subsidized flour. To make matters worse, the GASC cannot replace locally produced wheat by imported wheat, as it is obliged to clear the Egyptian wheat market to promote domestic production. Now, if the wheat trading sector were a market with perfect competition, prices should approach the level offered by the GASC. Yet, according to former Minster of Supply Gouda Abdel Khaleq, domestic wheat trade is controlled by an oligopoly of three traders, which can use their price-setting power to squeeze considerable profits out of the GASC.[249]

As regards rice, Egypt is self-sufficient and able to export considerable amounts to the world market. Domestic trade and production are predominantly in the hands of the private sector.[250] Similar to the wheat market, the trade of rice is dominated by five oligopolistic companies.[251] As a result, traders are able to collude on a high price and sell the rice expensively to the GASC, which increases the costs for the Egyptian taxpayer. This system is aggravated by the fact that rice can be stored for a long time, which means that rice traders can effectively ration the supply of rice without having to fear financial losses. Their price-setting power has led to major disruptions in the supply of rice. For instance, in early 2011, the Ministry of Supply cancelled a tender for domestic rice after prices had increased from 2,900 to 4,900 EGP per ton within a few months.[252] Again, there is an understanding that the GASC should clear the domestic rice market first. Importing rice whilst domestically produced rice is still available is strongly opposed by the Rice Chamber of Egypt's Industrial Union.[253] Lacking other alternatives, the Egyptian government imposed an export ban on rice, yet with little effect as traders have mostly kept their rice stocks, hoping for higher prices.[254]

While the exact political influence of these trader oligopolists is hard to gauge, senior officials whom I interviewed confirmed that they were well connected within the former regime apparatus.[255] For instance, the former secretary of President Mubarak, Gamal Eddin Abdel Aziz, operated a business partnership with the wheat trader Venus International Company, which was then given a large number of tenders by the GASC on the direct order of Abdel Aziz.[256] Another example is given by former Minister of Supply, Abdel Khaleq, who stated in a personal interview that traders attempted his ouster in 2011 in response to his intention to import rice and break up their monopoly.[257] Though anecdotal,

---

[248] Ghoneim 2012, pp. 11–19.

[249] Personal interview, Cairo, 18 November 2012. Abdel Khaleq served in the first post-revolutionary cabinet from 2011 until 2012.

[250] World Food Programme 2008a, p. 18.   [251] Ghoneim 2012, p. 25.

[252] Al-Youm Al-Saba'a 2011.   [253] See, for instance, Al-Masry Al-Youm 2012.

[254] Mansour 2012.

[255] Personal interview with Youmna El Hamaki and Gouda Abdel Khaleq, Cairo, 21 January 2013 and 18 November 2012.

[256] Egypt Independent 2012.   [257] Personal interview, Cairo, 18 November 2012.

these examples suggest that, in the absence of an effective competition law,[258] well-connected trader oligopolies have become an important lobby in favour of the current status quo.

The last two groups of beneficiaries are the big 'whales of the Nile',[259] that is, politically connected firms (PCFs) and the army.[260] Both groups derive economic benefits from the existing subsidy system by (i) producing in energy-intensive sectors, thus reaping the benefits of subsidized energy inputs; (ii) operating in an oligopolistic sector with low competition and high access barriers due to required government licences, coupled with guaranteed profits based on allocated government quotas which remove pressures to produce cost effectively. Profits are further enhanced by the fact that the subsidy system structurally encourages overproduction. As in Tunisia, the lobbying activities of these actors are difficult to observe directly and, hence, detailed process tracing is nearly impossible. I therefore seek to make the same 'circumstantial case' as in the previous chapter: if we can observe that actors with *well-known* political connections are active in sectors benefiting from food and energy subsidies, it is plausible to assume that they will use their influence to safeguard their privileged position if necessary. Moreover, if I can show that it is indeed the subsidies, and not alternative confounders like trade protection, that attract cronies and the army to these sectors, we have even more reason to believe that these actors will seek to block meaningful reforms in the subsidy system.

Regarding the presence of PCFs in sectors related to subsidies, Tables 6.8 and 6.9 summarize the activity in sectors related to food subsidies for cronies and the army respectively. Tables 6.10 and 6.11 do the same for energy-intensive sectors that benefit disproportionately from cheap energy. To identify business cronies and enterprises linked to the army, I rely on a dataset developed by Malik and Eibl.[261] For the army, I rely on two different sources: data collected by Acemoglu and co-authors who use the Zawya business database and online research to identify holding companies controlled by the Egyptian military;[262] and an original dataset by Eibl and Malik which identifies economic sectors with army activity based on a collection of secondary sources.[263] All company-related information was taken from the same sources, supplemented by information from the Orbis database,[264] and online research.

Looking more closely at the activity of PCFs in subsidy-related sectors, the four summary tables document an extensive network of businesses operating across

---

[258] A competition law was adopted in 2006 but has been rather ineffective. See Ghoneim 2012, p. 25.

[259] Sfakianakis 2004.

[260] Described as 'businessmen in arms', the Egyptian army has built an extensive business empire since 1973 which by the late 2000s was geared predominantly to civilian production and reached into nearly all aspects of manufacturing. For more details on Egypt's military economy, see Abul-Magd 2012; Abul-Magd 2013; and Abul-Magd 2016.

[261] Malik and Eibl forthcoming.   [262] Acemoglu, Hassan, and Tahoun 2014.

[263] Eibl and Malik 2015.   [264] Bureau van Dijk 2013.

Table 6.8 Politically connected actors in sectors related to food subsidies: Egypt

Actor	Company	Type of political connection	Sector
Mansour family	Seclam/Labanita, subsidiary of Mansour Group	Party: Mohamed Mansour was Minister of Transport (2004–11)	Tea
Sawiris family	Nile Sugar	Party: Naguib Sawiris was member of the NDP Business Secretariat and head of the Industrial Training Council	Sugar
Sallam family	Shareholders in El Fayoum Company for Sugar Industries	Party: Hussein Sallam was member of the NDP National Youth Council	Sugar
Ibrahim Kamel	National Food Company	Party: member of NDP General Secretariat	Sugar
Moataz Al-Alfi	Egyptian Starch and Glucose Company, subsidiary of Americana Group for Food & Tourism Projects	Party: Al-Alfi's brothers served on several high-ranking NDP committees	Flour, bread, pasta, rice, and wheat

Note: Politically connected actors are identified based on Roll 2010. Business information is taken from Bureau van Dijk 2013 and online research.

a range of sectors. In the food subsidy area, crony businesses have controlled important parts of sugar manufacturing, with the Sawiris family, the Sallam family, and Ibrahim Kamel operating a range of sugar factories. Moataz Al-Alfi, who was linked through family connections to the NDP leadership, is the owner of the Egyptian Starch and Glucose Company. As one of Egypt's manufacturers of inputs for the baking industry, he has benefited indirectly from the high consumption of bread as a result of subsidization.

Turning to the army, it should be noted that the main public holding company controlling nearly all state-owned enterprises related to the food subsidy sector—the Holding Company for Food Industries—is controlled by the Egyptian military. With retired generals acting as chairmen, board members, and managing directors of affiliated companies, the military also holds important stakes in Egypt's sugar industry. What is more, by virtue of controlling the food holding, the military holds sway over the entire public milling sector as well as the country's strategic wheat reserves run by the Egyptian Holding Company for Silos and Storage. The military is directly involved in the production of subsidized bread with the army operating 'eight gigantic complexes to make bread for the Ministry of Supply,

Table 6.9 Army-related companies in sectors related to food subsidies: Egypt

Company	Type of army connection	Sector
Delta Sugar Company, Al Noubariyah Sugar Company, El Fayoum Sugar Company, Daqahlia Sugar Company, *all subsidiaries of Holding Company for Food Industries SAE*	Chairman, managing directors, and board members of firms affiliated with *Holding Company for Food Industries* are (former) generals; Egyptian Sugar and Integrated Industries Company owns part of Delta Sugar Company; Holding for Silos & Storage run by a general	Sugar
Egyptian Holding Company for Silos & Storage SAE, *subsidiary of Holding Company for Food Industries*		Flour, bread, pasta, rice, and wheat
General Greater Cairo Bakeries, Wadi El Melouk Company for Milling, Wadi El Melouk Company for Grinding and Its Industries SAE, Middle Egypt Flour Mills Company SAE, Upper Egypt Flour Mills Company SAE, North Cairo Mills Company SAE, East Delta Mills Company SAE, Middle Egypt Flour Mills Company SAE, Gharbia Rice Mills, Alexandria Flour Mills and Bakeries SAE, Middle & West Delta Flour Mills SAE, Rice Marketing Company, South Cairo & Giza Mills & Bakeries Company SAE, United Flour Mills and Integrated Industries, United Mills Company, *all subsidiaries of Holding Company for Food Industries SAE*		Flour, bread, pasta, rice, and wheat

Note: Army-related companies are identified based on Acemoglu, Hassan, and Tahoun 2014 and Eibl & Malik 2015. Business information is taken from the same sources.

producing about 700 million loaves every year for civilian consumption. In Cairo, [the army] built ten complexes for bread for the Ministry of Social Solidarity [and] military factories manufactured thousands of kiosks for bread sales'.[265] The army is also heavily involved in the agro-industrial sector, including wheat production.[266]

---

[265] Abul-Magd 2018, pp. 146–7.   [266] Ibid., pp. 94–5.

Table 6.10 Politically connected actors in energy-intensive sectors: Egypt

Actor	Company	Type of political connection	Sector
Ibrahim Kamel	Kato Aromatic, The Modern Company for Manufacturing Soap and Detergent	Party: member of NDP General Secretariat	Chemical products
Sawiris family	Egyptian Fertilizer Company OCI Nitrogen, subsidiary of Orascom Construction Industries	Party: Naguib Sawiris was member of the NDP Business Secretariat and head of the Industrial Training Council	Chemical products
El-Sewedy family	UEIC Elsewedy, United Industries, United Metals, ECMEI	Party: Mohammed El-Sewedy was a member of the NDP's Business Secretariat	Manufacture of basic metals
Ahmed Ezz	Ezzsteel, Al-Ezz Ceramics and Porcelain Company	Party: MP, Chairman of Planning and Budget Committee (2000–10)	Manufacture of basic metals, non-metalic mineral products
Mohammed Abou El-Enein	Cleopatra Group	Party: MP, chairman of Housing Committee (2000–5), Industry and Energy Committee (2005–10)	Non-metalic mineral products
Mansour family	Saint Gobain Glass Egypt, part of Mansour Group	Party: Mohamed Mansour was Minister of Transport (2004–11)	Non-metalic mineral products
Mohammed Khamis	Oriental Weavers	Party: MP for NDP	Manufacture of textiles
Othman Abaza	Nile Cotton Trade Company)	Party: Minister of Agriculture (2005–11)	Manufacture of textiles

Note: Politically connected actors are identified based on Roll 2010. Business information is taken from Bureau van Dijk 2013 and online research. Classification of energy-intensive industries is taken from UNIDO 2010.

Table 6.11 Army-related companies in energy-intensive sectors: Egypt

Company	Type of army connection	Sector
Misr Chemical Industries Company SAE, Egyptian Chemical Industries SAE, El Delta Company for Fertilizers and Chemical Industries, El Nasr Company for Fertilizers & Chemical Industries, Abu Kir Fertilizers and Chemical Industries SAE, Paints and Chemical Industries Company SAE, *all subsidiaries of the Chemical Industries Holding Company*	Affiliated firms run by generals; major shareholders supervised by members of the military	Chemical products
Misr Fertilizers Production Company, *subsidiary of Egyptian Petrochemicals Holding Company*	Main business partner of the military is a shareholder	Chemical products
Egyptian Ferro Alloys Company SAE, Delta Steel Mills Company SAE, Egyptian Iron & Steel Company SAE, Egyptian Copper Works SAE, El-Nasr Steel Pipes & Fitt Egyptian Ferro Alloys Company, *all subsidiaries of Metallurgical Industries Holding Company*	Subsidiaries of holding company managed by a general	Manufacture of basic metals
National Cement Company Helwan, National Cement Company SAE, *both subsidiaries of Chemical Industries Holding Company*	Affiliated firms run by generals; major shareholders supervised by members of the military	Non-metallic mineral products
General Company for Ceramic and Porcelain Products, Gloden Globe Holdings Ltd, Alexandria Company for Refractories, *all subsidiaries of Metallurgical Industries Holding Company*	Subsidiaries of holding company managed by a general	Non-metallic mineral products
General Company for Paper Industry SAE, Paper Middle East (SIMO) SAE, *both subsidiaries of Chemical Industries Holding Company*	Affiliated firms run by generals; major shareholders supervised by members of the military	Paper and paper products

Quena Paper Industry Company SAE, General Company for Paper Industry SAE, *both subsidiaries of Holding Company for Food Industries SAE*	Chairman, managing directors, and board members of firms affiliated with holding company are (former) generals; Egyptian Sugar and Integrated Industries Company owns part of Delta Sugar Company; Holding for Silos & Storage run by a general	Paper and paper products
The Egyptian Ethylene and Derivatives Company, Egyptian Styrene and Polystyerene Production Company, Egyptian Styrenics Company, Sidi Kerir Petrochmicals Company SAE, Egyptian Methanex Methanol Company, Tanmia Petroleum Company, *all subsidiaries of Egyptian Petrochemicals Holding Company*	Main business partner of the military is a shareholder	Coke and refined petroleum products
Misr Company for Foreign Trade SAE, Abu Simble and Thebes Shipping Agency, Alexandria Container and Cargo Handling Company SAE, National Navigation Company, Delta Transport Company, Damietta Container and Cargo Handling Company, *all subsidiaries of Holding Company for Maritime and Land Transport*	Holding company partially owned by military with an admiral as chairman; managing directors and board members of affiliated firms are generals	Transport

Note: Army-related companies are identified based on Acemoglu, Hassan, and Tahoun 2014 and Eibl and Malik 2015. Business information is taken from the same sources. Classification of energy-intensive industries is taken from UNIDO 2010.

The situation is similar for energy-intensive sectors. Regarding cronies, a particularly prominent example is Ahmed Ezz, the owner of Egypt's biggest steel manufacturer, Ezzsteel. Controlling 65–75 per cent of the Egyptian market,[267] Ezz not only dominated the Egyptian steel market, he was also present on nearly all influential committees within the NDP, including the General Secretariat and the Political Bureau. As head of the Budget Committee, he was a key figure in the Egyptian parliament. Producing ceramics, textiles, and glass, connected businessmen, such as Mohammed Abou El-Enein, the Mansour family, Mohammed Khamis, and Othman Abaza equally benefited from low energy prices for their energy-intensive manufacturing companies. Two of them—Mansour and Abaza—served as ministers in the last cabinet under Mubarak. Army-controlled companies are active across the whole range of energy-intensive sectors, from paper production, to chemicals, such as fertilizers and petrochemicals, to services in transportation.

While this descriptive analysis demonstrates the wide-ranging activity of PCFs in subsidy-related sectors, it is not clear whether it was actually subsidies that business cronies and the army were after. In theory, their presence in these sectors could be explained by other profitability-enhancing mechanisms, such as high tariffs. To single out the significance of tariffs in explaining PCF activity across sectors, I run a number of simple logistic regressions. Parallel to the previous chapter, I use two binary indicators, *Crony activity* and *Army activity*, as dependent variables, indicating the activity of any of these actors at the four-digit level of manufacturing sectors. As before, the data are taken from a novel dataset by Eibl and Malik, which, for the analysis at hand, was updated with the information from Acemoglu et al.[268] Regarding the explanatory variables, I focus on the effect of a binary indicator for sectors with low energy intensity, *Low intensity*, as well as an indicator measuring whether a sector is related to food subsidies, *Direct food*.[269] Finally, the regression uses the same controls as in the previous chapter: that is, *Tariff average* and *Imports*, taken respectively from the WITS and UNIDO database.[270] As Egypt has a number of extremely high tariffs, mainly on trade in antiquities, I exclude tariffs above 1000 per cent from the analysis.[271] The results are shown in Tables 6.12 and 6.13.

The findings are insightful in that they qualify the foregoing descriptive analysis. Starting with cronies in Table 6.12, we can see that through columns (1)–(3), food and energy subsidies significantly increase the probability of crony presence in

---

[267] Chekir and Diwan 2013.

[268] Eibl and Malik 2015; Malik and Eibl forthcoming; and Acemoglu, Hassan, and Tahoun 2014.

[269] In Egypt, companies do not benefit from subsidized sugar for industrial purposes, which is why I do not test the effect of the variable *All food* from the previous chapter.

[270] World Bank 2013; and UNIDO 2013. For Egypt, data are available for 1997, 2002, 2004, 2005, 2006, and 2010. As in the case of Tunisia, I pool all years in a cross-sectional analysis.

[271] Neither the army nor cronies are present in these high-tariff sectors. I include regressions with the full tariff spectrum as robustness tests in Appendix D.

Table 6.12 Crony presence and subsidies in Egypt

	(1)	(2)	(3)	(4)
Low intensity	−0.624***		−0.543***	−0.316*
	(0.165)		(0.168)	(0.180)
Direct food		1.164***	0.940**	0.222
		(0.421)	(0.432)	(0.416)
Tariff average	0.00215	0.00298*	0.00221	0.00235
	(0.00173)	(0.00175)	(0.00170)	(0.00159)
Imports (log)	0.272***	0.267***	0.275***	0.196***
	(0.0497)	(0.0488)	(0.0497)	(0.0516)
Army activity				1.344***
				(0.183)
Observations	687	687	687	687

Note: Logit model with robust standard errors in parentheses; constant omitted. $^*p < 0.10$, $^{**}p < 0.05$, $^{***}p < 0.01$

Table 6.13 Army presence and subsidies in Egypt

	(1)	(2)	(3)	(4)
Low intensity	−1.086***		−0.894***	−0.803***
	(0.174)		(0.178)	(0.186)
Direct food		5.020***	4.690***	4.392***
		(1.434)	(1.436)	(1.433)
Tariff average	0.000519	0.00199	0.000647	−0.000219
	(0.00216)	(0.00216)	(0.00232)	(0.00284)
Imports (log)	0.321***	0.330***	0.348***	0.276***
	(0.0449)	(0.0470)	(0.0478)	(0.0502)
Crony activity				1.298***
				(0.181)
Observations	687	687	687	687

Note: Logit model with robust standard errors in parentheses; constant omitted. $^*p < 0.10$, $^{**}p < 0.05$, $^{***}p < 0.01$

any given manufacturing sector. This finding changes once we take into account the simultaneous presence of cronies and the army in a sector. Doing so is important because the presence of another politically connected actor might influence the rationale to invest in a given sector. On the one hand, cronies might avoid competition with the army and thus avoid business activity in army-dominated sectors. On the other hand, as army businesses are generally well shielded from international competition,[272] sectors with military presence might be considered particularly 'safe' and more profitable. As we see from the full model

---

[272] Eibl and Malik 2015.

in column (4), it is the latter hypothesis that is backed up by the data. While the presence of the army increases the likelihood of crony-affiliated companies being present in a sector, food subsidies, in turn, cease to be significant and the effect of energy intensity is considerably reduced. This is also visible in the predicted probability graph in Figure 6.9(a) which shows only a modest difference in the average probability between low and medium–high energy-intensive sectors with overlapping confidence intervals.

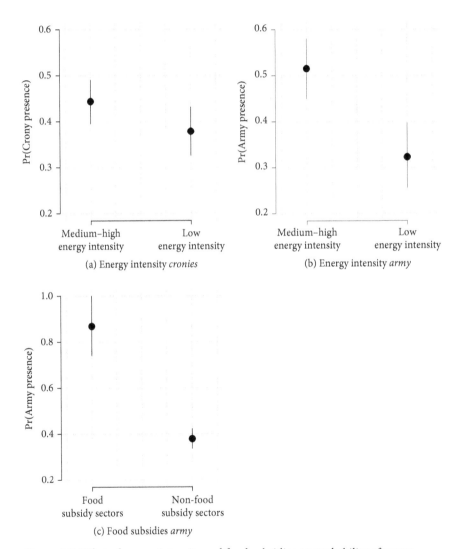

(a) Energy intensity *cronies*

(b) Energy intensity *army*

(c) Food subsidies *army*

Figure 6.9 Effect of energy intensity and food subsidies on probability of crony presence in Egypt

Note: Whiskers indicate 95 per cent confidence bounds. Marginal effects based on the full model presented in column (4) of Tables 6.12 and 6.13. All variables were set to their observed values.

Regarding army activity, the results displayed in Table 6.13 confirm the impression gained from the foregoing descriptive analysis. In fact, sectors related to food subsidies and sectors with a medium–high energy intensity are considerably more likely to exhibit economic activity by the army. This difference across sectors is shown graphically in Figures 6.9(b) and 6.9(c). On average, the army is 20 per cent more likely to be present in energy-intensive sectors. In the case of food subsidies, the army is 40 per cent more likely to operate in related sectors. Note that, because of 'tied' data, the models for army activity were estimated using a penalized maximum likelihood procedure, which allows me to estimate the effects of energy and food subsidies simultaneously.[273] The results are robust to the inclusion of *Tariff averages* and *Imports* (columns (1)–(3)), as well as the simultaneous presence of cronies (column (4)).

6.2.3 Summary

This section has highlighted the mechanisms of path dependence that have ensured the continuity of the Egyptian welfare trajectory, especially after peace with Israel in 1978. My findings concur with Chapter 5 in that welfare constituencies have prevented attempts at retrenchment and successfully defended their stakes, such as in the event of subsidy reductions or the attempted privatization and cost reduction in the area of health care in the 2000s. Using the example of the food and subsidy system, I have also been able to show that actors not initially targeted by social policies have over time become powerful stakeholders in the status quo. However, unlike in the Tunisian case, the political dynamics post-1978 have been very much shaped by the legacies of pre-1978. This has been visible in the role of the army as a budgetary gate keeper, the need to counter-balance the military by boosting the security apparatus, Egypt's debilitating debt problem, and the relative weakness of welfare constituencies, which have been too weak to push for systemic change, but too strong to withdraw from past achievements.

6.3 Conclusion

This chapter has pursued two major goals. First, it has aimed to understand the origin of Egypt's welfare trajectory by focusing on the causal mechanisms underpinning the regime's incentive and ability to provide social welfare. The above analysis supports the main line of my argument. One, I have been able to rule

---

[273] Regressions were run using the brglm package in R. Robustness tests for energy subsidies using a normal logit model are presented in Appendix D.

out ideological pre-commitments as a cause of the regime's incentive to distribute social welfare. As in Tunisia, there is ample evidence to suggest that, had the initial regime coalition remained cohesive, a rather right-wing, pro-business coalition might have been formed and social welfare might not have become a key priority. Two, I have relied on memoirs of regime insiders to substantiate the link between elite factionalism and the drive to distribute welfare as part of a lower–middle class coalition. Three, relying on secondary sources and cabinet minutes, I have demonstrated a shift in the regime's threat perception and provided a 'smoking gun' test of the resulting trade-off between defence and welfare. Four, I have presented both qualitative and quantitative evidence supporting my claim that the combination of a high incentive and low ability to provide social welfare has entailed a specific type of 'cheap' social policies, characterized by underfunding, the use of regulatory interventions instead of monetary transfers to generate rents, the reliance on expropriations, and the design of social policies such that they generate revenue.

Second, the chapter has brought to light the mechanisms of path dependence underlying the persistence of social policies past 1978. In this respect, the chapter has yielded two main conclusions. On the one hand, the political dynamics of path dependence in Egypt are very similar to other cases, most notably the Tunisian case, in that we find target groups of social policies rallying against retrenchments and systemic reforms. This dynamic was visible both in incidents of riots against subsidy cuts and in opposition to the 2004 health insurance reform in which *consumers* of social policies were the main actors. Likewise, social policies in Egypt have generated important rent streams for groups that are not considered target groups of social policies. This includes both the *producers* of social policies, such as workers in the production chain of subsidized goods, and powerful business actors capable of reaping the benefits from market distortions generated by social policies. In Egypt, these are commodity traders, the army, and crony businessmen. On the other hand, path dependence in Egypt reflects the origin of its welfare trajectory. This means that patterns of distribution to the military could not be easily reversed as a result of their own path-dependent dynamics. And the legacies of war making and threat have left little fiscal leeway for later spending adjustment, showing the long-lasting impact of initial path divergence.

7

MENA Welfare States: Explanations and Broader Implications

'Why are some authoritarian governments motivated to provide social welfare programs, while others provide little in the way of public goods?' asks Stephen Haber in an article on authoritarian government.[1] This study has sought to provide an answer to this question by explaining the divergent welfare trajectories of labour-abundant economies in the Middle East and North Africa. In so doing, it has pursued the dual objective of broadening our empirical knowledge of welfare provision in a region that has often remained 'under the radar' of global social policy research, whilst developing a general theoretical argument as to when we should expect authoritarian governments to provide welfare broadly and generously to their populations. To facilitate broader application, the theoretical model was purposefully kept simplified and stylized, relying on a rationalist framework that emphasizes authoritarian rulers' incentives and abilities to distribute welfare. Its key components—intra-elite conflict, communal cleavages, external threat, and resource abundance—are general enough for the argument to have a wider applicability to welfare trajectories outside the Middle East. Alongside this attempt at theory development, this study has also put to test the relevance of theories of path dependence to explain the striking persistence of welfare distribution over the last six decades in the region.

Beyond their academic relevance, social policies in the Middle East are of tremendous importance for ordinary people in the region. Citizens interact with the state most often through social policies as they pervade all stages of life. Variation in the willingness and capacity of MENA regimes to provide those policies determines, amongst others, whether mothers can give birth to their children in safe environments; whether life chances are enhanced by acquiring education; whether diseases and old age become poverty traps; and to what extent the negative effects of capitalism can be tamed. While the book does not provide easy fixes for any of these challenges or guidelines to build institutions, it underlines that, above all else, social policies are shaped by the incentives of political elites. At the most abstract level, mechanisms that force elites to take into account the interests

[1] Haber 2006, p. 694.

Social Dictatorships: The Political Economy of the Welfare State in the Middle East and North Africa. Ferdinand Eibl, Oxford University Press (2020). © Ferdinand Eibl. DOI: 10.1093/oso/9780198834274.001.0001

of as broad a cross-section of society as possible are likely to enhance social policies.

This concluding chapter is divided into two sections. Section 7.1 provides a concise synthesis of how the empirical material substantiates the theoretical claims, with respect to both the divergence and the persistence of welfare trajectories. Section 7.2 discusses the broader implications of this argument for a number of literatures this study speaks to.

7.1 The Puzzles and the Answers

The two puzzles driving this study were sketched out in Chapter 1 and more thoroughly presented in Chapter 2. The first one is a puzzle of *early divergence*. Based on novel social spending data going back to each regime's foundation, I showed that the divergence of welfare trajectories occurred alongside regime formation. More specifically, I argued that patterns of welfare provision in the region diverged into three specific subtypes. Authoritarian welfare states have combined *broad and generous welfare provision*, making a sustained financial effort to provide social policies to the vast majority of their population. A second type has been characterized by *broad welfare provision* only, as social policies are widely accessible but they are not underpinned by persistently high funding. A third type of regimes has engaged in *minimal-segmented welfare provision*, either providing generally rudimentary social policies or allowing only a limited subset of their citizens to benefit from public welfare. Using a combination of spending and outcome data, I demonstrated that spending has only been consistently high in the broad and generous type, which has also scored best in terms of social outcomes. Broad providers have achieved noticeable success in social outcome indicators as well, which reflects their universal access regimes, while lagging behind in terms of spending. Minimal welfare providers range at the bottom with respect to both spending and outcomes. Granted, the proposed typology is admittedly state-centric, but it allows us to map out, compare, and evaluate public welfare efforts in MENA and beyond.

The second puzzle is the *high persistence* of welfare trajectories. As I showed in Chapter 2, none of the regimes have changed track following the initial divergence. Granted, spending levels have shown fluctuations driven by periodic effects stemming from, for example, adverse economic circumstances or periods of conflict. Yet this should not obliterate the fact that for nearly all countries in my sample, the spending levels in the early 1960s are highly predictive of spending in the mid-2000s.

So how has the proposed theory fared in the light of the empirical material presented in this study?

7.1.1 Divergence of welfare trajectories

Regarding divergence, my theoretical argument has emphasized the coincidence of matching incentives and abilities for a regime to embark on social welfare. The former are shaped by coalition-building dynamics at the onset of regime formation while the latter are conditioned by the external environment. At the level of incentives, broad coalitions emerge in the presence of intra-elite conflict and the absence of salient communal cleavages and, if present jointly, provide a strong incentive for welfare provision. Conversely, a cohesive elite or salient communal divisions entail small coalitions with few incentives to distribute welfare broadly. At the level of abilities, a strong external threat to regime survival is expected to undermine the ability to provide social welfare in broad coalitions. Facing a 'butter or guns' trade-off, elites shift priority to security expenditures and the population accepts this because no alternative regime could credibly commit to neglecting external defence in the presence of external threats. Only fiscal surpluses from an abundant resource endowment can provide the necessary resources to avert this trade-off.

In Chapter 3, I proved the viability of my theory at the macro cross-country level, demonstrating that the different types of welfare provision closely align with the patterns of authoritarian coalition formation in varying external contexts. I showed that coalition formation in all three authoritarian welfare states—Tunisia, Algeria, and the Islamic Republic of Iran—was marked by intensive elite factionalism in the absence of salient communal divisions. In Tunisia and Algeria, welfare provision unfolded unhindered by external threats. And Iran was able to rely on ample resources to shield welfare from warfare. In Egypt and Syria, we find the conflicting combination of strong incentives and lacking abilities. This is most conspicuous in the Egyptian case where initial elite conflicts brought about a broad coalition, but the regime had to respond simultaneously to threats emanating from the external environment. In Syria, the incentive was somewhat 'lopsided' as in-fighting elites operated in a context of heightened communal cleavages, which translated into policies marked by communal favouritism, although the regime also sought to honour its cross-class nature by introducing universal access policies. As in Egypt, social spending was crowded out in the face of a threatening external environment. Finally, I showed that all minimal-segmented providers lacked an initial incentive to distribute welfare, owing to either cohesive elites coupled with communal cleavages (Jordan) or intra-elite conflict that was repressible due to the unequal distribution of coercive power between the rival factions (Morocco, Iran). In the case of Iran, the imbalance in coercive capacity was brought about by the involvement of external patrons (USA, UK).

In Chapter 4, I used evidence from longitudinal data to provide additional leverage for my divergence argument. Specifically, using a number of dynamic panel regressions, I documented the existence of a sizeable trade-off between defence and welfare spending. That said, defence spending did not have a significant negative effect on welfare in regimes with high levels of rents, as social spending levels in resource-rich regimes seem to be exempt from the 'butter or guns' trade-off because of fiscal surpluses from resource exports.

In Chapters 5 and 6, I substantiated the causal mechanisms underpinning my theory at the micro-level in the cases of Tunisia and Egypt. After discarding ideology as a credible explanatory factor, I demonstrated in both cases how severe intra-elite conflicts prompted Bourguiba and Nasser to engage in large-scale welfare provision, which went against their initial pro-business policies. In Tunisia, the direct effects of intra-elite conflict on social welfare were visible in the establishment of the National Fund for the Centre and the South, the foundation of which I could directly attribute to elite conflict based on archival material. The more lasting effects of elite factionalism on welfare were indirect, mediated by the labour union UGTT, which could effectively take control of social policy making as a result of intra-elite conflict. In Tunisia, intra-elite conflict served as an important door-opener for a strong pro-welfare constituency.

In Egypt, I relied on memoirs of regime insiders to demonstrate how the RCC used social spending strategically to respond to Naguib's attempt to snatch power away from them. On the one hand, they used the enormous wealth of the deposed royal family to establish a Council for Social Services with vast competences in the fields of health care, education, and housing. On the other hand, as the conflict with Naguib headed toward violent confrontation, they struck an explicit bargain with labour unions, offering considerable concessions in the form of increased social spending, a housing loan scheme, and, most importantly, the establishment of a social security system for Egyptian workers.

Regarding the security–welfare trade-off, I used declassified cabinet minutes to process-trace the mechanism, showing that elites did indeed perceive a need to arbitrate between social and defence policies and, importantly, that external threats were perceived as more pressing to the regime's survival than concerns for domestic legitimacy. I demonstrated that the conflicting mix of strong incentives and weak abilities prompted the regime to engage in what I termed 'cheap social policies'. Specifically, I used qualitative and quantitative evidence to establish that (i) social policies were underfunded; (ii) the regime relied to a large extent on 'free' social policies, such as rent control, that outsourced the costs to third parties; (iii) it systematically used expropriations to boost social spending; and (iv) it designed social policies such that they would alleviate funding shortages. To demonstrate the latter point, I relied on archival documents laying out the financial motives behind the foundation of social security in the 1950s. I showed that social security extensions systematically coincided with current account crises in a simple regression model, strongly suggesting that social security was extended to generate more revenue. Overall, the paired comparison between Egypt and Tunisia points to differences in the external environment to explain the divergence in their welfare trajectories.

7.1.2 Persistence of welfare trajectories

Regarding persistence, I relied on two important mechanisms in the welfare state literature to explain path dependence. The first one can broadly be summarized as 'constituency politics' in that beneficiaries of social policies successfully avert deviations from the spending path in the form of systemic reforms or large-scale spending cuts. Mobilization of these constituencies should be particularly vigorous if initial advantages conferred on these groups have been reinforced over time: for instance, because they grew in size or became entrenched in the state administration. The second mechanisms is spill-over effects to unintended beneficiaries who can over time become important gatekeepers against path divergence.

In Chapter 4, I provided initial cross-country evidence for these mechanisms by demonstrating the importance of coalitions in explaining changes in social spending over time. The chapter showed that periods of major welfare retrenchment are less likely in broad coalitions. Besides, broad coalitions channel additional resources in the form of resource windfalls systematically toward welfare.

In Chapters 5 and 6, I process-traced the outlined mechanisms at the micro-level in the cases of Tunisia and Egypt. In Tunisia, I chose the 1970s student protests, the 2004 health insurance reform, and the 1980s food riots to show how beneficiaries of social policies successfully mobilized to avert major spending cuts (student protests, food riots) and systemic reforms (health insurance). In both cases, the mobilization was carried out by groups that had benefited considerably from initial social policies (food subsidies), grown considerably in size (students), or gained an important foothold in the state institutions which provided important avenues for political lobbying (UGTT). In the latter case, a reform that started off with the objective of cost reduction was converted into a major overhaul of the public health care system and an upgrading of public health insurance. As regards unintended beneficiaries, I employed novel data on politically connected entrepreneurs in the late Ben Ali period to show how business cronies have become important beneficiaries of food and energy subsidies. Their lobbying could not be process-traced directly, yet by highlighting their interest in the subsidy system and their known political influence, I demonstrated that these actors should be considered important stakeholders in the system.

In Egypt, explaining path dependence is equivalent to explaining the absence of a major peace dividend after the country's 1978 peace treaty with Israel. Using a combination of primary and secondary sources, my explanation highlights the negative effects of past entrenchment of the military in the administration, which accounts for the 'stickiness' of defence spending in the post-1978 period. Related to that, I emphasized the regime's perceived need to counterbalance the army's influence by engaging in a coup-proofing strategy that boosted Egypt's non-military security apparatus. Finally, warfare had driven up the country's debt to barely sustainable levels, which meant that social spending post-1973 was competing acutely with debt service.

In addition, I analysed the failed health insurance reform in the 2000s and the Egyptian subsidy systems to explain why social spending was not only upwardly but also downwardly rigid. Regarding the health insurance reform, I showed that—while unable to transmute the reform's outcome from cost reduction and privatization into a major expansion of coverage and expenditure as in Tunisia—stakeholders in Egypt were able to make the reform founder in the face of a credible threat of major resistance. With respect to subsidies, I found very similar dynamics compared to Tunisia. Legacies of past constituency mobilization in the form of food riots have made the regime reluctant to roll out major reforms. And a number of unintended beneficiaries have been tapping into rent streams emanating from the subsidy system, which has complicated reform. As in Tunisia, these actors comprise a conglomerate of well-connected business moguls, in addition to the army, commodity traders, and workers in the milling sector, which have all developed important stakes in the existing system. This turned the subsidy system into a 'Gordian knot' which the Mubarak regime was unable to disentangle and unwilling to sever.

7.2 Broader Implications

Why is any of the foregoing of importance? This study contributes to a number of debates that pervade the study of authoritarianism, the Middle East, comparative politics, and political economy more broadly, and raises a number of questions for future research agendas.

7.2.1 Good and bad dictators

As the study of dictatorships historically emerged from the study of democracy, both are embedded in the same normative debates which have, at least since the second half of the twentieth century, associated democracy with 'good' and autocracies with 'bad' government. This has been reflected in the comparative politics and, in particular, comparative political economy literature which can partly be read as an effort to prove that democracy not only is normatively superior but also provides more desirable social outcomes. In consequence, part of the literature has viewed autocracies as necessarily pro-elite, neglecting the 'masses'.[2] The empirical picture, however, is not easily amenable to this conclusion as the number of contradictory findings in the literature suggests.[3] Echoing the uneasy fit of a dichotomous view, Haggard and Kaufman write that 'authoritarian regimes can, under specified circumstances, produce positive distributive effects'.[4]

This study has demonstrated what these circumstances are. Building on the established insight that authoritarian regimes differ from each other as much as they differ from democracies,[5] this study has developed a theoretical model that helps us explain when we should expect the emergence of what I have called social dictatorships or authoritarian welfare states. While acknowledging the important role of political institutions in the everyday politics of authoritarian regimes,[6] the book argues that long-term divergences in social policy trajectories are shaped in the crucible of societal conflict that most often precedes formalized political institutions. In that sense, it stands in a long tradition of macro-sociological research that has emphasized the significance of foundational conflict between societal actors.[7]

By the same token, the book contributes to the growing body of literature analysing public policies, rather than regime survival, across authoritarian regimes. To be sure, political economy research on authoritarianism has paid increasing attention to *economic policies* across autocracies,[8] but the comparative study of *social policies* across autocracies has lagged behind. Extant research has been conducted along the democracy–autocracy dichotomy,[9] analysed the short-term fluctuations in social spending instead of long-term patterns,[10] or carried out single country studies with the limited ambition of developing mid-range theories applicable to the whole authoritarian spectrum.[11] Another set of scholars has analysed varying outcomes of social policies across authoritarian regimes, but not the policies themselves.[12]

By bringing social policies into the focus of authoritarianism studies, this study may represent the springboard for a comparative research programme. One potential avenue of future research would be a more fine-grained cross-regime analysis of specific social policy subfields. For example, why do some authoritarian

---

[2] See, very prominently, Boix 2003; Acemoglu and J. A. Robinson 2006; and Ansell 2010.
[3] See references in footnote 9 in Chapter 1.   [4] Haggard and Kaufman 2008, p. 26.
[5] Geddes 1999b; and Art 2012.
[6] For example, Wright 2008a; Gandhi 2008; and Miller 2015a.
[7] For example, Slater 2010; Yom 2016; B. Smith 2007; and seminally Rueschemeyer, Huber, and J. D. Stephens 1992. See also institutionalist arguments in economics, e.g. Acemoglu, Johnson, and J. A. Robinson 2005.
[8] See, for example, Steinberg and Malhotra 2014; Hankla and Kuthy 2013; Richter 2013; and Knutsen and Fjelde 2013.
[9] See, for example, Ansell 2008; Knutsen and Rasmussen 2018; and Wigley and Akkoyunlu-Wigley 2011.
[10] See Miller 2015a; Gandhi 2008; and Mazaheri 2017 amongst others.
[11] See, for example, Frazier 2010; and K. Harris 2017.
[12] For example, Hanson and Gallagher 2009; and Miller 2015b.

regimes adopt more streamed educational systems or give greater preference to higher education than others? Much work needs to be done as well on subnational variation of social policies in autocracies.[13] In this respect, recent advances in GIS-based research hold the promise to overcome existing methodological and data challenges which have stifled subnational research.[14]

In seeking to answer what drives policies in authoritarian regimes, the book also emphasizes the role of authoritarian coalitions as compared to differences in the nature of the nominal ruler (e.g. military man, monarch, party leader). The literature has used the nature of the ruler as the defining criterion of authoritarian subtypes, which has produced important insights into the diversity of authoritarian rule.[15] Subtypes, however, offer only limited insight into the question of for whom, not by whom, an authoritarian regime is ruled. Party regimes are often viewed as incorporating a broader cross-section of interests,[16] but just a comparative glimpse at sub-Saharan party regimes' welfare effort relative to, say, Tunisia's reveals the tremendous diversity within authoritarian subtypes. Given the weakness of the left-right divide as a predictor of pro-poor policies in much of the Global South,[17] coalitional approaches, as proposed by this study and others,[18] or the comparative analysis of political settlements[19] appear more promising to identify the key constituencies for whom policies are designed. Besides this conceptual emphasis, this study has highlighted the important ways in which social spending is underpinned by 'sticky' institutions and can thus serve as an important commitment device between the ruler and the support coalition.

So is a regionally expanded research programme on authoritarian social policies likely to find many authoritarian welfare states? The answer is probably no. Many causal conditions undermining the emergence of an authoritarian welfare state have also been identified as a cause of authoritarianism itself: communal cleavages and ethnic exclusion have been associated with non-democratic governments.[20] Likewise, the prevalence of severe external threats and conflict has also been identified as a pathway toward authoritarianism.[21] And the long-term path dependence of social policies serves as a warning against any attempt to 'engineer' institutional contexts favourable to the emergence of large-scale welfare provision.

7.2.2 Authoritarian regimes, constituencies, and reform

Another important take-away message of this study is autocracies' limited capacity to reform. The popular narrative associates democracies with a fickle, wavering

---

[13] A notable exception here is Cammett and Issar 2010.
[14] For example, Hodler and Raschky 2014; and De Luca et al. 2018.
[15] For example, Escribà-Folch 2013; Lai and Slater 2006; and Weeks 2012.
[16] For example, Charron and Lapuente 2011.   [17] Rudra and Tobin 2017.
[18] For example, Albertus 2015a.   [19] For example, Di John and Putzel 2009; and Khan 2010.
[20] See, amongst others, Slater 2010; and Przeworski et al. 2000, p. 125.
[21] See, for example, Gibler 2010.

fashion of carrying out reform whilst autocracies are characterized by an iron-fist top-down efficiency. As the columnist Tom Friedman writes in the *New York Times*, 'one-party nondemocracy can just impose the politically difficult but critically important policies needed to move a society forward in the 21st century'.[22]

In view of my analysis of path dependence in Egypt and Tunisia—both long-standing dominant party regimes before their downfall—this narrative is in need of qualification. Instead of iron-fist policies, this study finds authoritarian elites to be cautious, at times anxious, and extremely opportunistic when it comes to reforms. More than anything else, the subsidy conundrum illuminates the inability of MENA regimes to engage in systemic reforms. Despite the widely recognized inefficiency, distributive regressiveness, and economic wastefulness of subsidies, neither the Tunisian nor the Egyptian government was able to muster the political courage to tackle vested interests and forge a coalition for reform.

While bureaucratic sloth and incompetence play a role in that story, the key element is the regimes' inability to unravel and reconstitute regime coalitions. This finding is in line with cross-country evidence demonstrating that structural economic change is inhibited by authoritarian–redistributive social contracts.[23] Authoritarian regimes are not slow at co-opting new constituencies, but they struggle enormously to get rid of old ones as the stakes of losing power are prohibitively high and the regularized reconstitution of coalitions in the form of elections is not viable. When it comes to critically important policies, my research cautions against betting too much on the inherent capacity of autocracies to implement them.[24]

7.2.3 War and cheap social policies

This book also calls for a more systematic study of the nexus between war, external threats, and social policies. Granted, linkages between domestic and international politics have long been acknowledged. Chaudhry, for example, draws important connections between the reshaping of national markets and the international economy in late developing countries.[25] With regard to autocracies, Bunce and Hozic note 'most authoritarian leaders are international, as well as domestic, actors [. . .] because the international system provides these leaders with both threats to their powers and opportunities to defend and expand them'.[26]

Surprisingly though, the effect of the most disruptive of events in international politics—interstate war—has received only very limited attention: 'Every aspect of domestic politics has felt war's influence',[27] yet political science has treated war

---

[22] New York Times 2009.   [23] Rougier 2016.
[24] For a similar finding in a large-*N* setting, see Giuliano, Mishra, and Spilimbergo 2010.
[25] Chaudhry 1993.   [26] Bunce and Hozic 2015, p. 18.   [27] Kasza 1996, p. 370.

mostly as an outcome to be explained, rather than a producer of politics. The only major exception in this respect is the literature on war and state building.[28] Social policy research has only produced a handful of studies that focus specifically on the effect of war on social policies, amongst others Skocpol's seminal study on the post-war welfare state in the United States and Harris's recent work on Iran's 'martyr's welfare state'.[29] Theory development on the broader nexus of warfare and welfare in the Global South has been notably absent.

By proposing the concept of 'cheap social policies', this study furnishes an analytical tool with the promise to shed more systematic light on how wars shape social policies. Of particular theoretical interest for a wider research programme is the ability of 'cheap social policies' to alleviate fiscal bottlenecks by generating, rather than distributing, resources, at least in the short to medium term. Coverage extensions of social security schemes in the face of current account deficits are an illustration of this mechanism. I also emphasized how Egypt systematically used expropriations to honour its coalitional commitments. Both of these aspects can be explored in further comparative study outside the MENA region. Finally, the theoretical argument provides a clear prediction about the conditions under which we should witness the emergence of 'cheap social policies'—a broad coalition, no resource endowment, and severe external threats—which can be readily tested in further cross-country research. The fact that social policies in Nazi Germany featured important elements of 'cheap social policies' provides a first indication that the concept might have traction beyond MENA.[30]

In concluding this section, it is worth reflecting upon the question of why systematic vulnerability did not entail developmental 'upgrading'[31] in MENA. Instead of adopting 'cheap social policies', Doner et al.'s theory would have predicted for regimes like Egypt and Syria to 'go developmental' and grow themselves out of the dilemma between 'butter or guns' by gradually upgrading into high value-added export production. The fact that this is not the case suggests that the choice of upgrading as a specific policy response to systematic vulnerability is shaped by antecedent conditions not theorized in their framework. While a systematic answer to this question lies outside the scope of this study, it seems that factors such as colonial heritage and elite cohesion vis-à-vis populist pressures played a more important role in the emergence of developmental states than the systematic vulnerability argument suggests.[32]

7.2.4 Misconceptions in Middle Eastern studies

This study has important implications for the field of Middle Eastern studies as it has sought to do away with a number of persistent misconceptions in the literature.

[28] Thies 2004; Thies 2005; and Lu and Thies 2012. Seminally Tilly 1985.
[29] Skocpol 1992; K. Harris 2013; and K. Harris 2017.   [30] Aly 2007.
[31] Doner, Ritchie, and Slater 2005; and Ritchie 2010.   [32] Kohli 1994; and Waldner 1999.

First of all, the division of the region into conservative regimes with low welfare provision and populist-progressive regimes with high welfare provision does not work, simply because the empirical evidence does not bear it out.[33] While all of the region's labour-abundant monarchies fall on the side of minimal welfare providers, the region's republics divide almost evenly into low- and high-spenders. A large part of this confusion comes from a massive Egypt bias that pervades the study of the Middle East. This might sound odd coming from an author who himself has dedicated a major part of this book to the study of Egypt, but the important difference lies in the comparative aspect of this study. Whereas Egypt has often been portrayed in the literature as the epitome of welfare provision in the region,[34] this study has collected novel historical data showing that Egypt never reached anywhere near the social spending levels of its neighbours, such as Tunisia or Algeria, not even under Nasser. And while any scholar of Egypt would confirm the importance of the external environment for the regime's formation, the connection between the regime's political economy and international relations has barely been made—neither in Egypt nor elsewhere in the region.[35]

A second, equally pervasive misconception is that welfare provision was gradually rolled back with the advent of neoliberal political reforms from the late 1970s. As Baylouny boldly puts its, 'economic liberalization reforms in the 1980s and 1990s signalled the progressive end of state social policies for Middle Eastern non-oil countries'.[36] Similarly, Hinnebusch sees a 'post-populist retreat from [...] welfare responsibilities'[37] and a tendency of cross-regional convergence in terms of welfare provision.[38] This study joins a growing group of scholars who caution against this broad-brush narrative.[39] My analysis points to two main misconceptions at the origin of this narrative. First, most examples adduced in favour of this reading have been taken from countries that were never high-spenders in the first place, such as Egypt and Syria. As a result, low levels of welfare provision are attributed to neoliberal reforms whereas their main root—coalitional origins and a challenging geostrategic environment—remains obscured. Second, the narrative stems from a lack of consideration for comparative data. In view of my descriptive account in Chapter 2, it is safe to say that there has been neither a sustained trend for convergence nor massive welfare retrenchment. Instead, my analysis has demonstrated that the occurrence and depth of retrenchment was itself a function of the way in which welfare states were created. While I do not deny the many ills that neoliberalism has inflicted on Middle Eastern countries,[40] I concur with Martínez in emphasizing the 'uneven pathways' of neoliberal transformation in the region.[41]

---

[33] For a representative example of this conceptual partitioning of the region, see, amongst others, King 2010; and Loewe 2010.

[34] See, for example, Pawelka 1985; and Waterbury 1983.

[35] A notable exception is the excellent study by Barnett. See Barnett 1992.

[36] Baylouny 2010, p. 16.   [37] Hinnebusch 2006, p. 385.   [38] Hinnebusch 2010, p. 211.

[39] For example, Cammett and Diwan 2016; Diwan and Akin 2015; and Hertog 2016.

[40] Hanieh 2013.   [41] Martínez 2017.

A third and final misconception that this study touches upon is the oft-assumed link between social policies and regime stability. My theory relies upon the assumption that authoritarian elites implement social policies to expand their support coalitions and, ultimately, survive in power. This idea has found expression in the notion of 'performance legitimacy' used in the literature.[42] Anecdotally, I encountered this assumption frequently when presenting my research: the depiction of Tunisia as an authoritarian welfare state, while being the original site of the 2011 Arab Spring, was frequently looked upon with incredulity. While a systematic analysis of the relationship between social policies and regime survival lies beyond the scope of this study, I can engage in some reflection on the presented research in the light of the Arab Spring.

From a purely empirical point of view, both high- and low-spenders—Tunisia and Egypt—from among my sample were distinctly affected by the events, which makes it difficult to draw any conclusions. Theoretically, Harris is probably right when he states that '[w]elfare policy is not a long-term stabilizing force'.[43] Social policies can engender and empower new societal groups with new economic or political demands towards the state. A main transmission channel in this regard seems to be education. Global large-N studies find that more educated citizens are more attentive to politics and more involved in associations.[44] At the cross-country level, higher levels of education are systematically associated with a greater likelihood of democratization.[45] Moreover, welfare states spawn widespread expectations of upward social mobility, particularly among the educated middle classes. As long as sufficient upward mobility is maintained, welfare states may serve as an important catalyst transforming social policies into regime legitimacy. If mobility stalls, however, human capital accumulated through social policies may fuel a regime's ultimate demise.[46] Answering the question of how beliefs about the role of the state, social mobility, and regime stability interact holds the promise to provide a more fine-grained understanding of the welfare–stability nexus.

---

[42] Gerschewski 2013.   [43] K. Harris 2017, p. 211.

[44] Larreguy and J. Marshall 2016.

[45] Sanborn and Thyne 2014. Diwan 2016 does not find the same emancipatory effects of education in MENA specifically, however.

[46] Campante and Chor 2012.

Introduction

Logic of Case Selection

Table A.1 explains the logic behind case selection.

Table A.1 The logic of case selection

Long-lasting authoritarianism, uninterrupted by democracy, fairly developed		Of which labour-rich		Of which data available	Selected sample
Algeria	South Africa	Algeria	Swaziland	Algeria	Algeria
Angola	Soviet Union	Angola	Syria	Belarus	Egypt
Azerbaijan	Spain	Belarus	Taiwan	China	Iran
Bahrain	Swaziland	Bulgaria	Tunisia	Egypt	Jordan
Belarus	Syria	Cambodia	Uzbekistan	El Salvador	Morocco
Bulgaria	Tunisia	China	South Africa	Iran	Syria
Cambodia	UAR	Congo Braz.	Soviet Union	Jordan	Tunisia
China	Uzbekistan	Côte d'Ivoire	Spain	Korea (S)	
Congo Braz.	Portugal	Czechoslovakia	Libya	Malaysia	
Côte d'Ivoire	Qatar	Dom. Republic	Malaysia	Mexico	
Czechoslovakia	Romania	Egypt	Mexico	Morocco	
Dom. Republic	Singapore	El Salvador	Morocco	Nicaragua	
Egypt	Kyrgyzstan	Gabon	Namibia	Paraguay	
El Salvador	Libya	Georgia	Nicaragua	Portugal	
Gabon	Malaysia	Hungary	Paraguay	Singapore	
Georgia	Mexico	Indonesia	Poland	Spain	
Hungary	Morocco	Iran	Portugal	Swaziland	
Indonesia	Namibia	Iraq	Romania	Syria	
Iran	Nicaragua	Jordan	Saudi Arabia	Tunisia	
Iraq	Oman	Kazakhstan	Singapore		
Jordan	Paraguay	Korea (S)			
Kazakhstan	Poland	Korea (N)			
Korea (S)	Korea (N)	Kyrgyzstan			
Kuwait					

Data Note

Social spending as understood throughout this book comprises four elements: education, health, housing, and social protection. The latter comprises direct social transfers to households, such as subsidies, and monetary transfers from the state budget to the social security system. Most social spending data used are taken from the International Monetary Fund. Data from the mid-1970s onward are taken from the *Government Financial Statistics*

(GFS).[1] I limit myself to the period ending in 2005 for two reasons. First, social spending data for all of my cases are only available until that date, whereas data for the Algerian and Syrian case are partly missing after that date. Second, for some MENA countries, the IMF changed the classification of spending data after that date, such that spending data are not comparable, neither across cases nor across time within the country. To the extent that this was possible, I checked, however, that the broad spending pattern remained consistent with the long-term historical trend.

Data before the onset of the GFS were collected as part of the Global State Revenue and Expenditure (GSRE) dataset, which is based on the annual reports of the IMF's regional departments, made available to researchers in the early 2000s.[2] In collecting the data, we followed the IMF's classification of social spending into education, health, housing, and social protection. The project was based at the German Institute of Global and Area Studies (GIGA). As an associate project member, I was responsible for labour-abundant MENA countries. In addition, I have consulted statistical yearbooks to complete the time series wherever necessary. This concerns the periods 2000–5 in Algeria, 1956–61 in Egypt, 1953–60 and 2000 in Iran, 1977 in Jordan, 1960 and 1965 in Morocco, 1951–4 in Syria , and 1974 and 1985 in Tunisia.[3]

Another point that needs to be addressed is the role of public employment and wages in measuring a regime's welfare effort. In the MENA-specific literature, employment provision has often been a key variable for measuring a regime's welfare effort.[4] I would argue, however, that using a functional classification of spending and focusing on the aim of spending, rather than the type of spending, such as wages, is a better way of account- ing for a regime's welfare effort. To start with, welfare spending and wages are highly correlated, ranging between 0.75 and 0.80 in my dataset depending on the specific ratio (share of GDP or budget). This should not come as a surprise as welfare provision is generally employment-intensive, and teaching and health care staff often represent the bulk of public employment.[5] This means, in turn, that many of the material benefits provided by public employment are captured in the social spending data. Public employment is also a private good while welfare spending has a public-good character with positive spill-overs onto society as a whole. What is more, the variation in public spending on wages and salaries does not exhibit the same level of variation as many MENA countries cluster around similar levels (see Figure A.1).[6] Above all else, this underlines the common legacies of statist development across the region. The variation in welfare spending also does not align well with known outcome indicators in the area of welfare (e.g. Morocco), which suggests wage spending does not comprehensively capture a regime's welfare effort.

Second, public employment that is not captured by social spending is often concentrated in the repressive apparatus, such as the police force or the army. Adding these figures to the overall welfare effort would seriously dilute the concept of welfare provision as it would mean that more repressive regimes provided a higher level of welfare. Granted, policemen and soldiers paid by the state would perceive this payment as an increase in their personal

---

[1] IMF 2011.   [2] V. Lucas and Richter 2016.

[3] Algeria various years; Arab Republic of Egypt various years; Statistical Centre of Iran various years; Hashemite Kingdom of Jordan various years; Kingdom of Morocco various years; Syrian Arab Republic various years; and Tunisian Republic various years.

[4] See, for instance, Ayubi 1995; El-Katiri, Fattouh, and Segal 2011.

[5] In Egypt, for instance, they have represented over 60 per cent of employment. See Handoussa and El Oraby 2004, p. 2.

[6] The data should be viewed with great caution as the time series are patchy and much shorter than for welfare spending.

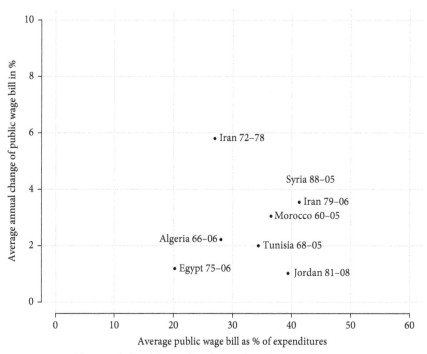

Figure A.1 Public wage bill in labour-abundant authoritarian regimes

Note: Spending data are taken from V. Lucas and Richter 2016; and IMF 2011.

welfare. However, the underlying idea of a welfare state is not primarily the increase of welfare for certain individuals but, rather, for the population as a whole. Thus, a primary focus on public employment is only warranted in cases where the state is indeed able to provide jobs for the whole or the vast majority of the population, which is not the case in labour-abundant MENA countries.

Third, more generally, the authoritarianism literature has tended to see any form of material distribution on the part of the state as a way of increasing output legitimacy.[7] Whilst this may be true, this broad definition of welfare distribution entails major difficulties when it comes to measuring a regime's output empirically as potentially *any* form of public spending could be considered as benefiting someone—perhaps with the exception of foreign debt service. By contrast, all spending items considered here share one common purpose, which is the improvement of welfare in the form of human development. Moreover, many social spending items, such as salaries for doctors, have a welfare-enhancing effect above and beyond the level of individual welfare provided to the direct recipients of transfers. In view of these arguments, welfare spending as measured here seems to capture welfare effort more accurately in labour-abundant MENA countries.

[7] See, for example, Schlumberger 2010.

Social Pacts over Time

Descriptive Statistics

Summary statistics are presented in Table A.2.

Table A.2 Summary statistics

Variable	N	Mean	St. dev.	Min.	Max.
Welfare/budget	315	32.786	12.417	11.340	74.060
Welfare/GDP	313	9.500	3.416	2.750	21.570
Welfare p.c. (log)	313	428.658	274.047	41.000	1,535.000
Defence/budget	315	17.807	11.633	3.340	57.400
Defence/GDP	314	5.580	4.265	0.940	19.790
Defence p.c. (log)	313	228.800	220.818	22.770	1,570.090
Rents p.c. (log)	316	4.091	2.684	0.000	8.235
GDP p.c. (log)	315	8.272	0.498	7.101	9.340
Foreign aid p.c. (log)	316	3.640	1.764	−4.605	7.479
Dependency	316	46.177	4.716	31.430	52.600
Urbanization	316	49.898	10.677	29.400	78.300
Current account balance	313	−6.635	8.142	−29.370	19.940
Polity	316	3.165	2.867	0	13
IMF	316	0.234	0.424	0	1
Trade	315	77.884	26.959	30.796	146.501
Trade openness	316	4.295	2.164	1.000	7.000
Capital openness	316	3.434	1.357	1.000	5.000
Tax/GDP	314	14.946	5.469	4.610	26.430
Output gap	315	−0.013	0.106	−0.500	0.304
Debt service	300	5.047	4.048	0.077	20.051
Retrenchment	305	7.659	5.259	1.000	25.000
Sustained retrenchment	305	7.659	5.259	1.000	25.000
Broad coalition duration	316	12.775	15.880	0	54
Narrow coalition duration	316	20.756	29.082	0	103
Resources p.c. (log)	316	4.407	2.155	0.000	8.124

Robustness Tests Hypothesis 1a

Alternative and Additional Indicators and Standard Errors

Table A.3 tests the robustness of the negative effect of defence spending to using alternative indicators for trade and capital openness (*Trade openness*, *Capital openness*), and additional control variables (*Tax/GDP*, *Output gap*). Columns (4), (8), and (12) use Beck–Katz panel-corrected standard errors on the baseline model. The findings are substantively identical to the main model presented in section 4.1.

Table A.3 Robustness tests H1a: varying controls and standard errors

	(1)	(2)	(3)	(4)	(5)	(6)	(7)	(8)	(9)	(10)	(11)	(12)
Δ Defence spending	-0.018	-0.017	-0.029	0.004	-0.058	-0.048	-0.072	-0.024	0.068	0.069	0.056	0.085
	(0.047)	(0.047)	(0.049)	(0.095)	(0.053)	(0.052)	(0.062)	(0.071)	(0.051)	(0.060)	(0.061)	(0.058)
Defence spending$_{t-1}$	-0.205***	-0.191***	-0.201***	-0.184***	-0.066	-0.046	-0.069	-0.057	-0.036	-0.048*	-0.055**	-0.056**
	(0.055)	(0.048)	(0.052)	(0.046)	(0.045)	(0.035)	(0.047)	(0.035)	(0.027)	(0.028)	(0.027)	(0.028)
Δ Trade openness	-0.180				-0.243**				-0.015			
	(0.281)				(0.118)				(0.019)			
Trade openness$_{t-1}$	0.938**				0.061				0.023*			
	(0.382)				(0.122)				(0.014)			
Δ Capital openness	-0.911*				0.092				-0.015			
	(0.535)				(0.175)				(0.031)			
Capital openness$_{t-1}$	-1.940***				-0.254				-0.051**			
	(0.717)				(0.207)				(0.020)			
Δ Tax/GDP		0.340				0.209**				0.023***		
		(0.260)				(0.092)				(0.007)		
Tax/GDP$_{t-1}$		0.007				0.047				0.008*		
		(0.135)				(0.036)				(0.004)		
Δ Output gap			6.680				-2.112				0.067	
			(16.146)				(5.474)				(0.586)	
Output gap$_{t-1}$			1.128				1.437				0.094	
			(3.350)				(1.259)				(0.110)	
Regime FEs	Yes	Yes	Yes	Yes	Yes	Yes	Yes	Yes	Yes	Yes	Yes	Yes
Beck–Katz SEs	No	No	No	Yes	No	No	No	Yes	No	No	No	Yes
Observations	305	306	306	306	303	304	304	304	303	304	304	304

Note: Error correction model with regime fixed effects. Standard errors in parentheses. Constant and FE coefficients omitted. Missing values for *Trade openness* and *Capital openness* multiply imputed. Columns (1)–(4) use *Welfare/Budget*; columns (5)–(8) *Welfare/GDP*; columns (9)–(12) *Welfare p.c. (log)*. * $p < 0.10$, ** $p < 0.05$, *** $p < 0.01$

Robustness Tests Hypothesis 1b

Alternative Indicator for Resource Abundance and Standard Errors

Table A.4 uses an alternative indicator for rent income throughout, drawing on data from Haber and Menaldo.[1] In addition, columns (4)–(6) use the alternative Beck–Katz standard errors. Due to space constraints, only the marginal effect for *Welfare/budget* are displayed in Figure A.2. The figure is based on Table A.4, column (6). Marginal effects for *Welfare/GDP* and *Welfare p.c. (log)* are nearly identical to the figures presented in section 4.1. The substantive results remain unaffected by these sensitivity tests.

Robustness Tests Hypothesis 2

Percentage Change Plot Based on Non-Stratified Model

Figure A.3 shows the change in the risk of retrenchment by coalition duration based on the non-stratified Cox model.

Robustness Tests Hypothesis 3

Alternative Indicator for Resource Abundance and Standard Errors

As a robustness test, all regressions displayed in Table A.5 use Haber–Menaldo instead of Ross's data for resource income.[2] Columns (3) and (4) use Beck–Katz panel-corrected standard errors instead of the Driscoll–Kraay standard errors employed in the baseline

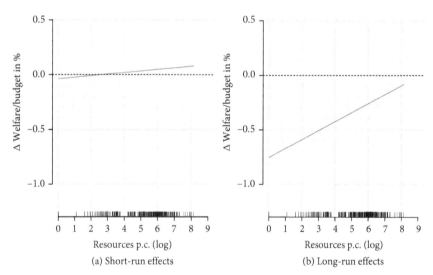

Figure A.2 Effect of defence spending on social spending as a percentage of budget by resource abundance

Note: Shaded area indicates 95 per cent confidence bounds. The figures are based on Table A.4, column (6).

---

[1] Haber and Menaldo 2011.   [2] Haber and Menaldo 2011.

Table A.4 Robustness test H1b: alternative measure of resource abundance and standard errors

	(1)	(2)	(3)	(4)	(5)	(6)
Welfare spending$_{t-1}$	−0.395***	−0.493***	−0.402***	−0.395***	−0.493***	−0.402***
	(0.045)	(0.068)	(0.046)	(0.043)	(0.058)	(0.045)
Δ Defence spending	−0.036	0.028	−0.107	−0.036	0.028	−0.107
	(0.080)	(0.080)	(0.138)	(0.175)	(0.084)	(0.124)
Defence spending$_{t-1}$	−0.297***	−0.019	−0.196***	−0.297***	−0.019	−0.196***
	(0.079)	(0.058)	(0.054)	(0.072)	(0.051)	(0.047)
Δ Resources p.c. (log)	−1.424	−0.408	−0.299**	−1.424	−0.408	−0.299*
	(1.927)	(0.520)	(0.148)	(1.612)	(0.476)	(0.172)
Resources p.c. (log)$_{t-1}$	−1.007***	0.303**	−0.146***	−1.007**	0.303***	−0.146***
	(0.404)	(0.138)	(0.052)	(0.497)	(0.106)	(0.052)
Δ Defence spending*Resources p.c. (log)$_{t-1}$	0.014	−0.007	0.038	0.014	−0.007	0.038*
	(0.026)	(0.007)	(0.027)	(0.039)	(0.007)	(0.023)
Δ Resources p.c. (log)*Δ Defence spending	0.044	0.015	0.052**	0.044	0.015	0.052*
	(0.067)	(0.019)	(0.025)	(0.057)	(0.017)	(0.030)
Δ Resources p.c. (log)*Defence spending$_{t-1}$	−0.104*	0.007	0.069	−0.104	0.007	0.069
	(0.061)	(0.019)	(0.113)	(0.138)	(0.036)	(0.098)
Resources p.c. (log)*$_{t-1}$ Defence spending$_{t-1}$	0.032**	−0.005	0.032***	0.032*	−0.005	0.032***
	(0.014)	(0.005)	(0.010)	(0.017)	(0.004)	(0.010)
Regime FEs	Yes	Yes	Yes	Yes	Yes	Yes
Standard controls	Yes	Yes	Yes	Yes	Yes	Yes
Beck–Katz SEs	No	No	No	Yes	Yes	Yes
Observations	306	304	304	306	304	304

Note: Error correction model with regime fixed effects and standard errors in parentheses. Constant and FE coefficients omitted. Columns (1) and (4) use *Welfare/budget*; columns (2) and (5) *Welfare/GDP*; columns (3) and (6) *Welfare p.c. (log)* as independent variable. * $p < 0.10$, ** $p < 0.05$, *** $p < 0.01$

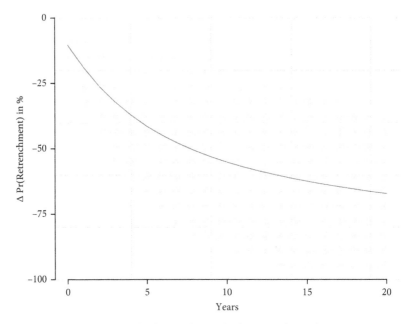

Figure A.3 Changes in the risk of retrenchment by broad coalition duration

Note: Shaded area indicates 95 per cent confidence bounds. Graph based on the non-stratified model.

model. Figure A.4 displays the marginal effects of resource windfalls by coalition type and coalition duration. The figure is based on Table A.5, columns (3) and (4), respectively. The headline findings are the same as in the baseline model. It should be noted, though, that for very long-lasting broad coalitions (> 20 years), the marginal effect of resource income ceases to be significant at the 95 per cent level. For long-lasting regimes, the steady conversion of windfall resources into welfare spending is therefore likely, but not guaranteed.

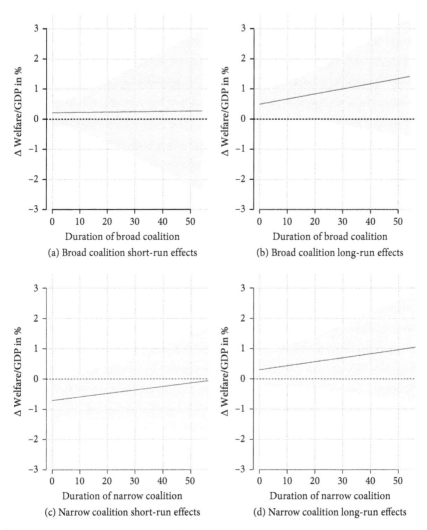

Figure A.4 Effect of resource windfalls on social spending as a percentage of GDP by coalition type and duration

Note: Shaded area indicates 95 per cent confidence bounds. The figures are based on Table A.5, columns (3) and (4).

Table A.5 Robustness test H3: alternative measure of resource abundance and standard errors

	(1) Broad coalition	(2) Narrow coalition	(3) Broad coalition	(4) Narrow coalition
Welfare spending$_{t-1}$	-0.466***	-0.460***	-0.466***	-0.460***
	(0.065)	(0.064)	(0.056)	(0.053)
Δ Resources p.c. (log)	0.213	-0.700*	0.213	-0.700*
	(0.156)	(0.413)	(0.208)	(0.368)
Resources p.c. (log)$_{t-1}$	0.230**	0.134	0.230**	0.134
	(0.113)	(0.146)	(0.109)	(0.140)
Δ Coalition duration	4.324***	0.654	4.324***	0.654
	(1.146)	(1.655)	(1.454)	(1.960)
Coalition duration$_{t-1}$	-0.013	-0.022	-0.013	-0.022
	(0.040)	(0.016)	(0.046)	(0.029)
Δ Resources p.c. (log)*Coalition duration$_{t-1}$	0.001	0.011	0.001	0.011
	(0.022)	(0.010)	(0.026)	(0.014)
Resources p.c. (log)*$_{t-1}$Δ Coalition duration	-0.330	-0.088	-0.330	-0.088
	(0.206)	(0.208)	(0.285)	(0.245)
Δ Resources p.c. (log)*Δ Coalition duration	-0.989*	0.655	-0.989	0.655
	(0.588)	(0.504)	(0.728)	(0.523)
Resources p.c. (log)*$_{t-1}$Coalition duration$_{t-1}$	0.008	0.006	0.008	0.006
	(0.007)	(0.004)	(0.008)	(0.008)
Regime FEs	Yes	Yes	Yes	Yes
Standard controls	Yes	Yes	Yes	Yes
Beck–Katz SEs	No	No	Yes	Yes
Observations	304	304	304	304

Note: Error correction model with regime fixed effects and standard errors in parentheses. The independent variable is *Welfare/GDP*. Constant and FE coefficients omitted.
* $p < 0.10$, ** $p < 0.05$, *** $p < 0.01$

Tunisia

Coding of Independent Variables

Table A.6 details the coding used to classify subsidy-related sectors. Please note: the same coding is used in Chapter 6 on Egypt.

Table A.6 Coding of subsidy-related sectors

Sectors producing subsidized food items	ISIC 3.1 Code
Processing and preserving of fruit and vegetables	1513
Manufacture of vegetable and animal oils and fats	1514
Manufacture of dairy products	1520
Manufacture of grain mill products	1531
Manufacture of bakery products	1541
Manufacture of sugar	1542
Manufacture of macaroni, noodles, couscous, and similar farinaceous products	1544

Sectors benefiting from subsidized inputs	ISIC 3.1 Code
Manufacture of bakery products	1541
Manufacture of cocoa, chocolate, and sugar confectionery	1543
Manufacture of soft drinks; production of mineral waters	1554

Egypt

Robustness Tests Cronies, Army, and Subsidies

Columns (1) and (2) in Table A.7 use the full spectrum of tariff rates, including tariffs above 1,000 per cent. Column (3) uses a standard logit model instead of a penalized maximum likelihood logit to estimate the effect of food and energy subsidies on army activity. While the coefficient of food subsidies is dropped due to 'tied' data, the coefficient for energy intensity remains highly statistically significant.

Table A.7 Robustness test: full tariff spectrum and different specification

	(1) Crony activity	(2) Army activity	(3) Army activity
Low intensity	−0.339*	−0.803***	−0.818***
	(0.180)	(0.186)	(0.182)
Direct food	0.226	4.398***	
	(0.419)	(1.433)	
Tariff average	−0.000905***	−0.000567	−0.00191**
	(0.000236)	(0.000684)	(0.000940)
Imports (log)	0.180***	0.277***	0.275***
	(0.0494)	(0.0486)	(0.0495)
Army activity	1.345***		
	(0.183)		
Crony activity		1.303***	1.318***
		(0.181)	(0.183)
Observations	699	699	663

Note: Logit (columns (1) and (3)) and penalized maximum likelihood logit (column (2)). Standard errors (column (2)) and robust standard errors (columns (1) and (3)) in parentheses. $^*p < 0.10$, $^{**}p < 0.05$, $^{***}p < 0.01$

List of Interviews in Order of Appearance

Table A.8 List of interviews in order of appearance

Person	(Former) position	Location and date
Driss Guiga	Minister of Social Affairs and Public Health (1969–73), Education (1973–6), and Interior (1980–4)	Hammamet, 17 June 2013
Mohamed Ennaceur	Minister of Social Affairs (1974–7, 1979–85)	Tunis, 21 May 2013
Ahmed Mestiri	Minister of Justice (1956–8), Finance and Commerce (1958–60), Defence (1966–8), and Interior (1970–1)	Tunis, 11 June 2013
Mohamed Sayah	Minister of Public Works (1971–3) and Housing (1980–3)	Tunis, 16 May 2013
Ahmed Ben Salah	Minister of Health (1957–61) and Social Affairs (1958–61), Minister of Finance, Planning, Economic Affairs (1961–9), and Education (1968–9)	Gabes, 27 April 2013
Rachid Sfar	Prime Minister (1986–7)	Tunis, 30 June 2013
Mustapha Filali	UGTT, former member of the Federation of Teachers, Minister of Agriculture (1957–9) and Information (1957–8)	Gabes, 19 June 2013
Naceur El Gharbi	Founding CEO of the CNAM (2004–9), Minister of Social Affairs (2010–11)	Tunis, 2 July 2013
Ridha Kechrid	Minister of Health (2004–7)	Tunis, 12 June 2013
Moncer Rouissi	Minister of Social Affairs (1989–91) and Employment (1992–2001); personal adviser of former President Ben Ali	Tunis, 22 May 2013
Ali Ben Romdhane	UGTT, Former Deputy Secretary General	Tunis, 2 May 2013
Ali Jebira	Head of the *Syndicat tunisien des médecins spécialistes libéraux* (Syndicate of the Independent Specialist Doctors; STMSL)	Tunis, 3 July 2013
Hédi Jilani	Former head of the employers' association UTICA	Tunis, 13 June 2013
Maher Kallel	Board member of the Poulina Group	Tunis, 18 June 2013

Continued

Table A.8 *Continued*

Person	(Former) position	Location and date
Abdel-Aziz Hegazy	Minister of the Treasury (1968–72), Minister of Finance and Foreign Trade (1973–4), Prime Minister (1974–5)	Cairo, 28 January 2013
Ali Lufti	Minister of Finance (1978–80), Prime Minister (1985–6)	Cairo, 26 February 2013
Medhat Hassanein	Minister of Finance (1999–2004)	Cairo, 24 February 2013
Awad Tag Eddin	Minister of Health (2002–5)	Cairo, 19 February 2013
Kamel Maait	Deputy Minister of Finance in charge of social security	Cairo, 14 November 2012
Youmna El Hamaki	Former member of the NDP General Secretariat	Cairo, 23 January 2013
Ali Moselhi	Former Minister of Social Affairs and Supply (2005–11)	Cairo, 13 January 201
Alia El Mahdy	Former member of the NDP Policies Committee	Cairo, 18 January 2013
Gouda Abdel Khaleq	Minister of Social Affairs (2011–12)	Cairo, 18 November 2012

References

Abbas, S. Ali et al. (2010). 'A Historical Public Debt Database'. IMF Working Paper WP/10/245. Washington, DC: International Monetary Fund.

Abdel-Fadil, Mahmoud (1980). *The Political Economy of Nasserism. A Study in Employment and Income Distribution Policies in Urban Egypt, 1952–72*. Cambridge: Cambridge University Press.

Abdel-Malik, Anouar (1968). *Egypt: Military Society*. New York: Random House.

Abdoun, Rabah (1989). 'Crise économique et satisfaction des besoins sociaux en Algérie'. In: *Cahiers du CREAD* 17, pp. 27–40.

Aboulenein, Soheir et al. (2010). 'Impact of the Global Food Price Shock on the Poor in Egypt'. Working Paper No. 157. Cairo: Egyptian Center for Economic Studies (ECES).

Abrahamian, Ervand (1982). *Iran Between Two Revolutions*. Princeton: Princeton University Press.

Abrahamian, Ervand (2008). *A History of Modern Iran*. Cambridge: Cambridge University Press.

Abrahamian, Ervand (2013). *The Coup: 1953, the CIA, and the Roots of Modern US–Iranian Relations*. Kindle edition. New York: The New Press.

Abu Jaber, Kamel (1966). *The Arab Ba'th Socialist Party: History, Ideology, and Organization*. Syracuse: Syracuse University Press.

Abul-Magd, Zeinab (2012). *The Egyptian Republic of Retired Generals*. Foreign Policy. URL: http://mideast.foreignpolicy.com/posts/2012/05/08/the%5C_egyptian%5C_republic%5C_of%5C_retired%5C_generals (visited on 24/06/2015).

Abul-Magd, Zeinab (2013). 'The Egyptian Military in Politics and the Economy: Recent History and Current Transition Status'. CMI Insight No. 2. Bergen: Chr. Michelsen Institute.

Abul-Magd, Zeinab (2016). 'Egypt's Adaptable Officers: Business, Nationalism, and Discontent'. In: *Businessmen in Arms: How the Military and Other Armed Groups Profit in the MENA Region*. Ed. by Zeinab Abul-Magd and Elke Grawert. London: Rowman & Littlefield, pp. 23–41.

Abul-Magd, Zeinab (2018). *Militarizing the Nation: The Army, Business, and Revolution in Egypt*. New York: Columbia University Press.

Acemoglu, Daron and James A. Robinson (2006). *Economic Origins of Dictatorship and Democracy*. Cambridge: Cambridge University Press.

Acemoglu, Daron, Georgy Egorov, and Konstantin Sonin (2006). 'Coalition Formation in Non-Democracies'. NBER Working Paper No. 12749. Cambridge, Mass.: National Bureau of Economic Research.

Acemoglu, Daron, Tarek A. Hassan, and Ahmed Tahoun (2014). 'The Power of the Street: Evidence from Egypt's Arab Spring'. NBER Working Paper No. 20665. Cambridge, Mass.: National Bureau of Economic Research.

Acemoglu, Daron, Simon Johnson, and James A. Robinson (2005). 'Institutions as a Fundamental Cause of Long-Run Growth'. In: *Handbook of Economic Growth*. Ed. by Philippe Aghion and Steven N. Durlauf. London: Elsevier, pp. 385–472.

Acemoglu, Daron, Simon Johnson, James A. Robinson, and David Albouy (2012). 'The Colonial Origins of Comparative Development: An Empirical Investigation'. In: *The American Economic Review* 91.5, pp. 1369–401.

Aclimandos, Tewfic Albert (2001). 'Regard rétrospectif sur la Révolution égyptienne, ou le 23 juillet 1952'. In: *Égypte monde arabe* 4–5, pp. 15–39.

Aclimandos, Tewfic Albert (2004). 'Les officiers activistes de l'armée égyptienne: 1936–1954'. PhD thesis. Sciences Po Paris.

Adaab, A. and M. Elloumi (1997). 'Les effets des politiques de prix, de subvention et de fiscalité sur l'agriculture tunisienne'. In: *Prix et subventions: effets sur les agricultures familiales méditerranéennes*. Ed. by N. Akesbi and N. Maraveyas. Montpellier: CIHEAM, pp. 7–53.

Adam, André (1970). 'Chronique sociale et culturelle Tunisie'. In: *Annuaire de l'Afrique du Nord*. Ed. by Michel Camau and Charles Debbasch. Paris: Éditions du CNRS, pp. 201–84.

Adserà, Alicia and Carles Boix (2002). 'Trade, Democracy, and the Size of the Public Sector: The Political Underpinnings of Openness'. In: *International Organization* 56.2, pp. 229–62.

AfDB (2014). *What Policies should be Implemented to Address Inequalities in Health Care in Tunisia?* Abidjan: African Development Bank.

Ageron, Charles Robert (1991). *Modern Algeria: A History from 1830 to the Present*. London: Hurst.

Ahmed, Akhter U. et al. (2001). *The Egyptian Food Subsidy System: Structure, Performance, and Options for Reform*. Research Report 119. Washington, DC.

Ahram, Ariel I. (2009). 'The Theory and Method of Comparative Area Studies'. Political Methodology Working Paper No. 19. The Committee on Concepts and Methods.

Aicha, Safi (1989). 'Disparité des régimes de couverture du risque maladie'. In: *Revue tunisienne de droit social*, pp. 75–104.

Aïssaoui, Ali (2001). *Algeria: The Political Economy of Oil and Gas*. Oxford: Oxford University Press.

Albertus, Michael (2015a). *Autocracy and Redistribution: The Politics of Land Reform*. Cambridge: Cambridge University Press.

Albertus, Michael (2015b). 'Explaining Patterns of Redistribution under Autocracy: The Case of Peru's Revolution from Above'. In: *Latin American Research Review* 50.2, pp. 107–34.

Albertus, Michael, Sofia Fenner, and Dan Slater (2018). *Coercive Distribution*. Cambridge: Cambridge University Press.

Albrecht, Holger and Rolf Frankenberger (2010). 'Autoritarismus Reloaded: Konzeptionelle Anmerkungen zur vergleichenden Analyse politischer Systeme'. In: *Autoritarismus Reloaded. Neuere Ansätze und Erkenntnisse der Autokratieforschung*. Ed. by Holger Albrecht and Rolf Frankenberger. Baden-Baden: Nomos, pp. 37–60.

Alexander, Michael Christopher (1996). 'Between Accommodation and Confrontation: State, Labor, and Development in Algeria and Tunisia'. PhD thesis. Duke University.

Alexander, Michael Christopher (2010). *Tunsia: Stability and Reform in the Modern Maghrib*. London: Routledge.

Algeria (various years). *Annuaire statistique de l'Algérie*. Alger: E. Pfister.

Ali, Merima et al. (2018). 'Colonial Legacy, State-Building and the Salience of Ethnicity in Sub-Saharan Africa'. In: *The Economic Journal*. Early view.

Allani, Alaya (1999). 'De nouvelles versions sur la crise youssefiste-Bourguibiste'. In: *Revue d'histoire maghrébine* 93–4, pp. 133–45.

Allinson, Jamie (2016). *The Struggle for the State in Jordan: The Social Origins of Alliances in the Middle East.* Kindle edition. London: I. B. Tauris.

Allman, James (1979). *Social Mobility, Education and Development in Tunisia.* Leiden: Brill.

Alon, Yoav (2007). *The Making of Jordan: Tribes, Colonialism and the Modern State.* London: I. B. Tauris.

Aly, Götz (2007). *Hitler's Beneficiaries: How the Nazis Bought the German People.* London: Verso.

Al-Amal (1963). *No Title.* 24 July. Tunis.

Al-'Usbua (1949). *Al-Ittihad yutalib t'amim al-t'alim [UGTT demands the Generalization of Education].* November. Tunis.

Amenta, Edwin (2003). 'What We Know About the Development of Social Policy: Comparative and Historical Research in Comparative and Historical Perspective'. In: *Comparative Historical Analysis in the Social Sciences.* Ed. by James Mahoney and Dietrich Rueschemeyer. Cambridge: Cambridge University Press, pp. 91–130.

American Embassy in Cairo (2009). *09CAIRO2320.* URL: http://www.telegraph.co.uk/news/wikileaks-files/egypt-wikileaks-cables/8326900/THE-MYSTERIES-OF-EGYPTS-HEALTH-CARE-REFORM.html (visited on 15/06/2015).

Amin, Galal (1995). *Egypt's Economic Predicament: A Study in the Interaction of External Pressure, Politically Folly and Social Tension in Egypt, 1960–1990.* Brill: Leiden.

Amin, Galal and Muhammad Nawwar (2006). *Thawrat Yuliyu: dirasah b'ada nisf qarn [The July Revolution: Study after Half A Century].* Cairo: Dar Jihad lil-Nashr wa al-Tawzi'.

Amin, Samir (1966). *L'économie du Maghreb.* Paris: Éditions de Minuit.

Amjad, Mohammed (1989). *Iran: From Royal Dictatorship to Theocracy.* London: Greenwood Press.

Amuzegar, Jahangir (1991). *The Dynamics of the Iranian Revolution: The Pahlavis' Triumph and Tragedy.* New York: State University of New York Press.

Amuzegar, Jahangir (1993). *Iran's Economy under the Islamic Republic.* London: I. B. Tauris.

Anderson, Lisa (1986). *The State and Social Transformation in Tunisia and Libya, 1830–1980.* Princeton: Princeton University Press.

Anderson, Lisa (1987). 'The State in the Middle East and North Africa'. In: *Comparative Politics* 20.1, pp. 1–18.

Ansari, Ali M. (2007). *Modern Iran: The Pahlavis and After.* London: Pearson Longman.

Ansell, Ben W. (2008). 'Traders, Teachers, and Tyrants: Democracy, Globalization, and Public Investment in Education'. In: *International Organization* 62.2, pp. 289–322.

Ansell, Ben W. (2010). *From the Ballot to the Blackboard: The Redistributive Political Economy of Education.* Cambridge: Cambridge University Press.

APII (2014). *Les industries agroalimentaires en Tunisie.* Tunis.

Arab Republic of Egypt (various years). *Statistical Handbook.* Cairo: Cenral Agency for Mobilization and Statistics.

Arafat, Alaa Al-Din (2009). *The Mubarak Leadership and Future of Democracy in Egypt.* New York: Palgrave Macmillan.

Arfa, Chokri and Heba Elgazzar (2013). 'Tunisia—Consolidation and Transparency: Transforming Tunisia's Health Care for the Poor'. Washington, DC.

Arnold, James R. (2009). *Saddam Hussein's Iraq.* Minneapolis: Lerner Books.

Arriola, Leonardo R. (2009). 'Patronage and Political Stability in Africa'. In: *Comparative Political Studies* 42.10, pp. 1339–62.

Art, David (2012). 'What Do We Know about Authoritarianism after Ten Years?' In: *Comparative Politics* 44.3, pp. 351–73.

Aruri, Naseer H. (1972). *Jordan: A Study in Political Development (1921–1965).* The Hague: Martinus Nijhoff.

Ashford, Douglas E. (1962). 'The Irredentist Appeal in Morocco and Mauritania'. In: *The Western Political Quarterly* 15.4, pp. 641–51.

Ashford, Douglas Elliott (1961). *Political Change in Morocco.* Princeton: Princeton University Press.

Assaad, R. (1997). 'The Effects of Public Sector Hiring and Compensation Policies on the Egyptian Labor Market'. In: *The World Bank Economic Review* 11.1, pp. 85–118.

Assaad, Ragui (2014). 'Making Sense of Arab Labor Markets: The Enduring Legacy of Dualism'. In: *IZA Journal of Labor and Development* 3.1, pp. 1–25.

Avelino, George, David S. Brown, and Wendy Hunter (2005). 'The Effects of Capital Mobility, Trade Openness, and Democracy on Social Spending in Latin America, 1980–1999'. In: *American Journal of Political Science* 49.3, pp. 625–41.

Awad, Louis (1975). *Aqni'at al-Nasiriyah al-sab'ah: munaqashat Tawfiq al-Hakim wa-Muhammad Hasanayn Haykal [The Seven Masks of Nasserism: Dialogue between Tawfiq al-Hakim and Muhammad Hasanayn Haykal].* Beirut: Dar al-Qadaya.

Ayachi, Mokhtar (2000). 'A la croisée des chemins: l'UGTT et les choix culturels de l'Etat national'. In: *Habib Bourguiba et l'établissement de l'Etat national: approches scientifiques du bourguibisme.* Ed. by Abdeljelil Temimi. Tunis: FTERSI, pp. 59–64.

Ayachi, Mokhtar (2003). *Histoire d'une école de cadres l'union générale des étudiants de Tunisie au cours des années 50–60.* Ben Arous: Imprimerie officielle.

Ayadi, Ines and Salma Zouari (2017). 'Out-of-Pocket Health Spending and Equity Implications in Tunisia'. In: *Middle East Development Journal* 9.1, pp. 1–21.

Ayal, Eliezer B. and Barry R. Chiswick (2013). 'The Economics of the Diaspora Revisited'. In: *Economic Development and Cultural Change* 31.4, pp. 861–75.

Ayubi, Nazih M. (1978). *Siyasat al-ta'alim fi Misr: dirasah siyasiyah wa-idariyah [Educaton Policies in Egypt: Study of its Politics and Administration].* Cairo: Markaz al-Dirasat al-Siyasiyah wa-al-Istiratijiyah, al-Ahram.

Ayubi, Nazih M. (1991). *The State and Public Policies in Egypt since Sadat.* Reading: Ithaca.

Ayubi, Nazih M. (1992). 'Withered Socialism or Whether Socialism? The Radical Arab States as Populist-Corporatist Regimes'. In: *Third World Quarterly* 13.1, pp. 89–105.

Ayubi, Nazih M. (1995). *Over-Stating the Arab State: Politics and Society in the Middle East.* London: Tauris.

Azimi, Fakhreddin (2004). 'Unseating Mosaddeq: The Configuration and Role of Domestic Forces'. In: *Mohammad Mosaddeq and the 1953 Coup in Iran.* Ed. by Mark J. Gasi- orowski and Malcolm Byrne. Syracuse: Syracuse University Press, pp. 27–101.

Ba Mohammed, Najib (2001). 'Notables et élites au Maroc'. In: *Revue Marocaine d'Administration Locale et de Développement* 41, pp. 17–25.

Baghdadi, Abdelatif (1977). *Mudhakirat Abd al-Latif al-Baghdadi [Memoirs of Abdelatif Baghdadi].* Cairo: Al-Maktab al-Masri al-Hadith.

Al-Bahrani, Imad ibn Jasim (2010). *Jamal Abd al-Nasir min al-thawrah ila al-naksah (1952–1967) [Gamal Abdel Nasser from the Revolution to the Catastrophy (1952–1967)].* Cairo: Maktabat Madbouli.

Bailey, Clive (2004). 'Extending Social Security Coverage in Africa'. ESS Working Paper No. 20. Geneva: International Labour Office (ILO).

Baker, Raymod William (1978). *Egypt's Uncertain Revoution under Nasser and Sadat.* Cambridge, Mass.: Harvard University Press.

Bakhash, Shaul (1990). *The Reign of the Ayatollahs: Iran and the Islamic Revolution.* New York: Basic Books.

Al-Bakoush, Aisa (2010). *Témoignages sur l'Union Générale des Etudiants de Tunisie*. Tunis: Fondation Temimi pour la recherche scientifique et l'information.

Balanche, Fabrice (2006). *La région alaouite et le pouvoir syrien*. Paris: Karthala.

Balanche, Fabrice (2017). "Go to Damascus, my son": Alawi Demographic Shifts under Ba'ath Party Rule'. In: *The Alawis of Syria: War, Faith, and Politics in the Levant*. Ed. by Michael Kerr and Craig Larkin. Kindle edition. New York: Oxford University Press.

Balanche, Fabrice (2018). *Sectarianism in Syria's Civil War: A Geopolitical Study Featuring 70 Original Maps*. Washington, DC. URL: http://www.washingtoninstitute.org/uploads/Documents/pubs/SyriaAtlasCOMPLETE.pdf (visited on 17/05/2019).

Baldwin, Kate (2013). 'Why Vote with the Chief? Political Connections and Public Goods Provision in Zambia'. In: *American Journal of Political Science* 57.4, pp. 794–809.

Bank, André (2009). 'Die Renaissance des Autoritarismus. Erkenntnisse und Grenzen neuerer Beiträge der Comparative Politics und Nahostforschung '. In: *Hamburg Review of Social Sciences* 4.1, pp. 10–41.

Banque Centrale de Tunisie (2015). *Rapport Annuel Archives*. URL: www.bct.gov.tn/bct/siteprod/page.jsp?id=77 (visited on 04/05/2015).

Baqir, Reza (2002). 'Social Sector Spending in a Panel of Countries'. IMF Working Paper 02/35. Washington, DC: International Monetary Fund.

Barbone, Luca and Luis-Alvaro Sanchez (1999). 'Pensions and Social Security in SubSaharan Africa: Issues and Options'. Conference Paper. XIII International Social Security Association African Regional Conference.

Barnett, Michael N. (1992). *Confronting the Costs of War: Military Power, State, and Society in Egypt and Israel*. Princeton: Princeton University Press.

Barroso, Sergio Espuelas (2009). 'The Determinants of Social Spending in Spain, 1950–1980. Are Dictatorships Less Redistributive?' Conference Paper. APHES Conference.

Barroso, Sergio Espuelas and Margarita Vilar Rodriguez (2009). 'The Determinants of Social Spending in Spain (1880–1960): Is Lindert Right?' Working Paper.

Basedau, Matthias and Patrick Köllner (2007). 'Area Studies, Comparative Area Studies, and the Study of Politics: Context, Substance, and Methodological Challenges'. In: *Zeitschrift für Vergleichende Politikwissenschaft* 1.1, pp. 105–24.

Batatu, Hanna (1981). 'Some Observations on the Social Roots of Syria's Ruling, Military Group and the Causes for Its Dominance'. In: *Middle East Journal* 35.3, pp. 331–44.

Batatu, Hanna (1999). *Syria's Peasantry, the Descendants of Its Lesser Rural Notables, and Their Politics*. Princeton: Princeton University Press.

Bates, Robert H. (1983). *Essays on the Political Economy of Rural Africa*. Cambridge: Cambridge University Press.

Batniji, Rajaie et al. (2014). 'Governance and Health in the Arab World'. In: *The Lancet* 383.9914, pp. 343–55.

Bayat, Asef (1988). 'Labor and Democracy in Post-Revolutionary Iran'. In: *Post-Revolutionary Iran*. Ed. by Hooshang Amirahmadi and Manoucher Parvin. London: Westview Press, pp. 41–55.

Bayat, Asef (2006). 'The Political Economy of Social Policy in Egypt'. In: *Social Policy in the Middle East: Economic, Political, and Gender Dynamics*. Ed. by Massoud Karshenas and Valentine M. Moghadam. Basingstoke: Palgrave Macmillan, pp. 135–55.

Baylouny, Anne Marie (2008). 'Militarizing Welfare: Neo-liberalism and Jordanian Policy'. In: *The Middle East Journal* 62.2, pp. 277–303.

Baylouny, Anne Marie (2010). *Privatizing Welfare in the Middle East: Kin Mutual Aid Associations in Jordan and Lebanon*. Bloomington: Indiana University Press.

Be'eri, Eliezer (1970). *Army Officers in Arab Politics and Society*. New York: Praeger.

Beach, Derek (2012). 'Taking Mechanisms Seriously?' In: *European Political Science* 12.1, pp. 13–15.

Beach, Derek and Rasmus Brun Pedersen (2013). *Process-Tracing Methods: Foundations and Guidelines*. Ann Arbor: Michigan University Press.

Beattie, Kirk J. (1994). *Egypt during the Nasser Years: Ideology, Politics, and Civil Society*. Oxford: Westview Press.

Beattie, Kirk J. (2000). *Egypt during the Sadat Years*. New York: Palgrave.

Beblawi, Hazem (1987). 'The Rentier State in the Arab World '. In: *The Rentier State*. Ed. by Hazem Beblawi and Giacomo Luciani. London: Croom Helm, pp. 49–62.

Beblawi, Hazem and Giacomo Luciani, eds. (1987). *The Rentier State*. London: Croom Helm.

Bechri, Mohamed Z. and Sonia Naccache (2003). 'The Political Economy of Development Policy in Tunisia'. Working Paper.

Beck, Lois (1991). 'Tribes in Nineteenth- and Twentieth-Century Iran'. In: *Tribes and State Formation in the Middle East*. Ed. by Philip S. Khoury and Joseph Kostiner. London: I. B. Tauris, pp. 185–225.

Beck, Martin (2007a). 'Der Rentierstaatsansatz und das Problem abweichender Fälle'. In: *Zeitschrift für Internationale Beziehungen* 14.1, pp. 43–70.

Beck, Martin (2007b). 'Paving the Way for Democracies or Strengthening Authoritarianism? Reforms in the Middle East'. In: *The Arab Authoritarian Regime between Reform and Persistence*. Ed. by Henner Fürtig. Newcastle: Cambridge Scholars, pp. 1–24.

Beck, Nathaniel L. and Jonathan N. Katz (1995). 'What to Do (and Not to Do) with Time-Series Cross-Section Data'. In: *American Political Science Review* 89.3, pp. 634–47.

Beck, Nathaniel L. and Jonathan N. Katz (2011). 'Modeling Dynamics in Time-Series-Cross-Section Political Economy Data'. In: *Annual Review of Political Science* 14, pp. 331–52.

Behdad, Sohrab (1996). 'The Post-revolutionary Economic Crisis'. In: *Iran after the Revolution*. Ed. by Saeed Rahnema and Sohrab Behdad. London: I. B. Tauris, pp. 97–128.

Behrooz, Maziar (2004). 'The 1953 Coup in Iran and the Legacy of the Tudeh'. In: *Mohammad Mosaddeq and the 1953 Coup in Iran*. Ed. by Mark J. Gasiorowski and Malcolm Byrne. Syracuse: Syracuse University Press, pp. 102–25.

Beinin, Joel (1989). 'Labor, Capital, and the State in Nasserist Egypt, 1952–1961'. In: *International Journal of Middle East Studies* 21.1, pp. 71–90.

Beinin, Joel and Zachary Lockman (1988). *Workers on the Nile: Nationalism, Communism, Islam and the Egyptian Working Class, 1882–1954*. London: I. B. Tauris.

Belghiti Allaoui, A. (2006). *La réforme de santé au Maroc, pertinence et opportunités*. Ministère de la Santé du Maroc. URL: http://www.sante.gov.ma/smsm/cmm%5C_web/La%5C_reforme%5C_de%5C_sante%5C_au%5C_Maroc.htm (visited on 06/09/2015).

Belhadi, Abdelmajid (2011). *Al-wa'i bi-almasalat al-iqtisadiyya fi fikr al-nukhab al-tunisiyya [The Economic Thinking of the Tunisian Elites 1980–1956]*. Tunis: Markas al-Nashr al-Gam'ayyi.

Belkhodja, Tahar (1998). *Les trois décennies de Bourguiba*. Paris: Publisud.

Bellin, Eva (2000). 'Contingent Democrats: Industrialists, Labor, and Democratization in Late-Developing Countries'. In: *World Politics* 52.2, pp. 175–205.

Bellin, Eva (2002). *Stalled Democracy: Capital, Labor, and the Paradox of State-Sponsored Development*. Ithaca: Cornell University Press.

Bellin, Eva (2004). 'The Robustness of Authoritarianism in the Middle East: Exceptionalism in Comparative Perspective'. In: *Comparative Politics* 36.2, pp. 139–57.

Bellin, Eva (2012). 'Reconsidering the Robustness of Authoritarianism in the Middle East: Lessons from the Arab Spring'. In: *Comparative Politics* 44.2, pp. 127–49.

Belouas, Aziza (2017). *Le secteur de la santé s'enfonce dans la crise*. 6 April. La Vie Éco. URL http://lavieeco.com/news/societe/le-secteur-de-la-sante-senfonce-dans-la-crise.html (visited on 21/05/2019).

Ben Braham, Mehdi and Mohamed Ali Marouani (2016). 'Determinants of Contribution Density to the Tunisian Pension System: A Cross Sectional Analysis'. ERF Working Paper 1005. Cairo: Economic Research Forum (ERF).

Ben Dhiaf, Issa (1982). 'Tunisie'. In: *Annuaire de l'Afrique du Nord 1981*. Ed. by Maurice Flory and Hubert Michel. Paris: Editions du CNRS, pp. 583–627.

Ben Dhiaf, Issa (1986). 'Tunisie'. In: *Annuaire de l'Afrique du Nord 1984*. Ed. by André Raymond and Hubert Michel. Paris: Editions du CNRS, pp. 865–923.

Ben Romdhane, Mahmoud (1984). 'Mutations économiques et sociales et mouvement ouvrier en Tunisie de 1956 à 1980'. In: *Annuaire de l'Afrique du Nord*. Ed. by Hubert Michel and Maurice Flory. Paris: Éditions du CNRS, pp. 259–84.

Ben Romdhane, Mahmoud (2006). 'Social Policy and Development in Tunisia since Independence'. In: *Social Policy in the Middle East: Economic, Political, and Gender Dynamics*. Ed. by Massoud Karshenas and Valentine M. Moghadam. Basingstoke: Palgrave Macmillan, pp. 31–77.

Ben Salah, Ahmed (2008). *Pour rétablir la vérité*. Paris: Cérès Editions.

Benhlal, Mohamed (1984). 'Le syndicat comme enjeu politique au Maroc: 1955–1981'. In: *Annuaire de l'Afrique du Nord*. Ed. by Hubert Michel and Maurice Flory. Paris: Éditions du CNRS, pp. 217–58.

Benkassmi, Mohamed, Touhami Abdelkhalek, and Fouzia Ejjanoui (2017). 'Evaluation de l'impact de l'Initiative Nationale pour le Développement (INDH) sur la pauvreté en milieu rural au Maroc: Une étude en enquête panel de ménages'. Cairo.

Bennett, Andrew and Jeffrey Checkel (2015). 'Process Tracing: From Philosophical Roots to Best Practices'. In: *Process Tracing: From Metaphor to Analytical Tool*. Ed. by Andrew Bennett and Jeffrey Checkel. Cambridge: Cambridge University Press, pp. 3–37.

Bennoune, Mahfoud (1988). *The Making of Contemporary Algeria, 1830–1987: Colonial Upheavals and Post-independence Development*. Cambridge: Cambridge University Press.

Benseddik, Fouad (1990). *Syndicalisme et politique au Maroc. Tome 1, 1930–1956*. Paris: L'Harmattan.

Berins Collier, Ruth and David Collier (1991). *Shaping the Political Arena: Critical Junctures, the Labor Movement, and Regime Dynamics in Latin America*. Princeton: Princeton University Press.

Bernhard, Helen, Urs Fischbacher, and Ernst Fehr (2006). 'Parochial Altruism in Humans'. In: *Nature* 442.7105, pp. 912–15.

Besley, Timothy and Torsten Persson (2014). 'Why Do Developing Countries Tax So Little?' In: *Journal of Economic Perspectives* 28.4, pp. 99–120.

Bessis, Sophie and Souhayr Belhassen (1988). *Bourguiba: À la conquête d'un destin*. Paris: Groupe Jeune Afrique.

Bessis, Sophie and Souhayr Belhassen (1989). *Bourguiba: Un si long règne*. Paris: Groupe Jeune Afrique.

Best, M. H. and W. E. Connolly (1982). *The Politicized Economy*. Lexington, Mass.: D.C. Heath.

Beyer, Jürgen (2010). 'The Same or Not the Same—On the Variety of Mechanisms of Path Dependence'. In: *International Journal of Human and Social Sciences* 5.1, pp. 1–11.

Binzel, Christine (2011). 'Decline in Social Mobility: Unfulfilled Aspirations among Egypt's Educated Youth'. IZA Discussion Paper No. 6139. Bonn. Institute for the Study of Labor (IZA).

Blatter, Daniel and Zachary Buzzell (2013). 'The Subsidy Trap: Why Tunisia's Leaders Are Unwilling , Unable, or Afraid to Abandon Fuel Subsidies'. Imes Capstrone Paper Series. Washington, DC: The Institute for Middle East Studies.

Blaydes, Lisa (2010). *Elections and Distributive Politics in Mubarak's Egypt.* Cambridge: Cambridge University Press.

Blaydes, Lisa (2018). *State of Repression: Iraq under Saddam Hussein.* Princeton: Princeton University Press.

Blaydes, Lisa and Eric Chaney (2013). 'The Feudal Revolution and Europe's Rise: Political Divergence of the Christian West and the Muslim World before 1500 CE'. In: *American Political Science Review* 107.1, pp. 16–34.

Blaydes, Lisa and Mark Andreas Kayser (2011). 'Counting Calories: Democracy and Distribution in the Developing World'. In: *International Studies Quarterly* 55.4, pp. 887–908.

Bockstette, Valerie, Areendam Chanda, and Louis Putterman (2002). 'States and Markets: The Advantage of an Early Start'. In: *Journal of Economic Growth* 7.4, pp. 347–69.

Boix, Carles (2003). *Democracy and Redistribution.* Cambridge: Cambridge University Press.

Booth, John A. (1998). 'The Somoza Regime in Nicaragua'. In: *Sultanistic Regimes.* Ed. by Houchang E. Chehabi and Juan J. Linz. Baltimore: Johns Hopkins University Press, pp. 132–52.

Borsali, Noura (2008). *Livre d'entretiens avec Ahmed Ben Salah: l'homme fort de la Tunisie des années soixante.* Tunis: Maison Samed d'Édition.

Boudahrain, Abdellah (2003). 'Social Security Pensions in the Maghreb: A Study of Morocco and Tunisia'. In: *International Social Security Review* 56.3–4, pp. 121–38.

Bouqra, Adel-Jelil (2012). *Al-nitham al-bourqibi—al-su'ud wa al-inhidar [The System, Bourguiba . . . the Rise and Fall: 1956–1987].* Tunis: Dar al-Afaq al-Nashr.

Bourguiba, Habib (1974a). *Discours Tome I.* Tunis: Secrétariat d'État à l'Information.

Bourguiba, Habib (1974b). *Discours Tome II.* Tunis: Secrétariat d'État à l'Information.

Bourguiba, Habib (1974c). *Discours Tome IV.* Tunis: Secrétariat d'État à l'Information.

Bourguiba, Habib (1974d). *Discours Tome VIII.* Tunis: Secrétariat d'État à l'Information.

Bourguiba, Habib (1976). *Interviews et déclarations 1952–1955.* Tunis: Publications du Secrétariat d'Etat à l'Information.

Bouzaine, Ahmed (1989). 'Les conflits collectifs du travail au Maroc: contribution à une sociologie des classes sociales dans le Maroc post-colonial'. PhD thesis. A.N.R.T. Université de Lille III, Université de Toulouse, Le Mirail.

Bowles, Samuel and Herbert Gintis (2004). 'The Evolution of Strong Reciprocity: Cooperation in Heterogeneous Populations'. In: *Theoretical Population Biology* 65.1, pp. 17–28.

Box-Steffensmeier, Janet M. and C. Zorn (2002). 'Duration Models for Repeated Events'. In: *The Journal of Politics* 64.4, pp. 1069–94.

Box-Steffensmeier, Janet M., Suzanna De Boef, and Kyle A. Joyce (2007). 'Event Dependence and Heterogeneity in Duration Models: The Conditional Frailty Model'. In: *Political Analysis* 15.3, pp. 237–56.

Bozarslan, Hamit (2011). 'Réflexions sur les configurations révolutionnaires tunisienne et égyptienne'. In: *Mouvements* 66.

Brambor, Thomas, William Roberts Clark, and Matt Golder (2005). 'Understanding Interaction Models: Improving Empirical Analyses'. In: *Political Analysis* 14.1, pp. 63–82.

Brand, Laurie A. (1999). 'The Effects of the Peace Process on Political Liberalization in Jordan'. In: *Journal of Palestine Studies* 28.2, pp. 52–67.

Bratton, Michael and Nicolas Van de Walle (1994). 'Neopatrimonial Regimes and Political Transitions in Africa'. In: *World Politics* 46.4, pp. 453–89.

Brewer, Marilynn B. (1999). 'The Psychology of Prejudice: Ingroup Love or Outgroup Hate?' In: *Journal of Social Issues* 55.3, pp. 429–44.

Brooke, Steven (2015). 'The Muslim Brotherhood's Social Outreach after the Egyptian Coup'. Brookings Working Paper. Washington, DC: Brookings Institution.

Brooke, Steven (2017). 'From Medicine to Mobilization: Social Service Provision and the Islamist Reputational Advantage'. In: *Perspectives on Politics* 15.1, pp. 42–61.

Brooke, Steven (2019). *Winning Heats and Votes: Social Service and the Islamist Political Advantage.* Ithaca: Cornell University Press.

Brouksy, Omar (2005). *Que s'est-il vraiment passé le 23 mars 1965?* 21 March. Jeune Afrique. URL: https://www.jeuneafrique.com/86510/archives-thematique/que-s-est-il-vraiment-pass-le-23-mars-1965/ (visited on 31/05/2019).

Brown, David S. and Wendy Hunter (1999). 'Democracy and Social Spending in Latin America, 1980–92'. In: *American Political Science Review* 93.4, pp. 779–90.

Brown, L. Carl (2001). 'Bourguiba and Bourguibism Revisited: Reflections and Interpretation'. In: *The Middle East Journal* 55.1, pp. 43–57.

Brownlee, Jason (2007). *Authoritarianism in an Age of Democratization.* Cambridge: Cambridge University Press.

Brubaker, Rogers (2004). *Ethnicity without Groups.* Cambridge, Mass.: Harvard University Press.

Bueno de Mesquita, Bruce, Randolph M. Siverson et al. (1992). 'War and the Fate of Regimes: A Comparative Analysis'. In: *The American Political Science Review* 86.3, pp. 638–46.

Bueno de Mesquita, Bruce, Alistair Smith et al. (2003). *The Logic of Political Survival.* Cambridge, Mass.: MIT.

Bunce, Valerie and Aida Hozic (2015). 'Hybrid Regimes and International Aggression'. In: *Comparative Democratization* 13.1, pp. 2–18.

Bureau van Dijk (2013). *Orbis Database.* URL: https://orbis.bvdinfo.com/ (visited on 24/06/2015).

Bush, Ray (2011). 'Coalitions for Dispossession and Networks of Resistance? Land, Politics and Agrarian Reform in Egypt'. In: *British Journal of Middle Eastern Studies* 38.3, pp. 391–405.

Bush, Ray and Habib Ayeb, eds. (2012). *Marginality and Exclusion in Egypt.* London: Zed Books.

Butter, David (1989). 'Debt and Egypt's Financial Policies'. In: *Egypt under Mubarak.* Ed. by Charles Tripp and Roger Owen. London: Routledge, pp. 123–36.

Buy, François (1965). *La République Algérienne Démocratique et Populaire.* Paris: La Librairie Française.

Camau, Michel, Hédi Zaïem, and Hajer Bahri (1990). *État de santé. Besoin médical et enjeux politiques en Tunisie.* Paris: Editions du CNRS.

Cameron, David R. (1978). 'The Expansion of the Public Economy: A Comparative Analysis'. In: *American Political Science Review* 72.4, pp. 1243–61.

Cammett, Melani (2014a). *Compassionate Communalism: Welfare and Sectarianism in Lebanon.* Ithaca: Cornell University Press.

Cammett, Melani (2014b). 'Sectarian Politics and Social Welfare: Non-state Provision in Lebanon'. In: *The Politics of Non-state Social Welfare.* Ed. by Melani Cammett and Lauren M. MacLean. Ithaca: Cornell University Press, pp. 137–55.

Cammett, Melani (2015). 'Sectarianism and the Ambiguities of Welfare in Lebanon'. In: *Current Anthropology* 56.11, pp. 76–87.

Cammett, Melani and Ishac Diwan (2016). 'Fiscal Policy and Crony Capitalism in MENA Countries'. In: *The Middle East Economies in Times of Transition*. Ed. by Ahmed Galal and Ishac Diwan. New York: Palgrave Macmillan, pp. 63–98.

Cammett, Melani and Sukriti Issar (2010). 'Bricks and Mortar Clientelism: Sectarianism and the Logics of Welfare Allocation in Lebanon'. In: *World Politics* 62.3, pp. 381–421.

Cammett, Melani and Lauren MacLean (2014a). 'The Consequences of Non-state Social Welfare'. In: *The Politics of Non-state Social Welfare*. Ed. by Melani Cammett and Lauren M. MacLean. Ithaca: Cornell University Press, pp. 31–53.

Cammett, Melani and Lauren M. MacLean, eds. (2014b). *The Politics of Non-state Social Welfare*. Ithaca: Cornell University Press.

Cammett, Melani and Marsha Pripstein Posusney (2010). 'Labor Standards and Labor Market Flexibility in the Middle East: Free Trade and Freer Unions?' In: *Studies in Comparative International Development* 45.2, pp. 250–79.

Cammett, Melani and Aytug Sasmaz (2016). 'Social Policy in Developing Countries'. In: *Handbook of Historical Institutionalism*. Ed. by Tulia G. Falleti, Orfeo Fioretos, and Adam Sheingate. Oxford: Oxford University Press, pp. 239–51.

Campante, Filipe R. and Davin Chor (2012). 'Why Was the Arab World Poised for Revolution ? Schooling , Economic Opportunities , and the Arab Spring'. In: *The Journal of Economic Perspectives* 26.2, pp. 167–87.

Capoccia, Giovanni and R. Daniel Kelemen (2007). 'The Study of Critical Junctures: Theory, Narrative, and Counterfactuals in Historical Institutionalism'. In: *World Politics* 59.3, pp. 341–69.

Carter, David B. and Curtis S. Signorino (2010). 'Back to the Future: Modeling Time Dependence in Binary Data'. In: *Political Analysis* 18, pp. 271–92.

Carter, Jeff (2017). 'The Political Cost of War Mobilization in Democracies and Dictatorships'. In: *Journal of Conflict Resolution* 61.8, pp. 1768–94.

Caselli, Francesco and Tom Cunningham (2009). 'Leader Behaviour and the Natural Resource Curse'. In: *Oxford Economic Papers* 61.4, pp. 628–50.

Caselli, Francesco and Andrea Tesei (2016). 'Resource Windfalls, Political Regimes, and Political Stability'. In: *Review of Economics and Statistics* 98.3, pp. 573–90.

Castles, Francis G. et al., eds. (2010). *The Oxford Handbook of the Welfare State*. Oxford: Oxford University Press.

Catusse, Myriam and Karam Karam (2009). 'Le développement contre la représentation? La technicisation du gouvernement local au Liban et au Maroc'. In: *Démocraties et autoritarismes. Fragmentation et hybridation des régimes*. Ed. by Michel Camau and Gilles Massardier. Paris: Karthala, pp. 85–120.

Catusse, Myriam and Lamia Zaki (2009). 'Gestion communale et clientélisme moral au maroc: les politiques du parti de la justice et du développement'. In: *Critique internationale* 42.1, pp. 73–91.

CDN (1970). *Discours de Habib Bourguiba*. Tunis: Centre de documentation nationale.

Central Bureau of Statistics (2004). *Statistical Abstract*. URL: http://cbssyr.sy/index-EN.htm (visited on 20/06/2019).

Cerami, Alfio (2013). *Permanent Emergency Welfare Regimes in Sub-Saharan Africa: The Exclusive Origins of Dictatorship and Democracy*. Basingstoke: Palgrave Macmillan.

CERMOC (1992). 'Systèmes de santé et systèmes de protection sociale dans le monde arabe'. In: *Maghreb-Machrek* 138.

Chaabane, Mohamed (2002). 'Towards the Universalization of Social Security: The Experience of Tunisia'. ESS Paper No. 4. Geneva: International Labour Office (ILO).

Charfi, Mounir (1989). Les ministres de Bourguiba (1956–1987). Paris: L'Harmattan.

Charnysh, Volha, Christopher Lucas, and Prerna Singh (2015). 'The Ties that Bind: National Identity Salience and Pro-social Behavior toward the Ethnic Other'. In: Comparative Political Studies 48.3, pp. 267–300.

Charrad, Mounira M. (2001). States and Women's Rights: The Making of Postcolonial Tunisia, Algeria, and Morocco. Berkeley: University of California Press.

Charron, Nicholas and Victor Lapuente (2011). 'Which Dictators Produce Quality of Government?' In: Studies in Comparative International Development 46.4, pp. 397–423.

Chaudhry, Kiren Aziz (1993). 'The Myths of the Market and the Common History of Late Developers'. In: Politics and Society 21.3, pp. 245–74.

Chaudhry, Kiren Aziz (1997). The Price of Wealth: Economics and Institutions in the Middle East. Ithaca: Cornell University Press.

Checkel, Jeffrey (2006). 'Tracing Causal Mechanisms'. In: International Studies Review 8.2, pp. 362–70.

Cheibub, José, Jennifer Gandhi, and James Vreeland (2010). 'Democracy and Dictatorship Revisited'. In: Public Choice 143.1, pp. 67–101.

Chekir, Hamouda and Ishac Diwan (2013). 'Distressed Whales on the Nile: Egypt Capitalists in the Wake of the 2010 Revolution'. ERF Working Paper 747. Cairo: Economic Research Forum (ERF).

Chen, Bradley and Melani Cammett (2012). 'Informal Politics and Inequity of Access to Health Care in Lebanon'. In: International Journal for Equity in Health 11.1, pp. 1–8.

Chiffoleau, Sylvia (1990). 'Le desengagement de l'État et les transformations du système de santé'. In: Maghreb-Machrek 127, pp. 84–103.

Clark, Janine (2004a). Islam, Charity, and Activism: Middle-Class Networks and Social Welfare in Egypt, Jordan, and Yemen. Bloomington: Indiana University Press.

Clark, Janine (2004b). 'Social Movement Theory and Patron-Clientelism: Islamic Social Institutions and the Middle Class in Egypt, Jordan, and Yemen'. In: Comparative Political Studies 37.8, pp. 941–68.

Clément, Françoise (2007). 'Réformer l'assurance en Égypte pour résorber son déficit? Enquête sur un alibi'. In: Égypte monde arabe 4, pp. 303–41.

Cohen, Abner (1974). 'Introduction: The Lesson of Ethnicity'. In: Urban Ethnicity. London: Tavistock Publications, pp. 9–23.

Collier, P. and A. Hoeffler (2002). 'Military Expenditure: Threats, Aid, and Arms Races'. World Bank Policy Research Working Paper No. 2927. Washington, DC: The World Bank.

Connelly, Matthew James (2002). A Diplomatic Revolution: Algeria's Fight for Independence and the Origins of the Post-Cold War Era. Oxford: Oxford University Press.

Cook, Linda J. (2007). Postcommunist Welfare States: Reform Politics in Russia and Eastern Europe. Ithaca: Cornell University Press.

Cook, Steven (2007). Ruling But Not Governing: The Military and Political Development in Egypt, Algeria, and Turkey. Baltimore: Johns Hopkins University Press.

Cook, Steven (2012). The Struggle for Egypt: From Nasser to Tahrir Square. Oxford: Oxford University Press.

Cook, Terrence (2002). Nested Political Coalitions: Nation, Regime, Program, Cabinet. London: Praeger.

Coppedge, Michael et al. (2017). Varieties of Democracy (V-Dem) Dataset, v. 7.1.

Cordesman, Anthony H. (2004). The Military Balance in the Middle East: The Arab–Israeli Balance. Washington, DC: CSIS.

Corstange, Daniel (2016). *The Price of a Vote in the Middle East.* Cambridge: Cambridge University Press.

Cottrell, Alvin J. (1978). 'Iran's Armed Forces under the Pahlavi Dynasty'. In: *Iran under the Pahlavis.* Ed. by George Lenczowski. Stanford: Hoover Institution Press, pp. 389–429.

Craissati, Dina (1989). 'The Political Economy of Nasserism and Sadatism: The Nature of the State in Egypt and Its Impact on Economic Strategy'. MA thesis. McGill University, Montreal.

Crawford, David (2002). 'Morocco's Invisible Imazighen'. In: *The Journal of North African Studies* 7.1, pp. 53–70.

CRES (2013). *Analyse de l',Im,pact des Subventions Alimentaires et des Programmes d'Assistance Sociale sur la Population Pauvre et Vulnérable.* Tunis.

CRES (2016). *Protection sociale et économie informelle en Tunisie: Défis de la transition vers l'économie formelle.* Tech. rep. Tunis: Centre de Recherches et d'Etudes Sociales (CRES).

Crystal, Jill (1989). 'Coalitions in Oil Monarchies: Kuwait and Qatar'. In: *Comparative Politics* 21.4, pp. 427–43.

Cuesta, José, AbdelRahmen El-Lahga, and Gabriel Lara Ibarra (2015). 'The Socioeconomic Impacts of Energy Reform in Tunisia: A Simulation Approach'. In: *World Bank Policy Research Working Paper* 7312. June.

Damis, John (1985). 'The Western Sahara Dispute as a Source of Regional Conflict in North Africa'. In: *Contemporary North Africa: Issues of Development and Integration.* Ed. by Halim Isber Barakat. London: Croom Helm, pp. 138–53.

Dann, Uriel (1989). *King Hussein and the Challenge of Arab Radicalism.* Oxford: Oxford University Press.

Dann, Uriel (1994). 'The Hashemite Monarchy 1948–88: The Constant and the Changing—an Integration'. In: *Jordan in the Middle East 1948–88: The Making of a Pivotal State.* Ed. by Joseph Nevo and Ilan Pappé. Essex: Frank Cass, pp. 15–25.

Dawisha, Adeed (2003). *Arab Nationalism in the Twentieth Century: From Triumph to Dispair.* Princeton: Princeton University Press.

Day, Arthur R. (1986). *East Bank/West Bank: Jordan and the Prospects for Peace.* New York: Council on Foreign Relations.

De Boef, Suzanna and Luke Keele (2008). 'Taking Time Seriously'. In: *American Journal of Political Science* 52.1, pp. 184–200.

De Elvira, Laura Ruiz, and Tina Zintl (2014). 'The End of the Ba'thist Social Contract in Bashar Al-Asad's Syria: Reading Sociopolitical Transformations through Charities and Broader Benevolent Activism'. In: *International Journal of Middle East Studies* 46.2, pp. 329–49.

De Luca, Giacomo et al. (2018). 'Ethnic Favoritism: An Axiom of Politics?' In: *Journal of Development Economics* 132, pp. 115–29.

Deacon, Robert T. (2009). 'Public Good Provision under Dictatorship and Democracy'. In: *Public Choice* 139.1–2, pp. 241–62.

Debbasch, Charles and Michel Camau (1974). *La Tunisie.* Paris: Éditions Berger-Levrault.

Decaluwé, Bernard et al. (1990). 'Chocs pétroliers et politiques économiques nationales. Simulation à l'aide d'un modèle d'équilibre général pour la Tunisie'. In: *Revue économique* 41.6, pp. 1051–69.

Dekmejian, Hrair (1971). *Egypt under Nasir: A Study in Political Dyanmics.* London: University of London Press.

Denoeux, Guilain and Abdeslam Maghraoui (1998). 'The Political Economy of Structural Adjustment'. In: *Economic Crisis and Political Change in North Africa.* Ed. by Azzedine Layachi. London: Praeger, pp. 55–88.

Desai, Manali (2005). 'Indirect British Rule, State Formation, and Welfarism in Kerala, India, 1860-1957'. In: *Social Science History* 29.3, pp. 457-88.

Desai, Raj M., Tarik Yousef, and Olofsgård Anders (2007). 'The Logic of Authoritarian Bargains: A Test of a Structural Model'. Washington, DC: Global Economy and Development Working Paper 3 January.

Destremeau, Blandine (2009). 'La protection sociale en Tunisie. Nature et cohérence de l'intervention publique'. In: *L'Etat face aux débordements du social au Maghreb*. Ed. by Myriam Catusse, Blandine Destremeau, and Éric Verdier. Paris: Karthala, pp. 129-71.

Di John, Jonathan and James Putzel (2009). 'Political Settlements'. Issues Paper. Birmingham: Governance and Social Development Resource Centre (GSDRC).

Diwan, Ishac (2016). *Low Social and Political Returns to Education in the Arab World*. Giza: Economic Research Forum.

Diwan, Ishac and Tarik Akin (2015). 'Fifty Years of Fiscal Policy in the Arab Region'. Giza: Economic Research Forum.

Dodlova, Marina and Anna Giolbas (2015). 'Regime Type, Inequality, and Redistributive Transfers in Developing Countries'. GIGA Working Paper 273. Hamburg: German Institute of Global and Area Studies.

Doner, Richard F., Bryan K. Ritchie, and Dan Slater (2005). 'Systemic Vulnerability and the Origins of Developmental States: Northeast and Southeast Asia in Comparative Perspective'. In: *International Organization* 59.2, pp. 327-61.

Doostgharin, Taghi (2012). 'Social Welfare and the Islamic Revolution in Iran'. In: *The Cup, the Gun and the Crescent: Social Welfare and Civil Unrest in Muslim Societies*. Ed. by Sara Ashencaen Crabtree, Jonathan Parker, and Azlindar Azman. London: Whiting & Birch, pp. 48-61.

Dreher, Axel and Martin Gassebner (2012). 'Do IMF and World Bank Programs Induce Government Crises? An Empirical Analysis'. In: *International Organization* 66.2, pp. 329-58.

Droz-Vincent, Philippe (2011). 'Authoritarianism, Revolutions, Armies and Arab Regime Transitions'. In: *The International Spectator* 46.2, pp. 5-21.

Drysdale, Alasdair (1981a). 'The Regional Equalization of Health Care and Education in Syria Since the Ba'thi Revolution'. In: *International Journal of Middle East Studies* 13.1, pp. 93-111.

Drysdale, Alasdair (1981b). 'The Syrian Political Elite, 1966-1976: A Spatial and Social Analysis'. In: *Middle Eastern Studies* 17.1, pp. 3-30.

Drysdale, Alasdair (1982). 'The Syrian Armed Forces in National Politics: The Role of Geographic and Ethnic Periphery'. In: *Soldiers, Peasants, and Bureaucrats: Civil–Military Relations in Communist and Modernizing Societies*. Ed. by Roman Kolkowcz and Andrezj Korbon- ski. London: George Allen & Unwin, pp. 52-76.

Dunning, Thad (2008). *Crude Democracy: Natural Resource Wealth and Political Regimes*. Cambridge: Cambridge University Press.

Duwaji, Ghazi (1967). *Economic Developmen in Tunisia: The Impact and Course of Government Planning*. London: Praeger.

Easterly, William and Ross Levine (1997). 'Africa's Growth Tragedy: Policies and Ethnic Divisions'. In: *Quarterly Journal of Economics* 112.4, pp. 1203-50.

Ebbinghaus, Bernhard (2010). 'Unions and Employers'. In: *The Oxford Handbook of the Welfare State*. Ed. by Francis G. Castles et al. Oxford: Oxford University Press, pp. 196-210.

ECES (2010). 'The Subsidy System in Egypt: Alternatives for Reform'. Policy Viewpoint No. 25. Cairo: Egyptian Center for Economic Studies (ECES).

Egypt Independent (2012). *Judge Keeps Mubarak Secretary in Prison for Corruption Investigations*. 2 September. Cairo.

Egyptian National Archives (1953a). *Juz awal qawanin wa murasim wa makatabat bi-sh'an sunduq al-ta'min wa sunduq al-idkhar wa al-mu'ashat li-muwadhafi al-hukuma al-madaniin [First Part of Laws, Decrees, and Correspondences Regarding the Insurance Fund and the Savings and Pension]*. Archival Document No. 0081-097940. Cairo.

Egyptian National Archives (1953b). *Session of the Council of Ministers, 14 October 1953*. Archival Document No. 0075–057910. Cairo.

Egyptian National Archives (1955a). *Insurance and Savings for Workers*. Archival Document No. 0081–053914. Cairo.

Egyptian National Archives (1955b). *Sessions of the Council of Ministers, January–February 1955*. Archival Document No. 0075–057919. Cairo.

Egyptian National Archives (1958). *Minutes of the Ministerial Committee for Services, October 1958*. Archival Document No. 0081–094526. Cairo.

Egyptian National Archives (1959a). *Session of the Council of Ministers, 15 July 1959*. Archival Document No. 0081–146705. Cairo.

Egyptian National Archives (1959b). *Session of the Council of Ministers, 19 December 1959*. Archival Document No. 0081–147213. Cairo.

Eibl, Ferdinand (2017). 'The Political Economy of Energy Subsidies in North Africa: The Untold Story'. OIES Paper. Oxford: Oxford Institute for Energy Studies.

Eibl, Ferdinand and Steffen Hertog (2018). 'When Do Oil Dictators Share the Wealth? Evidence from the Gulf Monarchies'. Unpublished manuscript.

Eibl, Ferdinand and Adeel Malik (2015). 'Behind the Barrier: Politically Connected Actors and Trade Protection in Pre-revolutionary Egypt and Tunisia'. Unpublished manuscript.

Eibl, Ferdinand and Adeel Malik (2016). 'The Politics of Partial Liberalization: Cronyism and Non-tariff Protection in Mubarak's Egypt'. CSAE Working Paper WPS/2016-27. Oxford. Centre for the Study of African Economies.

Eilers, Wilhelm (1978). 'Educational and Cultural Development in Iran during the Pah- lavi Era'. In: *Iran under the Pahlavis*. Ed. by George Lenczowski. Stanford: Hoover Institution Press, pp. 303–31.

Ejdemyr, Simon, Eric Kramon, and Amanda Lea Robinson (2018). 'Segregation, Ethnic Favoritism, and the Strategic Targeting of Local Public Goods'. In: *Comparative Political Studies* 51.9, pp. 1111–43.

El Mekkaoui, Najat (2019). *Ageing and Pensions Coverage in Arab Countries*. URL: https://theforum.erf.org.eg/2018/01/09/ageing-pensions-coverage-arab-countries/ (visited on 15/05/2019).

El Sadat, Anwar (1957). *Révolte sur le nil*. Paris: Pierre Amiot.

Elling, Rasmus (2013). *Minorities in Iran: Nationalism and Ethnicity after Khomeini*. New York: Palgrave Macmillan.

Entessar, Nader (1984). 'The Kurds in Post-revolutionary Iran and Iraq'. In: *Third World Quarterly* 6.4, pp. 911–33.

Eqbal, Ahmad (1967). 'Politics and Labor in Tunisia'. PhD thesis. Princeton University.

Erdle, Steffen (2010). *Ben Ali's 'New Tunisia' (1987–2009): A Case Study of Authoritarian Modernization in the Arab World*. Berlin: Klaus Schwarz Verlag.

Erdmann, Gero and Ulf Engel (2007). 'Neopatrimonialism Reconsidered: Critical Review and Elaboration of an Elusive Concept'. In: *Commonwealth and Comparative Politics* 45, pp. 95–119.

Ertman, Thomas (1997). *Birth of Leviathan: Building States and Regimes in Medieval and Early Modern Europe*. Cambridge: Cambridge University Press.

Escribà-Folch, A. (2008). 'Do Authoritarian Institutions Mobilize Economic Cooperation?' In: *Constitutional Political Economy* 20, pp. 71–93.

Escribà-Folch, A. (2013). 'Repression, Political Threats, and Survival under Autocracy'. In: *International Political Science Review* 34.5, pp. 543–60.

Esping-Andersen, Gøsta (1990). *The Three Worlds of Welfare Capitalism*. Cambridge: Polity.

Essam El-Din, Gamal (2002). *Political Economy of the Revolution*. Al-Ahram Weekly. URL: http://www.mafhoum.com/press3/nas105-3.htm (visited on 09/06/2015).

Faksh, Mahmud A. (1973). 'An Historical Survey of the Educational System in Egypt'. In: *Review of Education* 22.2, pp. 234–44.

Falleti, Tulia G. (2011). 'Varieties of Authoritarianism: The Organization of the Military State and Its Effects on Federalism in Argentina and Brazil'. In: *Studies in Comparative International Development* 46, pp. 1–26.

Fatima-Zohra, Oufriha (1990). 'Médecine gratuite—Forte augmentation des dépenses de soins et crise de l'Etat socialo-providence en Algérie'. In: *Cahiers du CREAD* 22, pp. 21–59.

Fattouh, Bassam and Laura El-Katiri (2012). 'Energy Subsidies in the Arab World'. Arab Human Development Report, Research Paper Series. New York: United Nations Development Programme (UNDP).

Fearon, James D. and David D. Laitin (1996). 'Explaining Interethnic Cooperation'. In: *American Political Science Review* 90.4, pp. 715–35.

Fearon, James D. and David D. Laitin (2000). 'Violence and the Social Construction of Ethnic Identity'. In: *International Organization* 54.4, pp. 845–77.

Femmes (2007). *Les spécialistes disent "non" à la CNAM! Les raisons de la colère.*

Fernandez, Juan J. (2012). 'Economic Crises, Population Aging and the Electoral Cycle: Explaining Pension Policy Retrenchments in 19 OECD Countries, 1981–2004'. In: *International Journal of Comparative Sociology* 53.2, pp. 77–96.

Fintz, Matthieu (2006). 'A Reform for the Poor Without Them? The Fate of the Egyptian Health Reform Programme in 2005'. In: *L'Égypte dans l'année 2005*. Ed. by Florian Kohstall. Cairo: CEDEJ.

Al-Fiqi, Hassan (1966). *Al-Tarikh al-thaqafi lil-ta'alim [The Cultural History of Education]*. Cairo: Dar al-Nahda al-Arabiyya.

Flora, Peter and Jens Alber (1981). 'Modernization, Democratization, and the Development of Welfare States in Western Europe'. In: *The Development of Welfare States in Europe and America*. Ed. by Peter Flora and Arnold J. Heidenheimer. Brunswick: Transaction Publishers, pp. 37–80.

Francos, Ania and Jean-Pierre Séréni (1976). *Un Algérien nommé Boumediène*. Paris: Stock.

Frazier, Mark (2006). 'One Country, Three Systems: The Politics of Welfare Policy in China's Authoritarian Developmental State'. Conference Paper. Indiana University.

Frazier, Mark (2010). *Socialist Insecurity: Pensions and the Politics of Uneven Development in China*. Ithaca: Cornell University Press.

Gal, John and Rana Jawad (2013). 'The Middle East'. In: *The Routledge Handbook of the Welfare State*. Ed. by Bent Greve. London: Routledge, pp. 242–51.

Galal, Ahmed and Taher Kanaan (2010). *Financing Higher Education in Arab Countries*. Giza: Economic Research Forum

Gandhi, Jennifer (2008). *Political Institutions under Dictatorship*. Cambridge: Cambridge University Press.

Gandhi, Jennifer and Adam Przeworski (2006). 'Cooperation, Cooptation, and Rebellion under Dictatorships'. In: *Economics and Politics* 18.1, pp. 1–26.

Gao, Eleanor (2016). 'Tribal Mobilization, Fragmented Groups, and Public Goods Provision in Jordan'. In: *Comparative Political Studies* 49.10, pp. 1372–403.

Garas, Félix (1956). *Bourguiba et la naissance d'une nation*. Paris: René Julliard.

Garrett, Geoffrey (2001). 'Globalization and Government Spending around the World'. In: *Studies in Comparative International Development* 35.4, pp. 3–29.

Gasiorowski, Mark J. (2004). 'The 1953 Coup d'État against Mosaddeq'. In: *Mohammad Mosaddeq and the 1953 Coup in Iran*. Ed. by Mark J. Gasiorowski and Malcolm Byrne. Syracuse: Syracuse University Press, pp. 227–60.

Gatti, Roberta et al. (2014). *Striving for Better Jobs*. Washington, DC: The World Bank.

Geddes, Barbara (1999a). 'Authoritarian Breakdown: Empirical Test of a Game Theoretic Argument'. Conference Paper. APSA Annual Meeting.

Geddes, Barbara (1999b). 'What Do We Know about Democratization after Twenty Years?' In: *Annual Review of Political Science* 2, pp. 115–44.

Geddes, Barbara (2003). *Paradigms and Sand Castles: Theory Building and Research Design in Comparative Politics*. Ann Arbor: University of Michigan.

Geddes, Barbara (2004). 'Minimum-Winning Coalitions and Personalization in Authoritarian Regimes'. Conference Paper. APSA Annual Meeting.

Geddes, Barbara, Joseph Wright, and Erica Frantz (2018). *How Dicatorships Work: Power, Personalization, and Collapse*. Cambridge: Cambridge University Press.

Genschel, Philipp and Laura Seelkopf (2016). 'Did They Learn to Tax? Taxation Trends outside the OECD'. In: *Review of International Political Economy* 23.2, pp. 316–44.

George, Alexander L. and Andrew Bennett (2005). *Case Studies and Theory Development in the Social Sciences*. Cambridge, Mass.: MIT Press.

German Trade Invest (2011). 'The Presence of the Ben Ali/Trabelsi Family in the Tunisian Economy'. Internal Report. Tunis.

German–Tunisian Chamber of Commerce (2011). 'Ben Ali and the 40 Thieves'. Internal Report. Tunis.

Gerring, John (2001). *Social Science Methodology: A Criterial Framework*. Cambridge: Cambridge University Press.

Gerring, John (2007). *Case Study Research: Principles and Practices*. Cambridge: Cambridge University Press.

Gerring, John (2011). 'How Good Is Good Enough? A Multidimensional, Best-Possible Standard for Research Design'. In: *Political Research Quarterly* 64.3, pp. 625–36.

Gerring, John, Strom C. Thacker, and Rodrigo Alfaro (2012). 'Democracy and Human Development'. In: *The Journal of Politics* 74.1, pp. 1–17.

Gerschewski, Johannes (2013). 'The Three Pillars of Stability: Legitimation, Repression, and Co-optation in Autocratic Regimes'. In: *Democratization* 20.1, pp. 13–38.

Ghoneim, Ahmed Farouk (2012). 'The Political Economy of Food Price Policy in Egypt'. Working Paper No. 2012/96. Helsinki. UNU-WIDER.

Gibler, Douglas M. (2010). 'Outside-in: The Effects of External Threat on State Centralization'. In: *Journal of Conflict Resolution* 54.4, pp. 519–42.

Gibson, Clark and Barak D. Hoffman (2013). 'Coalitions not Conflicts: Ethnicity, Political Institutions, and Expenditure in Africa'. In: *Comparative Politics* 45.3, pp. 273–90.

Giuliano, Paola, Prachi Mishra, and Antonio Spilimbergo (2010). 'Democracy and Reforms: Evidence from a New Dataset'. IMF Working Paper WP/10/173. Washington, DC: International Monetary Fund.

Gleditsch, Nils Petter et al. (2002). 'Armed Conflict 1946–2001: A New Dataset'. English. In: *Journal of Peace Research* 39.5, pp. 615–37.

Gobe, Éric (2008). 'Les syndicalismes arabes au prisme de l'autoritarisme et du corporatisme'. In: *Autoritarismes démocratiques et démocraties autoritaires au XXIe siècle. Convergences Nord/Sud.* Ed. by Olivier Dabène, Vincent Geisser, and Gilles Massardier. Paris: La Découverte, pp. 267–84.

Goemans, Henk E. (2008). 'Which Way Out? The Manner and Consequences of Losing Office'. In: *Journal of Conflict Resolution* 52.6, pp. 771–94.

Goemans, Henk E., Kristian Skrede Gleditsch, and Giacomo Chiozza (2009). 'Introducing Archigos: A Dataset of Political Leaders'. In: *Journal of Peace Research* 46.2, pp. 183–269.

Goertz, Gary and James Mahoney (2004). 'The Possibility Principle: Choosing Negative Cases in Comparative Research'. In: *American Political Science Review* 98.4, pp. 653–69.

Gongora, Thierry (1997). 'War Making and State Power in the Contemporary Middle East'. In: *International Journal of Middle East Studies* 29, pp. 323–40.

Gordon, Joel (1992). *Nasser's Blessed Movement: Egypt's Free Officers and the July Revolution.* Oxford: Oxford University Press.

Gough, Ian (2014). 'Mapping Social Welfare Regimes beyond the OECD'. In: *The Politics of Non-state Social Welfare.* Ed. by Melani Cammett and Lauren M. MacLean. Ithaca: Cornell University Press, pp. 17–30.

Gough, Ian et al. (2004). *Insecurity and Welfare Regimes in Asia, Africa and Latin America: Social Policy in Development Contexts.* Cambridge: Cambridge University Press.

Granai, George and Françoise Fanton (1965). 'Chronique sociale et culturelle Tunisie'. In: *Annuaire de l'Afrique du Nord.* Ed. by Maurice Flory and Jean-Louis Miège. Paris: Éditions du CNRS, pp. 220–30.

Grangaud, Marie-France (1984). 'Rôle de la sécurité sociale en Algérie'. In: *Cahiers du CREAD* 2, pp. 29–55.

Greene, Kenneth F. (2009). 'The Political Economy of Authoritarian Single-Party Dominance'. In: *Comparative Political Studies* 43.7, pp. 807–34.

Greif, Avner (1994). 'Cultural Beliefs and the Organization of Society: A Historical and Theoretical Reflection on Collectivist and Individualist Societies'. In: 102.5, pp. 912–50.

Grier, Robin M. (1999). 'Colonial Legacies and Economic Growth'. In: *Public Choice* 98.3, pp. 317–35.

Griffin, Larry J., Joel A. Devine and Michael Wallace (1982). 'Monopoly Capital , Organized Labor , and Military Expenditures in the United States, 1949–1976'. In: *American Journal of Sociology* 88. Supplement, pp. 113–53.

Griffith, William E. (1978). 'Iran's Foreign Policy in the Pahlavi Era'. In: *Iran under the Pahlavis.* Ed. by George Lenczowski. Stanford: Hoover Institution Press, pp. 365–88.

Guelmami, Abdelmajid (1996). 'Formation et dynamique de la politique sociale et du système de sécurité sociale en longue durée en Tunisie (1891–1991)'. PhD thesis. Université Lille 3.

Guen, Moncef (1961). *La Tunisie indépendante face à son économie. Enseignements d'une expérience de développement.* Paris: Presses Universitaires de France.

Guiga, Driss (2013). *Témoignages de M. Driss Guiga. Mon parcours dans la construction de l'Etat national à travers les Ministères de l'Education et de l'Intérieur entre (1954–1984).* Tunis: Fondation Temimi pour la recherche scientifique et l'information.

Gupta, Sanjeev et al. (2004). 'Fiscal Consequences of Armed Conflict and Terrorism in Low- and Middle-Income Countries'. In: *European Journal of Political Economy* 20.2, pp. 403–21.

Haber, Stephen (2006). 'Authoritarian Government'. In: *The Oxford Handbook of Political Economy.* Ed. by Barry Weingast and Donald Wittman. Oxford: Oxford University Press, pp. 693–707.

Haber, Stephen and Victor Menaldo (2011). 'Do Natural Resources Fuel Authoritarianism? A Reappraisal of the Resource Curse'. In: *American Political Science Review* 105.1, pp. 1–26.

Habibi, Nader (1994). 'Budgetary Policy and Political Liberty: A Cross-Sectional Analysis'. In: *World Development* 22.4, pp. 579–86.

Habyarimana, James et al. (2007). 'Why Does Ethnic Diversity Undermine Public Goods Provision?' In: *American Political Science Review* 101.4, pp. 709–25.

Haddad, Salem (2011). *Al-Ittihad al-'am al-tunisi lil-shughl wa nitham bourqiba bin al-wa'am wa al-sadam [The Tunisian Trade Union Federation and the System Bourguiba between Harmony and Conflict: The Tunisian Labour Movement from Independence until the 1990s]*. Tunis: Artibo.

Haggard, Stephan and Robert R. Kaufman (2008). *Development, Democracy, and Welfare States: Latin America, East Asia, and Eastern Europe*. Princeton: Princeton University Press.

Haile, Fiseha and Miguel Niño-Zarazúa (2017). 'Does Social Spending Improve Welfare in Low-Income and Middle-Income Countries?' In: *Journal of International Development* 398, pp. 367–98.

Hajzler, Christopher (2011). 'Expropriation of Foreign Direct Investments: Sectoral Patterns from 1993 to 2006'. In: *Review of World Economics* 148.1, pp. 119–49.

Hale, Henry E. (2004). 'Explaining Ethnicity'. In: *Comparative Political Studies* 37.4, pp. 458–85.

Hall, Peter (2010). 'Historical Institutionalism in Rationalist and Sociological Perspective'. In: *Explaining Institutional Change: Ambiguity, Agency, and Power*. Ed. by James Mahoney and Kathleen Thelen. Cambridge: Cambridge University Press, pp. 204–23.

Hall, Peter (2013). 'Tracing the Progress of Process Tracing'. In: *European Political Science* 12.1, pp. 20–30.

Hall, Peter and David W. Soskice, eds. (2001). *Varieties of Capitalism: The Institutional Foundations of Comparative Advantage*. Oxford: Oxford University Press.

Hall, Peter and Rosemary C. R. Taylor (1996). 'Political Science and the Three Institutionalisms'. In: *Political Studies* 44.5, pp. 936–57.

Halliday, Fred (1979). *Iran: Dictatorship and Development*. Harmondsworth: Penguin Books.

Halliday, Fred (2005). *The Middle East in International Relations: Power, Politics and Ideology*. 4. Cambridge: Cambridge University Press.

Hamrush, Ahmad (1983). *Qissat Thawrat 23 Yuliyu [The Story of the 23 July Revolution]*. Cairo: Maktabat Madbouli.

Handlin, Samuel (2016). 'Mass Organization and the Durability of Competitive Authoritarian Regimes: Evidence from Venezuela'. In: *Comparative Political Studies* 49.9, pp. 1238–69.

Handoussa, Heba and Nivine El Oraby (2004). 'Civil Service Wages and Reform: The Case of Egypt'. Working Paper No. 98. Cairo: Egyptian Center for Economic Studies (ECES).

Hanieh, Adam (2013). *Lineages of Revolt: Issues of Contemporary Capitalism in the Middle East*. Chicago: Haymarket Books.

Hankla, Charles R. and Daniel Kuthy (2013). 'Economic Liberalism in Illiberal Regimes: Authoritarian Variation and the Political Economy of Trade'. In: *International Studies Quarterly* 57, pp. 492–504.

Hanson, Jonathan K. and Mary Gallagher (2009). 'Coalitions, Carrots, and Sticks: Economic Inequality and Authoritarian States'. In: *PS: Political Science and Politics*, pp. 667–72.

Harding, Robin (2015). 'Attribution and Accountability: Voting for Roads in Ghana'. In: *World Politics* 67.4, pp. 656–89.

Harik, Iliya (1997). *Economic Policy Reform in Egypt*. Gainesville: University of Florida Press.

Harris, Joseph (2017). *Achieving Access: Professional Movements and the Politics of Health Universalism*. Ithaca: Cornell University Press.

Harris, Kevan (2010a). 'Lineages of the Iranian Welfare State: Dual Institutionalism and Social Policy in the Islamic Republic of Iran'. In: *Social Policy and Administration* 44.6, pp. 727–45.

Harris, Kevan (2010b). *The Politics of Subsidy Reform in Iran*. Middle East Report. URL: http://www.merip.org/mer/mer254/politics-subsidy-reform-iran (visited on 08/07/2015).

Harris, Kevan (2012). 'The Politics of Welfare after Revolution and War: The Imam Khomeini Relief Committee in the Islamic Republic of Iran'. In: *The Cup, the Gun and the Crescent: Social Welfare and Civil Unrest in Muslim Societies*. Ed. by Sara Ashencaen Crabtree, Jonathan Parker, and Linda Azman. London: Whiting & Birch, pp. 134–50.

Harris, Kevan (2013). 'A Martyr's Welfare State and Its Contradictions'. In: *Middle East Authorit- arianisms: Governance, Contestation, and Regime Resilience in Syria and Iran*. Ed. by Steven Heydemann and Reinoud Leenders. Stanford: Stanford University Press, pp. 61–81.

Harris, Kevan (2017). *A Social Revolution: Politics and the Welfare State in Iran*. Berkeley: University of California Press.

Hashemi, Nader and Danny Postel, eds. (2017). *Sectarianization: Mapping the New Politics of the Middle East*. Oxford: Oxford University Press.

Hashemite Kingdom of Jordan (various years). *Statistical Yearbook*. Jerusalem: Public Statistics Department.

Hazaimeh, Hani (2012). *Social Security Coverage Expanded 140% in 2000s*. 30 April. The Jordan Times.

Hazran, Yusri (2017). 'The Origins of Sectarianism in Egypt and the Fertile Crescent: The Origins of Sectarianism in Egypt and the Fertile Crescent'. In: *British Journal of Middle Eastern Studies*. Early view.

Hedström, Peter and Petri Ylikoski (2010). 'Causal Mechanisms in the Social Sciences'. In: *Annual Review of Sociology* 36.1, pp. 49–67.

Heggoy, Alf Andrew (1970). 'Colonial Origins of the Algerian–Moroccan Border Conflict of October 1963'. In: *African Studies Review* 13.1, pp. 17–22.

Heilbrunn, John (2014). *Oil, Democracy, and Development in Africa*. Cambridge: Cambridge University Press.

Helmy, Amina (2004). 'Tatwir nitham al-ma'ashat fi misr [Pension System Development in Egypt]'. Working Paper No. 94. Cairo: Egyptian Center for Economic Studies (ECES).

Herb, Michael (1999). *All in the Family: Absolutism, Revolution, and Democracy in the Middle Eastern Monarchies*. Albany: State University of New York Press.

Herb, Michael (2005). 'No Representation without Taxation? Rents, Development, and Democracy'. In: *Comparative Politics* 37.3, pp. 297–316.

Herb, Michael (2009). 'A Nation of Bureaucrats: Political Participation and Economic Diversification in Kuwait and the United Arab Emirates'. In: *International Journal of Middle East Studies* 41.3, pp. 375–95.

Herb, Michael (2014). *The Wages of Oil: Parliaments and Economic Development in Kuwait and the UAE*. Ithaca: Cornell University Press.

Herb, Michael (2017). 'Ontology and Methodology in the Study of the Resource Curse'. LSE Kuwait Programme Paper Series 43. London: LSE Middle East Centre.

Herbst, Jeffrey Ira (2000). *States and Power in Africa: Comparative Lessons in Authority and Control*. Princeton: Princeton University Press.

Hermassi, Elbaki (1972). *Leadership and National Development in North Africa: A Comparative Study*. Berkeley: University of California Press.

Hermessi, Mohamed Saleh (1990). *Tunis ... al-haraka al-'umaliyya fi nitham al-tabi'iyya wa al-hisb al-wahid (1956–1986) [Tunisia ... the Labour Movement in a System of Subordination and One Party Rule (1956–1986)]*. Beirut: Dar Al-Farabi.

Hertog, Steffen (2010). *Princes, Brokers, and Bureaucrats: Oil and the State in Saudi Arabia*. London: Cornell University Press.

Hertog, Steffen (2016). 'Is There an Arab Variety of Capitalism?' Giza: Economic Research Forum.

Hess, Peter and Brendan Mullan (1988). 'The Military Burden and Public Education Expenditures in Contemporary Developing Nations: Is There a Trade-Off?' In: *The Journal of Developing Areas* 22.4, pp. 497–514.

Heston, Alan, Robert Summers, and Bettina Aten (2006). *Penn World Table Version 6.2*. URL: http://pwt.econ.upenn.edu/php%5C_site/pwt62/pwt62%5C_form.php (visited on 09/08/2012).

Heydemann, Steven (1999). *Authoritarianism in Syria: Institutions and Social Conflict, 1946–1970*. Ithaca: Cornell University Press.

Heydemann, Steven (2000a). 'War, Institutions, and Social Change in the Middle East'. In: *War, Institutions, and Social Change in the Middle East*. Ed. by Steven Heydemann. Berkeley: University of California Press, pp. 1–30.

Heydemann, Steven ed. (2000b). *War, Institutions, and Social Change in the Middle East*. Berkeley: University of California Press.

Hibou, Béatrice (2006). *La force de l'obéissance: économie politique de la répression en Tunisie*. Paris: Découverte.

Hicks, Alexander (1999). *Social Democracy and Welfare Capitalism: A Century of Income Security Politics*. Ithaca: Cornell University Press.

Hicks, Alexander and Joya Misra (1993). 'Political Resources and the Growth of Welfare in Affluent Capitalist Democracies, 1960–1982'. In: *The American Journal of Sociology* 99.3, pp. 668–710.

Hicks, Alexander, Joya Misra, and Tang Nah Ng (1995). 'The Programmatic Emergence of the Social Security State'. In: *American Sociological Review* 60.3, pp. 329–49.

Hicks, Alexander and C. Zorn (2005). 'Economic Globalization, the Macro Economy, and Reversals of Welfare Expansion in Affluent Democracies, 1978–94'. In: *International Organization* 59, pp. 631–62.

Higgins, Patricia J. (1984). 'Minority–State Relations in Contemporary Iran'. In: *Iranian Studies* 17.1, pp. 37–71.

Hinnebusch, Raymond (1982). 'Syria under the Ba'th: State Formation in a Fragmented Society'. In: *Arab Studies Quarterly* 4.3, pp. 177–99.

Hinnebusch, Raymond (1985). *Egyptian Politics under Sadat: The Post-populist Development of an Authoritarian-Modernizing State*. Cambridge: Cambridge University Press.

Hinnebusch, Raymond (1986). 'Syria under the Ba'th: Social Ideology, Policy, and Practice'. In: *Social Legislation in the Contemporary Middle East*. Ed. by Laurence O. Michalak and Jeswald W. Salacuse. Berkeley: Institute of International Studies, pp. 61–109.

Hinnebusch, Raymond (1990). *Authoritarian Power and State Formation in Ba'thist Syria: Army, Party, and Peasant*. Boulder: Westview.

Hinnebusch, Raymond (2002). *Syria: Revolution from Above*. London: Routledge.

Hinnebusch, Raymond (2006). 'Authoritarian Persistence, Democratization Theory and the Middle East: An Overview and Critique'. In: *Democratization* 13.3, pp. 373–95.

Hinnebusch, Raymond (2010). 'Toward a Historical Sociology of State Formation in the Middle East'. In: *Middle East Critique* 19.3, pp. 201–16.

Hinnebusch, Raymond (2015). 'Syria's Alawis and the Ba'th Party'. In: *The Alawis of Syria: War, Faith, and Politics in the Levant*. Ed. by Michael Kerr and Craig Larkin. Kindle edition. New York: Oxford University Press, pp. 107–24.

Hinnebusch, Raymond and Anoushiravan Ehteshami, eds. (2002). *The Foreign Policies of Middle East States*. Boulder: Lynne Rienner Publishers.

Hinnebusch, Raymond and Spren Schmidt (2009). *The State and the Political Economy of Reform in Syria*. Boulder: Lynne Rienner Publishers.

Hodler, Roland and Paul A. Raschky (2014). 'Regional Favoritism'. In: *Quarterly Journal of Economics* 129.2, pp. 995–1033.

Holland, Alisha C. (2015). 'The Distributive Politics of Enforcement'. In: *American Journal of Political Science* 59.2, pp. 357–71.

Hong, Ji Yeon and Sunkyoung Park (2016). 'Factories for Votes? How Authoritarian Leaders Gain Popular Support Using Targeted Industrial Policy'. In: *British Journal of Political Science* 46.3, pp. 501–27.

Hooker, Mark A. and Michael M. Knetter (2001). 'Measuring the Economic Effects of Military Base Closures'. In: *Economic Inquiry* 39.4, pp. 583–98.

Hopwood, Derek (1988). *Syria 1945–86: Politics and Society*. London: Unwin Hyman.

Hopwood, Derek (1992). *Habib Bourguiba of Tunisia: The Tragedy of Longevity*. London: Macmillan.

Hopwood, Derek (1993). *Egypt: Politics and Society 1945–1990*. London: Routledge.

Hourcade, Bernard (1988). 'Ethnie, nation et citadinité en Iran'. In: *Le fait ethnique en Iran et en Afghanistan*. Ed. by Jean-Pierre Digard. Paris: Éditions CNRS, pp. 161–74.

Huber, Evelyne, Charles C. Ragin, and John D. Stephens (1993). 'Social Democracy, Christian Democracy, Constitutional Structure, and the Welfare State'. In: *American Journal of Sociology* 99.3, pp. 711–49.

Huber, Evelyne and John D. Stephens (2001). *Development and Crisis of the Welfare State: Parties and Policies in Global Markets*. Chicago: University of Chicago Press.

Huffpost (2019). *8,5 millions de Marocains disposent de la carte RAMED, selon le ministre de la Santé*. 14 January. Huffpost Maghreb. URL: https://www.huffpostmaghreb.com/entry/85-millions-de-marocains-disposent-de-la-carte-ramed-selon-anass-doukkali_mg_5c3cb0ede4b01c93e00c12f6?utm_hp_ref=mg-politique-maroc (visited on 21/05/2019).

Huneeus, Carlos and Lake Sagaris (2007). *The Pinochet Regime*. Boulder: Lynne Rienner Publishers.

Ibrahim, Saad Eddin (1996). *The Copts of Egypt*. London: Minority Rights Group.

Ibrahim, Saad Eddin (1998). 'Ethnic Conflict and State-Building in the Arab World'. In: *International Social Science Journal* 50.156, pp. 229–42.

Ibrahim, Vivian (2011). *The Copts of Egypt: Challenges of Modernisation and Identity*. London: I. B. Tauris.

IDSC (2005). *Bada'il tatwir nitham al-da'am al-ghitha'i fi Misr [Alternatives of Reforming the Food Subsidy System in Egypt]*. Cairo.

IDSC (2006). *Islah nitham al-ma'ashat fi Misr [Reforming the Pension System in Egypt]*. Cairo.

IDSC (2010). *Al-khubz al-muda'am fi Misr…haqa'iq wa arqam [Subsidized Bread in Egypt…Facts and Figures]*. Cairo.

IHS (2010). *Egyptian Government Considers Various Strategies in Health Insurance Over-haul, Faces Criticism from Advocacy Organisation*. IHS Inc. URL: https://www.ihs.com/country-industry-forecasting.html?ID=106594350 (visited on 14/06/2015).

Ikenberry, G. John (1994). 'History's Heavy Hand: Institutions and the Politics of the State'. University of Maryland. Conference on New Perspectives on Institutions.

IMF (1954). *SM-54-1, Egypt*. Staff Memorandum. Washington, DC.

IMF (1956). *SM-56-63, Egypt*. Staff Memorandum. Washington, DC.

IMF (1959). *SM-59-76, Tunisia*. Staff Memorandum. Washington, DC.

IMF (1962a). *IMF-62-25, Egypt*. Staff Memorandum. Washington, DC.

IMF (1962b). *SM-62-48, Tunisia*. Staff Memorandum. Washington, DC.

IMF (1966). *IMF-66-29, Egypt*. Staff Memorandum. Washington, DC.

IMF (1967). *IMF-67-64 Supplement 2, Egypt*. Staff Memorandum. Washington, DC.

IMF (1969). *IMF-69-47, Egypt*. Staff Memorandum. Washington, DC.

IMF (1970). *IMF-70-23, Egypt*. Staff Memorandum. Washington, DC.

IMF (1972). *SM-72-251, Tunisia*. Staff Memorandum. Washington, DC.

IMF (1973). *IMF-73-101, Egypt*. Staff Memorandum. Washington, DC.

IMF (1974). *IMF-74-182, Egypt*. Staff Memorandum. Washington, DC.

IMF (1975). *IMF-75-193, Egypt*. Staff Memorandum. Washington, DC.

IMF (1976). *IMF-76-183, Egypt*. Staff Memorandum. Washington, DC.

IMF (1978). *EBS-78-358, Egypt*. Executive Board Specials. Washington, DC.

IMF (1980). *SM-80-41, Egypt*. Staff Memorandum. Washington, DC.

IMF (1982). *SM-82-74, Egypt*. Staff Memorandum. Washington, DC.

IMF (1987a). *EBS-87-200, Tunisia*. Executive Board Specials. Washington, DC.

IMF (1987b). *EBS-87-93, Egypt*. Executive Board Specials. Washington, DC.

IMF (1988). *SM-88-98, Egypt*. Staff Memorandum. Washington, DC.

IMF (1989). *SM-89-242, Egypt*. Staff Memorandum. Washington, DC.

IMF (1995). *SM/95/218, Jordan—Background Information on Selected Aspects of Adjustment and Growth Strategy*. Staff Memorandum. Washington, DC.

IMF (1997). *SM 97-117, Tunisia*. Staff Memoramdum. Washington, DC.

IMF (1998). *SM/98/84 Jordan—Selected Issues*. Staff Memorandum. Washington, DC.

IMF (2000). *SM/00/157 Jordan—Recent Economic Developments*. Staff Memorandum. Washington, DC.

IMF (2001). *Jordan: Third Review Under the Stand-By Arrangement; and Press Release on the Executive Board Discussion*. 04/287. Washington, DC.

IMF (2004a). *Jordan: 2004 Article IV Consultation and Second Review under the StandBy Arrangement—Staff Report; Staff Statement; Public Information Notice and Press Release on the Executive Board Discussion; and Statement by the Executive Director for Jordan*. 04/122. Washington, DC.

IMF (2004b). *SM/04/96 Jordan—Selected Issues and Statistical Appendix*. Staff Memorandum. Washington, DC.

IMF (2011). *Government Finantical Statistics*. URL: http://www.elibrary.imf.org/ (visited on 11/06/2015).

IMF (2014). *Subsidy Reform in the Middle East and North Africa*. Washington, DC: International Monetary Fund.

IMF (2015). *International Financial Statistics (IFS)*. URL: http://www.elibrary.imf.org/ (visited on 11/06/2015).

Immergut, Ellen (2010). 'Political Institutions'. In: *The Oxford Handbook of the Welfare State*. Ed. by Francis G. Castles et al. Oxford: Oxford University Press, pp. 227–40.

IRIN (2014). *Living without the state in Cairo's slums*. IRIN Humanitarian News and Analysis. URL: http://www.irinnews.org/report/99518/living-without-the-state-in-cairo-s-slums (visited on 07/09/2015).

Al-Ishtiraki (2007). *No Title*. 1 May. Cairo.

Islam, Muhammad Q. (2000). 'Fiscal Policy and Social Welfare in Selected MENA Countries'. In: *Earnings Inequality, Unemployment, and Poverty in the Middle East and North Africa*. Ed. by Wassim N. Shahin and Ghassan Dibeh. London: Greenwood Press, pp. 95–110.

Islam, Muhammad N. (2015). 'Economic Growth, Repression, and State Expenditure in Non-democratic Regimes'. In: *European Journal of Political Economy* 37, pp. 68–85.

Ismaili, Ghita (2019). *Ramed: Un "échec" selon le Réseau de défense du droit à la santé*. 3 March. Tel Quel. URL: https://telquel.ma/2019/01/03/ramed-un-echec-selon-le-reseau-de-defense-du-droit-a-la-sante%7B%5C_%/7D1624285 (visited on 21/05/2019).

Issawi, Charles Philip (1963). *Egypt in Revolution: An Economic Analysis*. Oxford: Oxford University Press.

Issawi, Charles Philip (1978). 'The Iranian Economcy 1925–1975: Fifty Years of Economic Development'. In: *Iran under the Pahlavis*. Ed. by George Lenczowski. Stanford: Hoover Institution Press, pp. 129–66.

El-Issawy, Ibrahim H. (1984). *Employment Opportunities and Equity in Egypt: Labour Force, Employment and Unemployment*. Geneva: International Labour Office (ILO).

Iversen, Torben (2005). *Capitalism, Democracy, and Welfare*. Cambridge: Cambridge University Press.

Janoski, Thomas (1991). 'Synthetic Strategies in Comparative Sociological Research: Methods and Problems of Internal and External Analysis'. In: *Issues and Alternatives in Comparative Social Research*. Ed. by Charles C. Ragin. Leiden: Brill, pp. 59–81.

Jawad, Rana and Burcu Yakut-Cakar (2010). 'Religion and Social Policy in the Middle East: The (Re)Constitution of an Old–New Partnership'. In: *Social Policy and Administration* 44.6, pp. 658–72.

Jawhar, Sami (1975). *Al-Samitun yatakallamun [The Voiceless Speak Out]*. Cairo: Al-Maktab al-Masri al-Hadith.

Jensen, Carsten and Svend Erik Skaaning (2015). 'Democracy, Ethnic Fractionalisation, and the Politics of Social Spending: Disentangling a Conditional Relationship'. In: *International Political Science Review* 36.4, pp. 457–72.

Jeune Afrique (2012). *Tunisie: Carthage Cement voit le bout du tunnel*. 18 June. Paris.

Jimenez-Ayora, Pablo and Mehmet Ali Ulubaşoğlu (2015). 'What Underlies Weak States? The Role of Terrain Ruggedness'. In: *European Journal of Political Economy* 39.

Al-Jiritli, Ali (1974). *Al-Tarikh al-iqtisadi lil-thawrah, 1952–1966 [The Economic History of the Revolution, 1952–1966]*. Cairo: Dar al-Ma'arif bi Misr.

Julien, Charles-André (1976). 'Un Episode de la lutte pour l'indépendance tunisienne: l'affrontement de Bourguiba et de Salah Ben Youssef'. In: *Les Temps Modernes* 356.

Kaddar, Miloud (1989). 'Les rapports entre la sécurité sociale et le système de soins en Algérie'. In: *Cahiers du CREAD* 19, pp. 37–53.

Kamal, Oday (2015). *Half-Baked, the Other Side of Egypt's Baladi Bread Subsidy*. Barcelona: Centre for International Affairs (CIDOB).

Kamrava, Mehran (2000). 'Military Professionalization and Civil–Military Relations in the Middle East'. In: *Political Science Quarterly* 115.1, pp. 67–92.

Kandil, Hazem (2012a). 'Back on Horse? The Military between Two Revolutions'. In: *Arab Spring in Egypt: Revolution and Beyond*. Ed. by Bahgat Korany and Rabab El-Mahdi. Cairo: American University in Cairo Press, pp. 176–97.

Kandil, Hazem (2012b). *Soldiers, Spies and Statesmen: Egypt's Road to Revolt*. Kindle edition. London: Verso.

Kanovsky, Eliyahu (1987). 'Economic Implications for the Region and World Oil Market'. In: *The Iran–Iraq War: Impact and Implications*. Ed. by Efraim Karsh. London: Macmillan, pp. 231–52.

Karadam, Duygu Yolcu, Jülide Yildirim, and Nadir Öcal (2017). 'Military Expenditure and Economic Growth in Middle Eastern Countries and Turkey: A Non-linear Panel Data Approach'. In: *Defence and Peace Economics* 28.6, pp. 719–30.

Karshenas, Massoud and Valentine M. Moghadam, eds. (2006a). *Social Policy in the Middle East*. Basingstoke: Palgrave Macmillan.

Karshenas, Massoud and Valentine M. Moghadam (2006b). 'Social Policy in the Middle East: Introduction and Overview'. In: *Social Policy in the Middle East: Economic, Political, and Gender Dynamics*. Ed. by Massoud Karshenas and Valentine M. Moghadam. Basingstoke: Palgrave Macmillan, pp. 1–30.

Kasmi, Mohamed Salah (2008a). *L'assurance maladie en Tunisie*. Tunis: Imprimerie papeterie centrale.

Kasmi, Mohamed Salah (2008b). *L'assurance maladie en Tunisie: nouveautés et aspects pratiques*. Tunis: Latrach Édition.

Kasza, Gregory J. (1996). 'War and Comparative Politics'. In: *Comparative Politics* 28.3, pp. 355–73.

El-Katiri, Laura, Bassam Fattouh, and Paul Segal (2011). 'Anatomy of an Oil-Based Welfare State: Rent Distribution in Kuwait'. Research Paper No. 13, Kuwait Programme on Development, Governance and Globalisation in the Gulf States. London School of Economics and Political Science (LSE).

Katouzian, Homa (1981). *The Political Economy of Modern Iran: Despotism and PseudoModernism, 1926–1979*. London: Macmillan.

Katouzian, Homa (1998). 'The Pahlavi Regime in Iran'. In: *Sultanistic Regimes*. Ed. by Houchang E. Chehabi and Juan J. Linz. Baltimore: Johns Hopkins University Press, pp. 182–205.

Katouzian, Homa (2004). 'Mosaddeq's Government in Iranian History: Arbitrary Rule, Democracy, and the 1953 Coup'. In: *Mohammad Mosaddeq and the 1953 Coup in Iran*. Ed. by Mark J. Gasiorowski and Malcolm Byrne. Syracuse: Syracuse University Press, pp. 1–26.

Katzenstein, Peter J. (1985). *Small States in World Markets*. Ithaca: Cornell University Press.

Kaufman, Robert R. and Alex Segura-Ubiergo (2001). 'Globalization, Domestic Politics, and Social Spending in Latin America: A Time-Series Cross-Section Analysis, 1973–97'. In: *World Politics* 53.4, pp. 553–87.

Keddie, Nikki R. (2003). *Modern Iran: Roots and Results of a Revolution*. New Haven: Yale University Press.

Kelsall, Tim (2016). 'Thinking and Working with Political Settlements'. ODI Briefing. London. URL: https://www.odi.org/sites/odi.org.uk/files/odi-assets/publications-opinion-files/10200.pdf (visited on 28/08/2018). Overseas Development Institute (ODI).

Kerr, Clark (1964). *Industrialism and Industrial Man: The Problems of Labor and Management in Economic Growth*. Oxford: Oxford University Press.

Kerr, Michael (2015). 'For "God, Syria, and Bashar and Nothing Else"?' In: *The Alawis of Syria: War, Faith, and Politics in the Levant*. Ed. by Michael Kerr and Craig Larkin. Kindle edition. New York: Oxford University Press, pp. 1–23.

Khaldi, Raoudha (1995). 'La Caisse générale de compensation et ses mécanismes d'intervention'. In: *Les politiques alimentaires en Afrique du Nord: d'une assistance généralisée aux interventions ciblées*. Ed. by M. Padilla et al. Paris: Karthala, pp. 345–65.

Khalil, Muhammad (2006). 'Philosophie de l'assurance santé au temps de la mondialisation: du sérieux à la plaisanterie'. In: *Les politiques de réforme de l'assurance santé en Égypte*. Ed. by Center for the Study of Developing Countries. Cairo: University of Cairo, pp. 93–101.

Khan, Mushtaq (2010). 'Political Settlements and the Governance of Growth-Enhancing Institutions'. Unpublished manuscript. URL: https://eprints.soas.ac.Uk/9968/1/Political_Settlements_internet.pdf (visited on 27/08/2018).

Kherallah, Mylène et al. (2000). *Wheat Policy Reform in Egypt: Adjustment of Local Markets and Options for Future Reforms*. Washington, DC: International Food Policy Research Institute (IFPRI).

Khiari, Sadri and Olfa Lamloum (2000). 'Le zaïm et l'artisan ou de Bourguiba à Ben Ali'. In: *Annuaire de l'Afrique du Nord 1998*. Ed. by Christian Robin, Hélène Claudot-Hawad, and Jean-Noël Ferrié. Paris: Editions du CNRS, pp. 377–95.

Kienle, Eberhard (1991). 'Entre jama'a et classe. Le pouvoir politique en Syrie contemporaine'. In: *Revue du Monde Musulman et de la Méditerranée* 59.1, pp. 211–39.

Kim, Nam Kyu and Alex M. Kroeger (2018). 'Do Multiparty Elections Improve Human Development in Autocracies?' In: *Democratization* 25.2, pp. 251–72.

Kim, Wonik and Jennifer Gandhi (2010). 'Coopting Workers under Dictatorship'. In: *The Journal of Politics* 72.03, pp. 646–58.

King, Stephen J. (2010). *The New Authoritarianism in the Middle East and North Africa*. Bloomington: Indiana University Press.

Kingdom of Morocco (various years). *Annuaire statistique du Maroc*. Rabat: Service central des statistiques.

Kippenberg, Hans G. (1981). 'Jeder Tag 'Ashura, jedes Grab Kerbala: Zur Ritualisierung der Straßenkämpfe im Iran'. In: *Religion und Politik im Iran*. Ed. by Berliner Institut für Vergleichende Sozialforschung. Frankfurt/Main: Syndikat, pp. 217–56.

Kitschelt, Herbert and Steven Wilkinson (2007). 'Citizen–Politician Linkages: An Introduction'. In: *Patrons, Clients, and Policies: Patterns of Democratic Accountability and Political Competition*. Ed. by Herbert Kitschelt and Steven Wilkinson. Cambridge: Cambridge University Press, pp. 1–49.

Knauss, Peter R. (1980). 'Algeria under Boumedienne: The Mythical Revolution'. In: *The Performance of Soldiers as Governors: African Politics and the African Military*. Ed. by Isaac James Mowoe. Washington, DC: University Press of America, pp. 27–101.

Knight, Jack (1992). *Institutions and Social Conflict*. Cambridge: Cambridge University Press.

Knowles, Warwick (2005). *Jordan since 1989: A Study in Political Economy*. London: I. B. Tauris.

Knutsen, Carl Henrik and Hanne Fjelde (2013). 'Property Rights in Dictatorships: Kings Protect Property better than Generals or Party Bosses'. In: *Contemporary Politics* 19.1, pp. 94–114.

Knutsen, Carl Henrik and Magnus Rasmussen (2018). 'The Autocratic Welfare State: Old-Age Pensions, Credible Commitments, and Regime Survival'. In: *Comparative Political Studies* 51.5, pp. 659–95.

Kobrin, Stephen J. (1980). 'Foreign Enterprise and Forced Divestment in LDCs'. In: *International Organization* 34.1, pp. 65–88.

Kohli, Atul (1994). 'Where Do High Growth Political Economies Come From? The Japanese Lineage of Korea's "Developmental State"'. In: *World Development* 22.9, pp. 1269–93.

Korany, Bahgat (1984). 'Third Worldism and Pragmatic Radicalism: The Foreign Policy of Algeria'. In: *The Foreign Policies of Arab States*. Ed. by Bahgat Korany and Ali E. Hillal Dessouki. Cairo: The American University in Cairo Press, pp. 79–118.

Korpi, Walter (1974). 'Conflict, Power and Relative Deprivation'. In: *American Political Science Review* 68.4, pp. 1569–78.

Korpi, Walter (1983). *The Democratic Class Struggle*. London: Routledge.

Korpi, Walter (1985). 'Power Resources Approach vs. Action and Conflict: On Causal and Intentional Explanations in the Study of Power'. In: *Sociological Theory* 3.2, pp. 31–45.

Korpi, Walter (2006). 'Power Resources and Employer-Centered Approaches in Explanations of Welfare States and Varieties of Capitalism: Protagonists, Consenters, and Antagonists'. In: *World Politics* 58.2, pp. 167–206.

Korpi, Walter, Julia S. O'Connor, and Gregg Matthew Olsen (1998). *Power Resources Theory and the Welfare State: A Critical Approach: Essays Collected in Honour of Walter Korpi*. Toronto: University of Toronto Press.

Korpi, Walter and Joakim Palme (2003). 'New Politics and Class Politics in the Context of Austerity and Globalization: Welfare State Regress in 18 Countries, 1975–95'. In: *American Political Science Review* 97.3, pp. 425–46.

Kraïem, Mustapha (2011). *Etat et société dans la Tunisie bourguibienne*. Tunis: MIP Livre.

Kwon, Huck-Ju (1997). 'Beyond European Welfare Regimes: Comparative Perspectives on East Asian Welfare Systems'. In: *Journal of Social Policy* 26.4, pp. 467–84.

La Dépêche (1961). *No Title.* January. Tunis.

La Presse (1960). *No Title.* 24 October. Tunis.

La Presse (1961). *No Title.* 8 April. Tunis.

Lai, Brian and Dan Slater (2006). 'Institutions of the Offensive: Domestic Sources of Dispute Initiation in Authoritarian Regimes, 1950–1992'. In: *American Journal of Political Science* 50.1, pp. 113–26.

Larreguy, Horacio and John Marshall (2016). 'The Effect of Education on Civic and Political Engagement in Nonconsolidated Democracies: Evidence from Nigeria'. In: *The Review of Economics and Statistics* 99.3, pp. 387–401.

Le Parti Neo-Destour (1955). *Le congrés néo-destourien de Sfax (15–19 novembre 1955).* Sfax.

Le Petit Matin (1956). *Les étudiants en grève.* 24 January. Tunis.

Le Quotidien (2008a). *Accord sur la possibilité de choix de filières différentes par les conjoints.* 19 April. Tunis.

Le Quotidien (2008b). *L'UGTT appelle à la mise à niveau des établissements publics de santé.* 15 March. Tunis.

Le Temps (2005). *La réforme de l'assurance-maladie est une "bouffée d'oxygène".* 28 February. Tunis.

Le Temps (2006). *CNAM: La charrue devant les bœufs?* 22 December. Tunis.

Le Temps (2007). *Ce que nous attendons de la CNAM.* 10 January. Tunis.

Le Temps (2008). *Davantage de sensibilisation des assurés sociaux.* 21 April. Tunis.

Lektzian, David and Brandon C. Prins (2008). 'Taming the Leviathan: Examining the Impact of External Threat on State Capacity'. In: *Journal of Peace Research* 45.5, pp. 613–31.

Lenczowski, George (1966). 'Radical Regimes in Egypt, Syria and Iraq'. In: *The Journal of Politics* 28.1, pp. 29–56.

Lenczowski, George (1978). 'Introduction. From Assertion of Independence to the White Revolution'. In: *Iran under the Pahlavis*. Ed. by George Lenczowski. Stanford: Hoover Institution Press, pp. xv–xxii.

Leveau, Rémy (1970). *Le fellah marocain, défenseur du trône*. Paris: Presses de la Fondation Nationale des Sciences Politiques.

Levitsky, Steven and Lucan Way (2010). *Competitive Authoritarianism: Hybrid Regimes after the Cold War.* Cambridge: Cambridge University Press.

Liauzu, Claude (1996). 'The History of Labor and the Workers' Movement in North Africa'. In: *The Social History of Labor in the Middle East.* Ed. by Ellis Goldberg. Oxford: Westview, pp. 193–221.

Lieberman, Evan S. (2009). *Boundaries of Contagion: How Ethnic Politics Have Shaped Government Responses to AIDS.* Princeton: Princeton University Press.

Lieberman, Evan S. (2015). 'Nested Analysis: Toward the Integration of Comparative-Historical Analysis with Other Social Science Methods'. In: *Advances in Comparative-Historical Analysis.* Ed. by James Mahoney and Kathleen Thelen. Cambridge: Cambridge University Press, pp. 240–63.

Lieberman, Evan S. (2018). 'The Comparative Politics of Service Delivery in Developing Countries'. In: *The Oxford Handbook of the Politics of Development.* Ed. by Carol Lancaster and Nicolas van de Walle. Oxford: Oxford University Press, pp. 480–98.

Lieberman, Evan S. and Gwyneth H. McClendon (2013). 'The Ethnicity–Policy Preference Link in Sub-Saharan Africa'. In: *Comparative Political Studies* 46.5, pp. 574–602.

Lieberman, Evan S. and Prerna Singh (2012). 'The Institutional Origins of Ethnic Violence'. In: *Comparative Politics* 45.1, pp. 1–24.

Lieberman, Evan S. and Prerna Singh (2017). 'Census Enumeration and Group Conflict: A Global Analysis of the Consequences of Counting'. In: *World Politics* 69.1, pp. 1–53.

Lindert, Peter H. (1994). 'The Rise of Social Spending, 1880-1930'. In: *Explorations in Economic History* 31.1, pp. 1–37.

Lindert, Peter H. (2005). 'Growing Public: Is the Welfare State Mortal or Exportable?' Working Paper.

Lob, Eric (2017). 'Development, Mobilization and War: The Iranian Construction Jehad, Construction Mobilization and Trench Builders Association (1979-2013)'. In: *Middle East Critique* 26.1, pp. 25–44.

Loewe, Markus (1998). 'Sozialpolitik im Dienste des Machterhalts. Soziale Sicherung und Staat im arabischen Vorderen Orient'. In: *Der Bürger im Staat* 48.3, pp. 147–52.

Loewe, Markus (2010). *Soziale Sicherung in den arabischen Ländern.* Baden-Baden: Nomos.

Loewe, Markus and Lars Westemeier (2018). *Social Insurance Reforms in Egypt: Needed, Belated, Flopped.*

Longuenesse, Élisabeth, Myriam Catusse, and Blandine Destremeau (2005). 'Le travail et la question sociale au Maghreb et au Moyen-Orient'. In: *Revue des mondes musulmans et de la Méditerranée* 105–6, pp. 15–43.

Lorenzon, Flavia (2016). 'The Political Economy of Food Prices in Egypt: Reforms and Strengthening of Social Protection'. In: *The Public Sphere.*

Lott, John R. (1999). 'Public Schooling, Indoctrination, and Totalitarianism'. In: *Journal of Political Economy* 107.6, pp. 127–57.

Lowi, Miriam R. (2009). *Oil Wealth and the Poverty of Politics.* Cambridge: Cambridge University Press.

Lu, L. and Cameron G. Thies (2012). 'War, Rivalry, and State Building in the Middle East'. In: *Political Research Quarterly* 66.2, pp. 239–53.

Lucas, Viola and Thomas Richter (2016). 'State Hydrocarbon Rents, Authoritarian Survival and the Onset of Democracy: Evidence from a New Dataset'. In: *Research and Politics* 3.3.

Luciani, Giacomo (1987). 'Allocation vs. Production State'. In: *The Rentier State.* Ed. by Hazem Beblawi and Giacomo Luciani. London: Croom Helm, pp. 63–84.

Luebbert, Gregory M. (1991). *Liberalism, Fascism, or Social Democracy: Social Classes and the Political Origins of Regimes in Interwar Europe.* Oxford: Oxford University Press.

Luong, Pauline and Erika Weinthal (2010). *Oil Is Not a Curse: Ownership Structure and Institutions in Soviet Successor States*. Cambridge: Cambridge University Press.

Lust, Ellen and Lise Rakner (2018). 'The Other Side of Taxation: Extraction and Social Institutions in the Developing World'. In: *Annual Review of Political Science*.

Lustick, Ian S. (1997). 'The Absence of Middle Eastern Great Powers: Political "Backwardness" in Historical Perspective'. In: *International Organization* 51, pp. 653–84.

Ma'oz, Moshe (1988). *Asad. The Sphinx of Damascus: A Political Biography*. London: Weidenfeld & Nicolson.

Mabro, Robert (1974). *The Egyptian Economy 1952–1972*. Oxford: Clarendon Press.

Mabro, Robert and Samir Radwan (1976). *The Industrialization of Egypt 1939–1973*. Oxford: Clarendon Press.

Magaloni, Beatriz (2006). *Voting for Autocracy: Hegemonic Party Survival and Its Demise in Mexico*. Cambridge: Cambridge University Press.

Magaloni, Beatriz (2008). 'Credible Power-Sharing and the Longevity of Authoritarian Rule'. In: *Comparative Political Studies* 41.4–5, pp. 715–41.

Mahmoud, Mehdi (2019). *Anas Doukkali: "Il reste du chemin à faire pour atteindre l'universalité du système de santé"*. 18 March. Tel Quel. URL: https://telquel.ma/2019/03/18/anas-doukkali-il-reste-du-chemin-a-faire-pour-atteindre-luniversalite-du-syteme-de-sante%7B%5C_%7D1631838 (visited on 21/05/2019).

Mahoney, James (2000). 'Path Dependence in Historical Sociology'. In: *Theory and Society* 29.4, pp. 507–48.

Mahoney, James (2012). 'The Logic of Process Tracing Tests in the Social Sciences'. In: *Social Methods and Research* 41.4, pp. 570–97.

Mahoney, James and Gary Goertz (2006). 'A Tale of Two Cultures: Contrasting Quantitative and Qualitative Research'. In: *Political Analysis* 14, pp. 227–49.

Mahoney, James, E. Kimball and K. L. Koivu (2008). 'The Logic of Historical Explanation in the Social Sciences'. In: *Comparative Political Studies* 42.1, pp. 114–46.

Mahoney, James and Dietrich Rueschemeyer, eds. (2003a). *Comparative Historical Analysis in the Social Sciences*. Cambridge: Cambridge University Press.

Mahoney, James and Dietrich Rueschemeyer (2003b). 'Comparative Historical Analysis: Achievements and Agendas'. In: *Comparative Historical Analysis in the Social Sciences*. Ed. by James Mahoney and Dietrich Rueschemeyer. Cambridge: Cambridge University Press, pp. 3–40.

Mahoney, James and Kathleen Thelen (2010). 'A Theory of Gradual Institutional Change'. In: *Explaining Institutional Change: Ambiguity, Agency, and Power*. Ed. by James Mahoney and Kathleen Thelen. Cambridge: Cambridge University Press, pp. 1–37.

Mahoney, James and Kathleen Thelen eds. (2015). *Advances in Comparative Historical Analysis*. Cambridge: Cambridge University Press.

Makdisi, Ussama Samir (2000). *The Culture of Sectarianism: Community, History, and Violence in Nineteenth-Century Ottoman Lebanon*. Berkeley: University of California Press.

Malik, Adeel and Ferdinand Eibl (forthcoming). 'The Politics of Trade Protection in North Africa'. In: *Crony Capitalism in the Middle East: Business and Politics from Liberalization to the Arab Spring*. Ed. by Ishac Diwan, Adeel Malik, and Izak Itiyas. Oxford: Oxford University Press.

Maloney, Suzanne (2000). 'Agents or Obstacles? Parastatal Foundations and Challenges for Iranian Development'. In: *The Economy of Iran: Dilemmas of an Islamic State*. Ed. by Parvin Alizadeh. London: I. B. Tauris, pp. 145–76.

Malpezzi, Stephen and Gwendolyn Ball (1993). 'Measuring the Urban Policy Environment'. In: *Habitat International* 17.2, pp. 39–52.

Mann, Michael (1993). *The Sources of Social Power, Volume 2: The Rise of Classes and Nation-States, 1760–1914*. Cambridge: Cambridge University Press.

Mansour, S. (2012). *Egypt: Grain and Feed Annual—Wheat and Corn Production on the Rise*. Washington, DC: Global Agricultural Information Network.

Mares, Isabela (2005). 'Social Protection around the World: External Insecurity, State Capacity, and Domestic Political Cleavages'. In: *Comparative Political Studies* 38.6, pp. 623–51.

Mares, Isabela and Matthew E. Carnes (2009). 'Social Policy in Developing Countries'. In: *Annual Review of Political Science* 12.1, pp. 93–113.

Marschall, Melissa, Abdullah Aydogan, and Alper Bulut (2016). 'Does Housing Create Votes? Explaining the Electoral Success of the AKP in Turkey'. In: *Electoral Studies* 42, pp. 201–12.

Marshall, Monty G. and Keith Jaggers (2010). *Polity IV Annual Time-Series 1800–2010*. URL: http://www.systemicpeace.org/inscr/inscr.htm (visited on 08/02/2013).

Martin, Christian W. (2005). *Die doppelte Transformation: Demokratie und Außenwirtschaftsliberalisierung in Entwicklungsländern*. Wiesbaden: VS-Verlag.

Martinez, José Ciro (2017). 'Leavening Neoliberalization's Uneven Pathways: Bread, Governance and Political Rationalities in the Hashemite Kingdom of Jordan'. In: *Mediterranean Politics* 22.4, pp. 464–83.

Al-Masry Al-Youm (2008). *No Title*. 23 November. Cairo.

Al-Masry Al-Youm (2009a). *No Title*. 11 February. Cairo.

Al-Masry Al-Youm (2009b). *No Title*. 23 June. Cairo.

Al-Masry Al-Youm (2009c). *No Title*. 15 February. Cairo.

Al-Masry Al-Youm (2011). *No Title*. 14 November. Cairo.

Al-Masry Al-Youm (2012). *No Title*. 25 May. Cairo.

Matzke, Torsten (2008). 'The Political Economy of Structural Adjustment in the Egyptian Agrarian Sector'. MA thesis. University of Tübingen.

Mazaheri, Nimah (2017). 'Oil, Dissent, and Distribution'. In: *World Development* 99, pp. 186–202.

McGuire, James W. (2013). 'Political Regime and Social Performance'. In: *Contemporary Politics* 19.1, pp. 55–75.

Médard, Jean-François (1982). 'The Underdeveloped State in Tropical Africa: Political Clientelism or Neo-patrimonialism'. In: *Private Patronage and Public Power: Political Clientelism in the Modern State*. Ed. by Christopher Clapham. London: Frances Pinter, pp. 162–89.

Merouani, Walid, Nacer-Eddine Hammouda, and Claire El Moudden (2014). 'Le système algérien de protection sociale: entre Bismarckien et Beveridgien'. In: *Les Cahiers du CREAD* 107–8, pp. 109–47.

Messkoub, Mahmood (2006a). 'Constitutionalism, Modernization and Islamization: The Political Economy of Social Policy in Iran'. In: *Social Policy in the Middle East: Economic, Political, and Gender Dynamics*. Ed. by Massoud Karshenas and Valentine M. Moghadam. Basingstoke: Palgrave Macmillan, pp. 190–220.

Messkoub, Mahmood (2006b). 'Social Policy in Iran in the Twentieth Century'. In: *Iranian Studies* 39.2, pp. 227–52.

Mestiri, Ahmed (1999). *Témoignage pour l'histoire*. Tunis: Sud éditions.

Mestiri, Brahim (1983). 'La pensée politique et sociale du Président Habib Bourguiba'. MA thesis. University of Ottowa.

Micaud, Charles A., L. Carl Brown, and Clement Henry Moore (1964). *Tunisia: The Politics of Modernization*. London: Pall Mall Press.

Milani, Mohsen M. (1994). *The Making of Iran's Islamic Revolution: From Monarchy to Islamic Republic*. Oxford: Westview Press.

Miller, Michael K. (2015a). 'Elections, Information, and Policy Responsiveness in Autocratic Regimes'. In: *Comparative Political Studies* 48.6, pp. 691–727.

Miller, Michael K. (2015b). 'Electoral Authoritarianism and Human Development'. In: *Comparative Political Studies* 48.12, pp. 1526–62.

Milton-Edwards, Beverley and Peter Hinchcliffe (2001). *Jordan: A Hashemite Legacy*. London: Routledge.

Minor, Mari Sako (1994). 'The Demise of Expropriation as an Instrument of LDC Policy 1980–1992'. In: *Journal of International Business Studies* 25.1, pp. 177–88.

Mintz, A. and R. T. Stevenson (1995). 'Defense Expenditures, Economic Growth, and The "Peace Dividend": A Longitudinal Analysis of 103 Countries'. In: *Journal of Conflict Resolution* 39.2, pp. 283–305.

Mitchell, Timothy (2002). *Rule of Experts: Egypt, Techno-politics, Modernity*. Berkeley: University of California Press.

Moalla, Mansour (1992). *L'Etat tunisien et l'indépendance*. Tunis: Cérès Éditions.

Moalla, Mansour (2011). *De l'Indépendance à la Révolution. Système politique et développement économique en Tunisie*. Tunis: Sud éditions.

Moene, Karl and Michael Wallerstein (2001). 'Inequality, Social Insurance, and Redistribution'. In: *Annual Political Science Review* 95.4, pp. 859–74.

Mohi El Din, Khaled (1995). *Memories of a Revolution: Egypt 1952*. Cairo: American University in Cairo Press.

Moin, Baqir (1999). *Khomeini: Life of the Ayatollah*. London: I. B. Tauris.

Monastiri, Taoufik (1971). 'Tunisie'. In: *Annuaire de l'Afrique du Nord 1971*. Ed. by Jean-Claude Santucci and Maurice Flory. Paris: Editions du CNRS, pp. 424–43.

Monastiri, Taoufik (1974). 'Tunisie: chronique sociale et culturelle'. In: *Annuaire de l'Afrique du Nord 1973*. Ed. by Jean-Claude Santucci and Maurice Flory. Paris: Editions du CNRS, pp. 514–34.

Monjib, Maâti (1992). *La monarchie marocaine et la lutte pour le pouvoir*. Paris: L'Harmattan.

Moore, Barrington (1967). *Social Origins of Dictatorship and Democracy: Lord and Peasant in the Making of the Modern World*. Boston: Beacon Press.

Moore, Clement Henry (1965). *Tunisia since Independence: The Dynamics of One-Party Government*. Berkeley: University of California Press.

Moore, Clement Henry (1970). 'Tunisia: The Prospects of Institutionalization'. In: *Authoritarian Politics in Modern Society: The Dynamics of Established One-Party Systems*. Ed. by Samuel P. Huntington and Clement Henry Moore. London: Basic Books, pp. 311–36.

Morrison, Kevin M. (2009). 'Oil, Nontax Revenue, and the Redistributional Foundations of Regime Stability'. In: *International Organization* 63.1, pp. 107–38.

Moslem, Mehdi (2002). *Factional Politics in Post-Khomeini Iran*. Syracuse: Syracuse University Press.

Mouline, Mohammed Tawfik (2005). *Etude comparative, en terme de développement humain, du Maroc et d'un échantillon de 14 pays pour la période 1955–2004*. Rabat.

Mulligan, Casey B., Ricard Gil, and Xavier Sala-i-Martin (2004). 'Do Democracies have Different Public Policies than Nondemocracies?' In: *The Journal of Economic Perspectives* 18.1, pp. 51–74.

Munck, Gerardo L. (2004). 'Tools for Qualitative Research'. In: *Rethinking Social Inquiry: Diverse Tools, Shared Standards*. Ed. by Henry E. Brady and David Collier. Lanham: Rowman & Littlefield, pp. 105–21.

Murphy, Emma (1999). *Economic and Political Change in Tunisia: From Bourguiba to Ben Ali*. Basingstoke: Macmillan Press.

Myles, John (1984). *Old Age in the Welfare State: The Political Economy of Public Pensions*. Boston: Little, Brown.

Narizny, Kevin (2003). 'Both Guns and Butter, or Neither: Class Interests in the Political'. In: *American Political Science Review* 97.2, pp. 203–20.

Nasser, Gamal Abdel (1956). *Egypt's Liberation: The Philosophy of the Revolution*. Washington, DC: Public Affairs Press.

Neguib, Mohammed (1955). *Egypt's Destiny*. London: Victor Gollancz.

Neimat, Khaled (2013a). *Social security umbrella to cover those who lose their jobs*. 30 June. The Jordan Times.

Neimat, Khaled (2013b). *House endorses Social Security Law after a month of deliberations*. 30 July. The Jordan Times.

Nerfin, M. (1974). *Entretiens avec Ahmed Ben Salah sur la dynamique socialiste dans les années 1960*. Paris: Francois Maspero.

Nevo, Joseph (2003). 'Changing Identities in Jordan'. In: *Israel, the Hashemites and the Palestinians: The Fateful Triangle*. Ed. by Efraim Karsh and P. R. Kumaraswamy. London: Frank Cass, pp. 187–208.

New York Times (1977). *No Title*. 26 September. New York.

New York Times (2009). *Our One-Party Democracy*. 8 September. New York.

New York Times (2013). *Morocco's Health Care System in Distress*. 28 March. New York.

Nickell, Stephen (1981). 'Biases in Dynamic Models with Fixed Effects'. In: *Econometrica* 49.6, pp. 1417–26.

Noland, Marcus and Howard Pack (2007). *The Arab Economies in a Changing World*. Washington, DC: Peterson Institute for International Economics.

Nome, Martin Austvoll (2011). 'Causal Homogeneity in Mechanismic Research'. In: *Qualitative and Multi-Method Research Newsletter* 9.1, pp. 34–40.

Nooruddin, Irfan and Joel W. Simmons (2006). 'The Politics of Hard Choices: IMF Programs and Government Spending'. In: *International Organization* 60.4, pp. 1001–33.

Nooruddin, Irfan and Joel W. Simmons (2009). 'Openness, Uncertainty, and Social Spending: Implications for the Globalization–Welfare State Debate'. In: *International Studies Quarterly* 53.3, pp. 841–66.

Nordlinger, Eric A. (1977). *Soldiers in Politics: Military Coups and Governments*. Englewood Cliffs: Prentice-Hall.

North, Douglass Cecil, John Joseph Wallis, and Barry R. Weingast (2009). *Violence and Social Orders: A Conceptual Framework for Interpreting Recorded Human History*. Cambridge: Cambridge University Press.

Nucho, Joanne Randa (2018). *Everyday Sectarianism in Urban Lebanon*. Princeton: Princeton University Press.

Nunn, Nathan and Diego Puga (2012). 'Ruggedness: The Blessing of Bad Geography in Africa'. In: *Review of Economics and Statistics* 94.1, pp. 20–36.

O'Brien, Patrick (1966). *The Revolution in Egypt's Economic System*. Oxford: Oxford University Press.

O'Donnell, Guillermo and Philippe Schmitter (1986). *Transitions from Authoritarian Rule: Tentative Conclusions about Uncertain Democracies*. Baltimore: Johns Hopkins University Press.

O'Donnell, Guillermo A., Philippe C. Schmitter, and Laurence Whitehead (1986). *Transitions from Authoritarian Rule: Prospects for Democracy*. Baltimore: John Hopkins University Press.

Obinger, Herbert and Uwe Wagschal (2010). 'Social Expenditure and Revenues'. In: *The Oxford Handbook of the Welfare State*. Ed. by Francis G. Castles et al. Oxford: Oxford University Press, pp. 333–52.

Omar (2012). 'Food Subsidy Reform'. MA thesis. American University in Cairo.

Ottaway, David and Marina Ottaway (1970). *Algeria: The Politics of a Socialist Revolution*. Berkeley: California University Press.

Oualdi, Mohamed (1999). 'L'orage des indépendances: Salah Ben Youssef et les yousse- fistes, en Tunisie en 1955–1956'. PhD thesis. Université Paris 1.

Ouchfoun, A. and D. Hammouda (1993). 'Bilan de vingt-huit années de politique sanitaire en Algérie'. In: *Cahiers du CREAD* 35–6, pp. 59–96.

Owen, Roger (1991). 'The Economic Consequences of the Suez Crisis in Egypt'. In: *Suez 1956*. Ed. by Wm. Roger Louis and Roger Owen. Oxford: Clarendon Press, pp. 363–75.

Owen, Roger (2000). 'The Cumulative Impact of Middle Eastern Wars'. In: *War, Institutions, and Social Change in the Middle East*. Berkeley: University of California Press, pp. 325–34.

Owen, Roger (2004). *State, Power and Politics in the Making of the Modern Middle East*. London: Routledge.

Owen, Roger and Pamuk Şevket (1998). *A History of Middle East Economies in the Twentieht Century*. London: I. B.Tauris.

Palmer, Glenn (1990). 'Alliance Politics and Issue Areas: Determinants of Defense Spending'. In: *American Journal of Political Science* 34.1, pp. 190–211.

Papanicolas, Irene and Jonathan Cylus (2017). 'The Challenges of Using Cross-National Comparisons of Efficiency to Inform Health Policy'. In: *Eurohealth* 23.2, pp. 8–11.

Pappé, Ilan (1994). 'Jordan between Hashemite and Palestinian Identity'. In: *Jordan in the Middle East 1948–88: The Making of a Pivotal State*. Ed. by Joseph Nevo and Ilan Pappé. London: Frank Cass, pp. 61–91.

Park, Chan-Ung and Dongchul Jung (2009). 'Making Sense of the Asian Welfare Regimes'. In: *Korean Journal of Sociology* 43.3, pp. 57–85.

Parks, Thomas and William Cole (2010). 'Political Settlements: Implications for International Development Policy and Practice'. Occasional Paper No. 2. San Francisco. URL: http://asiafoundation.org/resources/pdfs/PoliticalSettlementsFINAL.pdf (visited on 28/08/2018). The Asia Foundation.

Pawelka, Peter (1985). *Herrschaft und Entwicklung im Nahen Osten: Ägypten*. Heidelberg: C. F. Müller.

Pawelka, Peter (2002). 'Der Staat im Vorderen Orient: Über die Demokratie-Resistenz in einer globalisierten Welt'. In: *Leviathan* 30.4, pp. 431–54.

Pennell, C. R. (2000). *Morocco since 1830: A History*. London: Hurst & Company.

Pennington, J. D. (1982). 'The Copts in Modern Egypt'. In: *Middle Eastern Studies* 18.2, pp. 158–79.

Pepinsky, Thomas B. (2008a). 'Capital Mobility and Coalitional Politics: Authoritarian Regimes and Economic Adjustment in Southeast Asia'. In: *World Politics* 60.3, pp. 438–74.

Pepinsky, Thomas B. (2008b). 'Durable Authoritarianism as a Self-Enforcing Coalition'. Unpublished manuscript.

Pepinsky, Thomas B. (2009). *Economic Crises and the Breakdown of Authoritarian Regimes*. Cambridge: Cambridge University Press.

Perkins, Kenneth J. (1997). *Historical Dictionary of Tunisia*. London: The Scarecrow Press.

Perlmutter, Amos (1969). 'From Obscurity to Rule: The Syrian Army and the Ba'th Party'. In: *Western Political Quarterly* 22.4, pp. 827–45.

Perlmutter, Amos (1977). *The Military and Politics in Modern Times*. New Haven: Yale University Press.

Perret, Cécile (2012). 'Les évolutions du système de protection sociale en Algérie'.

Perry, Glenn E. (2004). *The History of Egypt*. London: Greenwood Press.

Persson, Torsten and Guido Tabellini (2000). *Political Economics*. Cambridge, Mass.: MIT Press.

Perthes, Volker (1997). *The Political Economy of Syria under Asad*. London: I. B. Tauris.

Perthes, Volker (2000). 'Si Vis Stabilitatem, Para Bellum: State Building, National Security, and War Preparation in Syria'. In: *War, Institutions, and Social Change in the Middle East*. Ed. by Steven Heydemann. Berkeley: University of California, pp. 149–73.

Peters, Anne and Pete Moore (2009). 'Beyond Boom and Bust: External Rents, Durable Authoritarianism, and Institutional Adaptation in the Hashemite Kingdom of Jordan'. In: *Studies in Comparative International Development* 44.3, pp. 256–85.

Petersen, Roger D. (2001). *Resistance and Rebellion*. Cambridge: Cambridge University Press.

Picard, Elizabeth (1979). 'Clans militaires et pouvoir ba'thiste en Syrie'. In: *Orient* 20.3, pp. 49–62.

Pickel, Susanne (2009). 'Die Triangulation als Methode in der Politikwissenschaft'. In: *Methoden der vergleichenden Politik- und Sozialwissenschaft*. Ed. by Gert Pickel et al. Wiesbaden: VS-Verlag für Sozialwissenschaften, pp. 517–42.

Pierson, Paul (1994). *Dismantling the Welfare State? Reagan, Thatcher, and the Politics of Entrenchment*. Cambridge: Cambridge University Press.

Pierson, Paul (2004). *Politics in Time: History, Institutions, and Social Analysis*. Princeton: Princeton University Press.

Pierson, Paul (2015). 'Power and Path Dependence'. In: *Advances in Comparative-Historical Analysis*. Ed. by James Mahoney and Kathleen Thelen. Cambridge: Cambridge University Press, pp. 123–46.

Poncet, Jean (1970). 'L' économie tunisienne depuis l'indépendance'. In: *Annuaire de l'Afrique du Nord*. Ed. by Michel Camau and Charles Debbasch. Paris: Éditions du CNRS, pp. 93–114.

Posner, Daniel (2005). *Institutions and Ethnic Politics in Africa*. Cambridge: Cambridge University Press.

Posusney, Marsha Pripstein (1997). *Labor and the State in Egypt: Workers, Unions, and Economic Restructuring*. New York: Columbia University Press.

Przeworski, Adam et al. (2000). *Democracy and Development: Political Institutions and Well-being in the World, 1950–1990*. Cambridge: Cambridge University Press.

Qindil, Amani, ed. (1991). *Siyasat al-ta'lim al-jami'i fi Misr: al-ab'ad al-siyasiyah wa-al-iqtisadiyah [Higher Education Policies in Egypt: The Political and Economic Dimensions]*. Cairo: University of Cairo.

Quandt, William (1969). *Revolution and Political Leadership: Algeria 1954–1968*. Cambridge, Mass.: MIT Press.

Quandt, William (1972). 'The Berbers in the Algerian Political Elite'. In: *Arabs and Berbers: From Tribe to Nation in North Africa*. Ed. by Ernest Gellner and Charles A. Micaud. London: Duckworth, pp. 285–303.

Rabinovich, Itamar (1972). *Syria under the Ba'th 1963–66: The Army–Party Symbiosis*. Jerusalem: Israel Universities Press.

Rahnema, Ali (2015). *Behind the 1953 Coup in Iran: Thugs, Turncoats, Soldiers, and Spooks*. Kindle edition. Cambridge: Cambridge University Press.

Ramadan, Abdel-Athim (1975). *al-Sira' al-ijtima'i wa-al-siyasi fi Misr mundhu thawrat 23 Yuliyu 1952 ila nihayat azmat Maris 1954 [Social and Political Conflict in Egypt from, the 23 July Revolution in 1952 until the March Crisis in 1954]*. Cairo: Ruz al-Yusuf.

Ramadan, Abdel-Athim (1976). *Abd al-Nasir wa Azmat Maris [Abdel Nasser and the March Crisis]*. Cairo: Ruz al-Yusuf.

Ramadan, Abdel-Athim (1997). *al-Watha'iq al-sirriyah li-thawrat Yuliyu 1952: al-nusus al-kamilah li-m,ahadir al-Amanah al-'Ammah lil-Ittihad al-Ishtiraki [The Secret Documents of the July Revolution: The Complete Texts of the Minutes of the General Secretariat of the Arab Socialist Union*. Cairo: Al-Hay'ah Al-Misriya Al-Ammah lil-Kitab.

Rashad, Ahmed Shoukry and Mesbah Fathy Sharaf (2015). 'Catastrophic and Impoverishing Effects of Out-of-Pocket Health Expenditure: New Evidence from Egypt'. ERF Working Paper 974. Cairo: Economic Research Forum (ERF).

Rasler, Karen A. and William R. Thompson (1985). 'War Making and State Making: Governmental Expenditures, Tax Revenues, and Global Wars'. In: *American Political Science Review* 79.2, pp. 491–507.

Rastegar, Ashgar (1996). 'Health Policy and Medical Education'. In: *Iran after the Revolution*. Ed. by Saeed Rahnema and Sohrab Behdad. London: I. B. Tauris, pp. 218–28.

Ratib, Najla Abdelhamid (1998). *Azmat al-ta'lim fi Misr: dirasah susyulujiyah fi idarat al-azamat al-ijtima'iyah [Crisis of Education in Egypt: A Sociological Study of the Management of Social Crises]*. Cairo: Markaz al-Mahrusah lil-Buhuth wa al-Tadrib wa al-Nashr.

Rauch, J. E. and S. Kostyshak (2009). 'The Three Arab Worlds'. In: *Journal of Economic Perspectives* 23.3, pp. 165–88.

Réalités (1984). *No Title*. August. Tunis.

Reem, Leila (2010). *State of health*. Al-Ahram Weekly. URL: http://weekly.ahram.org.eg/2010/983/eg12.htm (visited on 10/07/2015).

Reich, Michael R. et al. (2016). 'Moving towards Universal Health Coverage: Lessons from 11 Country Studies'. In: *The Lancet* 387.10020, pp. 811–16.

Reiter, Yitzhak (2004). 'The Palestinian–Transjordanian Rift: Economic Might and Political Power in Jordan'. In: *The Middle East Journal* 58.1, pp. 72–92.

Republic of Tunisia (1987). *7th Plan 1987–1991*. Tunis: Imprimerie officielle.

Republic of Tunisia (2013). *Débat National Stratégique Energétique*. URL: http://www.tunisieindustrie.gov.tn/upload/documents/debat-energie/VF%5C_Presentation-Energie2013-Public%5C_V1.pdf (visited on 04/05/2013).

Republic of Tunisia (2015). *Gestion des biens confisqués*. URL: http://www.finances.gov.tn/index.php?option=com%5C_content%5C&view=article%5C&id=201:gestion-des-biens-confisques%5C&catid=28%5C&Itemid=577%5C&lang=fr (visited on 06/05/2015).

Richards, Alan and John Waterbury (2008). *A Political Economy of the Middle East*. Boulder: Westview.

Richter, Thomas (2007). 'The Political Economy of Regime Maintenance in Egypt: Linking External Resources and Domestic Legitimation'. In: *Debating Arab Authoritarianism,: Dynamics and Durability in Nondemocratic regimes*. Ed. by Oliver Schlumberger. Stanford: Stanford University Press, pp. 177–93.

Richter, Thomas (2009). 'Materielle Resourcen und der Beginn orthodoxer Wirtschaftsreformen in Marokko, Tunesien, Ägypten und Jordanien. Der Rentierstaats-Ansatz under Anpassungsdruck?' In: *Der Nahe Osten im Umbruch. Zwischen Transformation und Autoritarismos*. Ed. by Martin Beck et al. Wiesbaden: VS-Verlag, pp. 50–77.

Richter, Thomas (2012a). 'Außenhandelsrestriktionen bei Autokratien. Eine empirische Analyse zum Einfluss von Devisenreserven, politischer Offenheit, Renten und Regimetyp'. In: *Politische Vierteljahresschrift* Sonderheft "Autokratien im Vergleich".

Richter, Thomas (2012b). 'The Rentier State: Relevance, Scope and Explanatory Power'. In: *Challenges of the Caspian Resource Boom: Domestic Elites and Policy-Making*. Ed. by Andreas Heinrich and Heiko Pleines. Basingstoke: Palgrave Macmillan, pp. 23–34.

Richter, Thomas (2013). 'When Do Autocracies Start to Liberalize Foreign Trade? Evidence from four cases in the Middle East and North Africa'. In: *Review of International Political Economy* 20.4, pp. 760–87.

Ritchie, Bryan K. (2010). *Systemic Vulnerability and Sustainable Economic Growth: Skills and Upgrading in Southeast Asia*. Cheltenham: Edward Elgar.

Roberts, David (1987). *The Ba'th and the Creation of Modern Syria*. London: Croom Helm.

Roberts, Hugh (2001). 'Co-opting Identity: The Manipulation of Berberism, the Frustration of Democratisation and the Generation of Violence in Algeria'. Crisis States Programme Working Paper Series No. 1. London: London School of Economics and Political Science (LSE).

Robins, Philip (2004). *A History of Jordan*. Cambridge: Cambridge University Press.

Robinson, Glenn E. (1998). 'Elite Cohesion, Regime Succession and Political Instability in Syria'. In: *Middle East Policy* 5.4, pp. 159–79.

Rodinson, Maxime (1968). 'The Political System'. In: *Egypt since the Revolution*. Ed. by P. J. Vatikiotis. New York: Frederick A. Praeger, pp. 87–113.

Rodrik, Dani (1998). 'Why Do More Open Economies Have Bigger Governments?' In: *Journal of Political Economy* 106.5, pp. 997–1032.

Rogowski, Ronald (1989). *Commerce and Coalitions: How Trade Affects Domestic Political Alignments*. Princeton: Princeton University Press.

Rohlfing, Ingo (2013). 'Varieties of Process Tracing and Ways to Answer Why- Questions'. In: *European Political Science* 12.1, pp. 31–9.

Roll, Stephan (2010). *Geld und Macht: Finanzsektorreformen und politische Bedeutungszunahme der Unternehmer- und Finanzelite in Ägypten*. Berlin: Verlag Hans Schiller.

Rollinde, Marguerite (2002). *Le mouvement marocain des droits de l'homme: entre consensus national et engagement citoyen*. Paris: Karthala.

Ross, Michael (2004). 'Does Taxation Lead to Representation?' In: *British Journal of Political Science* 34.2, pp. 229–49.

Ross, Michael (2006). 'Is Democracy Good for the Poor?' In: *American Journal of Political Science* 50.4, pp. 860–74.

Ross, Michael (2013). *Oil and Gas Data, 1932–2011*. URL: http://hdl.handle.net/1902.1/20369 (visited on 19/06/2019).

Rougier, Eric (2016). ' "Fire in Cairo": Authoritarian-Redistributive Social Contracts, Structural Change, and the Arab Spring'. In: *World Development* 78, pp. 148–71.

Roushdy, Rania and Irene Selwaness (2014). 'Duration to Coverage: Dynamics of Access to Social Security in the Egyptian Labor Market in the 1998–2012 Period'. Cairo: Economic Research Forum.

Rudebeck, Lars (1967). *Party and People: A Study of Political Change in Tunisie*. Stockholm: Almqvist & Wiksell.

Rudra, Nita (2002). 'Globalization and the Decline of the Welfare State in Less-Developed Countries'. In: *International Organization* 56.2, pp. 411–45.

Rudra, Nita (2004). 'Openness, Welfare Spending, and Inequality in the Developing World'. In: *International Studies Quarterly* 48.3, pp. 683–709.

Rudra, Nita (2007). 'Welfare States in Developing Countries: Unique or Universal?' In: *The Journal of Politics* 69.2, pp. 378–96.

Rudra, Nita (2008). *Globalization and the Race to the Bottom in Developing Countries: Who Really Gets Hurt?* Cambridge: Cambridge University Press.

Rudra, Nita and Stephan Haggard (2005). 'Globalization, Democracy, and Effective Welfare Spending in the Developing World'. In: *Comparative Political Studies* 38.9, pp. 1015–49.

Rudra, Nita and Jennifer Tobin (2017). 'When Does Globalization Help the Poor?' In: *Annual Review of Political Science* 20.1, pp. 287–307.

Ruedy, John (2005). *Modern Algeria: The Origins and Development of a Nation*. Bloomington: Indiana University Press.

Rueschemeyer, Dietrich (2003). 'Can One or a Few Cases Yield Theoretical Gains?' In: *Comparative Historical Analysis in the Social Sciences*. Ed. by James Mahoney and Dietrich Rueschemeyer. Cambridge: Cambridge University Press, pp. 305–36.

Rueschemeyer, Dietrich, Evelyne Huber, and John D. Stephens (1992). *Capitalist Development and Democracy*. Cambridge: Polity.

Russet, B. (1982). 'Defense Expenditures and National Well-being'. In: *American Political Science Review* 76.4, pp. 767–77.

Al-Sabah (2005). *Ma'a katib 'am jami'a al-siha bi-ittihad al-shughl [Interview with the SG of the UGTT Health Section]*. 30 January. Tunis.

Sabhi, Magdi (2002). 'Thawrat yuliyu wa al-tanmia al-iqtisadia: islah al-zira'i wa al-tasni'a [The July Revolution and Economic Development: Land Reform and Industrialization]'. In: *Siyasat Yuliyu: khamsun 'aman 'ala al-Thawrah [The Politicies of July: 50 Years since the Revolution]*. Cairo: Markaz al-Dirasat al-Siyasiyah wa-al-Istiratijiyah, al-Ahram, pp. 145–54.

Sadowski, Yahya M. (1991). *Political Vegetables? Businessmen and Bureaucrats in the Development of Egyptian Agriculture*. Washington, DC: The Brookings Institution.

Safar Zitoun, Madani (2009). 'La protection sociale en Algérie. Évolution, fonctionnement et tendacnes actuelles'. In: *L'Etat face aux débordements du social au Maghreb*. Ed. by Myriam Catusse, Blandine Destremeau, and Éric Verdier. Paris: Karthala, pp. 53–93.

El-Said, Hamed and Jane Harrigan (2014). 'Economic Reform, Social Welfare, and Instability: Jordan, Egypt, Morocco, and Tunisia, 1983–2004'. In: *Middle East Journal* 68.1, pp. 1983–2004.

Salbah, Nisrine and Juliana Yartey (2004). 'Overview'. In: *Public Health in the Middle East and North Africa: Meeting the Challenges of the Twenty-First Century*. Ed. by Anne Maryse Pierre-Louis, Francisca Ayodeji Akala, and Hadia Samaha Karam. Washington, DC: World Bank Institute, pp. 1–23.

Salim, Gamal (1976). *al-Samitun fi ... al-mizan [The Voiceless ... on Trial]*. Cairo: al-Qahira lil-Thaqafa al-Arabiyya.

Samii, A. William (2000). 'The Nation and Its Minorities: Ethnicity, Unity and State Policy in Iran'. In: *Comparative Studies of South Asia, Africa and the Middle East* 20.1–2, pp. 128–42.

Sanborn, Howard and Clayton L. Thyne (2014). 'Learning Democracy: Education and the Fall of Authoritarian Regimes'. In: *British Journal of Political Science* 44.4, pp. 773–97.

Sater, James N. (2010). *Morocco: Challenges to Tradition and Modernity*. London: Routledge.

Satloff, Roberts B. (1994). *From Abdullah to Hussein: Jordan in Transition*. Oxford: Oxford University Press.

Savory, Roger M. (1978). 'Social Developent in Iran during the Pahlavi Era'. In: *Iran under the Pahlavis*. Ed. by George Lenczowski. Stanford: Hoover Institution Press, pp. 85–127.

Saylor, Ryan and Nicholas C. Wheeler (2017). 'Paying for War and Building States: The Coalitional Politics of Debt Servicing and Tax Institutions'. In: *World Politics* 69.2, pp. 366–408.

Schattschneider, E. E. (1960). *The Semisovereign People: A Realist's View of Democracy in America*. New York: Holt, Rinehart & Winston.

Scheve, Kenneth and David Stasavage (2010). 'The Conscription of Wealth: Mass Warfare and the Demand for Progressive Taxation'. In: *International Organization* 64.4, pp. 529–61.

Schlumberger, Oliver (2007). *Debating Arab Authoritarianism,: Dynamics and Durability in Non-democratic Regimes*. Stanford, CA: Stanford University Press.

Schlumberger, Oliver (2008a). *Autoritarismus in der arabischen Welt: Ursachen, Trends und internationale Demokratieförderung*. Baden-Baden: Nomos.

Schlumberger, Oliver (2008b). 'Structural Reform, Economic Order, and Development: Patrimonial Capitalism'. In: *Review of International Political Economy* 15.4, pp. 622–49.

Schlumberger, Oliver (2010). 'Opening Old Bottles in Search of New Wine: On Nondemocratic Legitimacy in the Middle East'. In: *Middle East Critique* 19.3, pp. 233–50.

Schneider, Carsten Q. and Ingo Rohlfing (2013). 'Set-Theoretic Methods and Process Tracing in Multi-Method Designs: Principles of Case Selection after QCA'. In: *Sociological Methods and Research* 42.4, pp. 559–97.

Schumpeter, Joseph (1990). 'The Crisis of the Tax State'. In: *The Economics and Sociology of Capitalism*. Ed. by Richard Swedberg. Princeton: Princeton University Press, pp. 99–140.

Seale, Patrick (1965). *The Struggle for Syria: A Study in Post-War Arab Politics 1945–1958*. London: I. B. Tauris.

Seale, Patrick (1995). *Asad of Syria: The Struggle for the Middle East*. London: University of California Press.

Seawright, Jason (2011). *Multi-method Social Science: Combining Qualitative and Quantitative Tools*. Book manuscript.

Seawright, Jason (2016). *Multi-method Social Science: Combining Qualitative and Quantitative Tools*. Cambridge: Cambridge University Press.

Seawright, Jason and John Gerring (2008). 'Case Selection Techniques in Case Study Research: A Menu of Qualitative and Quantitative Options'. In: *Political Research Quarterly* 61.2, pp. 294–308.

Segal, Paul (2012). 'How to Spend It: Resource Wealth and the Distribution of Resource Rents'. In: *Energy Policy* 51, pp. 340–8.

Segura-Ubiergo, Alex (2007). *The Political Economy of the Welfare State in Latin America: Globalization, Democracy, and Development*. Cambridge: Cambridge University Press.

Selwaness, Irène (2012). 'Rethinking Social Insurance in Egypt: An Empirical Study'. Conference Paper. Cairo. ERF 18th Annual Conference.

Sfakianakis, John (2004). 'The Whales of the Nile: Networks, Businessmen, and Bureaucrats during the Era of Privatization in Egypt'. In: *Networks of Privilege in the Middle East: The Politics of Economic Reform Revisited*. Ed. by Steven Heydemann. New York: Palgrave Macmillan, pp. 77–100.

Sghaier, Amira Aleya (2010). *fi al-taharur al-ijtima'i wa al-watani: fusul min tarikh tunis al-mu'asar [On the Social and National Liberation: Details of Contemporary Tunisian History]*. Tunis: al-Maghribiyah lil-Taba'ah wa-Ishhar al-Kitab.

Sghaier, Amira Aleya (2011). *al-yousefiyyun wa tahrir al-maghrib al-'arabi [The Youssefists and the Liberation of the Arab Maghrib]*. Tunis: Echaab.

Al-Sh'ab (2006a). *Bahth fi awlawiyyat tahil al-qita'a al-sihi al-'umumi [Looking for the Priorities in the Improvement of the Public Health Care System]*. 25 November. Tunis.

Al-Sh'ab (2006b). *No Title*. 25 November. Tunis.

SHAT (n.d.). *Note manuscrite et non signée*. Paris.

Shefter, Martin (1994). *Political Parties and the State*. Princeton: Princeton University Press.

El-Sherif, Ahmed Abou-Zeid (1995). 'The Pattern of Relations between Sadat's Regime and the Military Elite'. MA thesis. American University in Cairo.

Shlaim, Avi (2007). *Lion of Jordan: The Life of King Hussein in War and Peace*. London: Penguin.

Shwadran, Benjamin (1959). *Jordan: A State of Tension*. New York: Council for Middle Eastern Affairs.

Silva, Joana, Victoria Levin, and Matteo Morgandi (2013). *Inclusion and Resilience: The Way Forward for Social Safety Nets in the Middle East and North Africa*. Tech. rep. Washington, DC: The World Bank.

Singh, Prerna (2011). 'We-ness and Welfare: A Longitudinal Analysis of Social Development in Kerala, India'. In: *World Development* 39.2, pp. 282–93.

Singh, Prerna and Matthias vom Hau (2016). 'Ethnicity in Time: Politics, History, and the Relationship between Ethnic Diversity and Public Goods Provision'. In: *Comparative Political Studies* 49.10, pp. 1303–40.

Skocpol, Theda (1988). 'Social Revolutions and Mass Military Mobilization'. In: *World Politics* 40.2, pp. 147–68.

Skocpol, Theda (1992). *Protecting Soldiers and Mothers: The Political Origins of Social Policy in the United States*. Cambridge, Mass.: Harvard University Press.

Slater, Dan (2010). *Ordering Power: Contentious Politics and Authoritarian Leviathans in Southeast Asia*. Cambridge: Cambridge University Press.

Slater, Dan (2018). 'Violent Origins of Authoritarian Variation: Rebellion Type and Regime Type in Cold War Southeast Asia'. In: *Government and Opposition*. First view.

Slater, Dan and Erica Simmons (2010). 'Informative Regress: Critical Antecedents in Comparative Politics'. In: *Comparative Political Studies* 43.7, pp. 886–917.

Slater, Dan and Nicholas Rush Smith (2016). 'The Power of Counterrevolution: Elitist Origins of Political Order in Postcolonial Asia and Africa'. In: *American Journal of Sociology* 121.5, pp. 1472–516.

Slater, Dan and Joseph Wong (2013). 'The Strength to Concede: Ruling Parties and Democratization in Developmental Asia'. In: *Perspectives on Politics* 11.3, pp. 717–33.

Slater, Dan and D. Ziblatt (2013). 'The Enduring Indispensability of the Controlled Comparison'. In: *Comparative Political Studies* 46.10, pp. 1301–27.

Slim, Mongi et al. (2010). *Les bâtisseurs de la Tunisie contemporaine: Quelques nouveaux témoignages, Mongi Slim, Taieb Mhiri, Bahi Ladgham, Ahmed Tlili, Lamine Chebbi*. Tunis: Fondation nationale des sciences politiques.

Smith, Benjamin (2007). *Hard Times in the Land of Plenty: Oil Politics in Iran and Indonesia*. Ithaca: Cornell University Press.

Soares de Oliviera, Ricardo (2007). *Oil and Politics in the Gulf of Guinea*. London: Hurst.

Soifer, Hillel David (2012). 'State Power and the Economic Origins of Democracy'. In: *Studies in Comparative International Development* 48.1, pp. 1–22.

Soliman, Samer (2011). *The Autumn of Dictatorship: Fiscal Crisis and Political Change in Egypt under Mubarak*. Stanford: Stanford University Press.

Springborg, Robert (1989). *Mubarak's Egypt: Fragmentation of the Political Order*. London: Westview.

Sraïeb, Noureddine (1968). 'Mutations et réformes de structures de l'enseignement en Tunisie'. In: *Annuaire de l'Afrique du Nord 1967*. Ed. by Charles Debbasch and Bruno Etienne. Paris: Editions du CNRS, pp. 45–114.

Sraïeb, Noureddine (1971). 'Chronique sociale et culturelle Tunisie'. In: *Annuaire de l'Afrique du Nord 1970*. Ed. by Michel Camau, Jean-Claude Santucci, and Maurice Flory. Paris: Éditions du CNRS, pp. 400–32.

Stasavage, David (2005). 'Democracy and Education Spending in Africa'. In: *American Journal of Political Science* 49.2, pp. 343–58.

Statistical Centre of Iran (various years). *Statistical Yearbook of Iran*. Tehran: Plan and Budget Organization.

Steinberg, David A. and Krishan Malhotra (2014). 'The Effect of Authoritarian Regime Type on Exchange Rate Policy'. In: *World Politics* 66.3, pp. 491–529.

Stephens, John D. (1979). *The Transition from Capitalism to Socialism*. Urbana: University of Illinois Press.

Stephens, Robert (1971). *Nasser: A Political Biography*. New York: Simon & Schuster.

Stobauch, Robert B. (1978). 'The Evolution of Iranian Oil Policy, 1925–1975'. In: *Iran under the Pahlavis*. Ed. by George Lenczowski. Stanford: Hoover Institution Press, pp. 201–52.

Stokes, Susan et al. (2013). *Brokers, Voters, and Clientelism: The Puzzle of Distributive Politics*. Cambridge: Cambridge University Press.

Stora, Benjamin (2001). *Algeria, 1830–2000: A Short History*. London: Cornell University Press.

Storm, Lise (2007). *Democratization in Morocco: The Political Elite and Struggles for Power in the Post-independence State*. London: Routledge.

Stubbs, Richard (1989). *Hearts and Minds in Guerrilla Warfare: The Malayan Emergency 1948–1960*. Oxford: Oxford University Press.

Stubbs, Richard (1999). 'War and Economic Development: Export-Oriented Industrialization in East and Southeast Asia'. In: *Comparative Politics* 31.3, pp. 337–55.

Svolik, Milan (2009). 'Power-Sharing and Leadership Dynamics in Authoritarian Regimes'. In: *American Journal of Political Science* 53.2, pp. 477–94.

Svolik, Milan (2012). *The Politics of Authoritarian Rule*. Cambridge: Cambridge University Press.

Syrian Arab Republic (various years). *Statistical Abstract of Syria*. Damascus: Department of Statistics.

Tajfel, Henri et al. (1971). 'Social Categorization and Intergroup Behaviour'. In: *European Journal of Social Psychology* 1.2, pp. 149–78.

Tal, Lawrence (2002). *Politics, the Military, and National Security in Jordan, 1955–1967*. Basingstoke: Macmillan.

Tarrow, Sidney (2011). *Power in Movement: Social Movements and Contentious Politics*. Cambridge: Cambridge University Press.

Temimi, Abdeljelil et al. (2000). 'Les débats du congrès'. In: *Habib Bourguiba et l'établissement de l'Etat national: approches scientifiques du bourguibisme*. Ed. by Abdeljelil Temimi. Tunis: FTERSI, pp. 137–96.

The Telegraph (2002). *Now Turkey and Tunisia are to take NHS patients*. 20 January. London.

Theborn, Göran (1983). *When, How and Why Does a Welfare State Become a Welfare State?* Paper presented at European Consortium for Political Research Joint Workshops, Freiburg, Germany, 20–5 March.

Thelen, Kathleen (2003). 'How Institutions Evolve: Insights from Comparative Historical Analysis'. In: *Comparative Historical Analysis in the Social Sciences*. Ed. by James Mahoney and Dietrich Rueschemeyer. Cambridge: Cambridge University Press, pp. 208–40.

Thies, Cameron G. (2004). 'State Building, Interstate and Intrastate Rivalry: A Study of Post-colonial Developing Country Extractive Efforts, 1975–2000'. In: *International Studies Quarterly* 48.1, pp. 53–72.

Thies, Cameron G. (2005). 'War, Rivalry, and State Building in Latin America'. In: *American Journal of Political Science* 49.3, pp. 451–65.

Thomson, Henry (2017). 'Food and Power: Agricultural Policy under Democracy and Dictatorship'. In: *Comparative Politics* 49.2, pp. 273–96.

Thyen, Kressen (2019). *Tunesiens junge Demokratie: Zwischen Sozialprotesten und Struktu-ranpassung*. GIGA Focus Nahost 2019/2. Hamburg.

Tignor, Robert L. (1992). 'The Suez Crisis of 1956 and Egypt's Foreign Private Sector'. In: *The Journal of Imperial and Commonwealth History* 20.2, pp. 274–97.

Tilly, Charles (1978). *From Mobilization to Revolution*. New York: McGraw-Hill.

Tilly, Charles (1985). 'War Making and State Making as Organized Crime'. In: *Bringing the State Back In*. Ed. by Peter B. Evans, Dietrich Rueschemeyer, and Theda Skocpol. Cambridge: Cambridge University Press, pp. 169–87.

Toumi, Mohsen (1989). *La Tunisie de Bourguiba à Ben Ali*. Paris: Presses Universitaires de France.

Tu'aymah, Ahmad (1999). *Shahid haqq: sira' al-sultah: Najib, 'Abd al-Nasir, 'Amir, al- Sadat [Authentic Witness: The Struggle for Power, Naguib, Abdel Nasser, Amir, and Sadat]*. Cairo: A. Tu'aymah.

Tullock, Gordon (1987). *Autocracy*. Lancaster: Kluwer Academic.

Tunisian National Archives (1955a). *Motion de politiques budgétaires*. Archival Document No. FPC/K/0004/0058. Tunis.

Tunisian National Archives (1955b). *Motion politique*. Archival Document No. CM 1956/2000/158/Sommaire 87. Tunis.

Tunisian National Archives (1956a). *Rapport économique et social*. Archival Document No. FPC/K/0004/0058. Tunis.

Tunisian National Archives (1956b). *Séance du Conseil des Ministres, 14 novembre 1956*. Archival Document No. CM 1956/2000/158/Sommaire 87. Tunis.

Tunisian National Archives (1956c). *UGTT programme économique et social*. Archival Document No. FPC/K/0004/0058. Tunis.

Tunisian National Archives (1957a). *Coupures de presse concernant le budget de la Tunisie*. Archival Document No. FPC/K/0004/0052. Tunis.

Tunisian National Archives (1957b). *Coupures de presse concernant les activités syndicales et les revendications en Tunisie*. Archival Document No. FPC/K/0004/0058. Tunis.

Tunisian National Archives (1957c). *No Title*. Archival Document No. CM 1956-57/2000/157/Sommaire 86. Tunis.

Tunisian Republic (various years). *Annuaire statistique de la Tunisie*. Tunis: Secretariat Général du Gouvernment.

Tzannatos, Zafiris (2000). 'Social Protection in the Middle East and North Africa: A Review'. Conference Paper. Cairo: Mediterranean Development Forum.

UGTT (1956). *6ème congrès national de l'UGTT (20–23 septembre 1956): Rapport Economique*. Tunis.

UNDP (2015). *UNDP Open Data*. URL: https://data.undp.org/ (visited on 30/10/2015).

UNESCO (2015). *UNESCO Institute of Statistics*. URL: www.data.uis.unesco.org (visited on 01/05/2015).

UNIDO (2010). 'Compilation of Energy Statistics for Economic Analysis'. Working Paper 01/2010. Vienna: United Nations Industrial Development Organization (UNIDO).

UNIDO (2013). *INDSTAT4 Industrial Statistics Database*. URL: http://www.unido.org/en/resources/statistics/statistical-databases.html (visited on 24/06/2015).

United Nations (2012). *World Population Prospects: The 2012 Revision, Volume II: Demographic Profiles*. New York: United Nations Department of Economic and Social Affairs.

Vagliasindi, Maria, ed. (2012). *Implementing Energy Subsidy Reforms*. Washington, DC: The World Bank, pp. 1945–72.

Van Dam, Nikolaos (1978). 'Sectarian and Regional Factionalism in the Syrian Political Elite'. In: *Middle East Journal* 32.2, pp. 201–10.

Van Dam, Nikolaos (1996). *The Struggle for Power in Syria: Politics and Society under Asad and the Ba'th Party*. London: I. B. Tauris.

Van Evera, Stephen (1997). *Guide to Methods for Students of Political Science*. Ithaca: Cornell University Press.

Varshney, Ashutosh (2009). 'Ethnicity and Ethnic Conflict'. In: *The Oxford Handbook of Comparative Politics*. Ed. by Carles Boix and Susan Stokes. Oxford: Oxford University Press, pp. 274–94.

Vatikiotis, P. J. (1961). *The Egyptian Army in Politics*. Westport: Greenwood Press.

Vatikiotis, P. J. (1967). *Politics and the Military in Jordan: A Study of the Arab Legion 1921–1957*. London: Frank Cass.

Vatikiotis, P. J. (1978). *Nasser and His Generation*. London: Croom Helm.

Vatikiotis, P. J. (1985). *The History of Egypt: From Muhammad to Mubarak*. London: Weidenfeld & Nicolson.

Veit, Alex, Kalus Schlichte, and Roy Karadag (2017). 'The Social Question and State Formation in British Africa'. In: *European Journal of Sociology* 58.2, pp. 237–64.

Vennesson, Pascal (2008). 'Case Studies and Process Tracing: Theories and Practices'. In: *Approaches and Methodologies in the Social Sciences: A Pluralist Perspective*. Ed. by Donatella Della Porta and Michael Keating. Cambridge: Cambridge University Press, pp. 223–39.

Vittas, Dimitri (1997). 'Options for Pension Reform in Tunisia'. Policy Research Working Paper No. 1154. The World Bank.

Vreeland, James Raymond (2003). *The IMF and Economic Development*. Cambridge and New York: Cambridge University Press.

Wagner, Adolph (1883). *Finanzwissenschaften*. Leipzig: C. F. Winter.

Wahba, Mourad M. (1994). *The Role of the State in the Egyptian Economy: 1945–1981*. Reading: Ithaca Press.

Wahid, Latif (2009). *Military Expenditure and Economic Growth in the Middle East*. London: Palgrave Macmillan.

Waldner, David (1999). *State Building and Late Development*. London: Cornell University Press.

Waldner, David, Brenton Peterson, and Jon Shoup (2017). 'Against the Grain of Urban Bias: Elite Conflict and the Logic of Coalition Formation in Colonial and Post-colonial Africa'. In: *Studies in Comparative International Development* 52.3, pp. 327–48.

Walton, John and David Seddon (1994). *Free Markets and Food Riots*. Oxford: Blackwell.

Warner, Zach (2016). 'Conditional Relationships in Dynamic Models'. Unpublished paper.

Waterbury, John (1970). *The Commander of the Faithful: The Moroccan Political Elite—A Study in Segmented Politics*. London: Weidenfeld & Nicolson.

Waterbury, John (1983). *The Egypt of Nasser and Sadat: The Political Economy of Two Regimes*. Princeton: Princeton University Press.

Waterbury, John (1993). *Exposed to Innumerable Delusions: Public Enterprise and State Power in Egypt, India, Mexico, and Turkey*. Cambridge: Cambridge University Press.

Weeks, Jessica L. (2012). 'Strongmen and Straw Men: Authoritarian Regimes and the Initiation of International Conflict'. In: *American Political Science Review* 106.2, pp. 326–47.

Whitefield, Stephen (2002). 'Political Cleavages and Post-Communist Politics'. In: *Annual Review of Political Science* 5, pp. 181–200.

Whitten, Guy D. and Laron K. Williams (2011). 'Buttery Guns and Welfare Hawks: The Politics of Defense Spending in Advanced Industrial Democracies'. In: *American Journal of Political Science* 55.1, pp. 117–34.

WHO (2005). *Health Care Finance and Expenditure in Egypt*. Geneva.

Wibbels, Erik (2006). 'Dependency Revisited: International Markets, Business Cycles, and Social Spending in the Developing World'. In: *International Organization* 60.2, pp. 433–68.

Wibbels, Erik and John Ahlquist (2011). 'Development, Trade, and Social Insurance'. In: *International Studies Quarterly* 55, pp. 125–49.

Wigley, Simon and Arzu Akkoyunlu-Wigley (2011). 'The Impact of Regime Type on Health: Does Redistribution Explain Everything?' In: *World Politics* 63.4, pp. 647–77.

Wild, Patricia Berko (1966). 'The Organization of African Unity and the Algerian–Moroccan Border Conflict: A Study of New Machinery for Peacekeeping and for the Peaceful Settlement of Disputes among African States'. In: *International Organization* 20.1, pp. 18–36.

Wilensky, Harold L. (1975). *The Welfare State and Equality: Structural and Ideological Roots of Public Expenditures*. Berkeley: University of California Press.

Wilkinson, Richard and Michael Marmot, eds. (2003). *Social Determinants of Health*. Copenhagen: World Health Organization.

Willis, Michael (2012). *Politics and Power in the Maghreb: Algeria, Tunisia and Morocco from Independence to the Arab Spring*. London: Hurst.

Wimmer, Andreas (2002). *Nationalist Exclusion and Ethnic Conflict: Shadows of Modernity*. Cambridge: Cambridge University Press.

Wimmer, Andreas (2016). 'Is Diversity Detrimental? Ethnic Fractionalization, Public Goods Provision, and the Historical Legacies of Stateness'. In: *Comparative Political Studies* 49.11, pp. 1407–45.

Woertz, Eckart (2013). *Oil for Food: The Global Food Crisis and the Middle East*. Oxford: Oxford University Press.

Woertz, Eckart (2014). 'Historic Food Regimes and the Middle East'. In: *Food Security in the Middle East*. Ed. by Zahra Babar and Suzi Mirgani. Oxford: Oxford University Press, pp. 19–38.

Wood, Elisabeth Jean (2000). *Forging Democracy from Below: Insurgent Transitions in South Africa and El Salvador*. Cambridge: Cambridge University Press.

Wood, Geof and Ian Gough (2006). 'A Comparative Welfare Regime Approach to Global Social Policy'. In: *World Development* 34.10, pp. 1696–712.

Wood, Geoffrey (2004). 'Business and Politics in a Criminal State: The Case of Equatorial Guinea'. In: *African Affairs* 103.413, pp. 547–67.

World Bank (n.d.). *République tunisienne: Étude du secteur de la santé*. Washington, DC.

World Bank (1991). *Egypt: Alleviating Poverty during Structural Adjustment*. Washington, DC.

World Bank (1996). *Republic of Tunisia: From Universal Food Subsidies to a Self-Targeted Program*. Washington, DC.

World Bank (2001). *Kingdom of Morocco Poverty Update*. Washington, DC.

World Bank (2002). *Reducing Vulnerability and Increasing Opportunity: Social Protection in the Middle East and North Africa*. Washington, DC.

World Bank (2006a). *Opportunity, Security, and Equity in the Middle East and North Africa*. Washington, DC.

World Bank (2006b). *Tunisie Examen de la politique agricole*. Washington, DC.

World Bank (2008). *The Road Not Traveled: Education Reform in the Middle East and North Africa*. Washington, DC.

World Bank (2010a). *Egypt's Food Subsidies: Benefit Incidence and Leakages*. Washington, DC.

World Bank (2010b). *The Cost Efficiency in the Production and Distribution of Subsidised Bread in Egypt*. Washington, DC.

World Bank (2010c). *World Development Indicators*. URL: http://data.worldbank.org/ (visited on 05/09/2011).

World Bank (2012a). *Inclusion and Resilience: The Way Forward for Social Safety Nets in the Middle East and North Africa*. Washington, DC.

World Bank (2012b). *World Development Indicators*. URL: http://data.worldbank.org/data-catalog/world-development-indicators (visited on 19/01/2013).

World Bank (2013). *World Integrated Trade Solution (WITS)*. URL: http://wits.worldbank.org/ (visited on 24/06/2015).

World Bank (2015a). *A Roadmap to Achieve Social Justice in Health Care in Egypt*. Washington, DC.

World Bank (2015b). 'Morocco: Social Protection and Labor Diagnostic'. Washington, DC.

World Bank (2017). *World Development Indicators*. URL: http://data.worldbank.org (visited on 18/07/2017).

World Food Programme (2008a). *Marketing of Food in Egpyt: Food Subsidies, Social and Economic Considerations*. Cairo.

World Food Programme (2008b). *Vulnerability Analysis and Review of the Food Subsidy Program in Egypt*. Cairo.

Wright, Joseph (2008a). 'Do Authoritarian Institutions Constrain? How Legislatures Affect Economic Growth and Investment'. In: *American Journal of Political Science* 52.2, pp. 322–43.

Wright, Joseph (2008b). 'To Invest or Insure? How Authoritarian Time Horizons Impact Foreign Aid Effectiveness'. In: *Comparative Political Studies* 41.7, pp. 971–1000.

Yashar, Deborah J. (1997). *Demanding Democracy: Reform and Reaction in Costa Rica and Guatemala, 1870s–1950s*. Stanford: Stanford University Press.

Yogo, Urbain T. and Martine M. Ngo Njib (2018). 'Political Competition and Tax Revenues in Developing Countries'. In: *Journal of International Development* 30.2, pp. 302–22.

Yom, Sean (2009). 'Iron Fists in Silk Gloves: Building Political Regimes in the Middle East'. PhD thesis. Harvard University.

Yom, Sean (2011). 'Oil, Coalitions, and Regime Durability: The Origins and Persistence of Popular Rentierism in Kuwait'. In: *Studies in Comparative International Development* 46.2, pp. 217–41.

Yom, Sean (2016). *From Resilience to Revolution: How Foreign Interventions Destabilize the Middle East*. New York: Columbia University Press.

Al-Youm Al-Saba'a (2011). *No Title*. 21 April. Cairo.

Zine Barka, Mohamed (1991). 'Démographie, dépenses d'éducation et de santé'. In: *Cahiers du CREAD* 27–8, pp. 33–65.

Zisser, Eyal (1999). 'The 'Alawis, Lords of Syria: From Ethnic Minority to Ruling Sect'. In: *Minorities and the State in the Arab World*. Ed. by Ofra Bengio and Gabriel Ben-Dor. London: Lynne Rienner, pp. 129–45.

Zisser, Eyal (2001). *Asad's Legacy*. London: Hurst.

Zribi, Mohamed Jalel (2011). 'Originalités du socialisme "destourien" au cours des années soixantes'. In: *Revue d'histoire maghrébine* 143–4, pp. 109–15.

Index